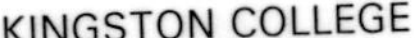

THE FORGOTTEN FRONT

Cameroons
Italian
Somaliland
British
East
Africa
Uganda
Belgian
Congo
Rutschuru
Congo
Nairobi
Brazzaville
Mombasa
Tabora
Tanga
Lukuga
Kabalo
GERMAN
Zanzibar
Rufiji
Dar-es-Salaam
EAST
Kilwa
Luanda
AFRICA
Lindi
Aldaraba
Island
Elisabethville
Angola
Broken
Hill
Portuguese
Northern
Rhodesia
Tete
Zomba
Mozambique
Salisbury
Quelimane
German
South-West
Africa
Southern
Rhodesia
East
Beira
Madagascar
Africa
Walvis Bay
Bechuanaland
Luderitz
Johannesburg
Lourenco
Marques
South
Africa
Durban
East London
Cape Town
0 300 450 600
Kilometres

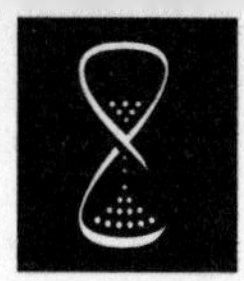

THE FORGOTTEN FRONT

THE EAST AFRICAN CAMPAIGN 1914-1918

Ross Anderson

TEMPUS

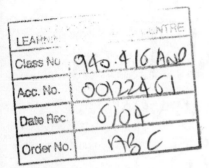

Frontispiece: the East African Front

First published 2004

Tempus Publishing Limited
The Mill, Brimscombe Port,
Stroud, Gloucestershire, GL5 2QG

British Library Cataloguing in Publication Data.
A catalogue record for this book is available from the British Library.

ISBN 0 7524 2344 4

Typesetting and origination by Tempus Publishing Limited
Printed in Great Britain by Midway Colour Print, Wiltshire

Contents

Acknowledgements

The writing of this book has been a lengthy process, but I was greatly aided by the generous assistance of a number of individuals and institutions. I must begin by thanking Professor Hew Strachan, first as my PhD supervisor and now as series editor, for his invaluable advice and criticism throughout. I have benefited from his unrivalled knowledge of the First World War and Africa, as well as his generosity in providing extended access to rare and hard to obtain books. Professor Brian Holden-Reid and Dr Simon Ball provided valuable comments on my dissertation that have helped in this book.

Dr Kent Fedorowich directed me to a number of unexpected and valuable primary sources as well as reading portions of the manuscript. He has shared his expertise in Imperial politics and South Africa to my considerable advantage. Lieutenant Colonel Ian van der Waag has been of great assistance in tracking down South African sources, providing valuable insights into the Union Defence Force and its members. I must also thank him for allowing me to present my ideas at two conferences.

I would also like to thank Ms Ann Crichton-Harris and Mr Andrew Kerr for their continued interest and assistance in my work. Mr Gerald Rilling placed his extensive knowledge of East Africa at my disposal in addition to tracking down a wide variety of books on the subject. Despite the pressures of her own PhD studies, Ms Alexandra Luce kindly undertook research on my behalf in Lisbon and provided a great deal of useful material in translation.

The help provided by the staff of a number of libraries and repositories has been invaluable to my researches. In the United Kingdom I would like to thank the University of Glasgow and Library; the British Library; the National Archives (formerly the Public Record Office); the Imperial War Museum; the National Army Museum; the Bodleian and Rhodes House Libraries, University of Oxford; the Cambridge University Library; the Liddell Hart Centre for Military Archives, King's College, London; the Wiltshire Record Office; Regimental Headquarters, the Queen's Lancashire Regiment; Regimental Headquarters, the Staffordshire Regiment; and the Royal Engineers Corps Library.

Overseas, I have been greatly assisted by the staff of the Bundesarchiv and the Geheimes Staatsarchiv, Preußischer Kulturbesitz, Berlin; the Bundesarchiv-Militärarchiv, Freiburg im Breisgau; the Musée Royal de l'Armée, Brussels; the Arquivo Ministério dos Negócios Estrangerios and Arquivo Histórico Militar, Lisbon; the Documentation Centre, South African National Defence Force and South African National Archives, Pretoria.

I am particularly grateful to the Documentation Centre of the South African National Defence Force and the Musée Royal de l'Armée for allowing me to reproduce photographs from their collections. Crown copyright material is reproduced with the permission of Her Majesty's Stationery Controller.

Thanks are also due to my publisher, Jonathan Reeve, and the staff at Tempus for their work in bringing this book to print. Finally, I must again thank my family for their long-standing support and encouragement. Without them, this book could not have been written.

Foreword

The First World War continues to fascinate historians and readers alike. The industrialisation of warfare brought the trenches, mass mobilisation and huge casualty lists. This gave rise to a long-lasting and spirited debate about its origins, conduct and consequences that remains very much alive today. Perhaps it was the sheer scale of effort, and resulting sacrifices, coloured by differing national outlooks that keeps it so controversial. In the English speaking world, study has largely focused on the Western Front with lesser consideration given to Gallipoli and Palestine. The other, more peripheral theatres have received a fraction of the attention. In proportion to the level of effort, this may be understandable, but in historical terms it represents a gap.

This is particularly true of the East African campaign that lasted from August 1914 until November 1918, with the fighting stopping two days after the armistice in Europe. It was never of first importance, yet it ranged from the modern states of Kenya and Uganda in the north, through the Congo, Ruanda, Burundi, and Tanzania in the centre, to Zambia, Malawi and Mozambique in the south. Few inhabitants, European or African, escaped its effects or ravages, while the colonial empires were irrevocably changed by the conflict. If it was insignificant in global terms, the war there was of overwhelming local consequence.

East Africa has not been entirely ignored, as a number of official histories, memoirs and regimental journals were published in the post-war years. Much of the modern view of the campaign has been shaped by two personal accounts written forty years apart. The most important of the two came from the pen of the undefeated German commander, Generalmajor Paul Emil von Lettow-Vorbeck in his *My Reminiscences of East Africa.*[1] It gave a frank and apparently unbiased account of his gallant campaign to defend German East Africa. It became a minor classic and is still available in reprint today. The other was Colonel Richard Meinertzhagen's book, *Army Diary.*[2] This interesting and entertaining memoir provided an insight into British operations of the period as well as criticising senior officers and many units harshly. However, Meinertzhagen remains a controversial figure and his account is based on his personal diaries and not as a history of the campaign.

The official British history did not appear until 1941 and only one volume out of two was ever published: Volume One of the History of the Great War: *Military Operations – East Africa.*[3] It too has been influential, although it suffers from the discretion expected of government-sponsored publications. The Germans were less fortunate as their military archives were destroyed in April 1945 by bombing. Although a large, multi-volume official history had already been published, its dealings with East Africa were cursory at best. A former participant and later historian of the campaign, Ludwig Boell, produced the most comprehensive German version of the campaign, *Die Operationen in Ostafrika.*[4] This was published in 1959 and was based on a draft manuscript taken from the now destroyed official documents and maps. Furthermore, the author had had extensive exchanges with the British official historians up until September 1939. Unfortunately, with copies being scarce and written in German, it has been relatively little used.

A number of popular accounts appeared in the 1960s with another batch in the 1980s. While colourful and interesting, only one made use of *Die Operationen* and none conducted any archival research.[5] Certainly apart from a few detailed studies of subjects such as labour, medicine and transport, there has been a scholarly neglect of the East African campaign. This has only recently been rectified by the publication of Hew Strachan's *The First World War – To Arms* whose magisterial work devotes substantial space to the war in Africa.[6]

Since the opening of the British First World War records in the mid-1960s, there has been an enormous amount of primary material available. To this may be added records in the South African National Defence Force

Documentation Directorate and the South African National Archives as well as that of the Belgian Musée Royal de l'Armée. There is also much in Portugal and Germany, notably the very substantial Lettow and Boell papers in the Bundesarchiv/Militärarchiv in Freiburg, as well as the vast quantities of non-military departmental papers in Berlin. In fact, the amount of material available is beyond the capacity of one person to read.

This book tries to employ new material in an attempt to gain a fuller understanding of the fighting and operational aspects of the East African campaign. It deals with the background to the conflict, the political goals that drove it, the forces involved and the manner in which they fought it. It attempts to produce a balanced view of the differing perspectives as well as judgements of performance, national aims and the means of fulfilling them. It is a story of imperial conflict and its telling reflects its records. However, one important voice is largely silent; that of the Africans who were drawn into the war by their colonial masters. Written records rarely reflect their point of view, yet without them few of the events described could ever have occurred. Silence must not be confused with lack of importance and the African contribution to the campaign was absolutely essential, if far from fully explained. This work cannot possibly hope to cover all aspects of the war nor give all equal prominence as it was simply too vast. I hope that it will stimulate interest and encourage others to study its many aspects.

As this was a war between empires, and given the large numbers of differing nationalities involved, I have used the terms 'British', 'German', 'Belgian' and 'Portuguese' to cover Europeans and Africans alike. The 'British' pose a special problem as at various times Indians, South Africans, Nigerians, West Indians as well as East Africans fought under their flag. I have used the term 'British' in the general sense and specified nationalities where it makes sense. Place names have been given as those used by the controlling power at the time and many have changed since then.

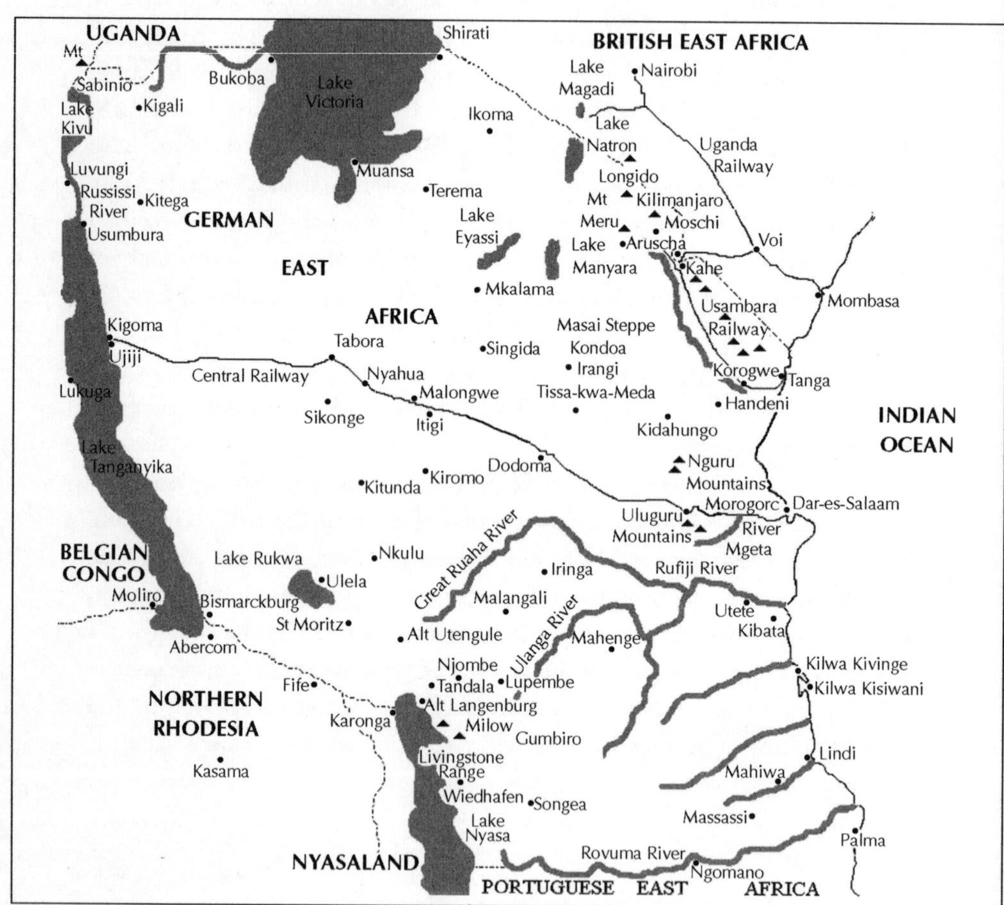

The Theatre of Operations 1914–1915

1

The Strategic Background

As Europe slid towards war in July 1914, life in colonial East Africa continued at its normal pace. Senior officials and military officers were aware of the increasingly disturbing news, but for the vast majority of the population there was little expectation that conflict would come to them. Few of the white settlers or officials had any great enthusiasm for fighting their neighbours, while the African population was largely unaware of this remote quarrel between Europeans. In German East Africa, the authorities were preparing for a major exhibition to celebrate the achievements of the past twenty years. Certainly, East Africa seemed an unlikely place for hostilities between the rival empires. European rule dated back less than thirty years and, despite a steady influx of settlers, the overwhelming majority of the population remained African. By 1914, the population of German East Africa was over 7.5 million Africans, 14,000 Indians and over 5,300 Europeans, as compared to the nearly 7 million Africans, 28,000 Indians and 6,000 Europeans in British East Africa and Uganda.[1] The proportions were similar in the surrounding territories of the Belgian Congo, Northern Rhodesia, Nyasaland and Portuguese East Africa.

Whether colonies, protectorates or chartered territories, they were all notable for their sheer size and lack of development. German East Africa was nearly twice the size of metropolitan Germany, measuring some 1,100 km north to south and 960 km east to west. Its terrain and climate varied tremendously, ranging from arid steppes to humid jungles and rugged mountains. Roads were very few and the main means of transportation was by the two railways, the Usambara Railway in the north and the Central Railway in the centre of the colony. They had been built in an attempt to stimulate economic development, but revenues were still very limited in relation to the cost of building.[2] To the north British East Africa was equally varied, with its economic lifeline being the Uganda Railway that ran from Mombasa to Lake Victoria. In the west, the Belgian Congo was an enormous expanse of tropical forest and river, where movement was slow and difficult. Further south, British Northern Rhodesia and Nyasaland were notable for vast areas and poor communications, while the northern part of Portuguese East Africa was virtually untouched by Europeans. The region offered considerable potential, but in 1914 it had little economic or military value. As a consistent drain on the respective imperial exchequers, it was hardly a rich prize. But, whatever its value, East Africa was inextricably drawn into war, with few imagining the scope of the fighting that would bring unprecedented devastation.

COLONIAL DEFENCE

East Africa's lack of economic strength was reflected in the weakness of its military power. With varying degrees of enthusiasm, European governments had tried to develop their territories through agriculture, trade and settlement. Faced by persistent budget shortfalls and constant demands for spending, they kept military expenditure to the minimum necessary to maintain European supremacy. Power was exerted through a combination of locally raised military units and paramilitary police, all commanded by whites. These were expected to keep law and order, but colonial governments were quite prepared to use force to control the African population. Punitive expeditions against recalcitrant tribes were common, especially on the frontier, although methods often varied.

In the opening months of the war, there was considerable criticism about the apparent lack of military preparation or planning. This was not actually the case for either Britain or Germany. The former, as the leading imperial and naval power, had put considerable thought into the problems of colonial defence. The Committee of Imperial Defence (CID) had carried out a series of detailed surveys and draft schemes of defence. These ranged from the general principles, to details as to the position of regular army officers seconded to local defence forces, to the defence of cable communications.[3] Furthermore, detailed studies of the various colonies and protectorates, including East Africa, were produced against the most recent intelligence estimates.[4]

Sea power was fundamental to British imperial defence. The Royal Navy was the means by which the security of overseas territories and trade would be secured. The power of the fleet was augmented by a worldwide system of undersea telegraph cables, all landing in friendly territory, which provided unparalleled and secure communications. With this combination of naval strength and centralised decision-making, the British Admiralty expected to gain mastery of the ocean lines quickly in order to maintain the uninterrupted flow of shipping and trade. It accepted that in the early stages of a conflict, an enemy might find it possible to gain local superiority in distant waters and threaten overseas possessions. But ultimate victory would accrue to the greater naval power and the fate of the African, or any, colonies would depend on this rather than local military operations.[5]

This meant that colonial defence policy was directed to the prevention and suppression of African uprisings and such forces were specifically not intended to match the strengths of the forces in neighbouring colonies. Based on these assumptions, the defence of British East Africa and its all-important Uganda Railway had been considered in detail and a comprehensive defence plan had been drafted and updated by 1912. Reflecting the political circumstances of the day, it focused on the potential threat from German East Africa. It was based on the latest, and quite accurate, intelligence estimates of German military strength as well as the terrain and likely enemy approaches. Particular detail was devoted to the importance and vulnerability of the Uganda Railway although it also took into account the difficulties of movement and the dispersed nature of the potential enemy forces. It recognised that with the King's African Rifles (KAR) focused on tribal operations in the far north of the protectorate, they would need up to two weeks to redeploy to the south. But the more dispersed German Schutztruppe (Protective Force) would take much longer to move north, giving sufficient time to parry any invasion. The plan was underpinned by recognition of the fundamental importance of the Royal Navy's obtaining ultimate supremacy.[6]

Germany had rather different conceptions of colonial defence, owing largely to its status as a land power in Europe. As a relative newcomer to overseas imperialism, its empire was widely spread and vulnerable. Despite the naval arms race, the German Admiralty realised that it could never compete with the British outside European waters. Consequently, it adopted a strategy known as *Kreuzerkrieg* (cruiser warfare) which would attack British shipping at its weakest points. This meant that the cruisers and armed auxiliaries stationed abroad would put to sea as soon as hostilities threatened and would patrol their secret war stations with orders to attack isolated merchant vessels. They would avoid enemy squadrons and concentrate on the shipping lanes that maintained Britain's wealth and power. While aggressive, it was also a policy of weakness that implicitly acknowledged that colonial possessions would be left to their own defences. For Germany, victory on land would determine the fate of the colonies.

Bereft of naval protection, German East Africa's first line of defence was diplomatic, for it lay within the area described by the Berlin Act of 1885 that attempted to regulate responsibilities and rights in the exploitation of the Congo Basin. Critically, the Act permitted the neutralisation of that area in time of a general European war under certain conditions. Chapter III, Article 10 stated that each of the ruling powers had the option of declaring their part of the Congo Basin neutral so long as: 'the Powers which exercise or shall exercise the rights of sovereignty or protectorate over those territories, using their option of proclaiming themselves neutral, shall fulfil the duties which neutrality requires'.

This option was circumscribed by Article 11 which specified that such neutrality required common consent of the powers before becoming effective.[7] Thus, while any power could attempt to neutralise its colonial territories there, its effectiveness depended on its neutrality being recognised by the others. Practically, the declaration of neutrality depended on whether it suited the respective imperial interests. German planners had considered this possibility in 1912 and had concluded that the British were unlikely to declare or accept such neutralisation as it would restrict their freedom of action. If neutrality failed, they would fall back on the Hague Convention to protect their coastal ports. This agreement had made it illegal to bombard undefended cities, so the Germans proposed to withdraw their coastal garrisons and to concentrate the troops inland. This would prevent the Royal Navy from using its formidable firepower while leaving many of the most important economic and trade centres intact.

The plan was far from being entirely passive as it envisaged a vigorous resistance in the interior of the colony. The two railway systems would be used to provide operational mobility and the Schutztruppe commander had full authority to conduct an aggressive defence.[8] The plan was agreed in Berlin before being accepted fully by both the governor and the commander of the day. These military preparations were matched by detailed planning in the civil government departments. There had been a number of meetings in Berlin between various government departments to discuss and co-ordinate mobilisation and emergency measures. This included the production of a draft proclamation of emergency powers for the use of the governor in dealing with war, uprisings or simple unrest.[9]

The German pre-war preparations were nothing if not thorough. If the means allocated to the defence of German East Africa were meagre and inadequate, that was the considered judgement of the government. In this regard, the policies of both the British and Germans were remarkably similar. Both realised that the colonies had negligible strategic value and allocated the minimum resources possible to guard their national interests.

Elsewhere in East Africa, Belgium and Portugal appear to have put less effort or emphasis into colonial defence. Neither had strong military or naval forces nor the financial strength to match Britain or Germany. The Belgian Congo had only emerged from the devastating exploitation of private ownership in 1908, while Portuguese East Africa was weakly governed and sparsely settled. Defence of colonial rule was the overriding consideration and they had no real territorial ambitions.

THE STRATEGIC SITUATION

Anglo-German naval rivalry had played its part in the coming of war. But in the colonial arena there had been some attempt to reduce tensions and the nations had initialled the draft of a secret treaty aimed at carving up the Portuguese colonies in the case of an expected financial default. This initiative ultimately foundered due to British reservations and the

Portuguese learning of the double-dealings of its erstwhile ally.[10] Apart from these fruitless negotiations, there were no burning colonial issues that separated Britain and Germany in Africa. Nonetheless, a group in government, including the colonial secretary, Dr Wilhelm Solf, aspired to a German *Mittelafrika* that would stretch from coast to coast. This would be achieved through generous helpings from the Portuguese and Belgian-held territories.[11] But it was hardly a vital interest and the Germans realised that British naval power would be dominant overseas. As such, short-term losses would have to be accepted and the re-ordering of the imperial system would have to await a decisive German victory in Europe and the inevitable peace conference.

As the world's leading trading nation, Britain's position depended on the ocean lanes being kept free from threat. This was not only for sound commercial reasons, but also once war had broken out, for food imports and the unimpeded movement of men and material from the far-flung corners of the Empire. In practical terms, this meant concentrating its efforts on attacking the German system of overseas naval bases and communications without detracting from the efforts in the main theatre of war.[12] Such a policy was also attractive to the government as it could be largely achieved by naval power and limited amphibious operations against coastal installations. Most importantly, it required neither the conquest of substantial inland territories nor the deployment of large bodies of troops.

In the pre-war years, the British Admiralty had followed a programme of withdrawing its best ships to home waters in order to counter the growing threat of the German High Sea Fleet in the North Sea. This deliberately left the more remote stations with ageing and second-rate vessels. Such ships were deemed adequate to deal with the principal expected opposition in the form of the German overseas cruiser force. The bulk of their naval power, the East Asiatic Cruiser Squadron, was based at Tsingtau in north China and possessed two new armoured cruisers together with three light cruisers, one of which, *Emden*, would ultimately influence East Africa. The remaining ships included two light cruisers in the Caribbean with another, SMS *Königsberg*, stationed at Dar-es-Salaam, in German East Africa. There were also a considerable number of merchant ships at sea that were intended to act as auxiliaries for the warships. Together, such a force posed a considerable threat to seaborne trade and the all-important troop convoys destined for Europe.[13] The

Indian Ocean was a particular area of weakness as German cruisers could easily swoop undetected onto the vital shipping and troop convoys moving between Australia, New Zealand, India and the Suez Canal. In this context, even a single enemy warship could wreak considerable havoc and damage on British interests if left undisturbed. This put great pressure on tracking down and destroying the enemy raiders as quickly as possible.[14]

However, the Royal Navy still remained superior in numbers and could easily reinforce the overseas stations, whereas the High Sea Fleet could not. Furthermore, Germany had only a handful of overseas ports, notably Tsingtau, New Guinea and Dar-es-Salaam. In the age of coal-fired ships, this was a critical limitation as ships needed regular replenishment of fuel that was both slow and laborious to carry out. The plans for *Kreuzerkrieg* recognised this problem and attempted to solve it through a system of supply ships and pre-arranged coal stocks in neutral ports. Such vessels would sail unobtrusively and link up with the raider before finding an isolated anchorage to conduct coaling. Stealth and access to neutral ports were critical to the success of the strategy as the only alternative was to offload the coal from prizes, a most unreliable method. In contrast, Britain had an extensive system of bunkering stations across the globe.

Communications were the other key link. The British undersea cables were complemented by a growing network of wireless stations that enabled their warships to range freely, yet remain linked to the Admiralty in London. The Germans had nothing comparable and the cable to Dar-es-Salaam passed through British-held Zanzibar, only 16 km distant. This left their communications vulnerable to interception or disconnection in times of tension or hostility.[15] To counter this, and impressed by British advances in wireless telegraphy, they had established their own system with the main transmitter at Nauen, outside Berlin. This station could send signals up to 6,000 km, but not reliably. In order to reach Dar-es-Salaam or the Pacific colonies, a system of relays was set up. The main link station was at Kamina, in tiny Togoland on the West Coast of Africa. It then re-broadcast messages to Windhoek in South-West Africa and to Dar-es-Salaam in East Africa and thence onward. Dar-es-Salaam had a regular range of about 2,000 km, making it useful for controlling shipping as well as passing information to two short-range stations at Bukoba and Muansa, with ranges of 200 and 600 km respectively. Within the colony, a system of telegraphs and telephones linked most of the major stations, although the south and interior remained isolated. The system was technically advanced and was the indispensable link between Europe, the Navy and other colonies.[16]

Wireless was still very primitive and storms and unfavourable atmospheric conditions could delay the reception of important messages for several days. By nature of its range, its signals were easy to intercept by the enemy and the very traffic could give a ship's presence away. Transmitters were large, bulky and fairly immobile, making them vulnerable to attack and destruction.

In August 1914, the opposing naval forces in the Indian Ocean were relatively weak. The protection of East African waters was the responsibility of the Cape of Good Hope Squadron, commanded by Rear Admiral Herbert King-Hall. It comprised three ageing light cruisers, the oldest of which had been in service for twenty years. His flag and most modern ship, HMS *Hyacinth*, of 5,600 tons and mounting eleven 6-inch guns, had a top speed of 19 knots; *Astraea*, the oldest, was of 4,360 tons with two 6-inch guns and could make 19 knots; while *Pegasus*, the smallest at 2,135 tons, had an armament of eight 4-inch guns and a maximum speed of 21 knots.[17]

In contrast, their most likely opponent, SMS *Königsberg*, was a light cruiser of more modern construction, being built in 1907. Displacing some 3,350 tons, it mounted ten 10.5-cm (4.1 inch) guns, but had a maximum speed of 24 knots. Although its main armament was of lesser calibre than that of its British opponents, it was actually superior in range and accuracy. Equally important was its greater speed that would enable it to escape if required. Individually, *Königsberg* posed a threat to any of the Cape Squadron vessels, although as a squadron they could overwhelm the German ship. There were a number of other vessels that ranged from an antiquated survey ship to coasting freighters, ocean liners and tugs, but none were capable of combat. In support there was only the harbour at Dar-es-Salaam with its floating dock, steam cranes and workshops; the remaining ports were too undeveloped to support a warship.

The chief problem facing Admiral King-Hall, however, was the vastness of his area of operational responsibility, which ranged from St Helena in the Atlantic to Zanzibar in the Indian Ocean. His tiny force was incapable of monitoring even a small portion of the area and success depended on being in the right place at the right time. Nearly 4,800 km north at Bombay, Vice Admiral Sir Richard Peirse's East Indies Squadron held an old battleship, *Swiftsure*, two light cruisers, *Dartmouth* and *Fox* and three sloops. However he also had an enormous area to protect, having to cover the approaches to Aden, the waters south of Ceylon and the Singapore Straits, all of which were critical to shipping. His ships were too far from East Africa to be immediately effective against the *Königsberg*, especially as he had to be prepared for a swoop into his waters by the East Asiatic Cruiser Squadron.[18]

THE OPPOSING MILITARY FORCES

On land, matters were more evenly matched. The British Colonial Office controlled and funded the King's African Rifles (KAR). It numbered three battalions with a total of twenty-one infantry companies, of which two were trained as mounted infantry while a third was camel-borne. While each unit was territorially based for recruiting purposes, with 1 KAR from Nyasaland, 3 KAR from British East Africa and 4 KAR from Uganda, in practice they could be deployed throughout the region.[19] Whatever their role in the defence plans, they were not intended to fight a modern, well-equipped enemy in general warfare. Their expertise lay in maintaining internal security through the suppression of African risings and preventing the depredations of marauding nomads.

Despite its obvious expertise, the War Office actually played only a minor role in overseeing the force. Its input was limited to seconding officers and supplying arms and equipment. General control of training, administration and operations was the responsibility of the inspector-general of the KAR, but as he had to split his time between London and the widely separated colonies, his direct influence was limited. In East Africa, there was only a tiny headquarters with no effective central staff, artillery, medical services or reserves. Given the vast distances and time needed to travel, practical decision-making had to be devolved to the officer on the spot. If these weaknesses were militarily undesirable and caused some inefficiency, they were acceptable to the Colonial Office as its financially straitened colonies had to meet the costs of defence. It deemed the system adequate for the low-level operations expected of the KAR.

In 1914, the KAR numbered just under 2,400 men of whom sixty-two were British officers, two were British non-commissioned officers (NCOs) and 2,319 were Africans.[20] Like other colonial forces of the period, British officers occupied all senior positions and were supported by African NCOs who rose from the ranks. The theory of the 'martial race' was still widely maintained and this meant that the troops were generally recruited only from traditional, favoured tribes. In terms of organisation, the KAR battalions were still using the outmoded eight single company format. Commanded by a captain, the company normally fielded between seventy-five and 125 soldiers and could be broken down into two half companies each of two sections. This system was in the process of being supplanted by the four company system coming into the British and Indian Armies, as it was unwieldy and lacked flexibility.

The relatively settled state of the British colonies meant that internal security was proving a lesser role than that of pacification of the border regions, particularly in the north around the border with Italian Somaliland. The principal activity was countering raids by Somali and Turkhana tribesmen into British territory. All three KAR battalions were divided between their home territories and the northern border, with no troops along the German border and the Uganda Railway left completely unprotected. Both Zanzibar and Nairobi had the equivalent of a company, but they were mainly involved in training and garrison activities.[21] Like their counterparts elsewhere, the African troops were usually referred to by their Swahili name, Askari.

Apart from the KAR, the colonial governments controlled paramilitary police forces; in British East Africa and Uganda there were seventy-one Europeans and 2,621 Africans with smaller numbers available in Nyasaland and Northern Rhodesia. Initially they were deployed around the main population centres and they were quickly pressed into security duties with the coming of war. Subsequently, a considerable number of these police found their way into military service, although initially this was limited by fears of internal unrest and enemy-inspired disorder.[22] Whatever its shortcomings in organisation and equipment, the KAR was a well disciplined and long-service force that was fully acclimatised to fighting in the African bush. It was highly experienced in patrol work and operated independently in small sub-units. In short, it was an ideal force with which to support any campaign against German East Africa.[23]

To the west, the Belgian troops of the Force Publique were by far the most numerous in the region, numbering nearly 15,000. Each of the twenty-six districts had a company of soldiers, but these were an armed gendarmerie and not expected to fight as formed units. The entire force was split up into a large number of isolated detachments scattered over the enormous area of the Belgian Congo. Its training was complicated by the existence of three different patterns of rifle, while the few black powder artillery pieces were antiques and most of the ammunition was unreliable through poor storage. They also lacked machine guns and had completely insufficient stocks of ammunition. The transportation difficulties were enormous as the River Congo was the main means of movement through the colony. But it was not fully navigable and had to be supplemented by three discrete sections of railway. Unfortunately, the last section of these, which ran from the riverhead at Kabalo, was still 29 km short of Lukuga on Lake Tanganyika. Apart from equipment deficiencies, the Belgian forces would have to overcome enormous physical challenges to support any operations on their eastern border.[24]

Far to the south, the troops in Portuguese East Africa reflected similar limitations. The forces available in Moçambique province amounted to eight companies totalling 1,680 men and thirteen sections of antique light mountain guns, of which only three could be crewed. All were scattered in small garrisons across the province from Lourenço Marques in the south to Quelimane in the north.[25] Matters were worse in the territory of the Niassa Company that bordered German East Africa. The Portuguese administration had barely penetrated that wild area and its military forces were very few. The military had also been engulfed in internal turmoil, including intervening in politics, that had reduced its effectiveness considerably. The Portuguese colonial troops were extremely limited in transport, equipment and medical supplies. They could do little more than maintain its ascendancy over poorly equipped tribesmen and were in no way prepared for modern warfare.

On the German side, the Schutztruppe was similar to the KAR as it was primarily a force for colonial control. But it was deployed by fundamentally different principles that reflected the differences between the two colonial systems. Like the Kaiserreich from which it sprang, German East Africa was much more militarised than its British neighbours. Whereas the KAR understood itself to be firmly under the control of the Colonial Office through the local governor, this was not quite the case for the Schutztruppe. The protectorate had been founded largely through adventurism and the military had taken a leading role in government from the outset. From 1893 to 1905 it was ruled by a succession of military governors and civilian voices were often in the minority. The policies of the imperial government were quietly ignored as well, with local commanders claiming a great deal of autonomy even from the governor. Again, this insubordination found its roots in the very unsatisfactory nature of civil-military relations in Wilhelmine Germany. Despite the fact that the government was nominally responsible for defence, the Kaiser was determined to keep military decision-making out of the jurisdiction of politicians. This, and a dysfunctional military organisational structure, meant that officers were quite prepared to ignore or circumvent political wishes if they deemed it militarily expedient.[26]

The inadequacies of these methods had been cruelly exposed during the Maji-Maji rebellion of 1905-07 when the harshness and insensitivity of military rule provoked a large-scale uprising by the African population in the south-eastern portion of the colony. The Schutztruppe had to be hurriedly reinforced before exacting a bloody and ruthless vengeance on the rebels and their families. Villages were razed, headmen hanged and crops left to rot as the military reasserted its power and punished the rebels. At least 75,000 Africans, possibly many more, died and the area was totally devastated. Indeed, the imperial government later determined that the military had largely provoked the rebellion through its brutality and administrative ineptitude.[27]

One of its legacies was the formation of a new department, the Reichskolonialamt (RKA or Colonial Office), and the appointment of a series of civilian governors. The governor was charged with the economic and physical development while the military was placed under his personal control. The number of districts under direct military control was reduced from twelve to two out of a total of twenty-two while less harsh economic and taxation policies were adopted. The intention of reducing military influence was, however, undermined by the chronic shortage of civil servants in the colony. This meant that many officers had to be retained in administration and others did not accept their subordination with good grace. Furthermore, there were sharp differences between the settler and official communities that encouraged constant in-fighting. By 1912, matters had reached such a head that the governor, Rechenberg, was forced to resign in acrimony. He was replaced by the lawyer and experienced colonial official, Dr Heinrich Schnee. Schnee was certainly more sympathetic to the needs of the Africans than the military and made development his main priority. However, he too had significant obstacles to overcome and bitter disputes would remain a characteristic feature of his administration.[28]

Although the RKA controlled the small Berlin headquarters of the Schutztruppe, there were policy clashes there too. Its military head, General von Glasnapp, was sympathetic to his subordinates' views. For example, as late as the summer of 1914, the headquarters was arguing for the disbandment of the police in militarily occupied territories, a retrograde argument that can have only added to the tension.[29] Equally, there had been discussions between the General Staff and the RKA about removing the Schutztruppe from all administrative matters with the governor losing his powers of discipline over the force. This might have eased civil-military tensions, but the outbreak of war meant that they came to nothing.[30]

Matters were not eased by the appointment of a new commander of the Schutztruppe in January 1914. From a noble Pomeranian family with a long tradition of military service, forty-four-year-old Lieutenant Colonel Paul Emil von Lettow-Vorbeck was an officer of considerable professional attainment. He had followed the traditional Prussian route to becoming an officer through a cadet academy and had served as a page at Court. He began his career in the socially exclusive Foot Guards and had passed into the Great General Staff in 1899 where he worked as an intelligence officer following the Boer War. He had an unusual amount of foreign service for a German officer of the period, having been on the staff during the Boxer rebellion in China of 1900-01 and later in the suppression of the Herero revolt in German South-West Africa in 1904-05. There he had served on General von Trotha's staff, before becoming a company commander in the field and receiving a wound.

On his return home, Lettow was assigned as a General Staff officer to XI Corps in Kassel. Thereafter, he was promoted and given command of a marine infantry battalion that lasted until 1913. His next move was again unconventional as he requested to serve with the colonial forces, although it was turned down by the RKA as he was considered 'unsuitable'. Within a year matters had changed completely and, after several alterations, he was selected to command the Schutztruppe in East Africa. The reason for the dramatic change is unclear, but he had the backing of the powerful Military Cabinet and Lettow arrived in Dar-es-Salaam in January 1914.[31]

Lettow was well educated and could speak both French and English. He was a highly professional officer who was exceptionally hard working and highly ambitious. He had definite charm and presence, polished by impeccable manners and bearing. However, he was also single-minded and capable of exceptional stubbornness and ruthlessness. His approach was also strongly influenced by his military and staff training; like his contemporaries, Lettow had a jaundiced view of civilian officials and considered them unqualified to comment on military matters. Equally, he had very firm views on strategy and tactics, but regarded any entertainment of political considerations as being an unwarranted interference.

From the outset he clashed with Schnee by pointedly criticising the 1912 defence scheme shortly after his arrival. Their relations were not helped by Lettow's decision to send a written critique of the plans to Berlin and of requesting a more aggressive strategy. As Lettow had only been in the country for a few weeks and had not yet visited much of the territory, Schnee believed that the protest was ill-considered and did not reflect the colony's interests. It was to be the beginning of a long and bitter dispute between the two highest authorities in German East Africa that would continue until the war's end.

Under these influences, the Schutztruppe had been deployed in a series of independent company bases throughout the protectorate, while two of the administrative districts remained under direct military control. There was no battalion or higher organisation as companies largely conducted independent operations in their local area. In numbers, it was comparable to the KAR as it had sixty-three German officers, thirty-two doctors, four officials, sixty-seven German NCOs and 2,542 Africans organised into some fourteen Feldkompagnien (FK or Field Companies). Unlike their British counterparts who served relatively short attachments to the KAR, many of the Schutztruppe's officers had been in Africa for many years and were responsible for the civil administration of their districts. This meant that their political duties had often taken primacy over their military functions and few had experience or knowledge of modern warfare. This contributed to a growing personal interest in the development of their districts while also dampening some of their ardour for the discomforts of military life.

Tactics were based on the mobile company column that could move independently through the bush and deal with tribal levies. Numbering two officers, one doctor, two German NCOs, 150 Askari, two machine guns, 322 carriers, 100 Askari 'boys' and thirteen European 'boys', such columns lived off the land apart from the supplies for Europeans and ammunition. The usual standard was to carry six months' supplies for the Europeans, but only one days' worth for the Africans. For the Europeans, life was relatively comfortable as they were entitled to twenty-two carriers each to carry their equipment, tent, cook set and food supplies. When the tsetse fly permitted, five riding animals and fifty-four oxen were provided, while the entire formation was designed to be moved by rail in two or three military trains.[32]

Districts were garrisoned by prominent high-walled forts (boma), suitably loopholed and occasionally equipped with an antique field piece. On campaign, the standard tactic against a tribal enemy armed with a few muzzleloaders and spears was to adopt an all-round defence, the so-called 'hedgehog'. By tightly bunching together in a square, the column was much less easy to outflank, while it could deliver heavy fire in all directions. This would normally inflict sufficient enemy casualties as to win the day; pursuit was often a matter of rounding up the cattle that made up so much of the native Africans' wealth.

The Schutztruppe were not armed for modern warfare, as the bulk of its weapons were the old '1871' pattern rifles which used black powder propellant for the ammunition. The great disadvantage of this was that the weapon emitted a dense cloud of smoke on firing, simultaneously obscuring the target and revealing the firer's position. With 10,500 of these rifles, only 1,600 old carbines and 579 '1898' pattern rifles of modern design, its weaponry was seriously inadequate.

Manpower was also a concern as there was no real reserve. There was a system whereby discharged soldiers were liable to two weeks' training every year with the local company or police detachment, but having completed a long-service engagement, many of the reservists were too old for serious duty. Furthermore, although district offices held lists of the names and villages of ex-soldiers, distance and inertia made training difficult. But, in the circumstances of normal life, the governor considered the system adequate and resisted any changes.[33] Not included in these calculations was the presence of some 2,700 German and Austro-Hungarian males capable of bearing arms, most of whom belonged to the Landsturm. Many had served as either officers or non-commissioned officers before coming out to Africa and understood the need for discipline and training.

Lettow was profoundly dissatisfied with this state of affairs as he had seen at first hand the results of magazine-fed rifle and machine-gun fire during both the Boxer rebellion and the war in South-West Africa. Should the Schutztruppe attempt to use such tactics against a modern enemy, the effects would be devastating. Furthermore, he was concerned about the tactical ability of his officers, very few of whom he considered capable of leading more than a single company. With the companies so widely spread, the difficulties of just visiting his command were huge, let alone supervising their training. Undaunted, he soon instituted a number of changes – not all of which were popular – as well as setting out on an ambitious programme of visits throughout the protectorate. His programme was supported by varying degrees of enthusiasm, although he was fortunate in having the backing of the more energetic officers who had promoted shooting clubs for the European reservists, in order to maintain their proficiency.[34]

The various colonial forces shared one characteristic. The lack of roads and the effects of the bite of the tsetse fly – which was fatal to all pack animals – forced them to rely on human porterage for all their transport needs. Africans were recruited to carry all the food, ammunition and baggage of a column with an individual load of about fifty pounds. While well adapted to conditions, it was an inefficient system that relied on skilled professional porters marching reasonable distances and living on local resources. It was mobile but relatively slow, and it required columns of large numbers of men marching in single file.

Both the KAR and the Schutztruppe were well adapted to their roles of maintaining colonial rule and in low-level warfare against ill-armed and undisciplined tribesmen. If they were not ready for modern warfare, it was because of conscious political decisions to limit their size and capability, mainly for financial reasons. Most importantly, nobody had seriously considered the possibility of general warfare in East Africa. The events of August were to change that assumption irrevocably.

THE THEATRE OF OPERATIONS

East Africa was a daunting place in which to conduct military operations. Although covering a vast area, the region between the British and German protectorates could be divided into three parts; namely the coastal strip, the highlands and the low country around Lake Victoria. Starting in the east, it began with a low-lying coastal strip that progressively widened as it ran south. Measuring up to 160 km in depth, this region was very hot and humid and covered with thick bush, making movement difficult and slow. The area was also highly pestilential and malarious. Away from the coast itself, the sparsely inhabited land began to rise with the vegetation changing into mimosa scrub. On the British side, beginning some 80 km inland, the arid Taru Desert supported little life and hindered movement.

The desert continued to the great highlands that began around Voi and extended nearly 480 km west to the Great Rift Valley. As the ground rose, it turned to open grass-covered country that was relatively easily traversed. Water was seasonal, with super-abundance in the rainy season and very little in the dry. The great extinct volcanic feature of Mount Kilimanjaro that stood north of the Pare Mountains dominated the region. Beyond that, there was an arid and sparsely inhabited desert that encompassed the salt lakes at Natron and Magadi, before reaching the Great Rift Valley. There, the Mau Escarpment land descended sharply over 600 metres with the ground dropping to the low-lying area around Lake Victoria. It became swampy and covered in thick bush, though the ground in the south towards the German border was higher and more healthy. Tropical diseases were a major problem in the area, although it was cultivated and heavily populated.

The vast inland sea of Lake Victoria offered the easiest and fastest movement in the region with a number of ports and anchorages. On its western shores, the protectorate of Uganda was covered in tropical forest that eventually opened out into rolling pastoral country covered in grass. To the west, the country rose gradually to a wild and rocky plateau some 1,200 to 2,400 metres in elevation, ending at the volcanic chain on the border with the Belgian Congo. In the south, the Kagera River posed a major obstacle with papyrus swamps and thick bush.

Man-made communications were few and largely limited to railways. The Usambara Railway ran roughly south-east to north-west from Tanga to Neu Moschi in the shadow of Kilimanjaro, while the Central Railway linked Dar-es-Salaam with Ujiji on Lake Tanganyika. On the British side, the Uganda Railway paralleled the border as it headed west to Voi before turning north-west to Nairobi and then onward to Lake Victoria.[35] East Africa also suffered badly from the depredations of the malarial mosquito and the tsetse fly that lived in vast numbers, especially in hot, humid conditions. This, and the extreme seasonality of water supply, meant that the region would be extremely difficult for military campaigning.

2
Operations of 1914

THE STRATEGIC SITUATION ON THE OUTBREAK OF WAR

As tensions rose, the British Admiralty initiated a number of precautionary measures. One of these was to locate and 'shadow' the German overseas cruisers before the actual outbreak of hostilities so that they could be attacked immediately should war be declared. Accordingly, Admiral King-Hall's Cape Squadron was ordered to steam north, heading directly towards Dar-es-Salaam. His ageing and under-powered ships reached Zanzibar early on 31 July, only to be sighted by a German merchant vessel. On receipt of the report, the *Königsberg* immediately made for sea just as the British ships arrived. The German captain, Max Looff, had no intention of being trapped and destroyed; using the cover of a squall and good seamanship, he shook free of his pursuers and soon left them far behind. Unbeknownst to the British, he was headed for the northern Indian Ocean approaches off Aden that led to the Red Sea and the Suez Canal.[1]

With war imminent and his prey vanished, King-Hall had to consider the protection of main base at Cape Town and sailed there in his flagship, *Hyacinth*, leaving the other cruisers to search for the *Königsberg*. To the north, the East Indies Squadron had its fastest cruiser in dry dock and the cruisers from Tsingtau were already at sea. Whatever the Admiralty's calculations, there was now a serious threat to shipping in the Indian and Pacific oceans, that could potentially devastate the long and vulnerable trade routes.[2] Until this threat was eliminated, it would add considerable risk to any operations planned against German East Africa.

In Dar-es-Salaam, the situation appeared less favourable as the political crisis in Europe escalated. As soon as the *Königsberg* had departed, Dr Schnee ordered implementation of the war plans and to sink the floating dock so as to block the harbour. At the time, Colonel Lettow was away in the interior on a tour of inspection and was urgently recalled. Cabled telegrams from Berlin warned of the imminence of war as did the British interference with communications from Zanzibar. Finally, as the tension continued to mount, a wireless message reached Dar-es-Salaam – war had broken out. The pretences were now over and full-scale defensive preparations were launched.[3]

The motives for going to war in August 1914 have been the subject of enormous debate, but colonial issues were not a significant factor. Apart from minor matters of internal security, East Africa only mattered as far as it impacted the achievement of British naval supremacy. Germany was far more concerned about mobilisation and achieving a rapid victory in France before turning on the Russians than any remote colony. All eyes were focused on the fight for Europe and the expected naval clash in the North Sea. If the Chancellor later called for an expanded German *Mittelafrika*, it was hardly a priority as it required the subjugation of Belgium, the destruction of French power and British acquiescence, willing or otherwise.[4]

On 5 August 1914, the day after the Cabinet had agreed to send the British Expeditionary Force (BEF) to France, a sub-committee of the CID was established to consider the possibilities of worldwide action against Germany. It included representatives from the Admiralty, War, Foreign, India and Colonial Offices and its remit was 'to decide what objectives can be assigned to joint expeditions with a view to produce a definite effect on the result of the war'.[5] Once these goals had been decided, they were to submit their proposals to the Cabinet for approval and, once authorised, were to work out the necessary details.

The idea of an operation against German East Africa was discussed on the same day and an attack against Dar-es-Salaam was one of many proposed for Cabinet approval. It was based on familiar principles:

> The Sub-Committee believed that by the reduction of this *point d'appui* of the German naval forces off the coast of East Africa, the Admiralty arrangements for the protection of commerce would be facilitated, and by thus taking the offensive the defence of British possessions in East Africa would be best guaranteed. They considered that the project was a feasible one, provided that the naval situation was favourable, and they suggested that the details should be left to the Indian Government to work out in consultation with the Naval Commander-in-Chief.[6]

The Cabinet considered the Offensive Sub-Committee's recommendations on 6 August in some detail. Winston Churchill, the First Lord of the Admiralty, later described the scene vividly:

> On an August morning, behold the curious sight of a British cabinet of respectable Liberal politicians sitting down deliberately and with malice aforethought to plan the seizure of the German colonies in every part of the world... But our sea communications depended largely upon the prompt denial of these bases or refuges to the German cruisers; and further with Belgium already largely overrun by the German armies everyone felt that we must lose no time in taking hostages for her eventual liberation.[7]

The British Government was seeking pawns for eventual peace negotiations rather than permanent acquisitions for the Empire. It was also aware of the need to maintain the moral high ground as well as allaying its allies' fears about its own motives. To that end, it specifically ruled out acquiring territories for the purposes of imperial expansion, stating that all permanent decisions would be subject to any post-war peace conference.[8] However, this high-minded declaration certainly did not rule out temporary conquest, while recognising, if only informally, that the self-governing dominions, such as South Africa and Australia, might have their own territorial ambitions.[9] The purely littoral strategy quickly crumbled; Togoland was attacked almost immediately, surrendering by the end of August, while colonial expeditionary forces were preparing to attack the Cameroons in the north and German South-West Africa in the south.[10] Local fears and sub-imperialist desires were beginning to undermine the pre-war strategy.

It was one thing to draw lines on a map but another to make serious military plans for which well-trained commanders and staffs were needed.

Hitherto, the process of convening a joint consultative committee to make recommendations for Cabinet approval and then to pass them to the two services for detailed planning was sound. But, there were serious inadequacies of the existing general and naval staff system, for the War Office, which should have run the military operations, was preoccupied with the sending of the BEF to France and rapid expansion of the Army. It had been singularly handicapped by the decision to send many of its most senior officers off to assume appointments with the field army. Although they were replaced, their successors lacked the same detailed and thorough knowledge of their posts and needed time to settle in. A solution was quickly found; responsibility was passed to the India Office and, through it, to the Indian Army. This was not unprecedented for, in 1900 at the height of the second Anglo-Boer War, the India Office had controlled the successful military operations during the Boxer rebellion in China.[11]

However, there were important differences between the two departments of state. The India Office was not a military headquarters and although the secretary of state had his own military secretary, General Sir E.G. Barrow, together with a small staff, they were there to provide advice about the Indian Army and manage officers' careers. It was neither equipped nor expected to direct military operations as this was the responsibility of Army Headquarters, India which had its own general staff working under the direction of the viceroy and commander-in-chief. In the Admiralty, matters were little more satisfactory, for, despite efforts to set up a naval staff system, it had never really been accepted by the senior admirals. The bulk of staff work involved in the planning and control of operations remained concentrated in the hands of a few very senior officers. The situation was not eased by the presence of the First Lord, Winston Churchill, who could not resist involving himself in low-level decision-making and tactics.

The Colonial Office still controlled the KAR and it wanted reinforcements quickly. With no chance of British troops, the India Office found a small force of three battalions of Indian troops, to be known as Indian Expeditionary Force (IEF) C under Brigadier General J.M. Stewart, on 17 August.[12] Although part of the Indian Army, they would come under the Colonial Office's control through the Governor of British East Africa, Sir H.C. Belfield, on arrival. With many units still mobilising, Stewart and the lead battalion sailed from Karachi on 19 August, with the rest due to follow as soon as possible thereafter.[13]

Finding troops for the descent on Dar-es-Salaam was more difficult. On 8 August, the India Office authorised the formation of IEF B, to be composed of two brigades numbering nearly 8,000 men. But this came at a demanding time for the Indian Army as it was trying to mobilise a corps, IEF A, for service in Egypt. The next day, instructions were given that IEF B should sail from India as soon as the former had departed.[14] Brigadier General Arthur Aitken was nominated as the expedition's commander, with his brigade, 16 (Poona), forming the nucleus of the force. He was an infantry officer who had served in the Indian Army since 1882. He had had a conventional military career with perhaps less active service than his contemporaries, having taken part in the Sudan campaign of 1888. At fifty-three years of age, he had commanded his brigade for nearly three years before being appointed to command IEF B. He seems to have been an average officer with no distinguishing talent or drive. Certainly, he showed no great intellect or grasp of modern warfare in his preparations and he was inclined to pompousness in manner. If anything, he was dominated by his chief of staff, a former Staff College instructor. Aitken did not inspire great confidence and some of his subordinates questioned his judgement. However, he had been given an independent command and he meant to make it a success.[15]

Almost immediately, other priorities arose. The deteriorating relations with the Ottoman Empire meant that the reinforcement of the Suez Canal and protection of oil supplies in the Persian Gulf was essential. The despatch of IEF B was now put on hold and would have to await developments in the Near East.[16] By the end of August, Aitken had lost his brigade to IEF A although he remained the nominated commander of IEF B. He did gain the services of Mr Norman King, former consul-general in Dar-es-Salaam as his political officer, and together they discussed the planned landings at that port.[17] Subsequently, as the Persian Gulf crisis had been surmounted, IEF B was resurrected and more troops had been found. Now it would consist of the regular 27 (Bangalore) Brigade plus a brigade of Imperial Service troops; it only remained to find sufficient transport ships and naval escorts before launching the invasion.[18]

In London, General Barrow had assumed general control over IEF B although detailed planning remained with Army Headquarters, India. Inter-departmental sensitivities had already placed IEF C under Colonial Office control while the commander-in-chief, Cape Station, who was responsible for the landings, reported directly to the Admiralty. There was no unified command structure and disputes had to be resolved by time-consuming referrals back to the London-based departments. Each office was determined to maintain its independence and prerogatives without considering the effect on military efficiency. This was brought out when, soon after the arrival of IEF C, General Stewart copied his plans to the War Office and Army Headquarters, India as was standard practice. This resulted in a firm rebuke by the colonial secretary and Stewart was forbidden to make direct communications with either department and to channel all requests through the former's office.[19] This decision blithely ignored the fact that the Colonial Office had no control over reinforcements, technical stores, weapons, ammunition or equipment. It meant that non-expert officials would have to assess technical demands before passing them on to the appropriate authorities – all taking extra time and wasting effort. Such methods may have been workable when dealing with punitive expeditions against tribesmen, but were hopeless when facing a modern and capable enemy such as the Germans.

However, the Byzantine command structure was overshadowed by Barrow's next move. Working alone in London and isolated from the Army Headquarters, India, he came up with a breathtaking change of plan. Aitken and his force were no longer to conduct a raid to destroy a wireless station and occupy a port. Now, they were told:

> THE object of the expedition under your command is to bring the whole of German East Africa under British authority… you should, in the first instance, secure the safety of British East Africa by occupying the north-eastern portion of the German Colony viz., the country between Tanga and Kilimanjaro. For this purpose, it is suggested that you should first occupy Tanga with Expedition 'B', and that, when this movement has had its due moral effect on the Germans in hinterland of Tanga, Expedition 'C' should, if feasible, advance from Tsavo and threaten Moshi. It is, however, for you to judge whether such an operation is practicable and advisable, also whether Expedition 'C' should be strengthened by you for this object.[20]

Having taken Tanga, Barrow now expected Aitken to launch a follow-up assault on Dar-es-Salaam before going on to secure the entire territory. It was an enormous task that expected the 8,000 soldiers of IEF B, assisted by some of the 2,000 in IEF C, to capture a tropical country considerably larger than Germany itself.[21] Furthermore, he seems not to have carried out a proper military appreciation of the situation or consulted the pre-war CID studies on East Africa. This would have revealed both the strength and calibre of the Schutztruppe as well as the difficulties of the terrain. Finally, he may have been influenced by the belief that the African population would rise up and even massacre the European and Indian populations.[22] Whatever the reasons, the plan would transform East Africa from a strategic backwater to a substantial commitment.

POLITICAL CO-OPERATION

The question of military co-operation among allies was altogether more complicated. If the British, French and Belgians were fighting shoulder-to-shoulder in Europe, there was considerably less solidarity in Africa. Colonial rivalries remained strong and there was a degree of mutual mistrust of the others' motives. In Britain, the Colonial Office was notably antagonistic towards any offers of assistance in East Africa as it wanted to eliminate the Germans as rivals without giving its allies any claim in the potential spoils.

The question of the possible neutralisation of the Congo Basin was one of the first to arise. Despite having been invaded by Germany, the Belgian Government was initially opposed to extending hostilities to Africa. On 9 August, it informed the British of its desire to invoke the neutrality clauses of the Berlin Act, a position that was soon supported by the French.[23] The British were wholly unsympathetic as it would limit their freedom to attack German naval power as well as to accumulate political bargaining chips. The situation was further complicated by the fact that the Belgians had already approached the German Government via Spain with these proposals.[24]

This approach was strongly supported in German East Africa as the governor was strongly opposed to war there. Schnee rightly foresaw that conflict would destroy the development made in recent years while possibly leading to an African uprising, and he feared the strength of the other belligerents. Accordingly, he spent much of August trying to get the neighbouring territories to agree to neutrality. Again, this was in conformity with the pre-war defence plan although intermittent communications made it difficult to clarify the progress of negotiations. But whatever his reservations about war, Dr Schnee was an experienced official who understood his duty as governor. There was no question that the pre-war defence plans would be activated and the necessary civil measures put into place. On 5 August, he declared martial law, called up the Landsturm, and turned over the bulk of the police force to the Schutztruppe. Three days later, he turned over more of the police, the posts and telegraphs and the railways to military control.[25]

All of this was insufficient for Lettow, who viewed matters from a purely military viewpoint. He was adamantly opposed to any hint of non-belligerence and had a number of stormy discussions with the governor on his return to Dar-es-Salaam. He believed that his first duty was to divert as many Allied resources as possible from the main theatre of war: 'I considered it our military object to detain the enemy, that is English, forces, if it could by any means be accomplished. This however, was impossible if we remained neutral'.[26] He also resented the fact that the governor remained at the head of the military structure, believing that all questions of policy should be in his own hands. The RKA thought differently, issuing the pre-planned proclamation granting full emergency powers to all colonial governors on 15 August.[27] Equally, many in the protectorate shared these views, with particular fears about a repetition of Maji-Maji. As well, they believed that armed conflict between the colonial powers would only weaken the prestige of the small European population with their African subjects. These feelings were by no means limited to civilians and were shared by a number of reserve officers who had settled in the colony.[28]

In the meantime, Lettow did not accept Schnee's decisions with good grace. Convinced of the rightness of his views, he authorised the armed steamer *Hedwig von Wissmann* to act aggressively on Lake Tanganyika. On 15 August, the crew cut Belgian telephone cables and seized a number of canoes; a week later, on 22 August, this was followed by the shelling and disablement of the Belgian vessel *Alexandre Delcommune* at Lukuga. Similar actions took place against the Portuguese in the south, where initially it was unclear whether they would remain neutral. Rumours of the detention of German reservists reached Dar-es-Salaam in early August, and Schnee sent an official to visit the Portuguese in order to clarify the situation. Unwilling to accept any delays, Lettow used some minor tribal unrest as a pretext for authorising troops to attack the Portuguese. Learning of this, Schnee forbade any incursion until the resolution of the diplomatic mission, but the force had already left. On 24 August it crossed the Rovuma River before attacking and destroying a small Portuguese boma (fort). As the Portuguese authorities had confirmed their neutrality with the German representative on the same day, this caused considerable upset. In the end, it took several formal apologies and the promise of punishment of the erring officer to bring relations back to a normal keel.[29]

The action was particularly unwise as Schnee's officials were trying to arrange the passage of mail, personnel and supplies through Portuguese territory while Lettow himself was to redeploy the sole regular company out of the area. The military value of the raid was negligible and it could have had severe political repercussions, especially on the use of Portuguese ports by German auxiliary ships.[30] In contrast, the British showed what diplomacy and persuasion could achieve. By mid-August, the Portuguese Government had agreed a request for the movement of troops from Chinde across Portuguese East Africa into Nyasaland. Although the soldiers were unarmed – their weapons having been shipped ahead – this was certainly not the action of a neutral.[31] Whatever the legal arguments to justify this action, it contrasted sharply with protestations of strict neutrality to the Germans and the restrictions on visiting warships or merchantmen. Furthermore, a local official offered military support to Britain, a pledge that was subsequently endorsed by the government in Lisbon.[32]

Entente doubts about bringing the conflict to Africa were eventually overcome by concerns about the success of the German offensive in Europe. The French position had changed by mid-August as they and the British wanted to attack the German colony of Cameroon. This pressure, plus the loss of much of their own country, induced the Belgians to modify their original proposal quite considerably. Citing the military position in Europe, they now stated that the neutrality of the Belgian Congo was ended and that, although a strictly defensive attitude would be assumed by the ground forces, they would co-operate with the British and French in everything except offensive operations.[33] In return for a guarantee of its colonial possessions, the Belgian Government now offered the British and French free passage of troops, munitions and material through their 'neutral' territory while also permitting their ships to use their ports. This was favourable enough for the British to accept it on 2 September.[34]

In the meantime, the German Government still supported neutrality although it was not until late September that their offer, passed by the United States, reached the British. By then, attitudes had hardened and the proposal died on 13 October, when Belgium formally declared its hostility, citing the German attack on Lukugu of 22 August as its reason. Now it was left to the Americans to inform Berlin of the joint British, French and Belgian rejection of the proposed neutralisation of the Congo Basin.[35]

The combined rejection of neutrality did not imply smooth relations between Britain and its allies though. Offers of military assistance by the Belgian, Portuguese and even French were politely rebuffed.[36] This may be attributed to British over-confidence in their own abilities to eliminate the Germans as a rival as well as a wish to deny other countries a claim in the potential spoils. Despite the pressing need for military victory over the Central Powers, imperial rivalries and colonial aspirations would remain significant factors throughout the war, and East Africa would be no exception.

While a Belgian colonial adventure may appear unusual with most of the home country under occupation by the Germans and the remainder largely a battleground, the prospect of a campaign held a number of attractions for the government-in-exile. The advantages included both national pride and diplomacy; in short they needed some tangible gains in order to negotiate from a position of strength in any peace conference. As the official Belgian instructions directed, they wanted 'a pawn in the form of a portion of German territory'.[37] The proximity of German East Africa and the support promised by the British made the campaign attractive, as did the wealth and fertility of its provinces of Ruanda and Urundi. A limited campaign to seize and control some of the best parts of German territory at relatively low risk was a most attractive option. It also had the advantages of placing the much stronger British in their debt, of enhancing their Congo colony, and of inflicting pain on the despoilers of their country. Under these conditions, and from a Belgian point of view, an offensive made strong strategic sense.

Despite their ancient alliance with Britain, the Portuguese were held in low regard and considered to be both militarily and administratively incompetent. Britain was by far the dominant power and believed the Portuguese to be incapable of serious military effort. Relations had not been helped by Portuguese awareness of the abortive pre-war Anglo-German negotiations to carve up their African empire. Nevertheless, Portugal was willing to enter on the British side, as it saw this as a means of protecting its vulnerable African colonies as well as possibly obtaining slices of German territory.[38] This met strong British opposition, as they considered that Portugal's financial and military weakness would make it more of a liability than an asset. They were far more interested in denying the Germans access to its ports or Atlantic islands. Finally, their colonial policies and governance were held in barely disguised contempt. In the end, Portugal gave in to to this pressure and stood aloof, declaring neither neutrality nor belligerence.[39] This stance was to provide significant assistance to the British as it was interpreted unequally and usually to their benefit.

NAVAL OPERATIONS AND UNOFFICIAL 'TRUCES'

Perhaps surprisingly, it was naval operations that were to cause the greatest friction and confusion on both sides. With the *Königsberg* vanished, the Cape Squadron turned its attention to the Indian Ocean ports of the enemy. Dar-es-Salaam was the most important with its wireless and port facilities; on 8 August *Astraea* was ordered to neutralise the former. Using his initiative, the ship's captain ordered a short bombardment, before issuing an ultimatum to the German authorities. It was stark; either be subject to further shelling, or establish a truce, in which all warlike materials should be removed and all hostile activity renounced for the duration of the war.[40] In return, the British would leave the towns undisturbed, although the truce would have to be ratified by their government. The truce agreement was duly signed, for, despite the severity of the terms, it was acceptable to Schnee as it fitted in well with his efforts to seek neutrality while also conforming with the existing defence plan.[41]

This was anathema to Lettow and, despite being personally instructed that Dar-es-Salaam was not to be defended, he ignored the order, sending an officer there to assume executive power and to conduct all negotiations. However, Schnee learned of this manoeuvre and overruled Lettow during a heated telephone call. Matters were repeated on 17 August, when HMS *Pegasus* issued a similar ultimatum and terms at Tanga.[42] Once again, Lettow tried to disobey the governor's instructions, but was unable to react in time to prevent it. Unabashed, he made further attempts to usurp the governor's power when the British attempted to land at Bagamoyo on 23 August and later at Tanga on 8 September.[43]

With the coast apparently neutralised and no sign of the German cruiser, *Astraea* was now instructed to return to South Africa in order to cover the planned landings in German South-West Africa. This left only slow and outgunned *Pegasus* as guardship off Zanzibar. Concerns about its being overwhelmed by the *Königsberg* were dismissed as being a 'slight risk' and the security of the East Coast was left to an obsolete cruiser and a number of small craft. More importantly, at the end of August the Admiralty refused to ratify the truces, as they would inhibit British freedom of action, especially as it planned to make landings at Dar-es-Salaam.[44]

Admiral King-Hall was left to make the decision whether to make an immediate disclaimer to the Germans or not. Believing that this would allow the enemy to defend their towns, he declined to do so and informed the Senior Naval Officer (SNO) Mombasa that 'HMG does not ratify terms of truce Dar-es-Salaam and Tanga. You should inform Governors of the two towns of this at a convenient opportunity shortly before any further offensive action is taken against either of the towns'.[45]

As the Admiralty had been intimately involved in the planning of the proposed descent on Dar-es-Salaam, this was an important statement. King-Hall's advice was accepted and it agreed that action could be deferred until the expedition reached Zanzibar. Elsewhere in London, the truces caused some apprehension, but the Colonial, India and War Offices were reassured about the arrangements for denunciation and the matter was left to rest.[46] This would have important consequences for the landing of IEF B.

Lettow's and Schnee's actions deserve analysis, particularly as the soldier tried to portray himself as hindered by civilian 'interference'. In fact, Lettow's actions were at complete variance with the Imperial Government's policy. The RKA had explicitly rejected his earlier proposals to defend the coastal ports and reaffirmed the 1912 decision to fight inland. A letter had been sent in July, but was intercepted by the British and it is unclear whether its contents reached German East Africa in another way. In any event, Lettow would have known the accepted defence plans would remain extant until superseded.[47] Furthermore, as Schnee appreciated, a neutralised Congo Basin was in Germany's direct interests, militarily and politically. Even more important was the status of Portugal, for the plans of the Admiralty's *Kreuzerkrieg* depended on having neutral ports from which colliers could draw coal to supply the warships. It made no sense to provoke unnecessary enemies given the vast and indefensible borders of the colony. Unlike Lettow, he could see the advantages of having over half of the frontier secure from attack as well as a source of supplies and communications.

Schnee also rightly refused to abdicate his position completely and to rubber stamp all decisions made by the military. He retained both the right to run the colony and the ultimate executive power although he was prepared to delegate it temporarily in cases of urgent danger. To that end, he opposed denuding the entire colony of troops as Lettow wished, while also attempting to negotiate with the British, Belgians and Portuguese.[48] The fact that negotiations ultimately failed for other reasons, was not to deny their potential value.

Lettow had shown himself quite prepared to disobey his legal superior and willing to usurp civil authority as he saw it necessary. So far from being a universally recognised war leader, Lettow was initially seen as lacking judgement and being dangerously aggressive. This was reflected in his nickname of the 'Mad-Mullah' and amplified by his attempts to defend Dar-es-Salaam. Indeed, members of the business community who worried about needless destruction of property complained to the governor. Political considerations such as maintaining domestic tranquillity, having neutrals through which supplies and information could pass, or keeping markets open were viewed as distractions. Overruled in the short term, he adopted a policy of concentrating his forces, despite the governor's concerns about an uprising.[49]

If Lettow may be criticised for narrow-mindedness and inability to think beyond the tactical level, the system under which he was trained must take much of the blame. He reflected the ethos and outlook of the Great General Staff in which technical military excellence was combined with a complete and disastrous disregard for politics. It was also a product of the confused decision-making process of Wilhelmine Germany, whereby the military deliberately excluded civilian ministers from many of its decisions and chose to ignore vital political factors in the build-up to war. In many ways, Lettow was simply following the tradition of military contempt for civil power.[50]

WAR COMES TO EAST AFRICA

While these diplomatic discussions were underway, the military lost no time in preparing for war. The British colonial authorities had already asked for reinforcements as they too were concerned about the possibility of risings as well as a direct threat from their German neighbour. The defence plan was initiated and orders were given for the recall of the bulk of the KAR from Jubaland, and the organisation of defences along the vulnerable Uganda Railway and the Kilimanjaro area. By the third week in August, the leading elements of IEF C were underway for Mombasa, while much effort was expended to re-enlisting former soldiers. African recruits were sought to make up under-strength companies while over 1,800 Europeans volunteered for service in a number of extemporised units. It would be some time before such troops, however enthusiastic, would be ready for serious military operations against a trained enemy. Fears of an uprising were also fanned by a minor revolt of the Giriama tribe that required the diversion of a number of KAR troops. While successfully put down, this was precisely the type of problem that colonial administrators feared most. [51]

For his part, Lettow began the frantic process of mobilising his force and readying it for operations. Companies were ordered to increase recruitment and arms, and munitions and stores were issued from the magazines. Despite the shortcomings of the reserve system, many ex-soldiers reported for duty, with over 600 former Askari and 400 police rejoining the colours. The Navy also provided several hundred valuable reinforcements as it placed the crew of the scuttled survey ship *Möwe* and a number of reservists at the Schutztruppe's disposal.[52] Many Europeans volunteered, often forming their own Schützenkompagnie (Sch K). Unlike the regular FK, the Sch K were drawn largely from the white settler community and shooting clubs, with several coming from distinct occupations such as the railways and farmers. Apart from carriers, the Sch K did not include any Africans, and sizes varied from forty to 120 strong. Furthermore, they were equipped with the modern '98 rifle while the bulk of the FK had to make do with the much less effective '71 pattern. This additional manpower was welcome, but a meaningful expansion of the Schutztruppe would require large numbers of recruits whose training and equipment would take a considerable period.[53] Equally, with the long distances and dispersion involved, it would be early September before the bulk of the troops were brought together.

In late August, Lettow was very worried about rumours of an imminent landing of 2,000 troops at Tanga and ordered the destruction of the Usambara Railway from Muhesa to the coast. This would have crippled his supply system and cut off Tanga completely. Several civil officials managed to delay the implementation of the order and informed the governor who then had Lettow countermand it. At that stage, the British were incapable of such a descent and it was the civilian officials who had kept their nerve.[54]

As soon as they were ready, the first few troops were ordered to move by foot and rail to cover the vital gap between Mount Kilimanjaro and the Pare Mountains. Lettow quickly took the initiative, as he ordered the newly arriving troops in the Kilimanjaro area to advance into British territory. On 14 August, the leading troops occupied the border post of Taveta, several kilometres inside the frontier. As this place was the last significant water hole for a considerable distace, the defenders retreated back towards Voi leaving an arid no-man's-land between them and the Germans. Neither side had the resources to do more, and a pause ensued.

By 8 September, Lettow had collected some eleven companies in and around Kilimanjaro with one protecting the Usambara Railway and another guarding Neu Moschi itself. Three companies remained to secure the Central Railway.[55] Two battalions were formed, each of four companies, with one near Himo close to the railway and the other near Tanga. On the coast, Lettow had ordered an advance north towards the British forward positions to be followed by attacks on the Uganda Railway. On 22 September, Majoreni was unsuccessfully attacked, but the threat of a follow-up convinced the British to withdraw three days later to Gazi. However, the Germans pursued in a lethargic fashion, giving the British time to regroup and despatch the newly arrived second wave of IEF C to the line. Now, with 500 Germans facing over 800 British troops, the situation was less favourable for an attack. This was confirmed on 7 October, when the coastal column attacked and was repulsed before falling back to Majoreni.[56] The expected success had not been obtained.

Elsewhere, there had been seen a great deal of mobilisation and reinforcement activity, but little real fighting. Around Lake Victoria, the principal German garrisons of the ports of Bukoba and Muansa were over a week's march from Tabora and felt isolated. The former's commander decided to evacuate Bukoba and concentrate his 450 soldiers at Muansa. This left the Uganda border undefended, but the few British soldiers were in no position to move across the Kagera River and little occurred. However, they retained superior operational mobility through their flotilla of seven vessels to the sole German steamer on the lake.

Colonel Lettow decided to redress the situation. He ordered the forces in Muansa to attack on the eastern shores of Lake Victoria. Some 400 rifles were landed at Kisii on 11 September just as the British had deployed 300 men to hold that place. The next day, the Germans were caught unawares and driven back after heavy losses.[57] Lettow promptly sacked the unfortunate commander and this marked an end to any offensive in the area for some time to come. Fearing an overland approach from Uganda, Bukoba was re-occupied and a forward line established along the general line of the River Kagera. This line was to mark the boundary of the British and Germans for the coming months as neither side had sufficient force to attack in the area and the difficulties of bringing up food and munitions precluded the build-up of a larger force.[58]

Farther to the west, Lake Tanganyika dominated military considerations along the Germano-Belgian border. Although this vast body of water had few good harbours and was prone to stormy weather, it offered easy mobility for troops and supplies. But, with few vessels available, a slight advantage could be decisive. The Germans held the advantage with three large steamers and two motor boats, against a single Belgian vessel. The Germans did not wait long to strike, falling on the *Delcommune* on 22 August, putting it out of action and gaining command of the lake.[59] North of the lake was the 300-km frontier that ran through the humid and dense Russisi Valley to Lake Kivu and then to the 4,600 metre-high volcanic uplands of the north. It was a remote region and difficult to reach with few troops.

It took until the end of September before the Force Publique could concentrate 1,000 troops in the area to face some 200 Germans in Ruanda under Captain Wintgens. Further south in Urundi the situation was similar, as barely 100 Germans were facing some 750 Belgians along the Russisi line. Wintgens had seized the offensive and secured the main island in the middle of Lake Kivu, thereby assuring their supremacy of that body of water. But, apart from that, only a few minor operations ensued with an unsuccessful Belgian attack on Kissenji taking place on 4 October. This was followed up by a number of German probes around the Kivu area, but of little military significance.[60]

In the southern province of Katanga, the Belgians under Major Olsen had quickly formed three battalions to secure the region from Lukuga down to the British border. In comparison, to the south and east, the British territories of Northern Rhodesia and Nyasaland were almost completely exposed, with the former defended by two companies of KAR and the latter having less than 450 paramilitaries from the Northern Rhodesian Police. The Germans were little stronger, with a platoon at Bismarckburg and an FK near Neu Langenburg. Physical communications in the area were significantly worse as there were no railways, few roads suitable for wheeled traffic and settlements were scarce.[61] The British did have a telegraph line that linked Abercorn, Fife, Karonga and Zomba to Southern Rhodesia and thence the outside world. For their part, the Germans had to make do with a heliograph system that linked Neu Langenburg to Iringa and then Kilossa, the site of the nearest telegraph station.

The Belgian presence was important, for it soon appeared that Northern Rhodesia was about to be invaded by the Germans. With virtually no troops, the local magistrate had appealed for immediate military assistance in the area of Abercorn, at the southern end of Lake Tanganyika. Major Olsen agreed and, on his own initiative, a battalion of troops was despatched to help defend the British colony. Arriving on 22 August, the unit was ordered to remain on the defensive and not to cross the international border. Now with over 600 Belgians and 200 British, Abercorn was relatively secure. It was a timely move as, two days later on 24 August, Lettow instructed the garrison of Bismarckburg to attack that place which was believed to be virtually undefended. With a force of only fifty ex-police Askari and 250 armed tribal auxiliaries, the attack occurred on 5 September, but failed to breach the defences. In the meanwhile, a company of British reinforcements was on the way, having been marching for over a month from the interior. Learning of the battle, they conducted a forced march, covering nearly 160 km in sixty-six hours and arrived at Abercorn early on 9 September. They were just in time to meet a renewed German attack that was repulsed with slight loss. They then broke off the battle and returned to Bismarckburg where they remained for the next few months.[62]

To the south-east, Lettow now set upon attacking Karonga in northern Nyasaland, with some 400 troops and 1,500 auxiliaries. At the same time, the local British commander decided to take the initiative and strike the Germans. Having passed each other in the thick bush, the British realised that the Germans were besieging Karonga and fell on them from the rear on 9 September. After a heavy battle the Germans were driven north, with over a third of the force becoming casualties. Morale of the troops took a heavy knock while the lack of military value of the auxiliaries was made plainly apparent. The force retired to friendly territory and began to make defensive preparations for the border. This action put paid to further advances, and both sides turned to improving their defences.[63]

Further friction was evident in late September when Lettow's deputy, Major Kepler, took the courageous step of writing to him, to state that he was being badly advised in tactical matters by his principal staff officer. This was followed on 11 October by a letter from the governor that questioned his policy of concentrating near Kilimanjaro and asking whether he was planning a major offensive against the British. His reply that his intentions were to induce the enemy into fearing attack and thereby he was implementing only defensive measures rang slightly hollow. He was well aware that morale of the troops was pessimistic and that many lacked confidence in his judgement.[64] To date, his aggressive style had achieved little except a series of minor setbacks.

The British were not inactive either, although despite the help from the Belgians, the Colonial Office was opposed to their presence, describing it as 'eminently undesirable'.[65] Nevertheless, in the absence of greater British force, it had to bow to necessity and the troops remained. This was to launch a major debate in London as the Rhodesian authorities continued to press for a Belgian presence with the Foreign Office supporting their involvement on practical grounds. Opposing this view, the Prime Minister, Asquith, agreed with the Colonial Office about discouraging any Belgian attacks against the Germans, despite their potential value in supporting the planned British landings on the coast.[66] Unsurprisingly, these inconsistent messages confused and irritated the Belgians, who still maintained their troops in British territory.

The colony at Nyasaland was dominated by the great lake bearing its name. It offered huge advantages of movement and speed to the controlling side and here the British had the edge with seven small steamers facing a single German ship.[67] They wasted little time, striking the enemy at Spinxhafen on 13 August. With the craft destroyed, command of the lake enabled the British to move 500 men up from Fort Johnston at the southern end of the lake to Karonga in the north two days later. In contrast to an overland journey that would have taken weeks, they were in position by 22 August.[68] But, the respite was only temporary, as within days there were reports of an enemy advance south. The Governor of Nyasaland appealed to the Portuguese for assistance, but was quickly rebuffed by Harcourt, the colonial secretary. Nevertheless, the situation was such that both Sir Edward Grey, the foreign secretary, and Churchill were prepared to bring Portugal into the war if Nyasaland considered itself seriously threatened. In the end they were not required and although this was a very minor crisis, the episode caused confusion and irritation as local officials sent one message and the government another. Matters were eased by the Portuguese declaration that they were prepared to use their colonial forces for regional defence as well as sending a 1,500-man expeditionary force from Europe.[69]

By early September, the troops available in British East Africa numbered about 4,300, being spread from a detachment on Lake Victoria to around 1,100 in Nairobi with a similar amount around Voi and about 400 on the coast. Distant Uganda contained just under 1,000, but many of these were far from being fully trained. The lead battalion of IEF C, the 29th Punjabis numbering over 700, had only just arrived and the remainder of that force, some 2,000 additional men, was still concentrated in India. The battalion was immediately split between the Voi-Tsavo area opposite Kilimanjaro and the remainder to Nairobi, where Brigadier General Stewart also established his headquarters. The arrival of the remaining two composite battalions of Imperial Service Troops and artillery at the end of the month eased worries further, although it was a decidedly mixed force with only limited offensive capability. However, it brought firepower and numbers to the thinly stretched KAR garrison.[70]

In early October, pressure also came from British East Africa where both the governor and local military commander asked for permission to support Belgian offensive proposals against German Ruanda. This was abruptly refused by Harcourt who stuck to the line of discouraging any Belgian offensive action, either alone or in conjunction with the British. His officials were concerned that by accepting such military aid, the Belgians would be in a position to make post-war claims on any captured German territory.[71] However, the Colonial Office's position was becoming less tenable, especially as the Foreign Office was trying to establish a coherent policy and becoming increasingly embarrassed by the poor treatment that it was according the Belgians. One senior official noted, 'The whole difficulty arises from the extraordinary jealousy of the Colonial Office of any action by the Congo troops beyond the Congo frontier. The result of this policy can only be the prolongation of the operations against German East Africa and the unnecessary loss of a good many lives'.[72]

While these minor operations were underway, the quasi-neutral Portuguese began the slow process of transferring troops to their northern border marked by the River Rovuma. Back at home, the government had decided that reinforcements were necessary and an expedition, commanded by Lieutenant Colonel Pedro Francisco Massano de Amorim, was raised. Its mission was primarily defensive, with the aims of quelling any possible African unrest and co-operating with the British as necessary. It did not sail from Lisbon until 11 September, reaching Lourenço Marques just over a month later, before continuing on to the forward base at Porto Amelia.[73] But the Portuguese state was in turmoil, with weak governments and considerable instability, including palace revolutions. The Army reflected these political divisions and, with patronage key to advancement, professionalism fell by the wayside. Consequently, there was little concern for the welfare or training of the soldiers and effectiveness was very low.

There was also the drawback that Portuguese East Africa was not under the rule of a single government. The northern half, the province of Moçambique which ran from the Lurio River to the southern side of the Zambezi River, was administered by a government-appointed governor. To the south of the Zambezi was the territory of the Moçambique Company and to the north of the Lurio to the Rovuma, the region was the property of the Niassa Company. The latter had only been finally occupied in 1912 and its rule was notoriously exploitative and harsh. Furthermore, there were always tensions between the companies, the colonial and the national interests. Porto Amelia mirrored this malaise as it was poorly organised with inadequate accommodation, supplies or sanitation. As it was in the unhealthy coastal belt, the result was high levels of sickness and discomfort. If many officers were unhappy with the unevenness of the Anglo-Portuguese relationship, in the circumstances there was little that Portugal could do.[74]

THE RAISING OF INDIAN EXPEDITIONARY FORCE (IEF) B

Back in India, General Aitken and IEF B had to wait until sufficient shipping was available to move them to East Africa. Their departure was further delayed by the exploits of the German cruiser, the *Emden*, which had entered the Indian Ocean, causing havoc. The very real fear that it would link-up with the *Königsberg* could not be discounted and the Admiralty was struggling to find enough escorts to protect the vulnerable convoys. Finally, it emerged that IEF B would not be able to sail until 16 October.[75]

This was just as well, for mobilisation was moving fitfully. The Indian Army had never been intended for large-scale expeditionary warfare and it was woefully short of material. Like the KAR, it was also in the midst of changing from the single to double company system and the process was far from complete. Many units were under strength and had to receive large drafts before reaching their war establishment. In 27 Brigade, one battalion only received all of its equipment and manpower on 7 October before embarking the next day. Machine guns were in short supply with only half the battalions initially in possession of them, and thus training had to be improvised. Another boarded on 30 September and had to remain on board for a further sixteen days before sailing. For the Imperial Service troops, there were no machine guns available at all.[76]

The commander of 27 Brigade, Brigadier General Richard Wapshare, was a cavalry officer of the same vintage as Aitken. His career had been unremarkable with active service in Burma during 1886–88 followed by regimental command and the commandantship of the cavalry school at Saugor. He had been a brigade commander for nearly two years, but had risen through seniority rather than any great talent. Wapshare was seen as being nervous and fussy and could not be considered an energetic or dynamic commander.[77] It was notable that, by departure, he had not been able to review his troops together or, indeed, conduct any collective training.

With the Indian Army short of regular troops, much reliance was placed upon the Imperial Service Corps that served the Princely States. Training standards ranged widely and they were much less well equipped than their Indian Army counterparts. The Imperial Service Brigade was a brand new formation that comprised one regular battalion and the equivalent of three battalions, most of whom had never worked together previously. Most notable was their reliance on the obsolete Martini-Henry rifles that had to be hastily exchanged for the new short-magazine Lee-Enfield rifle (SMLE).[78]

Command was vested in Brigadier General Michael Tighe, a fifty-year-old officer who had been brought back from retirement. Unlike Aitken and Wapshare, he had had extensive operational experience, fighting in six campaigns including East Africa, and had been decorated for his services. He was promoted to brigadier general in September 1914 and given command of the new brigade. Tighe was well known for his courageousness and desire to be in the thick of any fight, but he could not be described as a thinking officer. His experience was that of tribal warfare and not of a modern enemy.[79] Tighe did his best and managed to concentrate his troops, and conducted some preliminary training before departure. They were not crack troops and had serious limitations, but there was little else he could do in the time available.

Finally, on 16 October, IEF B was ready to sail. The formerly worrisome naval situation had cleared up as it was believed that the *Königsberg* was hiding along the East African coast while the *Emden* was in the eastern Indian Ocean. With an escort that included HMS *Goliath*, an elderly battleship, and an armed liner, the Admiralty was content to let the convoy sail. The fight for German East Africa was about to begin. [80]

THE BATTLE OF TANGA

On 1 November, the Schutztruppe was deployed with the bulk of its northern forces, some fourteen out of twenty companies, in the Kilimanjaro area. It was divided into four Abteilungen (detachments): Abt von Prince (three companies) in Taveta; Abt Kepler (four companies) at Tsavo; Abt Kraut (four companies) holding Longido; and headquarters (three companies) in reserve at Neu Moschi. A further two weak companies were engaged on railway defence duties with the remaining four of II Battalion under Baumstark in the coastal area. Tanga itself was virtually undefended, with only fifty police permitted under the truce and its sole company about to depart north for the border.[81]

Tanga was the second port of German East Africa, but could not be called important. Its facilities consisted of a single pier and a railway line that linked the town to the Usambara line. The bay was shallow, forcing large ships to anchor and unload by lighters. Furthermore, the entrance had a swift current and was ringed by a number of reefs in the outer waters. Geometrically laid out, the town was divided into European and African sections, all being surrounded by dense rubber and sisal plantations. Much of the Indian Ocean coastline was marked by thick mangrove swamps and steep cliffs with a coral reef lying about 500 metres off the shore. Although strategically unimportant in itself, Tanga provided important facilities to the main German forces around Mount Kilimanjaro. Ships and dhows provided a link to Dar-es-Salaam, while the railway workshops were essential to maintaining the all-important engines and cars.

By 29 October, IEF B had met up with HMS *Fox*, a light cruiser, off Mombasa. For the first time, Aitken learned of the truces and that the Navy intended to denounce them before any landing. However, he made no decision until he had had a chance to confer in Mombasa.[82] Meeting on 31 October, Aitken and his staff conferred with the local civil and military officials, including General Stewart, the commander of IEF C. After much discussion, Aitken agreed to the need to inform the Germans of the abrogation of the truces as well as his plan. The following line of action was decided upon:

> 'B' Force to land at Tanga, form Base there and work up Usambara Railway; Gen Stewart co-operating from Voi and Longido. A small expedition to be sent, as soon after landing as possible, from Tanga towards Vanga, to co-operate with a detachment of 'C' Force now at Gazi.

Assuming that the Germans would put up a feeble fight, Aitken foresaw the possibility that Stewart would be able to take the Kilimanjaro area unaided while IEF B might then land at Dar-es-Salaam. Despite clear evidence to the contrary, he assumed that the enemy would not put up a determined fight for the colony.[83] The role of IEF C was left unclear, as was the timing of its 'co-operation'. While Stewart had made a number of preliminary arrangements beforehand, with a force of some 1,500 based at Oldoinyo Erok, it was still a complacent approach to an important operation. He believed himself superior to the 400-500 estimated defenders of Abt Kraut who held the Longido position, not realising that it was considerably stronger, having four companies totalling some 660 rifles and six machine guns in good defensive positions.[84] Probably Aitken wished Stewart to delay or prevent a German re-deployment to Tanga, meaning that the attack would have to precede the landings. With the slowness of passing on information in the bush and then to issue orders, the enemy needed to be engaged at least twenty-four hours before the convoy arrived. In the end, the attack would take place on 3 November, a day after the landings were due to have commenced. It was to be a critical error.

The naval news was mixed; as it transpired that the main naval threat to the landings, the *Königsberg*, had been found hiding in the delta of the River Rufiji and was now blockaded in. On the other hand, *Goliath* had broken down and had to remain at Mombasa for repairs, depriving the convoy of its firepower and communications. This left only the *Emden* at large in the eastern Indian Ocean and out of range of IEF B.[85] From a naval perspective, it was safe to start the landings.

The motley convoy arrived off Tanga early on 2 November and *Fox* sailed in alone to deliver the ultimatum. However, the local official supported Lettow's stance and refused to give an answer, before telegraphing of the British demands. Lettow quickly ordered that Tanga was to be defended at all costs with the scratch force available.[86] Thus, by mid-morning the expeditionary force of nearly 5,000 fighting troops faced an opposition of a mere seventy-five barely trained and inadequately armed men with another 100 marching to their assistance. A landing at this stage would have almost certainly overwhelmed the defenders, no matter how determined and gallant their efforts. For the time being, the British were unable to land even a single company, thereby forgoing their overwhelming superiority in numbers.[87]

It was not until early afternoon that Aitken and Captain Caulfeild could confer with the various unit commanders about the changed situation. With no contingency plans or alternative landing sites planned, matters were further delayed by the need for reconnaissance and to sweep for mines. A very poor landing site in a mangrove swamp leading to a narrow beach running into 6-metre cliffs was the best that could be found. The rest of the day was lost through slow procedures and lack of rehearsal. The landings began after dark and were hindered by the falling tide that grounded many of the lighters on the coral reef. On the German side, Lettow had galvanised his troops into action. He reduced the numbers of troops in the forward positions and ordered the rest to concentrate at the railhead at Neu Moschi before moving south to Tanga. Ironically, it was only Abt Kraut at Longido that failed to receive these instructions, a day before General Stewart was to attack.[88]

The night of 2/3 November was spent in trying to land the Imperial Service Brigade. It was not until the early hours of 3 November that Tighe was ashore with his leading troops. After minor opposition they pressed on through the dense bush towards Tanga, now some seventeen hours after the expiry of the ultimatum. He pushed on with patrols sent out forward to locate the enemy.

By dawn, his troops were heavily engaged outside the eastern edge of the town and unable to advance further. Heavy casualties and a strong local German counter-attack shook the untried Indian troops and the line began to waver. At the same time, the first reinforcements from Neu Moschi had arrived and were moving against the British left wing which was showing no inclination to advance further. A further counter-attack broke the British line and the brigade began to retire in disorder. The landing of reinforcements was effected in time to avoid a rout, but the first attack had been a failure and, most importantly, the morale of the attackers was severely shaken.

By midday on 3 November, the first troops of 27 Brigade were landing and additional beaches had been cleared. Aitken himself landed later to find leading troops in bad condition. Deciding to build up his force, he instructed the remainder of the troops to land and a bridgehead to be built up, although, fearing an enemy attack, he forebore to disembark troops during darkness. On the other side, Lettow had no such concerns and kept the flow of German troops into Tanga at full speed, arriving himself in the early hours of 4 November.

The remainder of 27 Brigade landed by mid-morning on 4 November and Aitken planned his advance for midday, despite the intense heat. Accordingly, the two brigades deployed in an extended line and moved forward through the dense bush. After an exceptionally difficult and tiring move, they reached the German defences just after noon, only to find them fully manned. Attacking along the entire frontage of his line, Aitken hoped to break into the town and to turn the southern flank. But, the difficulties of maintaining formation and heavy machine-gun fire disrupted the advance. In the north, a melange of units managed to break into the town while, in the south, the line was badly separated and held up. At the critical moment, two Indian battalions disintegrated leaving gaping holes in the line, while the troops in Tanga were driven out by a strong counter-attack. By mid-afternoon, Lettow sent in his reserves in the south against the left of the British line. The weakened and isolated troops had to give way and the entire position of IEF B was put into jeopardy. With morale collapsing and having suffered heavy casualties, Aitken had little option but to break off the action and pull back.

The night of 4/5 November was one of confusion. The German defenders of Tanga mistakenly withdrew again from the town, while the dispirited British moved back to the landing beaches, convinced that they were beaten. Lettow spent the night and morning trying to overcome this blunder while Aitken reluctantly decided on re-embarkation. The transports were called in and the evacuation began after first light and was completed by early afternoon. The Germans eventually re-occupied Tanga and shelled the vessels in the harbour before realising that they had won the battle.[89]

The withdrawal was completed without serious opposition, but the British returned to offer a truce so as to collect the wounded and dead.

Finally, on 7 November the bedraggled convoy sailed for Mombasa, leaving behind an enormous amount of arms, ammunition and equipment to the Germans, as well as having suffered over 800 casualties to the defenders' 145. It was a humiliating defeat in the face of an overwhelming initial superiority in numbers and firepower.[90]

THE HUNT FOR THE *KÖNIGSBERG*

Since its disappearance at the end of July, the *Königsberg* had carried on its war patrol off the Horn of Africa. It managed to capture its prize, the first British vessel of the war, the SS *City of Winchester*, some 450 km east of Aden on 6 August. Replenishing itself from the captured coal and supplies, the German ship kept its prize for nearly a week until it decided to sink it and to proceed alone. There it lurked, unseen and undiscovered, but equally without any prey, as British merchantmen had been warned off the shipping lanes until the arrival of naval reinforcements. The situation for the *Königsberg* became daily more precarious as its high-speed escape had consumed a large proportion of its coal stocks and further prizes were not to be found. Facing a dangerous lack of fuel and the presence of many British cruisers, Looff decided to head south towards friendly territory in the hopes of meeting a German collier off the East African coast.[91] With ever-present threat of detection, he chose to hide his ship in the mouth of the Rufiji River amidst the tropical forest.

He was unaware that the *Emden* had entered the Bay of Bengal from the Pacific Ocean on 10 September, where it found plenty of prey, or that the British were concentrating on this latest threat. But, he was presented with an unexpected opportunity as intelligence reported that the lone British cruiser, *Pegasus*, was anchored at Zanzibar, conducting engine repairs.[92] Making a daring night-time passage through the reefs, Looff surprised his hapless opponent early on 20 September. With its boilers empty, *Pegasus* was a sitting target, easily outranged and outgunned by the superior *Königsberg*. It was no contest, and within a half hour the British vessel was a burning wreck. Later that day, news was received that the *Emden* had sunk five steamers and captured another in the previous five days, all of which was capped by the cruiser bombarding Madras on 22 September.[93] The only positive outcome was that the ships were clearly operating widely apart.

The reduced Cape Squadron was unable to help as it was tied up with escort duties and the planned invasion of German South-West Africa.

Forced to react, the Admiralty despatched three fast cruisers from the Mediterranean to East African waters with another three sent after the *Emden*. The first to arrive on 27 September, *Chatham*, found that the German vessel had vanished again. Wireless signals intercepts betrayed its presence in local waters, but there was a multitude of bays, creeks and inlets in which it might replenish in peace; it would be no easy task.[94] Conscious of this, the responsibility for the area was transferred to the East Indies Squadron, placing it under a single command. These measures turned the balance back into British favour as there were now three modern cruisers, plus the older cruiser *Fox*, on station. Captain F.W. Caulfeild of the latter ship was appointed Senior Naval Officer (SNO), with particular responsibility for the safety of IEF B. A small command, it was sufficiently important for the First Lord, Churchill, himself to draft its orders.[95]

Intelligence was also playing its role, for the British were now in possession of the German trade codes that had been recently seized in Australia. Able to decrypt the *Königsberg*'s signals to its auxiliary vessels, this led the British to the southern port of Lindi on 19 October. Boarding an alleged hospital ship, they found documents and charts showed that the *Königsberg* had recently been replenished on the River Rufiji. Equally importantly, the charts made it clear that the heavier British cruisers would be unable to proceed much beyond the mouth of that little-known river.[96]

The mouth of the Rufiji consisted of a large number of channels, generally shallow and twisting and bounded by dense mangrove swamps. The waterways were not well charted and regularly changed with the influx of mud and flood water. There were two obvious channels, but both had fast-flowing currents and were protected by sandbars. These natural obstacles were supplemented by a chain of German sentry posts along the coast and on Mafia Island, some 6 km offshore. Along the channels themselves, a number of well dug-in and camouflaged defensive positions and treetop observation posts had been constructed. Apart from small arms, they had also emplaced light guns and the *Königsberg*'s torpedoes, together with wire communications back to the ship.[97]

Approaching the river was a dangerous task and it took a landing party to learn of the *Königsberg*'s position in the river; this was confirmed by a visual sighting of its masts on 30 October. While important news, it was tempered by the fact that the enemy ship was at the extreme range of the British guns and that the intervening dense forest made the correction of fire by direct observation impossible. The only answer was an aircraft, but these were primitive and in very short supply. By the first week of November, the sole seaplane and pilot from South Africa was attempting to over-fly the German defences, but the combination of the hot climate and mechanical unreliability caused it to crash. This was countered by the news that the *Emden* had been sunk on 9 November, removing half of the German naval threat.[98] The Rufiji delta now became the decisive focus, but with neither side capable of forcing a decisive solution. It would be several months before this could occur.

DIPLOMATIC WRANGLING

The fiasco at Tanga had given the British a major knock. Despite the evidence of their military weakness, the wrangle between the Colonial and Foreign Offices continued, with Grey wishing to refer the situation to Offensive Sub-Committee as well as exchanging full military details with the Belgians, much to Harcourt's dismay.[99] While these lengthy correspondences took place, in mid-November renewed German activity near Karonga frightened the colonial authorities enough to request Portuguese help. Finally, it was agreed that their assistance could be requested, but only as an emergency measure as it would turn them into belligerents. Again, the lack of co-ordination was made clear by the local military commander's subsequent assessment that he could block any advance, while also noting that the Portuguese Expeditionary Force had arrived at Porto Amelia on 5 November.[100]

Matters were similar in Northern Rhodesia, as, under Colonial Office pressure, negotiations concerning a combined Anglo-Belgian offensive had failed. The Germans had made good use of their naval superiority for reconnaissance and a successful raid on Lukuga in late October. With the Belgian troops in the process of withdrawing back to the Congo, a German raid on the shores of Lake Tanganyika in mid-November and a further advance near Abercorn several weeks later changed matters. At local British request, the Belgian commander halted his troops and marched back to help repel the enemy activity. There they remained until the end of the year and the coming of the rainy season. Thereafter, operations were of a minor nature and were chiefly defensive.[101]

The Colonial Office also displayed marked reluctance to give up control of military operations despite its lack of staff or expertise. It rebuffed attempts to put the troops in Nyasaland and Northern Rhodesia under

War Office control despite the fact that the latter was responsible for the forces in British East Africa and Uganda, and all were facing a common enemy. Even more puzzling was its opposition to the appointment of an overall military commander for the region despite its undeniable logic and the Foreign Office's entreaties. Matters were not helped by Asquith's inability to force a decision and matters dragged on.[102]

In the north, the Belgians were relatively satisfied with security, where, in conjunction with the KAR troops in Uganda, they could match the estimated 2,000 Germans in the Kivu-Tanganyika sector. The Russisi sector was more of a concern, as they had insufficient troops to garrison it effectively and the Germans kept threatening. Finally, in early December, a mobile column of nearly 300 rifles was formed to counter any raids. However, further south in Katanga, they were worried that the Germans held the numerical advantage while maintaining the flexibility to shift their forces rapidly by steamer.[103]

In the meantime, their government was pressing for a common military policy in the region. Their frustration was vented in a note of 8 December in which it declined to accept any more requests for assistance until the two governments had reached some agreement. This unhappiness was shared by the Foreign Office, leading it to ask the War Office for details of British strategy in the region. The answer was not encouraging:

> As far as I can make out, HM Government have no definite military policy in that part of the world. However, up to the present, the attitude of the Colonial Office appears throughout to have been to discourage Belgian efforts for fear of their setting up claims at the end of the war... We have tried to deal with German East Africa by ourselves and we have failed. We have no additional troops to spare to send in reinforcement. The wisest course would seem to be to get the French and Belgians to help us.[104]

This was good advice as it identified both the lack of agreement and strategy within the Cabinet as well as recognising the value of allies. Lord Kitchener had been thinking on those lines for some time and had asked the French if they could provide a brigade from Madagascar. Perhaps to British surprise, this request was agreed to almost immediately and the troops were offered as soon as shipping was available. The offer ultimately declined for strategic reasons, but it illustrates the change in British attitudes since August.[105] Outmanoeuvred, Harcourt gave in and the British

Government agreed to formal military co-operation in mid-December. The Belgians responded enthusiastically, with details of their military forces and offers of support; they were keen to resolve the situation in East Africa as quickly as possible on account of cost and the need to win the war in Europe.[106]

GENERAL WAPSHARE ASSUMES COMMAND

General Aitken had been relieved shortly after his arrival in British East Africa. His replacement, Wapshare, had the immediate task of briefing Kitchener on his plans for the future. He had already proposed an attack on the Voi-Moschi axis together with an advance on Longido and a landing at Dar-es-Salaam, provided that two additional brigades were made available. Despite the recent defeat, the war secretary was not entirely dismissive of this view as he told the new General Officer Commanding (GOC) to consider on an advance of 5-8,000 troops on the Voi-Taveta line while also extending the railway towards Taveta and building the water pipeline. The capture of Tanga was also a possibility although the Navy was to be consulted as to the practicability of a renewed assault.[107]

Wapshare responded with an upbeat appreciation. He identified the strong defences in the Kilimanjaro area, which he estimated at 3,000 Germans and 4,000 Askari, as being too strong to penetrate frontally. He preferred to use the healthy Longido line to bypass Mount Kilimanjaro itself and strike at Aruscha, in the enemy rear area. At the same time, he envisaged the bulk of his force descending on Tanga before advancing up the Usambara line. He asked for two fresh brigades plus a regiment of Indian cavalry to carry out this plan, which could not take place until January at the earliest, and which needed to be completed before the south-west monsoon began in March. The all-important railway would probably reach Bura in four, Maktau in five and Taveta in six months after the commencement of work.[108]

Apart from the substantial extra troops, Wapshare's proposal mirrored Aitken's original plan although it was reasoned in much greater detail. He recognised that the Voi-Tsavo axis was very unhealthy and that water shortages would allow only a maximum of one brigade to operate there. Equally importantly, he noted that a substantial increase in transport, particularly motor vehicles, and the building of a water pipeline from Bura to the Voi area would be essential to his plans. The biggest stumbling block was manpower and the War Office's tentative offer of a composite brigade of troops by the end of February could not be matched by further reinforcements.

While these plans were being forwarded, Wapshare wanted to regain some form of initiative. He chose the coastal area south of Mombasa, which had been vacated back as far as Gazi in September. Here, Germans raiding from their forward post at Jassini had caused over 5,000 Africans to flee the area. However, their forces were quite weak, being only several companies strong and Jassini itself had no military value. On the other hand, the whole area was low-lying, hot and densely vegetated with a fearsome reputation for disease.[109] Nevertheless, Wapshare decided to advance southward along the coast to clear the area and restore British sovereignty. General Tighe was ordered to lead the attack with a force of about three battalions' strength: about 1,800 strong and six machine guns. As it was infested with the tsetse fly, animal transportation was ruled out and some 5,500 porters were employed to move supplies.

He duly set off on 17 December and reached the River Umba three days later after meeting only minor opposition from Abt von Boemken. British naval feints had left the Germans unsure of their exact intentions as they bombarded towns along the entire coastline. However, they had detected the preparations for extending the Voi-Bura railway line as well as the strength of the British defences there. Furthermore, Tighe's advance, coupled with naval superiority, threatened to cut off the coastal troops. Boemken had reached the same conclusion and had started withdrawing south. Lettow viewed this as an opportunity and, emboldened by his success at Tanga, he decided to launch a decisive counter-attack on the coastal axis. Boemken was swiftly ordered back to the frontier while reinforcements were sent to Tanga via the Usambara Railway.[110]

The British crossed the now-flooded river on 21 December and the leading troops cleared the deserted village of Vanga before closing up with Abt von Boemken, some 400 strong, in the village of Jassini further south. Matters remained relatively quiet until 26 December, when a surprise attack took this post with minimal casualties and the Germans withdrew to the south. Having cleared the coast to the border, Tighe then deployed his companies around Jasin and by 27 December, the whole area was securely fortified and the troops settled into their uncomfortable and unhealthy positions.[111]

Nevertheless, Wapshare continued to press London with various offensive schemes throughout December mainly through the Voi-Taveta line and downplayed the Tanga option owing to its unhealthiness. He remained constrained by the lack of available troops, with the first substantial reinforcements unlikely to be ready before July or August at the very earliest. In the circumstances, he showed caution, not wishing to proceed until his forces were entirely ready, and Kitchener happily approved the indefinite postponement of any offensive.[112] In light of the need to eliminate the *Königsberg*, however, he did view the occupation of Mafia Island, which lay off the Rufiji delta, as desirable for it offered a suitable base for the forthcoming seaplane operations. Given the urgency of removing the last potential threat in the area, Wapshare supported the landing of a small force that would remove a valuable enemy observation post and the provision of a small garrison. The War Office concurred with these measures and planning was put into action in late December.[113]

However, at the end of the month, the GOC made a dramatic revision in his plans and stated that he was now confident of landing at Tanga first and fortifying it with second-line troops, before returning his best units to the Kilimanjaro area for a decisive blow there. He would have only the equivalent of two battalions to take the port, although the battleship *Goliath* would remain to provide fire support, with a further two in the Umba Valley and only a half-battalion at Voi. Wapshare recognised that the Germans could easily block any advance out of Tanga with several companies while also attacking the weak garrison at Voi, key to the Uganda Railway.[114] It seems to have been a high-risk option, as the landing at Tanga would be too weak to make a substantial advance while leaving the area opposite the Germans' greatest strength virtually bare.

On the German side, matters had settled down rapidly after the victory of Tanga. Lettow was anxious to restore the defences in the vital Kilimanjaro-Pare gap, where only two companies had remained in the line. The bulk of the reinforcements that had rushed to the coast returned to the north a few days after the battle, leaving only Baumstark and his four companies. However, this time Tanga was left with a significant garrison and a light, covering force remained to cover the border. At the same time, British reinforcement of Erok, and the aforementioned supply difficulties at Longido, convinced him that the latter place should be evacuated. Accordingly, Abt Kraut withdrew from the hill and moved back about to Engare Nairobi, which commanded the gap between Mounts Kilimanjaro and Meru. Here it was much easier to support Kraut while also leaving it less vulnerable to overwhelming attack.[115]

Lettow's forward strategy depended on good lines of communication between the Kilimanjaro area and the heartland of the colony. While the Usambara Railway was invaluable, its terminus at Tanga was now unusable owing to the British Navy. Therefore roads were required and, between September and November, two major routes were cut; one from Morogoro to Handeni and thence to Korogwe, and the other from Dodoma to Kondoa Irangi to Ufiome to Aruscha. These were made usable for wagons and porters, and although lengthy, were a vital link in the supply chain. Furthermore, a uniform series of magazines were also established so as to provide a system of food and equipment storage. Fortunately, the richness of the land enabled the troops to live off local produce and cattle, making supply problems relatively straightforward. There were only four motor lorries in the colony and less than a hundred donkeys plus a few ox-wagons for transport. As with the British, the use of porters was essential and already 7,500 were employed in the northern area alone. They too suffered badly from disease and desertions were many.[116]

Another area of concern was that of feeding the troops. Prior to the war, the majority of food for the Schutztruppe, particularly European, had been imported from overseas before being distributed by rail and porters. The levels of supplies had been greatly helped by the preparations for the planned exhibition of 1914 when large quantities had been stockpiled in order to deal with the expected influx of visitors. Equally, the military units were dispersed across the protectorate and had placed little pressure on local resources. By the end of the year, the numbers serving had increased by two and a half times, with the majority concentrated in the northern area between Tanga and Kilimanjaro. This, coupled with the increasing demand for African manpower to act as porters and labourers, soon put considerable pressure on the farming system. Here again Schnee and Lettow clashed, as the former needed his few experienced officials to collect increasing amounts of food while maintaining civil peace. Lettow saw the matter in simpler terms, decrying the failure to mobilise every single European as a lack of determination, and dismissing the dangers of an uprising.[117]

The biggest problem to supply in the north was the British interdiction of sea movement between Tanga and Dar-es-Salaam. This forced the Germans to move all supplies by porters between Kimamba and Handeni, a journey which took twelve days each way and made serious inroads into the food being carried. At its peak, up to 350 loads of African food totalling 10,500 kg was carried daily on this route, requiring 7,700 porters alone. Additionally, European food, clothing, equipment and ammunition had to be moved on the same route: a considerable amount that must be tempered by the fact that the daily ration was 1 kg of grain. From the trolley head, supplies could be moved by rail to Neu Moschi, whereupon it had to be carried to the forward troops by porters, again reducing the quantities supplied. Like the British, the Germans suffered heavily from the deficiencies of a system based on human labour.[118]

Facing the Belgians on Lake Tanganyika, Lettow ordered reinforcements to Kigoma with the mission of destroying any enemy vessels, to attack the Belgian positions and to support the German land forces in the area. For this task, he sent the small steamer *Kingani*, which had to be dismantled in Dar-es-Salaam and sent by rail to Lake Tanganyika, before coming into service in November.[119] In the south, the combined Anglo-Belgian defences were too strong to breach and operations slowly wound down in anticipation of the coming rainy season.

By the end of 1914, the German colony was in good shape, despite its effective isolation. The Schutztruppe was growing in size and effectiveness, while its spirit had been bolstered by the victory at Tanga, as had Colonel Lettow's personal reputation. The pre-war defence policy was now effectively torn up and he was undisputedly in charge of military policy. His relations with the governor were still tense, although this was relieved by the physical distance between the two. If equipment and weapons were limited, food was still plentiful and the war economy was becoming established. For the Imperial Government, German East Africa was not forgotten, although wartime demands had reduced the RKA in size and effectiveness. The aspirations for a *Mittelafrika* remained, but Solf understood the realities of the strategic situation and that any exchanges of territory would follow a general peace settlement.

3
Operations of 1915

STRATEGIC POLICY FOR 1915

By the beginning of 1915, Britain's strategic position had changed considerably since the heady days of August 1914. The regular BEF had been badly mauled in France and it was becoming apparent that an enormous new army would have to be created. In the Near East, Turkey's entry into the war had increased the military commitments to Egypt and Mesopotamia, heavily stretching India's resources. In naval terms, an attack on the Dardanelles was being considered, while the North Sea remained in stalemate. Apart from the *Königsberg*, the German overseas fleet had been eliminated and the Indian Ocean was secure. East Africa remained low on the list of strategic priorities and few politicians remained sympathetic to a renewed offensive.[1]

The dismal failure at Tanga had shaken confidence in the Indian Army and Wapshare's downbeat telegrams had done little to improve matters. It appeared that many Indian units were virtually ineffective, while the Germans threatened to overwhelm British East Africa. This prognosis was much too gloomy, for despite the many weaknesses in the British forces,

Lettow had his problems to overcome, not least of which were insufficiently trained troops and lack of transport. Furthermore, it overlooked the substantial British advantage in operational mobility via the Uganda Railway and command of both Lake Victoria and the Indian Ocean. They could also count upon ample supplies of arms, ammunition and equipment to replace losses. Numerically, the British still outnumbered the Schutztruppe, which was forced to guard all its distant borders. On the negative side, malaria and lack of water affected both sides equally.

Effectively stalemated, the British also began to strengthen the key Voi-Kilimanjaro sector with small detachments scattered along the Uganda Railway from Mombasa to Lake Victoria. General Tighe had a substantial force along the coastal plain with reserves back at Mombasa. Nairobi was strongly garrisoned and developing into a major base whereas distant Uganda had only sufficient troops for its own security. To the south, the small forces in Northern Rhodesia and Nyasaland were deployed across the frontier with major posts at Abercorn, Fife and Karonga. The Belgian presence remained vital although reinforcements were slowly arriving. A number of white settler units of varying utility had been raised, but no serious attempt had been made to increase the KAR, despite the large potential pool of African manpower, being discouraged on cost and security grounds.

The *Königsberg* remained trapped in the Rufiji delta, although it was tying up a substantial blockading force of cruisers whose draught was too deep to pass into the river system. This meant that it remained out of engagement range while the military was unable to spare the troops for a land attack. The German ship was a tantalising target, outnumbered and relatively immobile, but protected by a combination of narrow river channels, jungle, swamps and strong shore defences. The swampy terrain and thick vegetation made any attempt to landing a military force very risky, as did the incipient monsoon and threat of malaria.[2] Furthermore, the Admiralty wanted to declare a blockade of the coastline as it was concerned about enemy supply ships getting through to the colony. With over 640 km to watch and the forthcoming demands of the Dardanelles campaign, ships were simply not available. So, despite undisputed naval superiority in the Indian Ocean, the Admiralty was far from satisfied with East Africa.[3]

British strategic decision-making was increasingly bedevilled by the inadequacy of the government's machinery for evaluating political goals against available military resources. This was particularly true in East Africa, where military weakness forced local officials to seek close co-operation with allies, whose responses were subsequently rebuffed or discouraged by the government, usually the Colonial Office. However, by early January, attitudes had changed and officials were discussing active military co-operation with the Belgians. In an about face, the Colonial Office even offered to hand over control of southern operations to the War Office, but Kitchener then declined to accept the extra burden.[4]

The Belgians now numbered 3,500 troops on their northern frontier with another 1,000 in or close to Northern Rhodesia. General Henry, now in command, wanted to attack the Germans with a combined column moving from Abercorn against the Bismarckburg area, together with a Belgian-only advance against Ruanda and Urundi. He hoped to raise 5-7,000 Belgian troops together with 8,000 British plus some 5,000 porters raised from Uganda. General Wapshare was authorised to despatch a liaison team to conduct preliminary discussions and gain information, but was not to commit the government to any action, which remained strictly defensive.[5] This attitude also reflected reality as Henry's plans ignored the immense difficulties in assembling and supplying such numbers as well as his lack of ammunition. Secure in the north, he reinforced the line of the Russisi, with a strong force around the main port of Lukuga. The expansion of the Force Publique was well underway, but was greatly hindered by lack of war materials and the difficulty of moving them to the forward areas.[6]

With the Portuguese, the British were content to continue their policy of semi-neutrality as it provided maximum flexibility with minimal commitment. By allowing the unhindered transit of war materials through their territory into Nyasaland and restricting German activities as much as possible, the Portuguese were rendering the greatest assistance. The Portuguese were not entirely happy about this subservient role, but domestic political instability and the subsequent installation of a military government limited their freedom of action. The weak and highly decentralised rule in their East African colony meant that the fiat of the state often did not extend far beyond the major centres of population. The military forces were poorly trained, ill-disciplined and unhealthy while having the difficult task of upholding a regime that was notorious for its severity and rapacity. Indeed, the most notable achievement of Amorim's troops was the cutting of a road and telegraph link from Porto Amelia to

Moçimboa do Rovuma, some 300 km long.[7] For the first half of 1915, they would achieve little else.

For the Imperial German Government, East Africa remained a complete strategic backwater and any thoughts of an expanded African empire had been put off until the ultimate peace conference. The limitations of its naval power had been starkly illustrated by the destruction of its overseas cruiser force and the High Sea Fleet's continued containment in the North Sea. Although the potential of the U-boats was becoming apparent, the technology of the day limited both the range and the time spent submerged quite significantly. These, and the lack of overseas bases, precluded any significant extension of the submarines' radius into East African waters. Furthermore, wireless communications were intermittent at best and letters had to be smuggled through the consulates in Portuguese East Africa and aboard neutral vessels. The only practical way of aiding the isolated colony was to send a supply ship through the British blockade of European waters.[8]

It was the position of the *Königsberg* rather than the Schutztruppe that pushed the German Admiralty to such a measure. Realising that it was unable to break out of the Rufiji unaided, it decided to send a relief ship with sufficient coal, provisions and ammunition for the cruiser to make its escape and return to Germany. It was a risky plan, but there was no alternative, and early in January its contents were passed to the consul in Beira, who had it smuggled to Lindi whereupon it was telegraphed to the Rufiji.[9] Interestingly, inter-departmental rivalry was also alive in Germany and the RKA was excluded from planning the expedition despite its importance to the colony.

An interned British freighter, formerly the *Rubens*, was found and re-flagged as a neutral Danish ship. Now known as the *Kronborg*, it had a bogus cargo of lumber that concealed coal and ammunition for the trapped cruiser, plus 1,800 rifles, cartridges, food and medical supplies for the Schutztruppe. It left Hamburg on 18 February, evading the blockade and breaking out into the Atlantic. From there it moved undetected, taking six weeks to reach the Indian Ocean. Its next objective was to link up with the *Königsberg* and unload its supplies.

Far away in East Africa, Colonel Lettow saw his duty as holding out and diverting as many Allied troops for as long as possible in order to assist decisive operations in Europe. He intended to achieve this through the build-up of an effective and well-trained fighting force that would maximise the defensive advantages of the country. Unlike the governor, Lettow saw German East Africa not as a resource to be developed or civilised, but as a potential battleground that was to be exploited to its fullest. To this end, he devoted his considerable energies to the expansion of the Schutztruppe, although he was hindered by shortages of arms, ammunition and equipment.[10]

Examining the situation, Lettow came to the conclusion that the only possible goal was the Uganda Railway. The coast was unhealthy and always vulnerable to British naval power whereas the west and south were too undeveloped to support large forces. An advance on Nairobi from Longido was simply not possible without large quantities of water and transport, neither of which was available. A move from Kilimanjaro was similarly constrained and might leave the Usambara Railway dangerously exposed. But, the long and vulnerable Uganda Railway was essential to the British position. Small patrols could easily disrupt its operations and would not detract from the build-up of the main force.[11]

But he was not really interested in fighting true guerrilla warfare as he was also looking to fight a decisive battle whenever a favourable opportunity presented itself. Furthermore, he showed little interest in subverting the enemy's African population, nor raising any political agenda. He looked at a campaign in purely military terms and while very good at defensive operations in the bush, he tended to be impatient and pressed distant subordinates to attack often regardless of the difficulties. Apart from the decided success at Tanga under his personal leadership, this policy had led to a number of failures and irreplaceable casualties.

Lettow resolved to carry on the policy of concentrating his main force around Kilimanjaro where defences would be improved, but also from which they could conduct an aggressive patrol policy against the railway. He also wished to reinforce Bismarckburg and Neu Langenburg as soon as the danger of a landing at Dar-es-Salaam had diminished, while also maintaining command of Lake Tanganyika. This would enable him to threaten the Belgians at any point along its length while maintaining mobility and supply for the troops opposite Northern Rhodesia.[12]

OPERATIONS ON THE COAST

British concern for the *Königsberg* led to an amphibious landing on Mafia Island, some 16 km from the mouth of the Rufiji on 10 January. The island had a tiny garrison of only thirty soldiers, but its importance lay in its proximity to the enemy cruiser. The 500 Indian troops landed well away from the defences and, within two days, had overwhelmed the defenders and seized the whole island. This minor victory now cleared the way for Mafia to become the advanced base for operations against the *Königsberg* with its anchorage and planned airstrip.

Lettow's counter-move against the advance to the Umba Valley was also developing during the first two weeks of January. Boemken had conducted reconnaissance as well as several half-hearted attacks on the British forward forces. With the re-deployment from Kilimanjaro to the coast almost complete, Lettow now decided to take personal control. With nine companies, totalling about 1,200 rifles, he had a substantial force. But the ground was difficult, being covered in dense palm and sisal plantations that severely restricted visibility, and he had little detailed information on the British positions. Nevertheless, Lettow resolved to press the attack and his force moved into position on the night of 17/18 January ready to attack at daybreak. His plan was focused on a sisal factory in Jassini and he intended to launch a frontal fixing attack, while two Abteilungen, each of two companies, outflanked the defenders from each side. He also sent a force to cover outlying enemy positions while retaining three companies in central reserve.[13]

The three companies of Indian defenders and reinforcing machine guns were well fortified with stockpiles of food and water. However, there were no guns in direct support and the main body was over 2 km away. The German attack on 18 January was a surprise, but the nearly impenetrable sisal fields and the well-constructed defences caused significant problems. Both sides reinforced quickly and casualties began to mount in the intense heat. By midday, the German advance had stalled in the face of determined British counter-attacks from the north while ammunition began to run short. Deadlocked, the German flanking columns had managed to cut off the main position and although Lettow was pressed to break off the battle, he reckoned that the defenders were also short of ammunition and suffering from thirst. He believed that he had a good chance of victory if his troops could just hold on.[14]

While the battle was underway, General Tighe had rushed down to the battle, having secured more reinforcements from Wapshare. He assumed command on the afternoon of 18 January and launched another counter-attack that failed to dislodge the attackers. He had calculated that Jassini would have sufficient ammunition for a week, but this proved to be wildly optimistic as the garrison had barely enough for a single day. His exhausted troops resumed battle early on 19 January, but the sisal factory was in trouble, having lost its commander and now under heavy artillery fire. Water was beginning to run out and, suffering from the blazing heat, the garrison surrendered in the morning. They were unaware that further reinforcements were close by at sea and about to be landed. It was all too late – Lettow's persistence had paid off and 276 prisoners were taken. With the surrender, the battle was effectively over with both sides physically incapable of continuing the fight. The evacuation of the numerous casualties and bringing up of supplies now became the priority.

If it was a stinging tactical defeat for the British, who had lost 476 out of a total force of 1,800, it was a pyrrhic victory for Lettow, as he had suffered 161 casualties out of 1,615 engaged. It was the loss of officers that hurt, with thirteen of the twenty-two engaged being taken casualty and his second-in-command, Major Kepler, and his staff officer being killed together with two company commanders. Lettow himself had several near misses, having had two bullets pass through his clothing. The expenditure of ammunition was equally prodigious, as the 200,000 rounds fired meant that a maximum of three more such battles could be fought.[15] Moreover, the approaching rains and the consequent growth in the mosquito population helped him to decide to return to Kilimanjaro. After clearing the battlefield and evacuating casualties, the main body began the long journey back to Tanga and thence to Neu Moschi on 23 January.

For his part, Wapshare had insufficient reliable troops to dislodge the Germans, while also realising that malaria was a much greater threat. With the sick rate soaring, the coming rains promised much worse. After a hurried consultation with Tighe and visiting the Umba Valley himself, Wapshare ordered a withdrawal north with a concomitant thinning out of the forward troops.[16] His decision was strongly reinforced by the subsequent rebuke administered by Kitchener, who stated:

> I think you ought to concentrate your forces more and give up risky expeditions that may lead to a serious situation being created in East Africa where we cannot reinforce you sufficiently to be sure of success. You are entirely mistaken in supposing that offensive operations are necessary. The experience at Jassini shows you are not well informed of the strength of the enemy.[17]

With the enemy already pulling back, the British withdrawal was unopposed when it began on 29 January until its completion on 8 February. Two months of campaigning, under the most difficult conditions, had proved most unproductive as it had further eroded British morale and self-confidence. Jassini was the product of bad tactics and a poorly considered operational plan; political reasons had prompted it, but little consideration had been paid to the climate or conditions. The only redeeming factor had been the performance of the KAR who had performed well and shown great spirit.

THE MAIN THEATRE

By early February, the main British force was deployed along the Uganda Railway with a smaller detachment on Uganda's southern frontier. British East Africa was divided into two commands: Nairobi Area, commanded by General Stewart, covered the frontier from Lake Victoria to Longido, while Voi Area, commanded by General Tighe, ran from the Voi-Tsavo area to Mombasa. The worst-affected troops had not recovered from Tanga, and Wapshare was handicapped by a serious lack of reliable infantry with numbers continually reduced by sickness. For the time being, the most his force was capable of was static defence and small-scale patrol activity centred on the Uganda Railway and the approaches to Mount Kilimanjaro.

In the longer term, the chief obstacles to any substantial operations along the Voi-Kilimanjaro axis were lack of water and the effects of the tsetse fly. Apart from the needs of the soldiers, considerable quantities of water would be required for the thousands of pack animals needed to support them. The nearest sources of water were the Bura Hills and German-held Lumi River, some 80 km distant. The solution to these problems was to extend the Uganda Railway from Voi towards Maktau so that the number of animals required could be reduced as well as their time spent in the fly-ridden areas. Parallel to this would be the building of a water pipeline and storage tanks that would enable a large force to be supported. Kitchener was finally convinced and agreed to the proposals on 15 February. With the rains less than a month away, work was started a few days later as soon as specialist railway troops and nearly 2,000 labourers could be collected.[18]

General Wapshare seems never to have given up hope for a renewed offensive, although his resources remained meagre. In early March, he reported that he was faced by an estimated 3,000 Germans and 8,000 Askari, but his reliable troops only amounted to about 1,200 British and 2,100 Indian infantry, 400 mounted troops, eight mountain and seven oxen-drawn guns. The remaining 1,600 British soldiers were in newly-formed battalions that lacked any transport, while a further 1,800 Indians were fit for defensive work only, with the remaining 2,400 Indians only capable of work behind the lines. The animal transport was completely inadequate and it was proving impossible to recruit enough porters to support the troops. Motor vehicles were still very few in number and slow to reach East Africa. More positively, he hoped to have the railway up to Maktau by early August when conditions would be best for campaigning.

The work on the railway line began well despite the shortage of materials and the need to clear the thick bush. By early March, 1,000 soldiers and over 1,800 labourers were committed to the work and 19 km had been cleared; by mid-April the Voi River had been bridged and progress continued to be good. The railhead reached Bura at the end of May while concurrently large quantities of railway material and piping reached Mombasa.[19]

He also had to contend with the possibility of subversion as there had been nagging doubts about the loyalty of the Indian soldiers, particularly the Muslims, since the outbreak of war. German and Turkish agitation for a jihad seems to have had very limited effect, but it was always a worry in the British command, as were the effects of political agitation in India. These fears were not far from groundless as a number of desertions occurred throughout the first half of 1915. Furthermore, there was passive resistance in the form of self-mutilation in both Baluchi and Sikh regiments, with over thirty men charged for this offence after Mbuyuni.[20] But on the whole, it appears that low morale rather than enemy propaganda was responsible for such occurrences and most regiments remained loyal.

In March 1915, Lettow began to fear for a British invasion of the Kilimanjaro area. He made several command changes and ordered his forward troops at Engare Nairobi to attack the British lines of communications in order to disrupt their supply system and therefore make an advance from Longido impossible. This was aided by Wapshare's decision to evacuate the latter place, which was promptly occupied by a newly mounted German force. This meant that the initiative had been lost in the area and patrols soon ranged as far north as the Magadi branch line. He was also aware from captured letters and intercepted wireless messages that the British and Belgians were conferring over possible future offensive plans. His response was to launch a long-range patrolling campaign against the Uganda Railway that would inhibit any build-up. The policy was facilitated by the arrival of the rains and the consequent increase in the ground water supply. By April, operations in the plains east of Kilimanjaro were made possible if still very arduous.[21]

It was not easy, for many German raiding parties had to cross over 80 km of the arid Taru Desert first. Owing to the scarcity of water, standard practice was to infiltrate small groups of about two to four Europeans, three to eight Askari and fifteen to thirty porters towards the railway. This enabled them to evade detection while carrying enough supplies and explosives to make their raids effective. They then had to find an isolated stretch of track before going forward and planting demolitions under the permanent way. Alternatively, pressure-sensitive mines could be laid so that the passage of a locomotive would cause detonation. The subsequent explosion would invariably attract a British reaction and the patrol had to make a hasty withdrawal, before returning over the same unforgiving terrain. With the railway now threatened at almost any point, the British responded by deploying numerous small posts along the line, but with few reserves left to intercept the enemy patrols.[22] However, despite German boldness, the initial impact was minimal despite the lack of adequate defensive preparations along the line.

The continuing weakness and low effectiveness of many regiments resulted in their being relegated to garrison duties on the lines of communication. Dispersed in small posts along the railway, and suffering from malaria and boredom, the fighting efficiency of such units seldom improved. While militarily inadvisable, the policy was seen as politically and morally necessary:

> We are, of course, handicapped by the raiding tendencies of the Germans. We cannot initiate there, as it is not playing the game to make non-combatants suffer. At the same time, we must try to protect our own natives and this means dissemination of force in small posts. It is an impossible problem.[23]

This meant that given the size of the country and the denseness of the bush, it was impossible to prevent German raiding parties from penetrating British lines and reaching an exposed portion of the railway, but they were very vulnerable to effective pursuit. A more active scheme of counter-patrolling was required but this depended on well-led soldiers. Over time, German tactics changed as they began to realise that the destruction of easily repairable track was ineffective and they switched their efforts to eliminating the vital locomotives and rolling stock that were in scarce supply.[24] Such missions were never easy, as, apart from the physical dangers, the British began to build fortified blockhouses every 16 km or so along the line. As well, the columns sent out in pursuit of the raiders were usually much stronger and could overwhelm any small patrol.

By 1 April, the Schutztruppe was still expanding and was just under 10,000 strong, comprising some 2,066 Europeans and 7,716 Askaris, together with seventy-eight machine guns and thirty-eight guns. It was now organised into thirty-six companies across the protectorate, with some 900 Europeans and 3,700 Askaris holding the Usambara Railway and the Kilimanjaro area, with another 580 Europeans and 1,800 Askaris on the Central Railway and the interior stations. There were another 570 Europeans and 2,100 Askaris manning the borders in an arc from Muansa to Bismarckburg to Neu Langenburg. In the depots, another 800 Askaris were under training as well as nearly 1,900 auxiliaries.[25] They faced some 15,000 British troops in British East African and Uganda together with another 400 in Nyasaland and Rhodesia, who were bolstered by another 400 Belgians. The Belgian Congo was secured by nearly 9,000 troops scattered along the length of its frontier. In the far south, the Portuguese maintained about 1,500 troops, although many of these were ineffective. The numbers were in British favour, but not decisively so.

Lettow was about to receive an unexpected bonus from the Navy, as the *Kronborg* had anchored north of Madagascar in early April. After carrying out essential repairs, wireless communications were established with the *Königsberg*, with Captain Looff learning that some of the cargo was intended for the Schutztruppe. Considering that his chances of breaking out of the Rufiji delta were slim, he ordered the *Kronborg* to make for Tanga where it would have a better chance of successfully unloading its cargo. But the British were ready, having read its signals. Admiral King-Hall and his flagship, *Hyacinth*, steamed north to intercept the freighter, meeting up at daybreak on 13 April north of Tanga. The *Kronborg* had little choice but to head into Mansa Bay at top speed. At the critical moment, *Hyacinth*'s port engine broke down and the cruiser lost most of its speed as the *Kronborg* reached shallow water. Now under fire, its scuttles were opened and the ship sank to the bottom. As the British cruiser slowly approached, it hit the freighter repeatedly with shells and it was soon ablaze. The heat was too great to permit inspection and, after a series of explosions, the Admiral was convinced that all the ammunition had been destroyed and the ship was a wreck. After making repairs, *Hyacinth* sailed off to rejoin the squadron off the Rufiji.[26]

This proved to be a huge error, as the flooding of the *Kronborg*'s hold had preserved its cargo from the fire. Most of the ammunition and weapons were left intact and the British departure meant that salvage operations could be started as soon as the wreck cooled. An all-out effort resulted in the retrieval of 2,000 tons of coal and 7,000 rounds of naval ammunition, plus some 1,500 rifles with 4.5 million rounds of ammunition and much-needed medical supplies, clothing and equipment. It would take considerable effort to dry and repackage the ammunition, but it was a major windfall for the Schutztruppe that would give it new life.[27]

At home, Wapshare's operational plans had not inspired confidence, showing little understanding of the need for concentration and a limited grasp of supply problems. He also needed at least two and a half extra brigades of reinforcements.[28] It was becoming clear that the British forces were suffering from a lack of purpose and poor morale, compounded by the constant splitting up of units and lack of clear direction. Strong and decisive leadership was required, and Wapshare was not up to the task. On 3 April, Kitchener ordered him to Mesopotamia as a brigade commander with loss of his temporary rank.[29] Tighe was promoted in his place and Brigadier General Malleson assumed control of the Voi area.

While the new GOC could not be described as a military thinker or tactician, he was much more aggressive and well regarded by the troops. His first priority was the reorganisation of the railway defences, which would become more vulnerable from the middle of May, with the end of the rains and better weather. However, it was the possibility of a combined Anglo-Belgian offensive that initially fired up his enthusiasm. After sending a number of proposals for combined action to the War Office, Kitchener dampened his expectations with a renewed injunction to remain on the defensive. By his own calculations, the defence of the railway was tying up the bulk of his force and he could only deploy a small reserve.[30]

By the beginning of June, Lettow was aware that the South-West African campaign was ending and the South African troops involved there might soon be transferred to East Africa. He considered their use there as a possibility, although he thought it unsuitable for them. The greatest threat continued to be in the Kilimanjaro area, where there was the progress of the railway and the development of water supplies and pipelines in the Bura Hills. These measures, and the surprisingly rapid progress of the Voi-Maktau railway line, pointed to the likelihood of a major offensive in the Kilimanjaro area. The camps at Tsavo and Maktau were too strong to be taken so he continued his patrolling campaign against the Uganda Railway. Precautions for a withdrawal into the interior of the colony were made, with a line being started from Kilossa-Kidodi-Mahenge. In the rear areas, about 100 km of hand-operated trolley lines were established from materials drawn from commercial plantations. Similarly, interim food and ammunition depots were established along the Usambara Railway and telegraphs erected to the south.[31]

With his force largely tied up in the static protection of the Uganda Railway and prevented from wider operations, Tighe needed to raise the morale of his command and a limited objective was the one means of achieving this. An attack on the Kilimanjaro area was impossible, owing to the defenders' strength and his own lack of manpower, while the coastal area was very unhealthy. On the other hand, the British had mastery of Lake Victoria and an amphibious raid offered a quick operation and no long-term commitment. Muansa was the most important port, but it was too strongly held, whereas Bukoba on the western shore was isolated from reinforcements and supplied the troops along the Kagera line. Most importantly, it had a wireless station that maintained communications with the rest of the colony.

The plan was to be carried out by six steamers carrying a force of 1,600 men, two mountain guns and twelve machine guns under Brigadier General Stewart. While the garrison was only 100 strong with a further 140 auxiliaries, a further 400 soldiers and 1,400 ruga-ruga were within 160 km of Bukoba.[32] In order to distract attention, a series of preliminary feints were carried out on the Kagera line from 16 June. The attacking troops embarked on 20 June, arriving off Bukoba the next evening. The landings started at dawn on 22 June nearly 6 km north of the town forming a beachhead. Progress inland was slow, as effective German opposition held the high ground north of the town while their sole gun shelled the flotilla. An attack dented the enemy line, but it was not until the following morning that a flanking movement helped to dislodge the defenders. Finally outnumbered, the Germans pulled out of the town around midday, leaving it to the advancing British. The wireless and fort were then destroyed, but not before a rather unseemly pillage of the town took place. Finally, the entire force re-embarked on the evening of 23 June and returned to Kisumu. While the raid was hardly a decisive battle, it did show that with proper planning and determination the British were capable of success. More worryingly, a released internee revealed that the *Kronborg*'s cargo had been largely salvaged.[33]

In order to disrupt British preparations, in mid-June Lettow ordered Major Kraut, now in command at Taveta, to advance to Mbuyuni with three companies and set up a forward position there. This prominent hill was about seven hours' march from Maktau and, with its water pools, it made an excellent base from which to strike the railway.[34] The shorter approach meant that patrol activity against the new line intensified throughout June and July, causing much inconvenience to the British. General Tighe recognised the threat to his plans and ordered Brigadier General Malleson to drive the enemy out from Mbuyuni as soon as possible.

The Germans were estimated to have about 600 defenders, when in fact they numbered just over 400 rifles and five machine guns. Their position was well sited on a ridgeline with well-camouflaged trenches and good fields of fire. It was a tough position but had no local reserves and was unsupported. The British commander, Malleson, had made his career in administration and had little tactical experience. Furthermore, he was an arrogant and supercilious officer who inspired very little respect. Perhaps because of these traits, he decided to attack Mbuyuni without adequate reconnaissance or even adequate orders. With 1,300 rifles, eleven machine guns and three guns at his disposal, his force was hardly overwhelming and his plan was simple; one flanking column would make a night march to move into the enemy's rear, while the main body would conduct a frontal attack the next morning.

The troops set out from Maktau on the afternoon of 13 July and the main body was in position by darkness. The flanking column made good progress overnight and pushed in the German left flank after dawn. By 0800 hours, it had reached the trench system and was unable to progress further. In the meantime, the main attack had gone in across some 2,000 metres of open ground supported by artillery from the high ground to the rear. However, the German position was a tough one, consisting of a series of well-camouflaged trenches sited in a thickly-vegetated area. Heavy fire made it difficult for the attackers to advance and the British artillery observers found it difficult to locate targets. By 1030 hours, the assault troops had lost all momentum and casualties were beginning to mount. An hour and a quarter later, Malleson learned that the flanking force had been halted and decided to break off the attack.

These orders had not reached the detached column at 1300 hours, when it was struck by a German force in its rear. Unaware that the enemy force was a returning patrol of only eighteen rifles, the column commander executed a fighting withdrawal until he received instructions to break off the battle completely, which he did without difficulty. However, the main body was not so fortunate, as firing caused the porters to panic and drop all their loads. Eventually, after much confusion, order was restored, but not without the loss of a machine gun, 80,000 rounds of ammunition and much equipment. The attack on Mbuyuni can only be described as a fiasco. Inadequate reconnaissance, planning and fire support led to the loss of 200 casualties as compared to the Germans' twenty-seven. Again, the quality of British generalship was shown to be poor and the threat against the railway remained.[35]

Despite this success, Lettow was not finding the situation easy. By the end of July his troops could claim to have derailed three trains and blown up the track on seven other occasions. These were not major blows and while they caused stoppages in traffic, they did not inflict any serious harm. In fact, the British GHQ considered that they had had the best of the patrol activity and that no material damage was done. Direct attacks on the British strongpoints at Maktau, Mzima and Tsavo were out of the question, as they were too heavily fortified to be attacked without heavy loss.[36]

In July, relations between Lettow and Schnee deteriorated further over a dispute concerning the garrison of Lindi. The soldier wanted it to march north and join the main body, but the governor was adamantly opposed as he considered that the police were inadequate to control an area that had played a major part in the Maji-Maji rebellion. After having his order countermanded, Lettow took the extraordinary step of writing a protest directly to the Kaiser in which he complained about the orders not to defend the coast in 1914, and the right of the governor to interfere in military decision-making. While he was within his rights to do so, most of the complaint was hardly relevant to the current circumstances; Schnee attached a rejoinder in which he rebutted the charges, citing the agreed pre-war plans and the need to prevent an uprising. It eventually reached

Berlin in August 1916 and although Schutztruppe headquarters supported Lettow, the RKA never passed on the complaint.[37]

Lettow did not hesitate to complain to Schnee about these matters in his written reports. In June, he noted that while civil-military co-operation was good in the northern area (where he was present), the same was not true of the rest of the colony. He was unhappy with various bureaucratic measures and the attitude of many officials. Again, in September, he wrote that many areas were still operating under peace-time priorities and that the needs of the troops in the field were being ignored, which seems to have been true.[38]

General Tighe was worried that the Germans were capable of arming up to 20,000 soldiers with the possibility of raising more, while his own forces dwindled through sickness; he considered that he had only 4,000 reliable soldiers and of these some 3,000 only could be concentrated on Maktau and Mzima. He considered the possibility of a German advance on those places as quite possible and potentially very serious.[39] Such pessimism must be considered against the actual situation. First, while illness had reduced British numbers considerably, the troops there were in well-defended positions with ample ammunition, food and water. Equally, the same problems of advancing across an arid plain that stymied a British advance did the same for the Germans.

If Tighe was formally prevented from pursuing a more aggressive policy, he was not above using unofficial methods to achieve his aim. In mid-July, he quietly despatched an officer and prominent settler to Southern Rhodesia and South Africa with a letter asking for support from those territories. He took pains to ensure that it would be shown to both the Prime Minister, General Louis Botha, and his deputy, General Jan Smuts, as their interest in East Africa was well known.[40]

Overall, GHQ was not unduly worried about the effectiveness of the enemy raids against the railway, even expressing satisfaction at having dominated operations in June and July.[41] But the realisation that the Germans had largely re-armed and re-equipped themselves, plus the rumour of a second supply ship, caused Tighe much concern as did the continuing toll of malaria. By mid-August, he considered that while he could hold his own against the estimated 20,000 German troops, his remaining 4,000 reliable infantry would be badly stretched in the case of a two-pronged enemy advance. His plight was seemingly deepened by the loss of the mid-desert signalling post and water hole at Kasigao through poor defences a few days later.[42]

Furthermore, from August, improvements in German mines made their patrols more effective. The development of the difficult-to-detect contact mine renewed British anxieties about their lifeline to the coast. September witnessed a number of attempts to disrupt the line with increasing patrol clashes. This was continued into October, and although a number of mines were detected, a number of trains were damaged.[43] Overall, Lettow was frustrated by the lack of decisive success. His efforts in the south had foundered and British strength in the north offered few opportunities for major attacks. He was pleased with the results of his patrols against the railway, while the salvaging of *Königsberg* guns now provided Dar-es-Salaam, Tanga, Muansa and Kigoma with long-range naval defences, reducing the burden of garrisons there. His troops had reached over 13,000 with 2,600 Europeans, 10,700 Askaris and 2,800 auxiliaries. On the other hand, supplies had hit a low in August with only eight days' ration in stock, but with careful management and the new harvest this was tripled by the following month.[44] The Imperial Government was pleased with his resistance and, as a mark of its approbation, Lettow was promoted to full colonel.

A further attempt to regain the initiative was launched by General Stewart in late September when a mix of cavalry and infantry were sent to push a German detachment out of the Longido position. Some 450 troops were sent in against an estimated eighty defenders with the infantry due to launch converging attacks while the cavalry were positioned to cut off any escape. Setting out on 16 September, the force attacked four days later, having paused for reconnaissance. It was not thorough enough and the British were driven back with painful losses.

In contrast, their new tactic of immediately launching infantry cut-off groups as soon as a German patrol was detected was proving effective. This was further enhanced through the use of armoured cars and mounted infantry in the pursuit, making the escape of the raiders difficult and dangerous. In response, the Germans increased the strength of their fighting patrols from the Taveta area to seventy, eighty or even 100 men, but still found it increasingly difficult to operate. They were also restricted by the weather, as many of the waterholes were now dried up and the Mbuyuni position had to be abandoned for that reason.[45]

Captured British weapons and the arrival of the *Kronborg* had done much to re-equip the troops with modern rifles. Lettow was keen to raise the size of his forces, but constraints on experienced troops led him to increase the strength of companies rather than field new units. Recruiting and training continued apace, as the force was now organised into thirty companies of 200 riflemen and fifteen to thirty officers and NCOs. The majority were concentrated in the arc Neu Moschi-Taveta-Kilimanjaro-Meru with strong detachments at Langenburg, Tanga and Dar-es-Salaam. Several companies were each in the areas of Muansa, Bukoba and along the Belgian border.[46]

The Germans certainly had to improvise considerably, as the garrison of Muansa showed. The local commander was concerned about British naval supremacy on the lake, having only several small and unarmed vessels at his disposal. Trenches had been dug and sound defences erected, but lack of effective artillery was a major drawback. Five companies of ruga-ruga recruits had been raised, but their training was patchy with only one considered good, two as fair, one as suitable for defence only and one completely unready for operations. Training was slow owing to the insufficient numbers of instructors and lack of Swahili knowledge by many Europeans. Half the troops were armed with worn-out M71 rifles and two companies had no weapons at all. There were also shortages of belts, buckles, clothing and webbing for which the local official was trying manufacture. Sickness was high, with sixty-one (out of 160) Europeans admitted to hospital in July and an average of 60-100 Askaris suffering from illness. Despite Lettow's desire for a more aggressive stance, there was little he could actually achieve in the area.[47]

THE STRUGGLE FOR THE UGANDA RAILWAY

It is instructive to consider several examples of operations along the Uganda Railway. While a number of raids were launched from the Taveta-Salaita sector opposite the British Maktau-Tsavo position, many others originated either from the coast or through the Pare Mountains. For example, 17 FK sent out a patrol from Mvomoni near the coast on 20 July, consisting of a German lieutenant, two African NCOs, fourteen Askari, twenty porters and three local guides. After two fruitless days trying to find a way north, the patrol set out across the trackless and waterless veldt which it crossed in a day and a night. Leaving half the party and food behind in a concealed camp, the remaining eleven soldiers and ten porters worked their way through more populated country, successfully posing as British soldiers for a period. On 25 July, they could see the Taru Hills and knew that they were close to the railway. Having been spotted by the local inhabitants, the patrol headed north-west on a compass bearing, having to crawl for three hours through thick bush. They reached the railway west of Samburu Station where it curved in a cutting. Explosives were laid and detonated before the party hurried back south. Three days were spent on the return journey, only to find that the remainder of the patrol had gone, taking all the food with them. Now very hungry and unable to halt, the group marched back to their own lines, reaching Mvomoni on 30 July. On return, the patrol commander noted the lack of enemy and of any follow-up at all.[48]

Despite this, Lettow was not content that the results of these arduous and dangerous patrols were commensurate with the effort put in. He wrote to Battalion Tanga on 6 August, forbidding further attacks on the railway tracks as the damage was very easy to repair. He ordered future efforts to be devoted to attacking bridges or other particularly vulnerable features as well as developing contact mines.[49] A few weeks later, the same officer led another patrol, departing on 27 August. This time the patrol encountered alert villagers who were clearly warned to watch for German raiding parties. After a four-day march to the railway, in which they had to avoid all inhabited areas, the patrol was resting within 20 km of the line, when it was suddenly attacked by a British patrol which had been tracking the raiders. Fire was opened at close range which terrified the porters, who bolted, taking all the vital food, maps and equipment with them. With only twelve soldiers, the Germans were outnumbered and had to carry an Askari who had been shot through the leg. After a battle in thick bush, the patrol broke away and spent the next four days on exhausting forced marches. With no food and only scant water, they were lucky to reach Mvomoni on 3 September alive. On returning, the patrol commander found that he had been tracked almost from the beginning of his raid and that the British had improved their surveillance greatly.[50]

For the British, operations along the Uganda Railway were equally hard work, with much monotonous guarding and patrolling interspersed with sudden actions. The experiences of the sole British regular battalion, 2nd Battalion, the Loyal North Lancashire Regiment, are illustrative. Following its hard fight at Tanga in November 1914, it had been sent immediately to Nairobi where it had acted as the central reserve for the security of the railway. By the end of the year it was split, with half in the Magadi area and the remainder operating out of Nairobi. Early in January 1915, two companies were sent out to the coast to support the Umba

Valley operations while another was deployed to the eastern shores of Lake Victoria. After a return to base, the companies were scattered again with another visit to the lake and a number of patrol duties. Life was marked by a great deal of hard marching with low-level skirmishes amidst a background of increasing sickness. March saw the beginning of increased German patrol activity against the railway and much time was spent on patrolling. In May, the commanding officer led a column in a fruitless chase of a raiding party, covering some 57 km in twenty-two and a half hours in very bad weather. At the end of the month, another two companies moved to Karungu on Lake Victoria, where after three nights' outpost duty, every man was down with fever.[51]

In June, half the battalion took part in the raid on Bukoba where it was heavily engaged in the break-in battle before re-embarking the next day. After returning to Nairobi, the unit was moved to Maktau in early July to help counter the German threat from Mbuyuni, numbering some twenty-one officers and 490 other ranks. After a thirty-six-hour train journey, it took over the defences there before being ordered to send half the battalion to Bura to defend the waterworks against enemy patrols. Back in Maktau the remaining companies were employed in mobile columns chasing off raiders. Two companies took part in the failed attack on Mbuyuni on 14 July and, after returning from this rebuff, the rest of the month was spent on patrols. The most striking detail was the increase in sickness; out of the battalion's 834 men serving in East Africa, some 577 had been in hospital one or more times. Of these, 209 were detached from the unit on other duties, while 123 were in hospital. The remaining 502 soldiers were split between Maktau and Bura, but some 213 were not fit for hard work owing to fevers – making a total of 332 non-effectives.[52]

Most of August was spent on guard duties interspersed with mobile columns being sent out to disrupt enemy patrols. On 14 August, seventy reinforcements arrived followed by 110 more on the 30th, but lacking essentials such as blankets, waterproof sheets and mosquito nets.[53] September began more eventfully, as the battalion's Mounted Infantry company had a sharp fight with a German patrol, losing eight men to the enemy's three. The next day, 4 September, saw the bulk of the battalion move to Bura where it rejoined its headquarters. The tedious and hot patrol work was finally relieved by a major success on 14 September, when the Mounted Infantry and 130th Baluchis ambushed a raiding party near Maktau, causing heavy casualties. As this was the first marked success for some time, it did much to raise morale. Just two weeks later, three platoons were sent out to intercept a patrol, but instead fell victim to an ambush, suffering nineteen casualties, including fourteen dead.

The battalion's health was still no better, with 161 men in hospital and another 120 being unfit for work out of 940 in the theatre in early October.[54] Belatedly, after a month and a half's field service, the August reinforcements received their blankets and mosquito nets. Apart from losing the machine-gun section to another column, the month was spent on security duties although forty armed African scouts were attached to the battalion. November was little different with the battalion leaving Bura on 13 November and marching 14 km forward to Mashoti. Despite constant patrolling and a minor find early in the month, it was not until 18 November that a small contact was made on the railway. One enemy Askari was killed, but the remainder escaped the follow-up. The next day, the battalion was informed that it would be part of the newly raised Voi Brigade under the command of Brigadier General Malleson. This was followed by a major operation on 21 November, when 300 men were detached to Voi and stayed out until the last day of the month, returning hungry and thoroughly wet.

Operations in December followed the familiar pattern of guards and railway patrols. The Mounted Infantry were involved in a substantial fight on 8 December when a large German force was engaged and routed, losing over thirty casualties.[55] The subsequent loss of Kasigau Hill caused major concern and two companies were immediately sent off to contain the situation. After a long and wearisome march, the attack was called off and they returned home on 12 December. Shortly thereafter, General Malleson then ordered 350 men to attack an un-reconnoitred and unconfirmed enemy position that turned out to be a wild-goose chase, with the column remaining out until well into the New Year. At the end of a frustrating year, the commanding officer simply noted: 'The British forces in East Africa have not yet gained ascendancy over the German Askari in scouting in the Bush and general Bush warfare'.[56]

Some of the Indian units were still in poor shape. The Kapurthala Imperial Service Infantry was considered to have lost its collective nerve and was removed from the front line. Even then, their performance was doubtful, as their piquets once memorably rushed into camp warning of an imminent enemy attack; the 'enemy' was later found to be a troop of baboons.[57] The regular 13th Rajputs were sent to the quiet sector of

Uganda while the 98th Infantry was relegated to the backwater between Lake Victoria and Nairobi. The former's commanding officer was eventually removed for incompetence as his unit was considered to be in a 'slack and unsatisfactory condition'.[58] The change of command seems to have had little positive effect, for in June the GHQ War Diary commented acidly:

> The 98th Infantry occasionally fight pitched battles with purely imaginary foes between Nairobi and Kisumu – but it is fairly certain that no enemy has attempted that part of the line, which is far from the frontier.[59]

As 1915 progressed, the Germans continued their attempts against the railway. On 1 October, 3 FK was ordered to send a patrol of two Europeans, two Askari and eight porters from its rest location on Mombo on the Usambara Railway. They moved by train to Mkomazi, then disembarked and marched through the gap between the Pare and Usambara Mountains. They reached the edge of the Taru Desert on 12 October and, after a day's rest, they set out for the forward post at Kifugua where excess baggage and reserve food was dumped. The next objective was Kasigao, an important hill some 30 km from the railway that possessed a good supply of water. This was reached on 17 October and bypassed using rhinoceros paths and moving through dense thorn bushes. The next evening, after an extended halt owing to the collapse of two porters from lack of water, the patrol reached the railway near Maungu Station. After successfully laying a mine, the patrol separated and, in confusion, a German NCO shot and wounded the commander by mistake. As this was being sorted out, a train initiated the mine, and the party quickly headed back, but suffering intensely from the heat. By 21 October they reached the area of Kasigao, having lost the two porters carrying the water who were never seen again. Matters were extremely serious and another carrier went mad and ran off shrieking into the bush. At their last gasp, the patrol reached Kifugua and water. Finally, on 25 October, the bedraggled patrol reached Mkomazi again and the wounded commander was sent to hospital where he took four months to recover.[60]

Although operations along the Uganda Railway were relatively low level and not spectacular, they were inevitably physically hard and mentally challenging. The Germans showed particular skill and determination in their patrolling in the harshest of environments, although the results achieved were not always commensurate with their efforts. The British had a tough time too, with much hard work in difficult conditions and hot sun, although their columns were never in the precarious position of the enemy patrols.

OPERATIONS IN THE SOUTH AND WEST

The British had a scare in late January, when an African rising broke out in Nyasaland and several whites were murdered. Led by John Chilembwe, a charismatic church leader, the revolt was unconnected with any enemy intrigue – indeed a captured German officer was instrumental in helping to suppress it. However, concerns for the safety of Europeans led to local officials requesting assistance from the Portuguese. They duly despatched a column although by the time it arrived, the uprising had been crushed.[61] Interestingly, this action was not seen as breaching neutrality as it was co-operation in support of maintaining European rule, and not general warfare.

For their part, the Belgians had considerable low-level activity in the volcanic region north of Lake Kivu against Wintgens' troops in Ruanda during January. But, with both sides well entrenched and movement difficult, there was no decisive action in this sector. On Lake Tanganyika, the Germans began the year with three major vessels on its waters; the steamer *Hedwig von Wissmann*, armed with four 37mm revolver guns; the tug *Kingani*, of 25 tons and carrying a revolver gun; and two motor boats. Moreover, the formidable 1,200-ton *Graf von Götzen* was nearing completion and would carry an armament of 87mm, 37mm and machine guns. The Belgians had nothing to counter these, although the large steamer *Baron Dhanis* was still awaiting its engine and boilers from Europe. These vessels were active and shelled Belgian coastal positions on several occasions, although causing little effective damage.[62] The biggest problem was the railway, as it had only reached Lukuga in February and its capacity was severely constrained by its wooden bridging. This would have serious consequences for the building of a harbour and the bringing up of sufficient supplies for the field army.

Along the Russisi line, events were more serious. The Belgians had taken up strong defensive positions in the hills west of the pestilential valley between the two lakes. Despite the enemy's superiority and good defences, Lettow had long been pressing for decisive action in the area.

Finally, on 12 January, Abt Schimmer moved towards the post at Luvungi, roughly in the centre of the line. After an exhausting advance, the attackers were hit by heavy fire, and after a brief battle that saw their commander killed, the Germans retreated in complete disorder.[63] Once again, an ill-conceived and difficult attack launched under pressure had miscarried.

In mid-February the British liaison mission under Brigadier General Malleson arrived at Rutschuru in the far north to confer with General Henry. From the outset, they were unable to reconcile their respective instructions as the latter now wanted a combined offensive against Ruanda. The British lacked the forces for such a move and Malleson could only agree that gaining control of Lake Tanganyika would be the essential precursor to any invasion. The reality of the situation was that the Belgians needed arms and ammunition from the British and the journey from Uganda to Rutschuru alone would take over a month. Three convoys were already underway, but any hope of an April offensive was out of the question and the earliest dates would be June or July.[64] These rather fruitless negotiations continued throughout March, when Henry was informed that General Tombeur had been appointed to the chief command. Unfortunately, the latter was at least six weeks' journey from Rutschuru and Malleson was ordered back to Nairobi.[65] The mission was a failure as much through the British unwillingness to assume the offensive in East Africa as wishful thinking of the Belgian commander.

The Belgians retained their enthusiasm to conquer Ruanda and Urundi, with or without the British. In early March, Tombeur had three distinct groups with 5,000 men in the north, 2,000 securing Lake Tanganyika and 2,000 under Olsen in the south. But by the beginning of the next month, it was quite clear that the British would not participate in a general offensive and General Tombeur was authorised to invade Ruanda with the means at his disposal. As a preliminary measure, he was instructed to withdraw his troops from Northern Rhodesia and to move them north. The government was also determined to obtain a squadron of seaplanes, with which the German bases on Lake Tanganyika could be bombed. However, without sufficient transport and still very short of machine guns and ammunition, the most that could be accomplished in the coming months was reconnaissance, small-scale raids and general preparations. The clearance of the lake would have to await further reinforcements.[66]

Apart from providing the necessary aircraft, ordnance and ammunition, the British now agreed to help wrestle control of the lake from the

Germans. A big game hunter, John Lee, had convinced the Admiralty of the possibility of moving small craft some 4,800 km overland from Cape Town to Lake Tanganyika and linking up with the Belgians. In April, Commander Spicer-Simson was appointed to command the tiny force of twenty-eight sailors and two 12-metre motor boats, of 4 tons, armed with a 3-pounder and a machine gun. His mission was straightforward; 'The object of the expedition is to obtain command of the waters of Lake Tanganyika'.[67]

The mission was daunting in the extreme. After the long sea voyage from Britain to Cape Town, the boats would be carried 4,000 km by rail to Fungurume in the Belgian Congo, where they would be dismounted and dragged by steam tractor over 220 km of bush to Sankisia. Then, they would steam another 640 km up the shallow and twisting Lualaba River, before reaching the Belgian rail network at Kabalo. A final rail journey of 290 km to Lukuga, on the western shore of Lake Tanganyika, would follow with the boats having to be unpacked and readied for action without the enemy noting their presence. Hopeful of surprise, the Admiralty believed that the force could overwhelm the Germans; unfortunately for them, the Germans had learned of the expedition before it departed through intercepted Belgian wireless messages.[68]

The expedition sailed on 11 June, reaching the Cape three weeks later and finally Fungurume on 4 August. It was nearly two weeks before the steam tractors could be brought up and put into action; the motley convoy set off on 18 August through narrow tracks and up steep inclines. Apart from the primitiveness of the vehicles, the difficulties were manifold as fuel wood had to be cut daily and all water for the boilers had to be laboriously collected by hand. The journey took six weeks, in which time roads had continually to be widened, which often required major felling of trees, and over 200 bridges had to be constructed. Frequent breakdowns and the difficulties of the route meant that 6-8 km per day was often the maximum achieved. Finally, after many hardships and huge effort, Sanskisia was reached on 28 September, and the boats were placed in the Lualaba River three days later.[69] The water was too low to use engines, so for the next week teams of rowers paddled the vessels up river. On 8 October, deeper water was reached and engines could be used for the remainder of the journey. Despite this, towing and poling was needed to overcome numerous groundings before the bedraggled force reached the railway at Kabalo on 21 October.[70]

During this period, Lettow was also concerned about the western theatre and was planning his own blow against the Anglo-Belgians. His targets were Abercorn-Saisi in the west and the wheat-growing area of Langenburg, further east. Early in April, Major von Langenn was nominated to command the force of six companies, two of which travelled by rail from Dar-es-Salaam to Kigoma before sailing south to Bismarckburg. However, lack of shipping space and the difficulties of moving troops in a remote area meant that the force was slow in assembling and only minor actions took place in May. Lettow remained impatient for a decisive battle, and deciding that the moment had passed in the west, he ordered Langenn's force to march the 200 km to Neu Langenburg. But the British were too strong and he contented himself to patrolling between Fife and Karonga.

Dissatisfied, Lettow now decided to place General Wahle in charge at Bismarckburg with an additional company as reinforcements. Using the lake steamers to move his troops, Wahle arrived at Bismarckburg on 7 June and was given clear orders: 'Task is not border protection or the driving back of the enemy, but rather a decisive success of arms'.[71] Although the British motor boat expedition had not been detected, Lettow was concerned about the Belgian attempt to ready their steamers for service. On 19 June, Wahle was ordered to attack the port of Lukuga and destroy the Belgian vessels, by the middle of July at the latest. However, Lettow had not given up hopes for a big success around Abercorn and instructed Wahle to first attack the Anglo-Belgian advanced post at Saisi. Under pressure to meet his deadline and lacking artillery, Wahle launched his attack on 28 June, with barely 390 men against over 400 well dug-in defenders. Unsurprisingly, the assault was sharply repulsed and Abt Wahle retired back to Bismarckburg.[72]

Through spies and signals intercepts, the Germans became aware that the Belgians were redeploying troops from the south towards Lake Kivu. While both Lettow and Wahle agreed that the threat to Ruanda and Urundi appeared to be increasing, the former was determined to destroy the *Baron Dhanis* and retain control of the lake. He continued to press for an attack, but Wahle disagreed, citing the bad weather in June and July as well as his own lack of forces. He preferred to lift the siege of Saisi and to concentrate his forces on the Russisi Valley.

There he learned that the Navy would not be ready for a landing at Lukuga in mid-July, and despite Lettow's pressure for a raid, Wahle stood firm, again citing the bad weather and lack of numbers. Finally, on 7 July the former changed tack and ordered Wahle to besiege Saisi in order to deliver a crushing blow to the Allies. It took several weeks to assemble the necessary force and reinforcements; now numbering over 800 with nine machine guns and two guns, the Germans began their encirclement on the night of 25/26 July. In the preceding week, the defenders had made substantial improvements to the defences as well as stocking up food and ammunition. An initial assault was thrown back by the defenders before a Belgian relieving force attempted to break through. The German line held, but neither side was able to make headway. The German artillery ammunition was largely ineffective against the defences and it was impossible to cut them off from their water supplies. Wahle accordingly decided to break off the action on 2 August and withdrew to Bismarckburg.[73]

With it, Lettow's plan had miscarried completely and had instead caused serious losses to his own troops without any commensurate effect on the Allies. While it had tied up a single Belgian battalion for several months, the effect was minimal. On the other hand, the British naval success gave it unchallenged supremacy on the Indian Ocean. Once again, Dar-es-Salaam was threatened and the bulk of Wahle's troops were ordered back to the coast, with the last men only arriving there on 21 August.[74]

Portugal had had a difficult and destabilising year that had been marked by a military coup in May. While nationalist elements wanted to enter the war for reasons of pride and possible territorial gains, a declaration of war would expose its East African colony to German attack. British assistance, however necessary, would be distasteful and the Portuguese remained deeply suspicious of South Africa's intentions towards their colonies.[75] In face of this, Amorim's force was ordered to re-occupy the Kionga triangle in June. This empty patch of land lay at the mouth of the Rovuma and had been earlier annexed by the Germans. It had no value, but the dispirited Portuguese force could not manage this limited task and had to content itself with maintaining a line of posts along the Rovuma River.

The British were also placing heavy pressure on the Portuguese to restrict German activities in their territories. While the metropolitan government and the governor general in Lourenço Marques issued orders to stop the flow of contraband and information crossing the border, they were only partially effective. In July, the Minister of Colonies issued an edict reinforcing the prohibition of trade and contraband, naming several German firms, but aided by a great number of employees of the Niassa

Company.[76] The restrictions did begin to bite, but they were never completely effective in shutting off communications across the border.

DESTRUCTION OF THE *KÖNIGSBERG*

Early in 1915, the battleship *Goliath* picked up an interesting passenger at Durban; one Pieter Pretorius, a Boer and big game hunter. He was a remarkable man who had spent his life in the African bush and knew German East Africa and the Rufiji Valley intimately. He was an expert tracker who was destined to become chief scout of the British forces in 1916 and 1917. However, his immediate task was to locate the *Königsberg* and discover its distance from the sea. Using stealth and disguise, Pretorius managed to evade the German defences and actually reached the ship itself. His initial mission accomplished, he was given an even more daunting task, that of finding a channel suitable for flat-bottomed monitors to pass. This involved taking soundings of the river entrance from a canoe, often in daylight and close to the defences. After a considerable period, this dangerous and monotonous job was successful and a route was found and charted – one more remained. Pretorius now was instructed to spend one month on shore, measuring the rise and fall of the tides on an hourly basis. Finally, this important task completed, Admiral King-Hall was ready to complete his arrangements for the attack on the *Königsberg*.[77]

The continued existence of the *Königsberg* was an unwelcome drain on British naval resources. The use of seaplanes had pinpointed the ship's position, but the problem of attacking the vessel remained unresolved. In April 1915, the Admiralty decided to send out two monitors, HMS *Severn* and *Mersey*, which had originally been built for the Brazilian Navy for use on its rivers. Taken over on the outbreak of war, these flat-bottomed craft mounted two 6-inch and one 4.7-inch guns on an un-armoured frame. However, despite their lack of seaworthiness, low freeboard and ungainly shape, they had one vital feature; a shallow draught. This meant that they could move up the shallow channels of the Rufiji and get into engagement range.[78] Getting to East Africa from the Mediterranean was a huge problem in itself, as the monitors had to be towed by tugs and the crews carried aboard an escort ship through the heat of the Red Sea and difficult conditions in the Indian Ocean. After an epic journey of five weeks, the convoy reached Mafia Island on 3 June. Equally important to the plan was the arrival of a squadron of four new aircraft, which were based on a newly-constructed airstrip on the island. Apart from the numbers, this represented a major increase in capability as these craft could reach over 1,000 metres in altitude, whereas the seaplanes hitherto in use could barely achieve 300 metres. Training and practice firing now ensued to be ready for the big attack.[79]

The British naval force now numbered four light cruisers, two armed merchantmen and the two monitors. Repairs after the long sea voyage and the fitting of armour plate took nearly a month, and by 5 July Admiral King-Hall was ready to attack. The plan was dependent on surprise; the monitors would enter the Rufiji channel under cover of darkness supported by the guns of the cruisers who would suppress the shore defences as much as possible. With the *Königsberg* hidden from direct visual observation, the two aircraft were given the task of directing the fire of the monitors onto the target. It was a complex operation that required good co-ordination, navigation and accurate shooting against a strong enemy.[80]

Severn and *Mersey* commenced their move early on 6 July followed by the larger ships at flood tide. They burst past the shore defences, coming under heavy fire, but emerged relatively unscathed. They then anchored and opened fire on the enemy cruiser, some 11,000 metres away. The *Königsberg* replied with accurate fire based on concealed shore observation posts and Mersey was hit, losing a gun. The fight continued throughout the day, with a number of hits on the German vessel, none of them serious. By mid-afternoon, the action was broken off and the monitors re-ran the gauntlet at the mouth of the river.[81]

The action had been only partially successful and King-Hall wanted to finish off his opponent as quickly as possible. However, the firing at extreme elevation and effects of the *Königsberg*'s guns rendered further repairs necessary and it was not until 11 July that the British were ready for a second attack. This time the high tides were in daylight and the Germans were ready for another attempt. The monitors again passed the hail of heavy shore fire and were soon engaged by the *Königsberg* itself. Advancing by leapfrog movements, *Mersey* used its aerial observers to good effect and began to score an increasing number of hits despite the loss of one of the aircraft. *Severn* joined in the action and the German fire began to weaken under the pressure. By midday, the end was near as salvo after salvo was hitting the cruiser. An aircraft was shot down by one of the last shrapnel shells, but it was too late. With the loss of nearly all the gun crews, the captain severely wounded and the need to flood the magazine, further resistance was futile. At 1330 hours, the ship was abandoned and orders were given to blow up the hulk. Using a torpedo warhead, the once proud *Königsberg* was ruptured and sank to the bottom half an hour later.[82]

The British quickly realised this, as they had heard the explosion and the lack of firing was indicative. The remaining aircraft confirmed that the ship was on fire and had sunk into the muddy waters of the Rufiji. With this, King-Hall recalled his ships and signalled the end of the naval threat to the Indian Ocean.[83]

CIVIL-MILITARY RELATIONS

As the operations progressed, away from the front line, normal life in the various colonies continued. There were shortages and numerous restrictions on liberty, including the increasing demands for manpower, both military and civil, but outwardly life had not changed too much. One factor that remained constant was that of maintaining the supremacy and prestige of colonial rule. Whites remained a tiny minority of the overall population and very conscious of the fragility of their power over the black majority. While the increasingly large armies could overwhelm any uprising or rebellion, the inescapable fact remained that the war could only be successfully prosecuted with the tacit consent of the populace. This meant that the government could only push demands for manpower, labour and taxes to a certain point; if it went beyond that, then disorder would follow. With disorder, the whole system of porterage, food and equipment production for the military and trade would collapse. Whatever the military situation, the civil administrators forgot this at their peril and this would become an important point of contention.

There was a tendency for the military to complain about lack of enthusiastic support by government officials, whose wider concerns for their districts were seen as obstructive and delaying. As a generalisation, the professional soldiers were naturally focused on operations and expected everyone else to share their priorities, regardless of the social or administrative costs. Equally, the civil administrators were concerned with maintaining internal tranquillity, farming, trade and finance, without which the military could not exist. It was also true that many believed that it was their duty to safeguard the interests of the African populace from the exploitation of plantation owners and the military labour system. Personal differences certainly played their part, but the military generally underestimated the complexities of administering vast areas and large populations with over-worked and diminishing staffs. For their part, some civil servants showed a distinct lack of enthusiasm for the war or the deference that the military hierarchy expected. This must be mitigated by the fact that over half of officials ultimately served in or closely with the military.

On the British side, criticism centred on the Governor of East Africa, Sir H.C. Belfield, and his staff. He was seen as uninterested in the military or the war effort and spent a good deal of his time fishing in Mombasa. Complaints reached London and the colonial secretary felt it necessary to warn Belfield about the situation. More devious methods were also used, as leading settlers connived with the military to demand an ordinance for universal compulsory service at a mass meeting in mid-September.[84] Although this was largely aimed at coercing African labour, the governor was forced to comply. This measure would open the way for mass registration of men and the enormous demands for carriers in 1916–17. Ultimately, Belfield maintained a correct, if slightly distant relationship with senior commanders.

Lettow had always considered the governor's retention of officials in their civil positions or even small numbers of police as inexcusable diversions from the all-important military effort.[85] He considered the legacy of the Maji-Maji rebellion as inconsequential and that Schnee's fears of further uprisings were unwarranted. While he extolled the virtues of German self-sufficiency in overcoming shortages, he consistently downplayed the complexities of managing an enormous labour force within colonial realities. Indeed, he aimed to deprive the government of its key role in economic matters and sought to bring all such activities under direct military control. For his part, Schnee considered Lettow as an exceptionally talented soldier, but one who was completely one-sided and incapable of thinking of any but a military solution.[86]

WESTERN OPERATIONS IN LATE 1915

German tactical failures in the west were claimed as strategic successes as they diverted Belgian strength away from both the Russisi and Kivu areas and preserved German power. While it is true, the concentration of forces on the Russisi also prevented Wahle from carrying out his planned attack in August. More worryingly, on 8 August, Lettow learned from the consul in Beira of the capitulation of South-West Africa. With the *Königsberg* destroyed and the British in full command of the sea, the eastern flank became distinctly vulnerable. On the other hand, this also freed up the 200-strong Abt Delta that had been protecting the cruiser as well as the nearly 300-strong crew of that vessel. Apart from the coast, Lettow was also concerned about Belgian intentions on the western border of the colony. On 26 October, he appointed General Wahle to command the Westtruppen with Langenn in charge of Urundi and Wintgens in Ruanda. Back in Dar-es-Salaam, Looff assumed control of the lines of communication.[87]

During these months, a fundamental restructuring of the Belgian forces was underway. General Tombeur realised that the existing organisation and structures were no longer relevant to modern war and reorganised his forces into a battalion and group (regiment equivalent) structure, giving him Groupes III and IV in the north. A reserve groupe was created for the defence of Lake Tanganyika although Olsen's troops were still in the south of Katanga. His great weakness was transport, for in the volcanic ranges, only porters could operate and only 4,300 were available. This was simply too few to sustain offensive operations to any distance.[88]

Belgian activity began to increase in September with a reconnaissance in force against the northern German troops. In the meantime, the withdrawal of Olsen's troops was underway. His northernmost battalion was deployed to cover the Russisi Valley while the remaining two marched north from Rhodesia. This redistribution caught the Germans unawares as Abt Schulz, some six companies strong, crossed the Russisi for an attack on Luvungi on 26/27 September. The resulting Belgian counter-attack completely disrupted the enemy preparations and they were driven back across the border, suffering heavy casualties. Renewed German moves against that place were repeated in mid and late October, but with little effect.[89] The Belgians were simply too strong.

By late November, matters had changed as the Germans renewed their advance on Abercorn and Belgian assistance had to be urgently sought. However, the British Foreign Office wished to improve the rather rocky relationship between the two countries, largely, it must be said, by the Colonial Office's narrow and mean-spirited attitude towards any Belgian aspirations. Fundamentally, the problem lay in the British Government's inability to formulate coherent and explicit war aims while the debate over strategy took place through inter-departmental correspondence rather than being argued out openly by the War Committee. However, as relationships in the Cabinet worsened and, after the failure at Loos, deep dissatisfaction with the conduct of military affairs continued to mount, attitudes were beginning to change.

The growing support for an offensive in East Africa did much to improve relations, although the slowness of the Colonial Office in passing on information on military operations continued to irritate both the Foreign Office and the Belgians. By mid-November, Tombeur deployed fifteen battalions split into four groupes: Olsen's Groupe I now had one of its battalions deployed along the Russisi, with Groupe II under Stingelhamber protecting settlements along Lake Tanganyika. Molitor's Groupe III of four battalions was in the Rutschuru area, north of Lake Kivu, while Rouling's similarly-sized Groupe IV was to its south. Preparations for the planned offensive continued, but with the knowledge that the British would finally join in, although not before March. In order to ease the planned advance, several small preparatory operations were planned for December and January.[90]

Lettow maintained his conviction that the Belgians should be hit strongly and driven back so as to free-up troops from the forward area. He continued to reinforce Wahle, so that by the end of November the latter had disposed of some ten companies, of which only four were equipped with smokeless rifles, and with about twenty machine guns along the Russisi. Shelling by both sides had continued since late October, and Abt Schulz, three companies strong, initiated a flank march against the main Belgian position at Luvungi on 23 November that failed to bring them to battle. In the meantime, the unhealthiness of the climate worked against the Germans, and by mid-December, with sickness rising inexorably, Lettow was forced to cancel his ambitious plans. He left Abt Wintgens, now reinforced to over 800 rifles, to maintain the pressure in the mountainous areas of Ruanda and, apart from three companies left to hold the Russisi line in Urundi, the remainder were sent to Kigoma.[91]

General Wahle was worried about the growing Belgian superiority of numbers and artillery north of Lake Kivu; Kissenje protected the entrance to Ruanda and maintained its strong garrison of over 900. He was less worried about the Russisi Valley, as he believed a Belgian forward movement was completely unlikely as the difficulties of crossing the river and the area's unhealthiness were negative factors. For his own troops, escalating illness and a shortage of doctors was a major worry, although there was little he could do. Further confirmation of allied plans came in September, with the capture of a Belgian telegram. Lettow had been aware of the progress of the British naval expedition since late October and decided to take pre-emptive action. He moved four naval guns to Kigoma in order to strengthen the defences, followed by two of the *Königsberg* guns as an independent detachment to raid the Belgians, who were now working hard on finishing the *Baron Dhanis*.

Lettow was determined to attack Lukuga from November onwards, but the Navy showed considerable reluctance to attack into overwhelmingly strong defences and prevaricated. He still believed that the South African reinforcements would go to Europe. Interestingly, the motor boat expedition was now known to have reached Lukuga on 22 October and that it was preparing a surprise, probably torpedoes, for the enemy. He considered that these developments threatened German superiority on the lake and could be decisive, not just for the western borders, but for the entire war. The Belgian movements towards Kivu and Bismarckburg indicated that an attack was likely. If possible, a decisive defeat would be best, but if not, the infliction of heavy losses was desirable, while the prevention of the enemy from taking command of the lake's waters was also important. He intended to reinforce both the Russisi and Kivu areas with the aim of disrupting the Belgians before they completed their concentrations.[92]

By the end of the month, the expedition was in Lukuga, which despite being protected by a Belgian battery of 75-mm guns, had no harbour facilities whatsoever. This meant that a site had to be selected and then a further six weeks were needed to build a breakwater and pier. It was not until 23 December that the boats HMS *Mimi* and *Tou-Tou* were finally launched and joined the small Belgian flotilla of two small, armed motor boats.[93] Finally, at the end of the year, all of the huge efforts placed into moving the expedition across Africa paid off. The Germans had intercepted many wireless messages and were aware that the motor boats were due to arrive imminently. Despite this, General Wahle dismissed these threats and was more worried about having to attack Lukugu, which was strongly fortified. Further south, in Bismarckburg, he noted the enemy withdrawal from Saisi back to Abercorn, which was attributed to supply problems. But Wahle had major supply problems of his own, chiefly in the shortage of ammunition; he lacked modern rounds for his machine guns and shortages were forcing him into a defensive posture. He also warned of the Belgian fighting power, as their Askaris had been underestimated. Recent fighting had shown them to be as good as, and even better than, their German equivalents in the west.[94]

The *Graf von Götzen* was heavily armed and had possessed a 105-mm *Königsberg* gun since the beginning of November. Yet, despite its overwhelming firepower, it was left behind while the *Kingani* was sent alone to reconnoitre Lukuga. This resulted in the German vessel being surprised and captured after a brief battle on 26 December.[95] It was a small success, but the first step in taking control of the lake. The *Kingani* was repaired and brought into British service as HMS *Fifi*, strengthening the flotilla. Equally importantly, the Belgians prevented the news from getting out and, through the use of agents, convinced the Germans that the shore battery had sunk the ship. This led to a further lack of vigilance that would have important effects in 1916. Unfortunately for the British, Spicer-Simson was a difficult and undiplomatic man who quarrelled bitterly with the Belgians. His naval prowess was undermined by the continual friction and complaints that reached both national governments. It was not a promising start to co-operation between the two nations.[96]

THE SITUATION AT THE END OF 1915

By the beginning of October, the British forces were only slightly stronger than the Germans with 17,000 as compared to 15,000 troops, but with the proposed reinforcements this total would climb to nearly 36,000.[97] As will be seen shortly, British plans for a general advance in 1916 were progrssing steadily. For the offensive, General Tighe now proposed to send a South African mounted and British infantry brigade from Longido around the northern flank of the Kilimanjaro position. The main force, consisting of the Voi brigade and the two South African infantry brigades, would go to Maktau whence they would strike towards the Lumi River. His biggest worry was the lack of transport, particularly in having insufficient animals and drivers. He foresaw the end of February as the likeliest date for the commencement of the offensive, given the heavy rains due in April and the increased effects of tsetse fly during that period.[98]

This was broadly accepted and Tighe was instructed to improve the water supply to Maktau and to extend the permanent way for the railway as far forwards as possible. He had already stockpiled sufficient pipeline material to provide up to 35,000 gallons per day at Mbuyuni and as soon as reinforcements arrived it would be laid at a rate of about 5.5 km per week. But an advance would require up to 100,000 gallons daily and the potential shortfall was overcome by using forward storage tanks and railway tanker cars.[99]

At the end of November, Tighe was ready to receive substantial reinforcements. The railway had been pushed on satisfactorily and the water pipeline was fully functional as far as Maktau. In agreement with visiting South African officers, he redistributed his forces so that their Mounted Brigade and his own cavalry were deployed on the Longido line while the Voi Brigade plus the two new infantry brigades would concentrate around Maktau. Given the shortage of locomotives, he estimated that he could not be ready to move before the end of February, while the heavy rains in April would hamper movement, increase sickness and the tsetse fly belt would expand considerably. He had also planned for the future, as materials for both the water pipeline and railway were stockpiled at Maktau ready to be laid in bounds of about 5 km per week.[100]

In the meantime, the Germans made seven attempts on the Uganda Railway, but only one on the Maktau line, in November, while the detachment of reserves to Ruanda has already been noted. In late November, Lettow decided to seize Kasigao Hill once again and allocated the task to a company. The aim was to use it as a patrol base from which to operate against the railway more effectively. On 6 December, an assault on the isolated British garrison on Kasigao Hill was successful and the place was quickly reinforced to three companies' strength with a further three sent in support further east with a similar mission. This now placed a substantial force within 48 km of the railway and made an excellent patrol base.[101]

December was devoted to planning for the impending arrival of the South Africans. The War Office wished for Longido and Mbuyuni to be captured in February/March before the rains started, with the main advance taking place in May. Tighe was ready for a March offensive although it would bring much sickness with the rains.[102] By mid-December, Tighe had some 400 mounted troops, twenty battalions, sixty-six machine guns and twenty-eight guns in hand with another four regiments of mounted troops, eleven infantry battalions, forty-eight machine guns and twenty guns arriving from South Africa and India shortly. Transport was improving as over 6,300 mules had been landed together with some 160 lorries, twenty-five cars and sixty ambulances in the country. He was also aware that the growing Belgian threat had drawn off a number of German reserves and that Lettow planned to maximise pressure on the railway.[103]

The progress of the railway continued and by the end of the year it was 6 km beyond Maktau and further progress was dependent on the arrival of reinforcements. It had gone as far as it could and would be a vital factor in the coming months. For his part, Lettow was determined to disrupt the line, but despite forty attempts being made in December, only one train was derailed. It was a disappointing result for so much strenuous effort. By the end of 1915, the Germans reckoned that the Uganda Railway had been blown up twenty-five times, with the Voi extension being disrupted on ten occasions. Furthermore, they claimed sixteen trains had been derailed with twenty-five locomotives being either destroyed or damaged.[104] But, however valiant the efforts, it was not enough to interrupt the preparations for the coming offensive.

For the Portuguese, the year had been a bad one for Colonel Amorim and his expedition which had been ravaged by disease. The government ordered their replacement by another force led by Major Moura Mendes, who arrived in late November. This officer had never served in Africa and was chosen for his political leanings rather than professional ability. With his headquarters in the unhygienic surroundings of Porto Amelia, the new commander was soon surrounded by sick and undernourished troops. It was hardly an auspicious start to the new expedition.

The Portuguese were slowly moving towards belligerency and a considerably stronger force was planned for 1916. Active co-operation with the British forces was expected and the Ministry of Colonies began to make preparations for the campaign. These took much longer than anticipated as it had to overcome the difficulties of communication and the disorganised nature of Portuguese colonial rule. In reality, the writ of Lisbon did not run far beyond the few bedraggled ports on the coast.[105] This did not prevent the Portuguese from sustaining ambitions of seizing German territory. They envisaged Mendes sending a column north along the coast, taking the ports of Mikindani and Lindi. Reinforcements would then be landed in order to launch a two-pronged attack on Songea and thence Tabora where they would link-up with the British. Such a plan completely ignored the difficultiy of movement and supply in those undeveloped and underpopulated regions as well as the incapacity of the troops to fulfil it.[106]

1915 ended with both sides preparing feverishly for the coming offensive; large numbers of South African troops, stores and vehicles were moving towards East Africa whereas the Germans were making maximum efforts to disrupt the preparations of both the British and Belgians. The small-scale patrolling and raiding operations of the previous year were about to give way to a major offensive from three directions.

4

The Allied Advance Begins

THE POLITICS OF CONQUEST

The military preparations for an offensive campaign reflected gradually changing British political priorities. East Africa's status as a backwater had begun to evolve with the formation of the first coalition government in May 1915. The introduction of Conservative ministers, such as Bonar Law, brought a different outlook on the war and its conduct to the Cabinet. As the year progressed, the shells crisis, the failure to preserve Serbia's independence and the stalemate at the Dardenelles led to growing disenchantment with Asquith's leadership and the direction of military strategy.[1]

Now Colonial Secretary Bonar Law had received a series of reports about the German threat to Northern Rhodesia and Nyasaland, while the aftershocks of the Chilembwe rising had stoked fears about internal security. If he shared his officials' view that Belgian or Portuguese military assistance was to be discouraged for fear of encouraging territorial claims, he was also dissatisfied with British military resources in the region. A solution was to come from the rather unexpected source of South Africa and the government of Louis Botha and Jan Smuts.

This support may be considered remarkable given their past in leading the opposition during the second Anglo-Boer war and traditional Afrikaner hostility to British imperialism. Yet, while the Union of South Africa had only been formed in 1910 and many remained hostile to their new overlords, it must be remembered that the Boer republics had been founded on expansionism, with the Great Trek being the best-known example. Both Botha and Smuts viewed the neighbouring territories of German South-West Africa, British-run Southern Rhodesia and Portuguese East Africa as attractive acquisitions for a Greater South Africa. Indeed there had been considerable frustration at the manner in which the Boers had been 'hemmed in' during the colonial expansion of the late nineteenth century.[2] The outbreak of war had presented an unparalleled opportunity to advance these claims under the auspices of loyalty to Britain's cause. But it was a highly contentious policy as preparations for an invasion of German South-West Africa had helped to precipitate an armed rebellion of disaffected Afrikaners. This had been forcibly suppressed and Botha took personal command of the forces in South-West Africa, with Smuts' assistance from Pretoria and later in the field.[3]

The British Government was highly gratified by the campaign, although they were well aware that the South Africans wished and intended to retain the territory.[4] The governor general, Lord Buxton, an ex-Liberal Cabinet Minister, was the vital link in this axis as he was on excellent terms with his leading ministers and the Asquith administration. Behind the scenes, he did much to encourage South African participation in the war while in his other role as High Commissioner for Southern Africa, he was very concerned about the security of the Rhodesias and Nyasaland.

German East Africa was a less obvious target for South African ambitions, separated as it was by the masses of the Rhodesias, Moçambique and Nyasaland from the northern tip of the Transvaal. As Smuts said:

> But they [the British Government] now practically intimate that in future German East Africa will be our destination. If that country were conquered by us, we could probably effect an exchange with Moçambique and so consolidate our territories south of the Zambesi and Kunene.[5]

Such an exchange would provide first-class ports for an enlarged South Africa and remove a rival power from the scene. It also had the merit of coinciding with the British belief that Portugal was unfit to be a colonial power and might welcome an expansion of its colonial interests under the South African banner. Furthermore, as the hard-pressed British and Indian armies were unable to spare significant reinforcements for the campaign, a strong South African contingent would be welcomed on military as well as political grounds. Buxton understood Smuts' ambitions well and had kept the colonial secretary fully informed as to his intentions.[6]

Smuts' dreams, however, were getting ahead of themselves, as the fighting in German South-West Africa was far from over. It was the Prime Minister, Botha, still engaged in personally directing the campaign at the front, who was more cautious, prudently preferring to finish off one campaign before starting another. At the same time, Buxton had been pressing for an offensive strategy for some time, encouraging the British Government's informal proposals to the South Africans.[7] His efforts had been partially rewarded in mid-1915, when the South African Government had agreed to the raising of a 1,000-man contingent for Nyasaland, while 300 recruits to the British South Africa Police were raised for military service. This inevitably raised speculation and the government felt obliged to issue a press statement stating that no decision had been made about sending troops to Europe or elsewhere in Africa.[8]

Furthermore, as the campaign in South-West Africa wound down in July 1915, a new and difficult problem arose, that of winning the required general election. The Botha government was under heavy pressure from the Nationalists and the Afrikaner population was split. Ministers were seriously concerned about the effects of sending away so many potentially friendly voters before the election.[9] With the election set for October 1915, no outward preparations could be made until the last quarter of the year and it would take several months to recruit, equip and train any contingent. In the interim, nothing was publicly announced about South African participation in East Africa, as it would almost certainly have been a vote-loser in a close-run contest. The British Cabinet realised the threat posed by Hertzog's Nationalists and wanted Botha's South Africa Party to be returned to power; accordingly, London heeded Lord Buxton's advice and refrained from public pressure.[10]

Quietly, Smuts was organising another Southern Rhodesian contingent, equipped by South Africa, while offering artillery, aircraft and several hundred motor vehicles to General Tighe. A few weeks later, two well-connected officers were sent to East Africa to report on military conditions; it was another surreptitious move towards open hostilities.[11] Finally,

Botha unofficially let Tighe know that should the elections proceed favourably, a substantial force might be expected shortly thereafter. On the latter asking for official direction, he was told to leave matters in the War Office's hands and that no decision had yet been made.[12]

By Autumn 1915, the British Cabinet was bitterly divided with two main factions having strongly opposed views on strategy, the management of the war effort, and conscription. Notably, there was strong opposition to further offensives on the Western Front and some ministers sought to find alternative theatres in which to achieve strategic success. The pressure for an offensive was mounting as Bonar Law wanted a sufficiently large force to conquer German East Africa once and for all.[13]

In October, the Cabinet was in crisis as major cracks appeared in the coalition's structure and the reconstitution of the cumbersome Dardanelles Committee into the smaller War Committee in early November did little to ease the tension. The success of the campaign in German South-West Africa and the positive manner in which the newly-created dominion was supporting imperial policies had not gone unnoticed in London. But, Lord Kitchener wanted East Africa to remain on the strategic defensive so as to limit its requirements to the minimum possible. While he had authorised the extension of the Voi Railway and the raid on Bukoba, these were minor operations that made few demands on national resources.

By this time, however, Kitchener had long lost the confidence of his Cabinet colleagues, many of whom wanted him removed from power. As it was politically impossible to sack him, they chose more subtle methods of undermining his position.[14] The Chief of the Imperial General Staff (CIGS), Lieutenant General Sir James Murray, opened the debate in October with a paper on East Africa that was based on a series of pessimistic and alarmist reports from General Tighe. It called for the immediate despatch of a brigade to reinforce British East Africa, with a total of about 10,000 reinforcements being required. Attached to the paper was a telegram from Tighe that revealed the offer of five batteries of artillery from South Africa and the possibility of more infantry. This was purely for effect, as the War Office had already agreed to accept the artillery as well as to recruit the infantry.[15] This was formalised in mid-October, when it asked the South Africans for a brigade of infantry plus support units in East Africa. Tellingly, Smuts' request that any of Tighe's military demands be treated as having War Office authority was agreed subject only to the provision that they be copied to London.[16]

Finally, in early November Kitchener's opponents struck and he was sent out to the Dardanelles in order to report on the military situation. Bonar Law was appointed to chair a committee of the CID to consider the situation in East Africa. It wasted little time endorsing Murray's memorandum and recommending an offensive using the promised South African reinforcements. The apparently unfavourable military situation did much to change minds; with the blockade runner having re-equipped the Schutztruppe, now an estimated 17-20,000 men, the British could only muster 11,000 effectives out of the total of 15,500 soldiers in East Africa. Far from being predominant, the British seemed outnumbered and vulnerable. These figures were enough for the Colonial Office to overcome its objections to active Belgian co-operation and only the absent Kitchener remained in the way.[17]

Buxton's request for a senior British officer to take command of the Allied forces in the southern area was accepted by Bonar Law with the War Office nominating Brigadier General Edward Northey on 12 November. Northey was an experienced regular officer who had been wounded while leading his battalion in battle and again while commanding a brigade at Ypres. On recovering he was sent not, as he had hoped, back to the Western Front, but to command the splendidly-named Nyasaland and North-Eastern Rhodesia Field Force. He was to ensure the security of the area of his command, secondly to assist in the Anglo-Belgian operations on Lake Tanganyika and finally to be ready for the main offensive in early 1916.[18]

It is unclear how much knowledge Kitchener had of these actions, as he was notoriously unable to delegate and overloaded with work. He was kept partially informed by telegram as Murray sought to find troops for the campaign. Smuts' unsolicited offer of a Boer mounted brigade with an English mounted regiment was well received and added to the numbers.[19] But the CIGS acted in the knowledge of broad political and royal support, while Bonar Law had been negotiating with the South Africans on this for some time.[20] Furthermore, the victory in October, albeit with a reduced majority, of Botha's South Africa Party, had cleared the main obstacle to an offensive there.

General Sir Horace Smith-Dorrien was nominated as commander-in-chief of the forces in British East Africa on 22 November with his appointment being formally confirmed by the Government on 18 December. In the meantime, Murray produced a detailed memorandum advocating an attack against German East Africa, using an additional 1,500 Indian and 13,400 South African troops to double troop numbers. He considered that this would give nearly 15,000 white troops as compared to the Germans' 2,200 and should be sufficient for success. Seeking to allay any criticisms about the diversion of effort from the decisive theatres, General Murray justified the plan through the need for obtaining negotiating stakes for any peace negotiations and that the forces involved would be relatively minor. There is little doubt that the soldiers had intrigued against the political head of the Army and had used Kitchener's absence as an opportunity for going against his express wishes.[21]

But on return, Kitchener was adamantly opposed, stating:

> This scheme for offensive operations in the centre of Africa is, in my opinion, a very dangerous project in the present state of the war... The general military policy now advocated, may therefore, lead us to place South African troops in positions where they will be liable to disaster, from which we will not be able to extricate them, as our troops will be fully engaged elsewhere. I think that the recent example we have had of similar proceedings based on wrong premises in Mesopotamia should teach us to be cautious in undertaking similar operations of this nature.[22]

He was swiftly outmanoeuvred by Bonar Law, who ordered the news of the campaign to be published in South Africa before Kitchener's minute was sent. General Robertson, the new CIGS, agreed the plan on 23 December with Smith-Dorrien and his staff sailing the next day. However, it was not until 28 December that the war secretary was formally overruled and the War Committee endorsed the new strategy.[23]

The new commander-in-chief was an experienced and highly regarded soldier whose dramatic stand at Le Cateau in 1914 had helped save the BEF. However, he had fallen out of favour with Sir John French and was subsequently relieved of his appointment and returned home. He was a thorough and professional officer who had had extensive experience during the South African war. Smith-Dorrien now had the equivalent of two divisions at his disposal and seemed the right man to finish off the campaign. But, as he had noted, it was a vast and ambitious project based on a co-ordinated attack from British East Africa in the north-east and from Northern Rhodesia and Nyasaland in the south-west, with the Belgians advancing from the Congo in the west. The difficulties of climate and terrain were well known, but nevertheless the politicians expected a quick and easy victory.[24] The scene was now set for a major struggle in the heart of Africa.

PREPARATIONS IN EAST AFRICA

In Germany there was continued concern for East Africa, although the authorities believed that the *Kronborg*'s mission had been a complete success. It was not until Schnee's urgent request for help finally arrived in Berlin that the issue took on new urgency.[25] Various plans were considered until it decided to send another blockade breaker to the colony's aid. A captured freighter, re-named the *Marie*, was loaded with 2,000 modern '98 pattern rifles, 3 million rounds of ammunition, four light field howitzers, two mountain guns and four heavy machine guns. Equally vital, and based on Schnee's advice, some 50,000 pre-packed loads suitable for porters were included. These contained much-needed food, medicine, clothing and equipment in convenient sizes, unlike that of its predecessor.[26]

The *Marie* left Hamburg on 16 January 1916, taking exactly two months to reach the area of Sudi Bay in the far south of the colony. It was an uneventful journey conducted under complete wireless silence. After laying a small minefield, the crew began assembling pre-fabricated wooden floats for unloading. Despite frantic activity, the vital cargo was not fully unloaded until 27 March when the assembly of the guns and carriages began. On 8 April, as *Marie* was ready to sail to the neutral Dutch East Indies, HMS *Hyacinth* arrived. The ensuing bombardment was ineffective owing to faulty ammunition, as was another a week later. Further British vessels appeared, but bad weather enabled the *Marie* to escape, eventually reaching Batavia where it was interned. However, Schnee's request for further assistance got through and reached the Imperial Government in late May.[27]

By early 1916, the situation in East Africa was worsening for the Germans. Through South African and Portuguese newspapers they had long heard of the many reinforcements proceeding to East Africa; facts that were confirmed in great detail in February.[28] Lettow considered that while a coastal descent was a distinct possibility, the problems of supply and health diminished its attractiveness. He believed that Kilimanjaro remained the main objective and that the railway extension confirmed this. However, the situation remained far from clear and

Belgian intentions against Ruanda seemed worrying. Lettow now recognised that the Russisi line was too difficult for decisive battle and began to thin out the troops there in favour of Ruanda and the Central Railway. He intended to place his main effort against the Uganda Railway, both to force the dispersal of troops and to disrupt preparations for any attack. He proposed to retain the strong fortified position on Kasigao and set up another near the coast to continue these harassing raids. However, he also admitted that the British surveillance of the railway had improved considerably and that it was almost impossible to place dynamite on the line successfully.[29]

The Schutztruppe was now reaching its peak strength with 2,712 Europeans, 11,367 Askaris and 2,591 auxiliaries. Most of the forty companies had fifteen to twenty Europeans and 200 Askaris as well as several hundred carriers each. The bulk of these were in the Kilimanjaro area, with 900 around Taveta, 400 protecting the Meru gap and 650 at Kasigao. In reserve, Lettow held 700 back at Neu Moschi with a further 1,000 along the Usambara Railway and 800 at Tanga. In the west, Muansa and Bukoba had 1,000 and 300 rifles respectively. Ruanda had about 1,000 troops with Urundi holding 500. In the south, Bismarckburg had 270, Langenburg 600 and in the interior another 600 spread between Songea, Mahenge and Iringa. Dar-es-Salaam now counted over 1,000 troops and the coastal ports had less than 200 each, save for Lindi which had a company of 200 for its protection. The remainder were scattered on the lines of communication.[30]

For the British, January marked the arrival of the first South African reinforcements and two fresh Indian battalions. Recruiting was going well and in mid-January Smuts offered an additional two mounted regiments for service. Still convalescing near Cape Town, General Smith-Dorrien instructed Tighe to press on with a series of preliminary moves. To that end, Longido was occupied on 21 January and Mbuyuni the next day, both forward positions being then strongly fortified against recapture.[31] Serengeti Camp, some 6 km to the west of Mbuyuni, was occupied on 25 January with the railway being extended to there shortly thereafter. This meant that British advanced posts were now within 19 km of Salaita Hill, itself 10 km east of Taveta. The build-up also severely restricted the Germans' ability to strike the Uganda Railway, as did improved British counter-measures and aggressive patrolling. The enemy was now in striking range, thanks to the railway and water pipeline.[32]

The Belgians had been busy too, with the last of Olsen's troops finally completing their long march from Northern Rhodesia to the Russisi line in mid-January. They needed a rest after a two-and-a-half-month journey, as well as receiving further reinforcements. General Tombeur had finalised his plan of gaining mastery of Lake Tanganyika followed by a simultaneous invasion of Ruanda and Urundi together with a bombardment of the German ports. After a meeting with the Governor of Uganda in February to discuss the recruitment of porters, the Belgian commander-in-chief was forced to postpone the land offensive until March so that the necessary men could be found.[33]

On Lake Tanganyika, the situation was moving into the Allies' favour, although storms and sickness limited operations until February. Despite their knowledge of enemy intentions, the Germans had still not made the obvious deduction that the British vessels had arrived. On 9 February, they decided to search for the remains of the *Kingani*, taking the *Hedwig von Wissmann* to Lukuga. The much larger and well-armed *Graf von Götzen* was supposed to sail in support, but for some reason it was not available. This was a major miscalculation as the Anglo-Belgian flotilla scrambled out of harbour and gave chase to the enemy. After a five-hour engagement, the motor boats outmanoeuvred and pounded the *Hedwig* into a wreck, before finally sinking it. German control of the lake, especially with the links to Usumbura and Bismarckburg threatened, was becoming precarious.[34]

The mysterious disappearance of a second vessel resulted in Wahle asking for the sea-going tug *Adjutant* and the steamer *Wami* as replacements. Lettow now realised that his western flank was threatened and agreed.[35] A few days later, intercepted Belgian signals added to the urgency by revealing the British presence on the lake. The *Wami* was immediately prepared for the 1,000 km rail journey, reaching Kigoma in late April and ready for service several weeks later. The *Adjutant* was a more difficult problem, as it had to evade the blockade at the mouth of the Rufiji before sailing by night to Dar-es-Salaam. It, too, was dismantled into sections and sent off to Kigoma.[36] These reinforcements were welcome, but would take some time to reassemble, while the rainy season made operations very difficult until May.

In South Africa, major problems were arising as Smith-Dorrien had fallen seriously ill from influenza onboard ship and his condition remained bad until the end of January. While his staff went on to Pretoria to arrange matters with their South African counterparts, the commander-in-chief had to remain at Cape Town. In the meantime, Smuts was working behind the scenes against Smith-Dorrien. Bonar Law had previously asked Smuts to take command of the force, but he had declined, citing his need to support Botha in Parliament. Now, with Smith-Dorrien unwell, he reconsidered his position and began to pressure for an early offensive in March. His official justification was domestic political necessity, but he was well aware that Smith-Dorrien would be unable to take command until the middle of that month.[37]

By the end of January and feeling much improved, Smith-Dorrien felt concerned enough to warn the War Office that he considered that the South Africans would not be sufficiently trained by then as well as having insufficient transport. More importantly, he also revealed that the South Africans were unprepared to serve under Tighe, while he thought some of Tighe's decisions were unsound. He offered two alternatives; either appoint Smuts or wait for the end of the rains when he himself would assume command. This telegram provoked a sharp response by Buxton, which was approved by both Botha and Smuts, that warned that a delay would be 'a serious mistake and fraught with grave disadvantages'. Furthermore, they believed that the rains might not even prove a hindrance to operations.[38]

This was followed by a private telegram from Buxton stating that he doubted Smith-Dorrien would be fit enough for the campaign and further pressure for an early offensive.[39] Faced with this and the strong opposition of the South African Government, whose support was important to London, the British Cabinet made an important reversal of policy. It had briefly considered another British officer, but had decided to offer the command to Smuts together with authority to launch an early offensive. Suddenly, his parliamentary duties became less demanding and he agreed to take up the post almost immediately. This was a highly unusual appointment, with a politician and colonial officer in supreme command of imperial troops, but it received the assent of both Lord Kitchener and the War Committee on 3 February 1916.[40]

Smuts had also helped manoeuvre himself into the position, having been instrumental in instigating an aggressive policy in East Africa and arranging a large South African contingent. If politically favourable, Smuts had serious limitations as a soldier. Although he had been a very successful leader of a commando in the Anglo-Boer War, he lacked formal military training, let alone any experience of higher command in war.[41] His troops had seldom numbered more than 300 and it had been mainly guerrilla tactics against a much stronger, but less mobile enemy. Subsequently, he had served briefly under Botha in German South-West Africa which, while arid, had a railway line and few of the deadly tropical diseases that plagued the East Coast. Now, Smuts was being called upon to lead over 50,000 soldiers of many nationalities and languages through extremely difficult and often unmapped terrain while battling a harsh climate and a host of deadly diseases. Apart from operational and tactical skill, his appointment also required the firm grasp of administration and supply which had been shown to be so important in previous African campaigns.[42]

Smuts' position was also not made easier by his position as a politician and leading government minister. It was unavoidable that politics would play an important role in his decision-making, be it the appointment of officers, selection of strategy or the issuance of communiqués. With the prime minister, Botha, under heavy pressure from the Nationalist Party, Smuts was acutely conscious of the dangers of a large casualty list. He was also well aware of the need for success, as any setback would be used to attack and possibly weaken the government.[43]

On taking over the chief command from Smith-Dorrien, Smuts received a copy of his instructions, which read in part:

> to undertake an offensive defensive with the object of expelling the enemy from British territory and safeguarding it from further incursion. The decision as to the ultimate scope of the offensive operations to be undertaken against German East Africa after the rainy season should be postponed until General Sir Horace Smith-Dorrien has reported in light of the experience gained before the rainy season.[44]

However, Smuts had no intention of waiting for the dry weather, having claimed that it would be bad for morale, recruiting and the health of the troops. Accepting the appointment on 5 February 1916, he then received the War Committee's permission to start before the rains, provided that he was confident of success.[45] Smuts arrived at Mombasa on 19 February where he was briefed by General Tighe and conducted a rapid reconnaissance of the main areas. After only four days, he signalled to London that he wished to undertake an immediate offensive, receiving approval on

25 February. His own troops were still in the process of arriving (the second infantry brigade would not arrive until after the opening of the offensive) and were largely untrained. Most significantly, he decided that mounted troops would play a leading role through a country that was known to be infested with the tsetse fly with its fatal effects on all domestic animals.[46] This was not just relevant to the mounted brigades, but also to the overwhelmingly animal-drawn supply system. In contrast, his predecessor had specifically requested that only the front-line units have mules with the remainder equipped with motor vehicles.[47] Smuts chose not to wait or rectify this critical weakness.

If the Germans were unaware of these developments, they did realise the scale of the enemy build-up and progress of the railway. Lettow had about 4,000 troops with which to cover both the Longido-Neu Moschi and Salaita-Taveta approaches, far too few to be effective everywhere. Accordingly, he chose to detach about 600 rifles to the northern and more difficult axis, with the remainder concentrated in the gap between Kilimanjaro and the North Pare Mountains. Salaita Hill was particularly strong while outposts covered the drifts along the Lumi River.[48]

In the meantime, Tighe decided that Salaita Hill had to be taken to facilitate the main advance. He now had two divisions in the process of formation based on the two existing brigades plus two new South African formations. In the middle of February, he decided to use Second Division under General Malleson for the task. Apart from securing an important feature, the attack would also give the untried 2nd SA Infantry Brigade its first experience of battle. He planned to use the veteran 1st EA Infantry Brigade to conduct a frontal holding attack while the South Africans swept in from the right flank.

It was a simple plan that left no reserve and depended on green troops for success. Moreover, Malleson presumed that Abt Kraut had only 300 rifles rather than the actual 1,300 with a further 600 in depth to the rear. Oblivious to this, the approximately 4,000 attackers left Serengeti Camp at dawn on 12 February. By 0800 hours, both brigades were in position and the South Africans deployed into assault formation, with their guns coming into action at 0900. But they had been detected just after first light and Abt Kraut was in complete readiness to meet the attack. As soon as the British guns opened up, Lettow ordered Abt Schulz to close up to Salaita Hill while two other detachments were instructed to march to the Lumi River. Lettow himself moved up to Taveta to control the battle.

The 1st EA Brigade advanced to within 1,000 metres of the enemy trenches, but in the open ground it could make little progress. The South Africans were equally held up by fire and the lead battalion was ordered to fall back. At 1000 hours, Kraut ordered Schulz into action on the British right flank, but before it could arrive, a returning German patrol engaged the South Africans from the rear. The brigade reserve was deployed, but it was difficult to maintain touch in the thick bush. Matters were worsened by the arrival of the three companies of Abt Schulz's from the north. Now under heavy fire from three directions, the inexperienced South Africans began to fall back in some disorder and had to be extracted covered by heavy artillery fire and the assistance of the other brigade.[49]

By midday, the Germans realised that the battle was won and launched a spirited pursuit that was stopped only by a tenacious Indian battalion. Eventually, the rearguard managed to break clean and the force retired to camp, defeated and dejected. The South Africans had suffered the bulk of the casualties and had jolted their over-confidence. Apart from Malleson's deficiencies as a commander, the action showed that much training and experience would be required to match the Schutztruppe.[50]

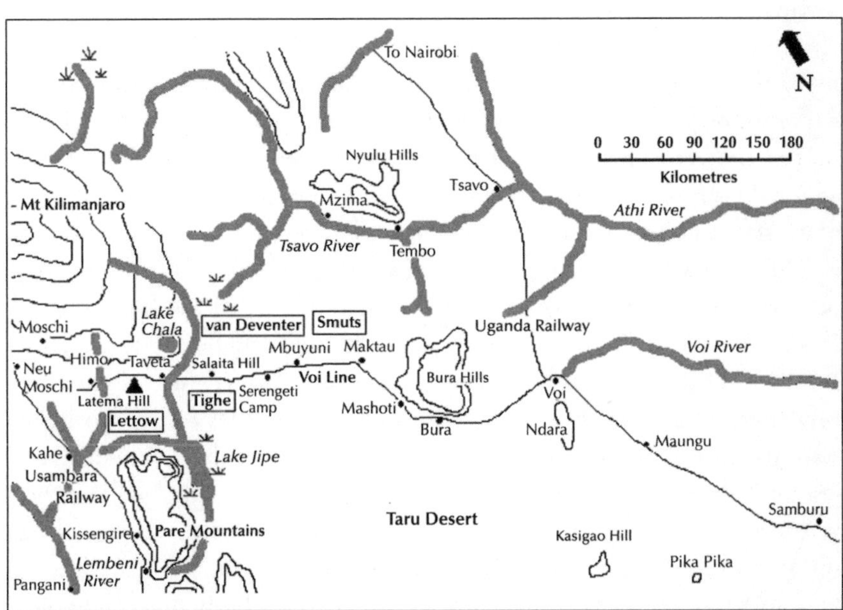

The Kilimanjaro-Voi area, March 1916

THE ADVANCE TO KILIMANJARO

As Smuts prepared for the advance, he learned that the Portuguese had some 2,700 men facing the Germans along the Rovuma. He had long had a low opinion of the Portuguese and took little hope from their offer to send 10,000 men across the Rovuma in mid-June. While they hoped to occupy Songea, a more realistic objective was the building of a road network between Porto Amelia, the Rovuma line and Mocimboa da Praia on the coast. These plans were finalised at the end of March, but much depended on the arrival of reinforcements from Portugal.[51]

Smuts had left himself little time and he adopted the bulk of Tighe's plan with one important change; he switched the South African mounted troops from the Longido axis to the central thrust towards Taveta. He wanted to use the traditional Boer tactic of avoiding frontal attacks and instead using wide turning movements by highly mobile mounted columns to hit the enemy's flanks and cut off his escape.[52] But, van Deventer's 1st SA Mounted Brigade would have to pass through a heavily infested tsetse fly belt from the outset. Smuts also placed the newly arrived 3rd SA Infantry Brigade under van Deventer, a move that effectively created another division without suitable headquarters or communications while keeping 2nd SA Infantry Brigade under his personal control. These changes left both Stewart's First and Tighe's Second Divisions as little more than reinforced infantry brigades. Another innovation was Smuts' decision to operate an advanced GHQ (A/GHQ), leaving the bulk of the staff to the rear. This meant that he could operate close to the front line and make decisions rapidly, but at the cost of being isolated from the bulk of his staff and potentially becoming too involved in local battles.

With about 40,000 troops, he faced about 4,000 in twenty-eight companies in the Kilimanjaro area. Five companies in Abt Fischer faced the First Division with the remaining twenty-three under Lettow further south.[53] With less than a month to succeed under his self-imposed timetable, Smuts had to work fast. Stewart's reduced First Division would start first from Longido on 5 March with a crossing of the 56 km of waterless bush through the Meru-Kilimanjaro gap. Two days later, van Deventer was to cross the Lumi River before striking for the Chala heights, while on 8 March Tighe would attack the Salaita position. The aim was for Stewart to hit the German rear area while the main body outmanoeuvred the Germans around Salaita-Taveta.[54]

Stewart's advance began as planned and progress was slow from the outset. He was a cautious commander, who wasted much time on trying to clear his flanks instead of pushing on. His opponent was similarly cautious and failed to strike despite several opportunities.[55] Although there had been heavy rainstorms, it took a week for the Division to cover 64 km and they were far from their objectives.

Van Deventer was much quicker and had covered the 19 km to the Lumi by early on 8 March before turning to the crater of Lake Chala above. The infantry was left to clear the area, while, further south, Tighe was shelling Salaita Hill. The next day, to their surprise, the formidable defences were found unoccupied and the hill was taken without a fight. Lettow had seen the danger posed by the mounted troops and had evacuated Abt Kraut back to the twin hills of Latema-Reata that dominated the main road to Moschi.[56]

By 10 March, Berrangé's 3rd SA Infantry Brigade had reached Lake Chala, while van Deventer moved south-west to dominate the high ground over Taveta. It now fell to First Division to attack the well-defended hills of Latema-Reata, without waiting for the arrival of Berrangé's troops. The attack began at midday on 11 March in great heat and the lead battalions soon slowed down. By late afternoon, Tighe had committed his reserve, only to be thrown back by a vigorous counter-attack. The first South Africans were arriving and helped defeat another counter-attack at dusk. Tighe now committed the reinforcements to a night attack that was successfully parried by a fierce German counter-attack. Early on 12 March, Tighe asked Smuts for more troops, but the latter refused and instead ordered a general retirement before dawn.[57]

Daylight revealed small clusters of infantry clinging to the summit. In the darkness and confusion, the Germans had missed them. But Lettow was worried about the progress of van Deventer's mounted troops and, receiving word of Fischer's failure to halt Stewart, he had ordered a withdrawal, much to his later dismay. Smuts did not miss the opportunity and released his reserve to Tighe. The formidable position was now his although at a heavy cost in casualties. The victory left the way to Moschi open although Stewart's force was well behind schedule and still at Boma Ngombe. He was sent on towards Kahe with the aim of cutting off the German retreat, but was hindered by more rain and dense bush.[58]

With the loss of Latema, the Germans began to withdraw rapidly towards Kahe so as not to be cut off from the railway. Van Deventer's mounted troops pushed on quickly, reaching the railway terminus at Neu Moschi on 14 March where it linked up with Stewart's division. The remaining two South African infantry brigades were moving towards the River Himo while Tighe's troops were left to reorganise at Taveta.

A short pause was now necessary for reorganisation as the rain began to hinder the bringing up of supplies. Smuts' plan for an early victory had foundered owing to the slowness of Stewart's advance. However, he had won a victory at Latema that had opened the way to the Kilimanjaro heartland. On the other hand, the Schutztruppe had withdrawn in good order and held the Usambara Railway as well as the densely wooded area north of the River Ruwu. The next phase of the advance was dependent on the Voi railway line being extended to Neu Moschi, a task that would be hindered by the rain.

Having declared his preliminary operations a success, Smuts now radically reformed his force. He placed the British and Imperial troops in the two brigades of First Division, while South Africans were split between the Second and soon to be formed Third Divisions. Stewart and Malleson were sent back to India in disgrace, and although Tighe was given a knighthood, his services were also dispensed with. In their place, Smuts arranged the promotion of his own men, van Deventer and Coen Brits, still en route from South Africa. He also ensured that Brigadier General Reginald Hoskins, a British officer who had been specially selected as his Chief of the General Staff, was supplanted by another South African, J.J. Collyer. Hoskins was instead given the now vacant command of First Division.[59]

Smuts also had to deal with the rain that was now falling in increasing quantities. He was well aware of both its magnitude and effects from his own staff and captured records. Despite the certainty that the roads would become impassable and that sickness rise rapidly, he decided to push on.[60] On 17 March, the two South African infantry brigades moved south along the Himo River supported by First Division on the right flank. After initial successes, their advance ran into heavy opposition on 19 March, leading Smuts to abandon that axis and attempt a bypassing movement towards the key junction of Kahe. Van Deventer was ordered to move from Neu Moschi in the north and swoop in on the western flank of the position while the three infantry brigades pressed their attacks in line. But, as the mounted force was moving, Lettow launched a violent counter-attack that shook, but could not break through, the determined defenders. Having suffered heavy casualties, the Germans moved south.[61]

Early on 21 March, van Deventer set out to Kahe Hill and cut off the line of retreat while the infantry drove south. The latter's progress was slow, having to cross a wide and crocodile-infested river before meeting with strong resistance. Van Deventer's troops reached their objective, but were held off by Abt von Bock until dark. The next day revealed a number of demolished bridges, but no defenders as they had retired to Lembeni.[62] Smuts' plan had been foiled by the failure of his mounted troops to press the attack and the difficult terrain.

More ominously, his transport was in trouble with a shortage of over 1,600 mules out of an establishment of 7,000. But with the anticipated losses from tsetse fly, this deficiency would soon rise to 5,000 animals. This led to unit transport being ordered back to pick up supplies at the cost of leaving tents and equipment behind. Consequently, troops were forced to sleep on sodden ground without protection and sickness quickly soared. The cost of rectifying this was to deprive 3rd South African Brigade of its mobility and ordinary supplies.[63]

Once again Smuts had to halt and consider his options in light of the increasing rainfall. Decisive success had eluded him as he had only pushed the Germans back, inflicting 330 casualties as compared to his own 800. A continued drive down the Pangani Valley was the obvious option, but it was very difficult and likely to be held. To the south-west, matters were more promising as the axis Aruscha-Ufiome-Kondoa Irangi offered an approach to the Central Railway. A thrust there could divide the enemy force and offer a speedy resolution to the campaign.[64]

Lettow had redeployed his forces around Lembeni ready to meet the next attack as well as trying to mitigate the worst effects of the rain. He was focussed on protecting the Usambara Railway from the British although he expected them to reach the Central Railway in April. In anticipation, he ordered the removal of all stores and equipment along the line to Tabora so as to form depots in Kissaki, Mahenge and Iringa.[65] If he was outnumbered, the thick bush of the Pangani Valley offered significant tactical advantages.

This pressure would also be helped by General Northey's troops in the south. Norforce, as it was usually known, had about 1,100 troops on the Rhodesian frontier with another 1,600 in Nyasaland preparing to move north. It too was facing heavy rain and would be unable to move until May, but would help drive the Germans north. Northey wanted the Portuguese to protect his eastern flank, particularly around Songea. Such hopes were in vain, for despite their optimism Mendes' troops were in a dreadful condition and they lacked means to advance. However, he did propose to send a column of 500 through Nyasaland to occupy Mtengula near the middle of Lake Nyasa although this was mainly to keep the British out of Portuguese territory.[66]

The Belgians were altogether more robust and their long-awaited offensive was nearly ready. Tombeur had concentrated some 8,000 men in two brigades, ready to drive into enemy territory, while a further 2,000 remained to secure Lake Tanganyika together with the Anglo-Belgian flotilla.[67] This build-up had not gone unnoticed and the Germans realised that a co-ordinated offensive was likely. Despite being substantially outnumbered, Wintgens, at least, believed his forces would be capable of holding any enemy offensive.[68] It was an optimistic assessment not shared by Wahle.

One piece of good news for the British was the completion of the railway link between the Uganda and Usambara railways in April. Although not as dramatic as any advance, it was absolutely essential to Smuts' plans. The first 93 km had been completed by February, with the remaining 59 km being laid behind the advance and at the height of the rainy season. The hard-worked railway troops had managed a sustained rate of 1.6 km per day, a laudable achievement.[69]

Smuts had bigger ideas as he now planned to send Second Division plunging south from Aruscha towards Kondoa Irangi in a move to unbalance the Germans, while First and Third Divisions would push down the Pangani Valley. It was a bold scheme that ignored the effects of the rains and his inadequate transport. By 4 April the main road to Aruscha was unusable and although another route was found, it was slow and also impassable in parts. Nevertheless, the troops persevered and, three days later, van Deventer had covered the 56 km to Lol Kissale where over 400 enemy had been surrounded and surrendered.[70]

Pushing hard, the Mounted Brigade reached Ufiome on 12 April and, five days later, was within 6 km of Kondoa Irangi. The town was reached and taken on 19 April after a short fight, with the enemy garrison withdrawing to the south. This success was tempered by the enormous loss of horses and growing sickness. The infantry were still trudging behind, struggling to move forward through deep mud, across raging torrents and without any shelter.[71] It took them two weeks to reach their objective and they arrived in poor condition and badly underfed. The additional

1,800 rifles brought Second Division to a bare 3,000 men, many of whom were seriously unwell. Worse was the crisis in the supply system, which was completely inadequate to cover the 345 km to Kondoa Irangi. It was a major struggle to get food as far forward as Aruscha as the roads between Taveta and Neu Moschi were so bad that only carriers could traverse them.[72]

While his forces were wallowing in a sea of mud, Smuts received further instructions from London. He was now expected to capture the whole of German East Africa, although no annexations were to be proclaimed and the African population was to be discouraged from hostility to any of the white population. This fit in well with his own territorial ambitions, although it was diminished by the unwelcome news that a second supply ship, the *Marie*, had offloaded a considerable amount of stores at Sudi Bay.[73]

Smuts had hoped to catch the Germans off-guard and penetrate to their undefended rear areas. Lettow was surprised by the move and quickly ordered substantial reinforcements to the area. On 14 April, he left Kraut holding the Pangani Valley with ten companies totalling about 2,400 rifles, while taking eighteen companies for his riposte. One company was sent across the Masai Steppe while the rest moved by rail to Handeni and then marched towards Kimamba on the Central Railway, where he arrived on 25 April. Trains then began to shuttle troops to Dodoma, from where they disembarked and marched towards Kondoa Irangi. With the large numbers of troops, it was a lengthy process, and would take until the first week in May for all to be in position for the planned attack. But supply difficulties plagued the Germans too, as they struggled to improve the indifferent tracks north.[74]

The British detected this shifting of forces; in the first week of May, twenty companies of about 4,000 men together with three guns and twenty machine guns were identified. This was bad news as van Deventer and his weakened troops were now outnumbered and dangerously exposed. He was aided by geography as Kondoa Irangi lay in a shallow valley that was ringed by a series of hills. To the south-west, the junction of two swollen rivers blocked the approaches, while the south was marked by a series of prominent hills that ran east and then north overlooking the Steppe. Van Deventer had placed his three infantry battalions in the south with the four mounted regiments holding the outlying hills on either flank.

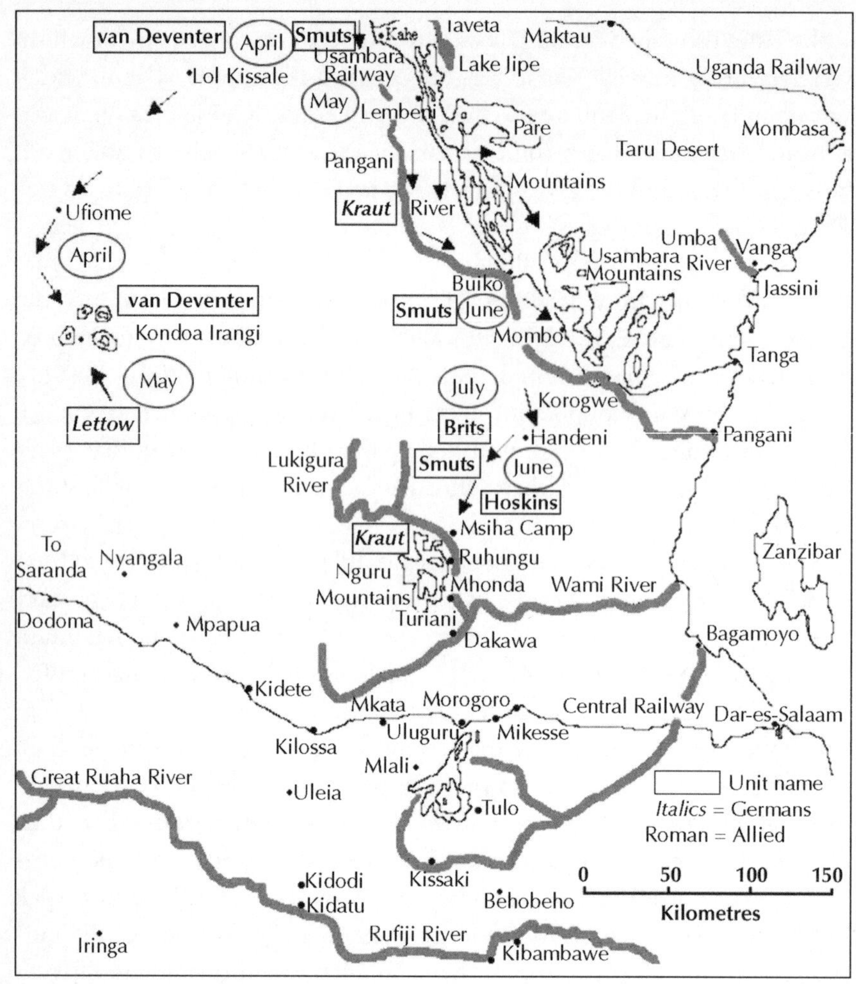

Smuts' advance from Kilimanjaro to the Lukigura, April-June 1916

Lettow planned his attack for 9 May, having already moved up to within 3,000 metres of the South African main position. He timed his assault for the next morning and opened the battle with heavy fire from his two large guns and a mountain battery at midday. The fire was effective and, in late afternoon, the defenders were observed to be evacuating their trenches and retiring towards Kondoa. Lettow resolved to follow-up as quickly as possible, ordering Abt von Bock and Abt Kornatzki to move forward while Abt Otto was to advance on a neighbouring hill to their east. However, the ground was very difficult and the troops did not arrive until darkness, thereby losing the support of the artillery. Lettow was wary of his troops' ability to launch a night attack and time was spent on reconnaissance. Finally, patrols reported the position clear and the advance resumed in darkness. But, they were running into a trap, as the South African positions were designed to draw them into a withering crossfire. Too far back to influence matters directly, Lettow could only hear the raging battle that ended early on 10 May, when his battered troops broke off the action. Both the attacking Abteilungen had suffered heavy losses, while Otto on the eastern flank had similarly run into a previously unidentified position.[75]

It was an expensive failure, as it cost the Germans over 100 casualties, including a number of officers, to the South Africans' thirty-one. Lettow had failed to reconnoitre adequately and had rushed the attack. Unable to afford more such losses, he contented himself with extending his front to the hills to the west of the town and subjecting the defenders to increasing artillery fire. Smuts now realised the danger that his troops were in and, despite the appalling conditions, every available man was rushed south. These reinforcements, plus Lettow's new passivity meant that the position was deadlocked. Conditions remained miserable and insufficient rations continued to sap men's strength – the number of sick in Kondoa Irangi rose from 100 in late May to over 1,200 in mid-June. Furthermore, horses were dying at an alarming rate as only 1,100 out of 3,800 remained fit for service.[76]

Despite this, on 19 May Smuts described his move on Kondoa 'as a complete success' although there had been enormous wastage of men and horses. He planned to continue Second Division's advance as soon as the remounts arrived. The reality was that the men were in rags and needed new boots while replacement animals were unshod and lacked reins.[77] For their part, the Germans were less troubled as the countryside was rich and they were able to forage successfully. By early June, neither was strong enough to gain a decisive advantage over the other and operations were limited to patrol activity.

Elsewhere, events in Portugal were picking up steam as the new commander-in-chief, General José Cesar Ferreira Gil, was nominated on 12 May with orders to support Smuts' advance. Subject to political control through the governor general of Moçambique, Gil was given a wide-ranging remit. Like his predecessors, his appointment appears to have been based on political grounds, as he had had no previous experience in Africa, but was a known Republican supporter.[78] He was given a force of three infantry battalions, three batteries of machine guns, three mountain artillery batteries and an engineering company, totalling 4,642 soldiers, 945 animals and 159 motor vehicles. Outwardly a reasonable command, these numbers concealed serious deficiencies in unit organisation, levels of training and fitness as well as insufficient draught animals. Whatever their readiness, the force sailed in succession on six ships with the first leaving Portugal at the end of May and reaching Moçambique on 27 June.[79]

Despite his general instructions to advance north and seize the coastal ports between the Rovuma and the Rufiji before striking westward to link-up with the British forces in the interior, Gil had to deal with the realities of his power. These limits had illustrated on 27 May, when two German posts just north of the Rovuma River were attacked. It had been a fiasco and the columns were driven back by the defenders who inflicted considerable loss.[80] It was ironic that it had only been the stubborn refusal of Schnee to allow Lettow to remove the troops from the Lindi area that enabled any defence at all. For the Portuguese, the fact remained that weak German forces were still more than a match for them.

On Lake Tanganyika, the Germans were largely inactive, with the *Götzen* making only three voyages in late March and April. Spicer-Simson's little flotilla had some success in surprising the *Wami*, which was grounded and subsequently destroyed. Work continued on the *Baron Dhanis*, now in Lukuga, as its engines had finally arrived. Once finished, it would add significantly to the transport power of the Allies and be vital to support the planned advance into German territory.

The Belgians wished to take Ruanda with all urgency, but also had plans to advance into Urundi from the Russisi Valley. Preliminary operations began on 16 April with Brigade Sud moving south of Lake Kivu to seize crossing sites. This was accomplished in four days, followed by consolidation of the local area and the building of permanent bridges. At the same time, the flotilla was engaged in moving the seaplane squadron forward in readiness for the next phase.[81] The main advance was more ambitious; Brigade Nord would launch frontal holding attack coupled with a flanking move through difficult mountainous terrain in an attempt to cut Wintgens off and reach Kigali. Brigade Sud would push east from its crossing sites along the Russisi towards Nyanza driving into Urundi.

The Belgians also used agents to spread anti-German sedition amongst the African inhabitants. It was successful as a number of tribes went over to the Belgian side and a rebellion soon developed on the northern edge of Lake Tanganyika. Wahle's problems were magnified as, apart from having insufficient numbers and no reserves, he had to detach a company to suppress the rebels at the worst possible time. In Ruanda, Wintgens only had 430 rifles to hold the country and he quickly appreciated the danger of the flank march. Within a week, the situation had deteriorated quickly as Wahle could send no reinforcements.[82]

Kigali was reached on 6 May and Nyanza nine days later as the outnumbered Germans evacuated their forward positions. As ever, transport was the problem and insufficient porters meant that the Belgian moves had to halt for supplies. The country was so wild and undeveloped that the Westtruppen managed to slip away without being decisively engaged. The Belgian brigades had moved into German territory although they remained well separated and incapable of supporting each other. While these operations were underway, Smuts was trying to launch his own column from Lake Victoria towards Tabora. Commanded by a prominent South African, Brigadier General Sir Charles Crewe, the brigade-sized Lake Force was due to land on the western coast of Lake Victoria in early June. General Tombeur, needing an easier supply chain for Brigade Nord, now began planning for the next phase based on the lake.[83]

The rains had ceased in the Kilimanjaro area and the country was drying up. Smuts now decided to resume the advance against the weakened Abt Kraut. The Pangani Valley was thickly vegetated and unhealthy, but he proposed to push 5,000 rifles down the river valley with another 1,800 moving down the railway line and a third column of 700 to move through the gap between the Pare and Usambara mountains as a feint. It was largely up to First Division for the Third consisted of only two infantry battalions with General Brits and the Mounted Brigade still at sea. In support, Smuts wanted Northey, the Belgians and Portuguese to exert all pressure from their positions.[84]

Once again, the commander-in-chief ignored the existing divisional structures and created three columns, two of which were equivalent to weak brigades and the third was in battalion strength, all to be commanded by Hoskins. His own general reserve consisted of two South African battalions. Operations commenced on 21 May, with the columns starting their marches in great heat. Expecting the worst, they encountered no resistance as Kraut had decided to pull back nearly 100 km to the north of Buiko. When Lettow realised this, he ordered that resistance be made, but his instructions arrived too late. Consequently, the British columns toiled for four days through thick bush and heavy dust without any opposition. On 28 May, the two eastern columns linked up and continued to press down the railway line, while the western one struggled through the Pangani Valley. Lack of water and the extreme heat began to take a toll on the marching men as sickness began to rise.

The eastern column was ordered north through the hills to emerge north of Buiko and outflank any defences. However, this route was particularly difficult and it fell behind the progress of the river column, which had reached German Bridge on the Pangani on 30 May. Here, the first engagement was fought with Kraut's forward troops, who were quickly turned out of their trenches and retired to Buiko. Both British columns linked up the next day and halted in order to bring up supplies and rest the exhausted troops.[85]

Smuts' troops had covered over 210 km in ten days through extremely difficult country that often proved impassable to wheeled vehicles of any sort. This meant that artillery and most supply vehicles could not follow until a road had been hacked out of the bush. Furthermore, the retreating Germans had done an effective job of destroying the railway line and, despite the best efforts of the railway troops, it took time to repair. This forced the British to overwork their already inadequate motor transport and although the administrative staff estimated that they could operate up to 160 km beyond the railhead, the troops were already on half-rations or less with insufficient ammunition for a major fight.[86]

Using the halt as an opportunity to visit van Deventer in Kondoa Irangi, General Smuts left on the ten-day round-trip journey by motor car. In the interim, all available effort was put into improving the river crossings as well as the lines of communications. The commander-in-chief found Second Division in a weak state, still some 1,500 horses and 1,800 mules short of establishment, with the remainder exhausted. There were over 1,200 men sick and reinforcement drafts were very slow in arriving.[87] The difficulties of being over 340 km from the railhead were immense.

Lettow's redeployment eastward was detected in late June and 3rd SA Infantry Brigade advanced south against the enemy rearguards and cleared them out of the dominating hills south of Kondoa Irangi. However, out of a nominally 10,000-man division, there was not enough strength to pursue Abt Otto south towards Dodoma. In the meantime, the sick had to lie on the ground without stretchers and the nearest receiving clearing hospital was 210 km away at Ufiome, but it could not move for lack of transport. The infantry regiments had no blankets, their clothes and equipment being in rags and rations remained woefully inadequate. It was an administrative disaster and meant that Second Division was going nowhere for at least a fortnight.[88]

THE PORTUGUESE COME TO WAR

Having passed nearly two years as quasi-neutral, Portugal's entry into the war came about from two imperatives. The various governments of the period had long resented their inferior status in the alliance with Britain although they recognised its value in defending their colonial interests and supported its cause. The British also found it difficult to relax their colonial concerns:

> We do not want Portugal to establish too great a claim on our gratitude or to be under obligation to protect their Colonies or divide up German territory with them… In view of the above we have discouraged the Portuguese from assisting us either in South West Africa or East Africa in spite of repeated offers on their part.[89]

However, it was Allied pressure to use the large numbers of German ships interned in Portuguese waters that tipped the balance. Finally, Britain encouraged the Portuguese to seize these vessels in late February 1916, provoking a declaration of war on 9 March. Apart from domestic factors, the Portuguese realised that by fighting on the Allied side and perhaps seizing German territory, they would be in a much better position to fend off South African or other attempts to take over its colonies. Equally, practical co-operation was complicated by mixed attitudes towards the British and their South African proxies. One group admired their colonial methods while many, including those running the chartered companies, were openly hostile or fearful of their intentions.[90]

The British had long suspected that German mail and contraband had been passing clandestinely through Portuguese East Africa and that many local merchants were engaged in cross-border trade. The opening of hostilities would probably be the only way in which such exchanges could be stopped, although it would take a major military and naval effort to achieve success.[91] On the other hand, as long as Portugal remained neutral, it would have been politically difficult for the Schutztruppe to move south of the Rovuma especially without authority from the Imperial Government.

Enthused by their new status, and despite the dismal failures of the expeditions of 1914-15, in which mismanagement and poor organisation resulted in large losses in troops and equipment, the Portuguese Government almost immediately decided to send another expeditionary force to East Africa. Admittedly, it had been lulled by British assertions that the campaign would be wound up within several months and delusions about its own military capacity. This placed a degree of political urgency on starting operations as quickly as possible, for, like their allies, the Portuguese wanted to obtain suitable bargaining chips for the eventual peace negotiations. But, they also distrusted Smuts' political ambitions intensely and a rapid intervention would guarantee that Moçambique would not be incorporated into the Union of South Africa. Finally, such operations would prove Portugal's value as an ally to the British while also promoting the national interest. Despite these efforts, Britain was to remain an impatient ally and quick to criticise Portuguese efforts whenever they were found lacking.[92]

The question of dealing with captured German territory was to prove highly contentious. The British wished to keep a free hand for the peace negotiations and refused to consider any question of annexations until then. However, for the time being, Smuts was willing to support the British official line in protecting his own ambitions. But the Portuguese thought differently, as their colonial officials devised a grandiose and ambitious plan. They saw operations taking part in three phases with the first being the reoccupation of the Kionga triangle, a reasonably straightforward goal. Thereafter, it became sweeping with the next phase envisaging an advance and occupation of the territory between the Rovuma and Rufiji rivers and the third seeing a decisive attack on Tabora. With less than 300 out of the over 13,000 Schutztruppe in the far south, the planned expeditionary force would have sufficient numbers for local operations. But, it would require substantial reinforcements for the latter two phases. Apart from the operational effectiveness of such a force, the plan ignored the enormous requirements for supply and transport to support a move over hundreds of kilometres of virgin bush.[93]

Apart from its lack of military reality, this plan presumed British acquiescence in the Portuguese administration of the occupied territories. Given the Colonial Office's jealous watch over the potential spoils, there was little chance of this being agreed as both Bonar Law and Smuts did their best to prevent either Portugal or Belgium from exerting any form of administration. Even Grey agreed to these demands and let it be known that Britain proposed to administer the whole of German East Africa.[94] But with the rapid change in Portuguese ministries of the period, the question was never fully addressed until late in 1916 when it would cause some upset. Matters were not helped by divisions in colonial opinion, with many local officials opposed to co-operating with the British as it would threaten their exploitation of the local population and the lucrative, if clandestine, trade with German East Africa.

As has been described, Smuts' territorial ambitions left nothing for either the Belgians or the Portuguese. Rather than being pleased with the extra manpower, he was more worried about them occupying territory owing to his advances elsewhere. As this attitude was still shared by the Colonial Office, it was to hamper good relations and mutual trust.[95] Smuts sought to attach British political officers to his allies' headquarters; these were not liaison officers, but officials meant to administer the captured regions. He believed, 'To begin there Belgian administration might be ominous and react unfavourably also on the future British influence and prestige'.[96] This was naturally unacceptable to either country as they could hardly accept subordination to the British in a country they had occupied and over which their lines of communications ran. The end result was a sterile debate that only succeeded in upsetting the Belgians with no material gain to the British.[97]

This also ignored the value of the Belgian advance. Tombeur's troops had resumed the advance in early June with Brigade Nord moving towards a link-up with Crewe at Namirembe, largely for supply reasons, while Brigade Sud continued its eastern push towards Kitegi, the capital of Urundi. Movement was difficult against German rearguards and difficult country. Kitegi was finally reached on 19 June, but the brigade was at the limits of its range and had to halt for supplies. Further north, Wintgens was still falling back before Brigade Nord which was approaching Lake Victoria. Crewe's troops, having successfully occupied Bukoba on 28 June, re-embarked and sailed south. The Belgians had reached Namirembe on 1 July ready to greet the British landing two days later. Everywhere the troops were exhausted after very strenuous marching and fighting. Tombeur had achieved his instructions as much of Ruanda and Urundi had been captured at reasonably low cost.[98]

5
The Advance to the Rufiji

From the outset, Brigadier General Northey grasped that he would be faced by exceptional physical and material challenges. There were very few roads and the nearest railhead was 970 km from the Anglo-German border. Furthermore, there was only a tiny settler population and no industry to support his forces. In contrast to Smuts, he had put considerable effort into preparing his force before launching operations. Leaving England in early December 1915, Northey had spent a week conferring in South Africa with Botha and Smuts, before travelling north to Rhodesia for a three-week stay that concentrated on planning his transport system between the railway terminus and the north-eastern border. Thereafter, he went into Portuguese East Africa to meet the governor general and to make further arrangements. He then sailed up the Zambezi River, arriving at Zomba on 28 January. After spending two weeks thoroughly organising the supply and transport system in Nyasaland, he finally reached the forward post of Karonga on 16 February.[1]

1 *Above:* The German Askari firing '71 pattern rifle with its characteristic cloud of smoke.

2 *Right:* A German Schützenkompagnie in training.

3 *Below:* Soldiers of the Force Publique being instructed on the machine gun.

4 *Above:* Open bush and road.

5 *Right:* HMS *Chatham* in action off the Rufiji delta against the *Königsberg*.

6 *Below:* A Caudron aircraft being uncrated at Mafia Island.

7 German Askari on the counter-attack.

8 General Jan Smuts.

9 Brigadier General Edward Northey.

10 Lettow addressing his headquarters – he is in the centre on the white horse facing the camera.

11 The advance on Kilimanjaro.

12 Weary Kashmiris on the march.

13 F27 Farman aircraft of 26 (South African) Squadron RFC.

14 A flooded camp en route to Kondoa Irangi.

15 Ammunition had to be kept clean for use.

16 A battery struggles up Utschungwe Mountain near Iringa.

17 Belgian troops of the Force Publique in action. The smoke from the German positions can be seen on the right.

18 A Belgian mortar detachment in action.

19 Meal time for British Askari in Nyasaland.

20 Moving a motorcycle with sidecar across a river.

21 South Africans crossing the Lukigura River.

22 The grim aftermath of battle – identifying the dead.

23 South African supply convoy.

24 A Nigerian gun carrier in full marching order. He is carrying a gun wheel of the 2.95-inch mountain gun which weighs 31.5 kg and is a most awkward load.

25 Troops ride a modified tractor on the Central Railway at Kilossa.

26 Captain F.W. Selous and his company of 25th Royal Fusiliers.

27 Belgian troops disembarking on Lake Tanganyika.

28 Belgian carriers bringing forward supplies through the highlands of Ruanda.

29 A German dug-out – strong and well constructed.

30 Along the Mgeta line – 75 yards from the German positions.

31 Rhodesian troops crossing swampy ground.

32 Road-making – hacking a way through the bush.

33 Brigadier General Beves.

34 General van Deventer (right) with a staff officer.

35 The Nigerians in action at Mahiwa, October 1917.

36 The Nigerians fighting from the trenches at Mahiwa.

37 The Kashmir Mountain Battery in action at Mahiwa.

Satisfied that his rear areas were properly organised, Northey now turned to the fighting troops. He inspected the whole frontier between Lakes Nyassa and Tanganyika, finding much that was inadequate. He spent most of March rectifying tactical deficiencies and making plans for his advance, including efficient road and telegraph communications. This was supplemented by the detailed preliminary instructions he issued to his column commanders; Northey expected thorough and methodical preparation.[2] By the end of April, his troops were ready for the main advance.

With the rainy seasons in the southern theatre starting and ending later than those in the north, Norforce had to wait until the end of May before starting its advance. It was a mixed force of about 2,400 effectives divided into four separate columns and comprised of the British South Africa Police, the Northern Rhodesia Police, two battalions of South African Rifles and the 1st King's African Rifles. Facing them were an estimated 1,500 Germans in four isolated garrisons spread between the two great lakes, Tanganyika and Nyasa.[3]

Northey's plan was to set out on 23 May with the aim of encircling all of the enemy posts and compelling them to surrender. With three columns concentrated between Fife and Lake Nyasa, the fourth was far to the west and based on Abercorn. With his superiority of numbers and preparations, it was a feasible plan, but it counted on rapid movement and the opposition remaining in place. However, none of the columns had sufficient troops to pin the Germans into the defences who had already begun to withdraw towards Iringa, apart from the troops at Bismarckburg, who moved towards Tabora. By the second week of June, the vigorous advance had dislodged the defenders everywhere along the front and the key posts of Bismarckburg and Neu Langenburg were in Norforce's hands. Furthermore, large quantities of supplies and ammunition had been captured during the precipitate flight of the enemy. If he had failed to destroy his opponents as originally intended, Northey had now fulfilled the first part of his instructions in full.[4] With Lake Tanganyika and the western portion now secure, the Belgian advance some 480 km further north secured his left flank.

Northey now established his headquarters in Neu Langenburg and asked Smuts for further direction as to his next move. On 3 June, as First Division was moving south towards Handeni and Second Division was preparing to advance from Kondoa Irangi, he was instructed to push for Iringa in order to block any enemy escape in that direction. This was subsequently modified a few days later so that Northey should not advance so quickly as to expose himself to an isolated attack.[5]

With the enemy on the run, Northey intended to give them no rest. He now looked north towards the villages of Ulongwe and Ubena, both key track junctions that linked Neu Langenburg with Iringa, Mahenge and Songea. However, this also meant ascending the broken and difficult mountains that rose to 1,800 metres above sea level. With no serious roads and steep climbs, Norforce was dependent on a narrow column of porters winding through narrow mountain trails. The next two weeks of June were spent in arduous marches into the wet and colder highlands. The Germans continued to fight small rearguard actions, but the British columns pressed them back, clearing the frontier as far as Lake Nyasa.

The principal column under Colonel Hawthorn occupied the villages of Brandt and Neu Utengule, both of which lay on the route to Iringa, while two smaller ones pushed eastwards to Ubena. Hawthorn then switched to the south-east and pushed on Ubena, seizing it and a large quantity of food in the last week of June. The next objective was Malangali, 72 km to the north, which was reported to have over 1,000 defenders. This was too strong for Hawthorn's 800 rifles and he was ordered to hold fast until further orders from Smuts had been received. At the same time, stockpiles were built up in the forward areas while the column in Bismarckburg marched to rejoin the main force. Thus, by the beginning of July, Norforce was deployed in two substantial columns, facing north and east.

Lettow realised the threat posed by Northey's steady push north. He despatched substantial reinforcements to hold the arc of Madibira-Malangali with several forward posts so as to block an advance on Iringa. Both places had to be taken, but the strength of their defences and the strain of the advance meant that a pause was necessary. The next two weeks were spent bringing up supplies and Colonel Murray's column in readiness for a major blow. At the same time, Northey's engineers had completed a motor road from Mwaya at the northern end of Lake Nyasa to Neu Langenburg thence to Brandt where previously only tracks had existed. Considering the limited resources and the need to construct it over a 1,800-metre vertical rise, this was a substantial achievement.[6]

With Murray now opposite Madibira and Hawthorn reinforced for a move on Malangali, by late July they were ready to attack. Hawthorn had only 1,200 rifles to deal with the 550 defenders, but making a concentric

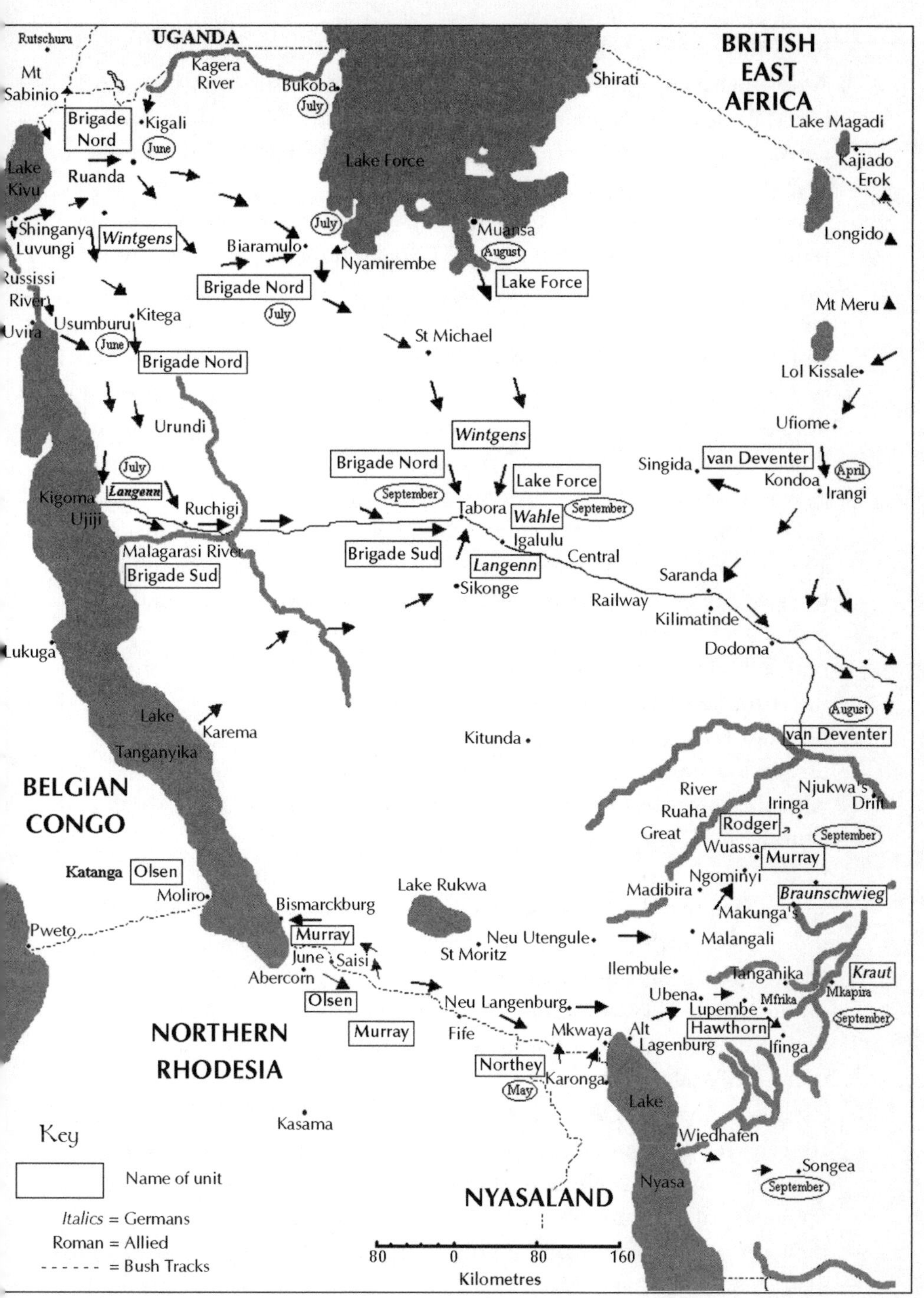

The Anglo-Belgian advance in the west, April–September 1916

move forward on 24 July, he caught them in the process of withdrawing. After a sharp engagement, the Germans managed to slip away in darkness, but Malangali was occupied the next day, as was Madibira which had been taken unopposed. The road to Iringa was now open and the southern granary of German East Africa was now lost.

Northey appreciated that his movements could well trigger substantial reinforcements against him. He had initially hoped that, as he advanced east, the Portuguese might occupy the large tract of German territory between Mahenge and Songea. However, they were incapable of such an ambitious movement and the area remained largely empty of forces, Allied or German. On the other hand, intelligence indicated that a threat was developing in the Lupembe area, some 64 km east of Ubena on the road to Mahenge. Apart from its military significance, it was an important rice-growing area with the crops soon ready for harvest.

Facing nearly 700 of the enemy to the north, he considered that about 400 rifles were in the Lupembe area. Hawthorn was sent there in the first week of August to locate their defences and confirm their strength. Now realising that the Portuguese were incapable of occupying Songea, Northey now had to divert an important part of his striking force from the Iringa axis, which he considered vital. With van Deventer still stalled north of the Central Railway, Smuts instructed Northey to not advance further towards Iringa for the moment, but instead to consolidate and deal with the threat from Lupembe.[7] With Hawthorn holding the south and Murray the north, he prepared for his next move.

To his surprise, the Germans evacuated Lupembe as Hawthorn approached together with a second, very strong natural position at Mfrika, some 11 km further east. This was highly significant, as Mfrika marked the edge of the great upland ridge that ran towards Iringa. From there the ground dropped away sharply, losing over 300 metres as it descended into the hot lowlands of the Ruhudje Valley that lay for the 160 km to the uplands of Mahenge.[8]

Now, with his eastern flank much more secure, Northey was able to concentrate on resuming the move north. With van Deventer at Kilossa and the Belgians marching on Tabora, on 21 August he sent Murray and Rodger's columns north on a parallel course towards Wuasa. Once more, the Germans had retired and it now seemed that Mahenge was their ultimate destination, and Murray was sent along the eastern side of the plateau to prevent any escape. The drive to reach Iringa continued and, on

29 August, the two columns entered the town unopposed. With Falkenstein moving eastward towards the edge of the mountains, Northey considered sending Hawthorn towards Mahenge, but realised that this would place the column nearly 480 km from its base and with little support. He abandoned the idea, but had achieved a remarkable advance.[9]

Norforce's greatest handicap was the lack of soldiers for the task at hand. In reality, it was a brigade-sized command that now fielded less than 4,000 rifles, split into three columns, separated by 320 km of wild and mountainous terrain. Despite the high quality of his columns and their commanders, Northey was rightly concerned that his lack of concentration and the dangers of being defeated in detail should the Westtruppen move east. As well, his troops were suffering from the effects of climate and disease, although nowhere near as badly as the main body to the north.

Northey had requested naval assistance for his planned subsidiary advance on Bismarckburg, now possible with the increasingly untenable position of the German vessels. The Belgian seaplanes began attacking the *Götzen*, it being temporarily disabled on 10 June. They then turned to the *Adjutant*, which was being reassembled after its rail journey from the coast. But the Germans struck first, as they scuttled the vessels before their withdrawal from Kigoma.[10]

By June 1916, the shipping available to the Allies on Lake Tanganyika had increased dramatically. In six months, it had risen from a mere 14 tons to 380 tons of capacity, while an important port had been developed at Lukuga. With control of Kigoma, the waters of Lake Tanganyika would change from being a barrier to an efficient link in the Belgian supply chain. On the other side, the 400 km of railway that linked Kigoma to Tabora had been badly damaged by the Germans and would require extensive repairs. Diplomatically, Spicer-Simson's position was increasingly untenable as he was an argumentative and difficult man and local relations were nearing breaking point. Naval support for the move on Bismarckburg in late June was ill-organised and slow; despite the expedition's earlier success, it was clear that a change was necessary.[11]

If the Belgians had achieved their initial goals, they had not forgotten their pledge to assist General Smuts. He and Tombeur had agreed that the next move would be a combined move of Crewe and Brigade Nord on the port of Muansa while Brigade Sud turned south back towards Ujiji and the western terminus of the Central Railway. Orders were issued on

5 July for a renewed advance, with a move in the south commencing first. Brigade Sud met virtually no resistance, as Wahle had withdrawn the troops in Urundi back towards Tabora, but had to struggle through numerous swamps. It was not until the last day of the month that Ujiji was occupied, with Kigoma falling a day later. With the launch of the *Baron Dhanis* a few days later, the Allies now held undisputed mastery over Lake Tanganyika. It also provided the Admiralty with a good excuse to withdraw its expedition and reduce Anglo-Belgian friction; by August responsibility was formally handed over to their allies.[12]

Matters were also fraught in the north as Tombeur wanted to press south and Crewe needed assistance to take Muansa. Finally, the British decided to conduct an amphibious landing near the port, while Brigade Nord marched down the coast in an attempt to cut off Wintgens. On 10 July, Crewe landed 2,000 men as the Belgians marched south. The expected battle never took place, as the Germans pulled out four days later. Instead, disputes over supplies and administration took its place, while a lack of carriers prevented an immediate further advance.

Wahle had two distinct groups; one under Wintgens in the north and the other under Langenn, neither of which was strong enough to halt a determined advance. Fortunately for him, Tombeur and Crewe could not get along and the advance from the north was largely unco-ordinated. The move on Tabora began in early August, with Brigade Sud moving along the railway line and the Anglo-Belgian force through difficult, waterless bush. Sickness and supply problems enabled only limited progress, but by the end of the month the southern troops were only 56 km from Tabora. Tombeur issued instructions on 2 September for its capture, regardless of Crewe's intentions. The race was on.

Brigade Sud had the easier approach, coming within a few kilometres of its objective on 10 September. Heavy fighting ensued, with Wahle's troops making a determined defence. The next day Brigade Nord was within range, launching its attack on 12 September, as its sister column paused for re-supply. A major battle raged, with a spirited German counter-attack driving the northern column back on 14 September. The next day, the Belgian columns linked up as Brigade Sud advanced slowly without opposition. A final assault was planned for 19 September, but Wahle had evacuated the town the night before as he was unwilling to subject the civilian population to a major battle. Tabora was occupied without resistance by the Belgian forces. In the meantime, Crewe's force was floundering in the bush, having paused for supplies and still being many kilometres north of Tabora. Despite the best efforts of his troops, he had failed to engage the Germans or beat the Belgians to Tabora.[13]

THE ADVANCE TO THE LUKIGURA

In early September, Smuts instructed Northey to advance on and occupy the Mahenge plateau. The concept was for Norforce to move westwards through the Ulanga Valley, then to ascend the Mahenge plateau before the withdrawing German main body reached that place itself. Its capture was part of his grand plan to cut off the Schutztruppe; this, coupled with the advance from Kilwa would make further retreat impossible and force a surrender.[14]

As was becoming usual, Smuts' plan was based on fallacious or questionable assumptions. Apart from expecting Northey to advance another 160 km across an enormous flood plain during the short rainy season, it ignored the threat posed by the Westtruppen to his exposed lines of communication. It also failed to recognise that Smuts' own troops were in absolutely no condition for further offensive operations and that restoring the Central Railway to full capacity was going to take months rather than weeks. Finally, it presumed that it would be possible to prevent the Germans from breaking through the 120–160-km gap that would remain between Norforce and the Second Division.[15]

That formation struggled to bring forward enough supplies for the long-delayed advance. Lack of petrol was a major problem as there was insufficient either for the aircraft or even the staff cars for the brigade commanders.[16] Nevertheless, they began to move as ordered in the third week of July. Van Deventer was expected to advance to with his main force to Dodoma on the Central Railway with smaller columns on the flanks. On 20 July, he sent his 1st SA Mounted Brigade south-east with the 3rd SA Infantry pushing south while a number of detached units cleared the area further west. After light resistance and continual rearguards, the Division reached the Central Railway on 29 July, cutting the lifeline of the enemy forces in two. By the middle of August, the line from Saranda to Kikombo was secure although he had added another 160 km to this already extensive line of communication. Nyangalo was now the forward base of operations, although still many kilometres north of the railway.

It took another week before van Deventer was able to move again, chiefly through want of supplies. Faced by six to ten companies, he was now to push east towards Mpapua with the ultimate objective of Kilosa, where thousands of porters were reported to be collecting.[17] Speed was of the essence and, on the eve of Smuts' move in the Nguru, van Deventer was being pressed to push along with all speed. His troops continued to move determinedly and Mpapua was taken on 11 August, having covered the 51 km of poor roads in thirty hours without rations or water while preventing the enemy from demolishing any railway or important bridges.[18]

For the Portuguese, General Gil's first action on arriving in late June was to confer with the governor general and British consul general. From there, he then sailed north to the port of Palma where he met the remnants of the previous expedition. It was a pitiable sight as the hospitals overflowed with sick, sanitation was poor and morale was low. His own medical resources were scant and still had yet to arrive, an ominous sign given that that 75% of the 1915 expedition had been incapacitated through illness. As the new troops began to arrive, it was apparent that their lack of fitness and training meant` that they were unready for the front. Unfortunately, Palma was very unhealthy and the longer they stayed, the longer malaria had time to wreak its effects and weaken their strength.[19] Few lessons had been learned.

Colonel Lettow was concerned about the Belgian pressure on Wahle's troops in the west; with the latter's reserves exhausted, he had to make a decision. Ten companies were left in the Kondoa area under Captain Klinghardt, with two being sent off to help Wahle, leaving twelve under his personal control. The priority was now in the east and Lettow began moving back to Dodoma on 20 June. He also arranged for the evacuation of the depot in Morogoro back to Kissaki that was slowed by a chronic shortage of carriers.[20]

After a week's halt at Buiko, Hoskins began to push south again on 5 June, moving along the railway to Mombo. Hannyngton reached it on 9 June, but not before the railway bridge and workshops had been destroyed. Sheppard's Brigade had been marching cross-country south-eastwards for Mkalamo on the trolley line to Handeni. But, Kraut had garrisoned that place strongly so as to cover his withdrawal to Handeni. A heavy clash ensued on 9 June, but despite both sides trying to outflank each other and the Germans breaking into the British rear area, neither side gained a decisive advantage. Pausing in position for the night, patrols the next morning found the defenders gone and the trolley line badly damaged. Kraut had escaped to the south towards Handeni.[21]

On 15 June, Hannyngton's brigade had reached the station at Korogwe while Sheppard's was just outside Handeni, reconnoitring the defences there. A sharp clash took place on 20 June with Beves' 2nd SA Brigade running into the rearguard south of Handeni and both sides suffering a number of losses. However, Handeni was now in British hands and Kraut was retiring south. Here a decision had to be made; Smuts wanted to push the Germans well south of the railway so as to protect his own supply lines, but his troops also needed water. With no sources between the Rivers Pangani and Lukigura, success depended on pushing south to the latter.[22]

Air and ground reconnaissance located the German position on the Lukigura River, some 64 km south of Handeni. Once again Smuts divided his force, with Sheppard's much weakened column (many units were at 50% strength) ordered to make a frontal demonstration while a picked column, not more than a brigade in strength, lead by Hoskins personally, would conduct a flanking attack. They left on the night of 23 June while Sheppard moved slowly ahead with Smuts personally controlling the battle. It was not until noon the next day that Hoskins' advance guard clashed with the defenders who were holding a ridge. Despite being exhausted and very hungry, the Indian and British troops plunged in with bayonets, surprising the defenders and rapidly capturing a gun and machine gun. The Germans were overwhelmed and the position dissolved into chaos and streamed away to the south. This was the first notable achievement for First Division which had been unable to bring the rearguards to battle before this. It also marked the importance of driving home the fight to the enemy.[23]

Smuts himself fell ill with malaria and was bed-ridden for a number of days. But there was no question of exploiting that success for the supply system had collapsed. The troops had marched an impressive 320 km in a month, but with the nearest railhead at Buiko being 145 km distant, matters were extremely strained. Repairs and extensions of the railway were ordered, but would not be effective until mid-July, and it would then take some time to build-up supplies. In the meantime, the troops were in rags and badly underfed; in many cases the troops were issued bully beef and raw flour without any fats or oils to cook it with. Even the medical units had extreme difficulty as one field ambulance had no rations for its patients. Unsurprisingly, the sick rate soared with First Division alone losing 1,500 out of its 5,500 men since 20 May.[24] There were simply too many troops to be supported and this created a vicious circle of sickness being increased by lack of food, which increased the demands for transport, which in turn reduced the supply capacity. The distances forward were also huge; from Sanja to Dodoma was 470 km and Korogwe to Morogoro was 315 km. At the moment, just over half of Second Division's requirements could be met and although things were less dire on the main front, the existing transport could only support First and Third Divisions for 57 km beyond Handeni.[25]

In the meantime, operations on the Indian Ocean coast had been very quiet since a minor advance to Gazi and the naval bombardment of Tanga in March. Lettow had reduced the garrisons to a minimum, enabling the British to move to Jassini in June. This was followed by the Navy's occupation of Tanga on 19 June, finding it largely empty with most of its facilities destroyed. Despite its value as a railhead and port, Smuts showed little interest in using it to support his hard-pressed supply service.

Smuts' consistently upbeat communiqués had had their effect on London, with the CIGS looking for him to wrap up the campaign reasonably quickly. Robertson foresaw the likely withdrawal south of the Central Railway and with it adverse effects. He recommended that it might be advisable to withdraw the bulk of his white troops and finish off the fighting with locally-raised African units.[26] Smuts himself was quite clear that this was Lettow's most likely option and that it would be very difficult to prevent him from doing so. Moreover, he believed that his transport would get him to the Central Railway and no farther, making a halt on that line imperative. Malaria was also destroying his force, as some 50% of Hoskins' First Division had been affected by it since late May.[27] Another prolonged pause was unavoidable and a bivouac was found on the Msiha River and occupied on 5 July by First Division.

Smuts recognised the link between numbers and supply problems, but effectively chose to ignore it as he continued the movement of the newly arrived 2nd SA Mounted Brigade forward to the Lukigura.[28] The day before, he had sent two battalions to land at Tanga and to secure the area. But the infantry were incapable of making the necessary repairs and despite a report on 10 July that, despite the damage to the railway line, the harbour could be used immediately and be in working order within a month, it was not until the end of the month that the first company of specialist railway troops arrived there. This meant that the first train did not reach Korogwe until 17 August at a time when all supplies were needed at Msiha Camp. Smuts betrayed his ignorance of supply in his statement that the port was 'of no importance after the Tanga railway had been reached further north'.[29] This was apparent as the early opening of the port meant that the short haul from Tanga to Mombo could be substituted for the long journey from Mombasa to Voi to Neu Moshi to Mombo.

This also left the substantial area between the garrisons at Handeni and Korogwe and Tanga open to the enemy. While the main force was halted at Msiha Camp, the enemy used this freedom to attack the British lines of communication, especially the road linking the two former places. By mid-July, a substantial attack on a bridge near Korogwe was beaten off, but stronger measures were needed. Smuts sent Hannyngton's 2nd EA Infantry Brigade back to Handeni while ordering the IGC to clear the area. This was a major error as the IGC was not a fighting commander and was fully occupied with running the overworked supply and transport system. He was forced to use two companies of his specialist, and irreplaceable, railway companies for this role at a time that the Usambara Railway and the port of Tanga needed urgent work. While Hannyngton eventually took over the operations, this was a waste of scarce resources.[30] It took until 19 July for his forces to link-up with those from Tanga and the area was not fully secured until the end of the month.

Fresh African troops had now been recruited and were in training. Having wasted over a year, the new KAR battalions were far from ready to take the field as they were very short of experienced officers and NCOs. To make up the shortfall, Smuts asked for 6,000 Belgian troops to assist in what was likely to become a difficult battle in extremely rough terrain. At the end of the month, he received an important visitor, Louis Botha, and together they spent several days discussing the campaign and political matters at home. The prime minister was also able to see a large number of troops and the extreme conditions under which they were serving.[31]

By the third week in July, the supply situation was far from good. The Third Division had three weeks' supplies, the Force Reserve one weeks' and First Division, the effective fighting force, none. The difficulty may be gauged that out of a theoretical 136,000 kg of lift, available vehicles could provide between 88,000 to 65,000 kg (or less). In comparison, the support of First Division and Force Reserve alone required 68,000 kg and these totals excluded extra medical and ordnance stores. This depressing picture was slightly alleviated by the expected arrival of over 150 ox wagons, 100 donkey wagons and 100 Fords within a fortnight, but it meant that, in the short term, it would be impossible to build-up sufficient reserves.[32]

Smuts then came up with an unusual idea, proposing that the Belgian Force Publique, but without the Belgian officers, should be taken under British command for future operations. This ill-judged suggestion cut little ice with the Belgians, who naturally resented the implied slur on the quality of their officers.[33] It was also evident that he hoped to escape from his increasingly difficult command:

> When our forces are thus transformed no useful purpose will be served any longer by my continuing in command, and I hope that I shall be permitted to return to my duties in the Union Government.[34]

While the War Committee agreed this in principle, it also stipulated that it would only be implemented once a decisive result had been achieved. But Smuts continued to look for other ways to end the fighting quickly. Upon reaching the Central Railway, he proposed to ask for similar terms of surrender as those achieved in South-West Africa, namely that officers, civilians and reservists would be disarmed and allowed home on parole with only regular soldiers interned. This was followed several weeks later by a mission to the Governor of British East Africa in which Smuts' emissary sought similar terms. His senior staff realised that he wanted out, but his hopes were dashed by the uncompromising rejection by the War Committee on 18 August.[35]

Whatever Smuts' motivations, the War Office was clear that European and Indian troops were not able to withstand devastating tropical diseases. African troops were seen to be much less vulnerable to malaria and their feeding was a much simpler matter. While this simplistic view overlooked the considerable differences amongst widely spread peoples, such a policy would also reduce the shipping requirements to East Africa. The ending of the Cameroons campaign released the West African Frontier Force for service although it needed rest, while reinforcements in the form of a West Indies battalion and one from the Gold Coast were already en route to the theatre. The rather more obvious question of raising more East African troops was finally tackled with the recommendation that a further three battalions be raised. However, given the need to recruit and train such units, it would be a considerable period before they were ready for the field. With nothing immediately available, Smuts proposed to continue south of the Central Railway with his existing force.[36] In the circumstances, it was the only possible decision.

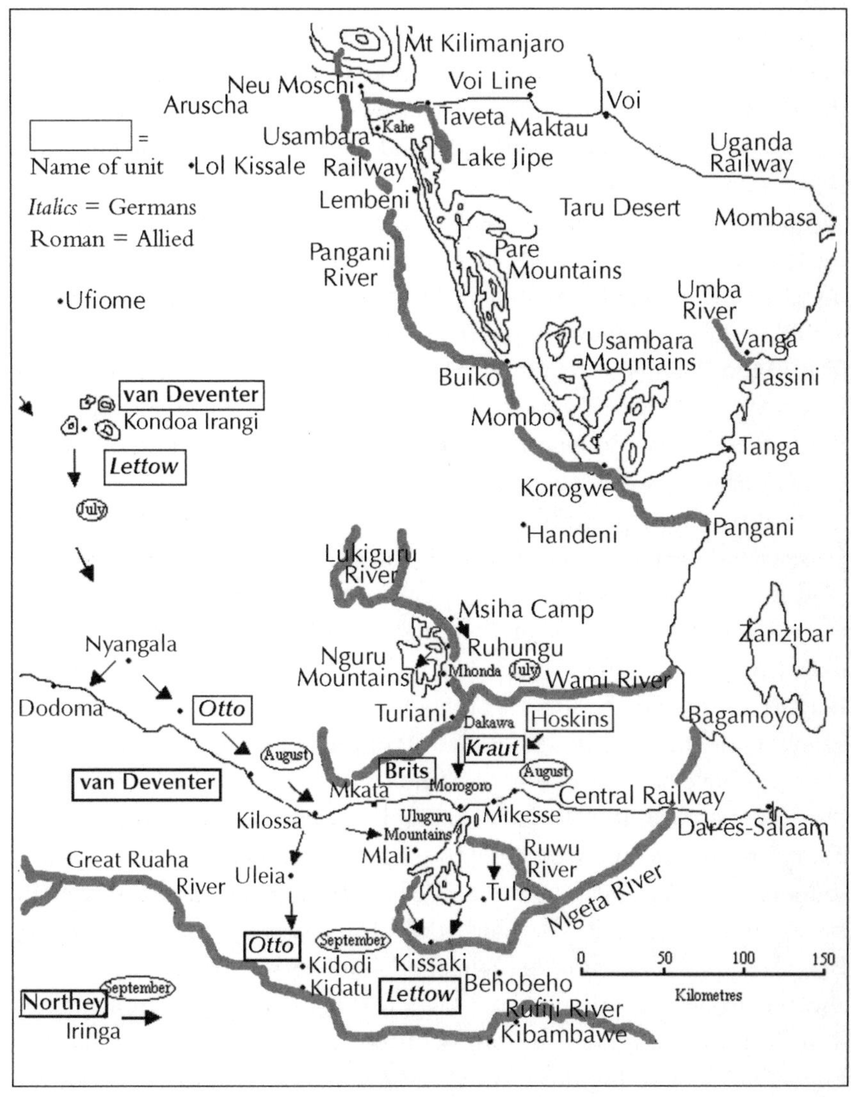

Smuts' advance to the Mgeta, July-September 1916

THE PUSH TO THE CENTRAL RAILWAY

Back in Germany, Schnee's request for help was being actioned in mid-1916 as a further relief expedition of two ships had been approved and large quantities of ammunition, supplies and medicine were readied. Vessels were found, but as Smuts advanced south, the government became indecisive and the mission was further delayed. Unaware of these deliberations, Lettow had returned to the east, joining Kraut in early July. He conducted lengthy reconnaissance and brought up several guns to harass the enemy. The Germans still possessed superior operational mobility via the Central Railway while the British were burdened with lengthy and precarious lines of communication and sufferd from insufficient food, sickness and regular shelling.[37]

Smuts needed to press on and in mid-month he ordered the newly-mobile Second Division, which was 240 km west of the main body, to move to the Central Railway at Saranda and Dodoma. From there, it would swing east, following the tracks as it moved toward the main body from Morogoro. Concurrently, Hannynton's brigade would clear the Usambara Railway to Tanga while supplies were stockpiled. Further west, the Belgians were clearing the eastern shores of Lake Tanganyika while Crewe's brigade was besieging Muansa.[38]

He also wanted to push south from Msiha to Morogoro as quickly as possible, but the terrain was daunting. The rugged Nguru Mountains were wild and covered in dense bush or elephant grass. 9 km south of the camp, the strongly fortified post of Ruhungu held by Abt Kraut blocked the main road south. Smuts intended to use Sheppard's 1st EA Infantry Brigade to follow the River Lukigura south before launching a feint attack on the main enemy position at Ruhungu. This would cover a wide flanking movement by the now completed Third Division under Brits. His 2nd SA Mounted Brigade under Brigadier General Enslin would plunge nearly 48 km west into the Nguru Mountains, before turning south towards Turiani and cutting off any retreat. It would be followed by Beves' 2nd SA Infantry Brigade while Hannyngton's 2nd EA Infantry Brigade would make an inner wheel of about 24 km into the hills before also turning south. The plan also saw Northey holding his present positions south of Iringa and dealing with the threat to his eastern flank at Lupembe. Several hundred kilometres west, the Belgians and Crewe would continue their combined advance towards Tabora. If the balance of forces was in Smuts' favour, it was hardly overwhelmingly as his 7,000 men faced 3,500 Germans in the Nguru area.[39]

In the west, van Deventer continued to press hard along the railway, trying to link-up with the main body. His next objective was Mpapua, but again the South Africans were forced to halt to bring up supplies as they were 113 km south of Kondoa Irangi.[40] His troops had done well in difficult circumstances, but were increasingly tired from their exertions.

The main advance began on 5 August with Third Division setting off on its ambitious wheel. Matters quickly deteriorated, for after a mere 3 km, the track was found to be completely impossible for motor vehicles and they had to return to camp. Enslin's Mounted Brigade disappeared into the wilderness and contact was soon lost between the columns. Brits and his troops struggled forward, but by 8 August he was ordered to turn south-east and to send all his heavy transport and artillery back to the Lukigura. Unknown to him, Enslin had pushed well to the west, and was actually paused at Mhonda, 6 km from his objective.

Hannyngton's infantry was finding matters equally difficult and also had to send their transport back to its starting place. On 7 August, he had turned south, but with virtually no food, he was forced to wait for two days until supplies were brought forward. Finally, he linked up with Beves' infantry and both attacked Abt Stemmermann around Matamondo. All of 10 August was spent in determined attacks against the defenders, who suffered heavily in the engagement. By the next morning, however, the enemy had slipped away, moving back towards Turiani.

In the west, Sheppard moved against Ruhungu on 7 August, but found the position very strong and put in a desultory attack. Short of water, he decided to return to Msiha Camp despite the need to pin Kraut. Very quickly, Hoskins ordered the brigade back south for a flanking move east of Ruhungu. Lettow was well aware of this danger, and on the night of 9/10 August, he ordered the evacuation of the position and a withdrawal south to the River Wami, destroying all the bridges over the many raging streams. Once again, the Germans had slipped away at night. Smuts' plan had depended on the holding attack keeping the enemy well forward and the mounted troops cutting off the escape at Turiani. But, Sheppard's premature breaking off of the attack and Enslin's failure to press hard at Mhonda prevented its fulfillment.[41] Inadequate reconnaissance, poor communications and lack of artillery contributed to the failure.

The British continued to push south with Dakawa on the Wami River being reached on 17 August. Smuts decided to send Enslin's mounted troops to cross in the west while Sheppard's much-reduced infantry pushed from the east. A crossing was found, but once more Enslin failed to push into the defenders' rear areas, although 1st EA Brigade made good progress. By evening, the defenders had slipped away again and Smuts was forced to pause for supplies and the need to bridge the Wami. Supply shortages were again becoming serious and despite the need for replacement manpower in units, GHQ had to stop them from coming forward for the time being.[42]

Further west, Second Division was also experiencing severe supply problems, particularly from lack of petrol and food, with only three days' rations on hand.[43] Opposite them, Abt Otto was conducting a skilful rearguard and using the difficult ground well. As they continued east from Mpapua, the South Africans were becoming increasingly exhausted as they marched towards Kilossa. That town was occupied on 22 August and Smuts wanted van Deventer to press ahead to Morogoro so as to trap the Germans. With the troops worn out, the latter pressed for a pause until 28 August, but it was overruled and told to carry on.

The commander-in-chief now resolved to pin the Schutztruppe against the apparently impassable Uluguru Mountains, south of Morogoro. By blocking the western and eastern flanks, he hoped to force a surrender that would end the campaign, although this ran against his own intelligence reports and knowledge of Lettow's character. Furthermore, heavy rains, in conjunction with widespread destruction of bridges and roads, were seriously hampering the supply situation. Undaunted, he ordered both South African Mounted Brigades to converge on Mlali on the western side while Hoskins' infantry would cut off the eastern flank. The plan was subsequently modified to have van Deventer's infantry brigade move south towards the River Ruaha where it would seize the crossings at Kidodi and Kidatu.[44]

The commander-in-chief was also under pressure from London to wind up operations. The CIGS considered that once the Ruaha River had been reached, it would be possible to wind up operations with a force of about 12,000 men comprised of an Indian brigade, Norforce and a mixed brigade of South African and West African troops. A further 7,000 troops would be needed for the lines of communication and once the Nigerian Brigade and the six new KAR battalions were ready, then the white and

Indian troops could be relieved. The main aim was not to denude East Africa of troops, but to get as many white and Indian troops for other theatres.[45] Smuts agreed with this analysis and seriously underplayed the enemy's prospects. Believing that his morale had gone, numbers were diminishing rapidly and that if the present pressure were maintained, that no more than 3,000 troops would be left. He wished to release the mounted troops, which were virtually useless owing to losses, while holding onto the South African infantry for the next two months as he said then 'the situation will have materially cleared up.'[46]

Lettow had other ideas, as lack of food had forced him to abandon his plans for a retreat to Mahenge. He also recognised the threat of encirclement and had no intention of being trapped in front of the Uluguru Mountains. He had already ordered the important supply dump at Morogoro to be evacuated to Kissaki and prepared for a withdrawal before the arrival of the British. In the north, the Wami had been bridged on 21 August, and First Division's way to Morogoro was open, although the Schutztruppe was still a formidable force with an estimated 1,430 Europeans and 7,950 Askari.[47] Hoskins' division, plus half of Beves' 3rd SA Infantry Brigade, had the trying task of pushing the 29 km of tsetse fly-ridden and waterless country to the hills that overlooked Morogoro. Starting on 23 August, they spent the next two days on a hot and exhausting march, before patrols discovered that Morogoro was being evacuated. Tired and thirsty, they occupied the undefended town the next day, followed by GHQ on 27 August.

Elsewhere, the mounted advance began on 24 August, with the depleted 1st SA Mounted Brigade under Nussey moving east. It was in poor shape, with barely 900 soldiers and losing 249 horses on the preliminary move forward alone. Enslin's 2nd SA Mounted Brigade, about 1,000 strong, arrived at Mlali on the same day, pushing the enemy out. The two formations linked up the next day and, after a brief rest, they continued the difficult march along the sides of the mountains, reaching halfway to Kissaki on 29 August. Smuts and Brits arrived there, with the latter being placed in command of the next move, south to Kissaki on the River Mgeta. The state of the troops was worsening, with Enslin's brigade down to 600 soldiers and Nussey's largely dismounted. Uniforms and boots were in tatters while the transport was completely insufficient, in both porters and mules.[48]

First Division was expected to clear around the eastern edge of the Uluguru Mountains, with both its infantry brigades pushing hard to cut off the routes south.[49] On the coast, a small force was to land near Dar-es-Salaam in order to take that important seaport. Northey wanted to concentrate in the south at Lupembe while van Deventer, still 160 km north of Iringa, took over that place. Such a move would permit Norforce to concentrate its 2,000 rifles rather than have two groups over 160 km apart. He was unaware that Berrangé's 2nd SA Infantry Brigade had 60% of its manpower in debilitated condition and clothed in rags; it was hardly fit to hold its present positions let alone advance. For his part, Smuts wanted Northey to drive on Mahenge as he feared Lettow would retire to there from positions on the Rufiji River although he was not particularly worried about Wahle's troops around Tabora.[50] All seemed ready for a decisive blow.

The move began well with the unopposed occupation of Dar-es-Salaam on 4 September. It had been badly damaged by the retreating Germans and would take considerable effort to restore its facilities to full use. Nevertheless, as the major port and terminus of the Central Railway, it would be vital to the future support of the campaign. By 15 September, the remaining ports of Kilwa, Mikindani, Sudi and Lindi were all in British hands. Unbeknownst to Smuts, this had an important effect in Germany as it convinced the government to postpone again the planned relief expedition to its beleaguered colony.[51]

In the interior, heavy rain was causing major problems as bridges were washed out and roads turned to mud. General Brits was struggling to move his division forward to Kissaki through the densely wooded slopes of the Uluguru Mountains. Communications between the columns had been lost and when Nussey's brigade neared its objectives, Brits and Enslin were barely 8 km away, yet neither was aware of each other's presence. Not waiting for his other column, Brits ordered Beves' infantry to attack while Enslin's mounted troops conducted a flanking march. Beves advanced through difficult bush before running into strong defences and having to halt. They immediately began digging in and waited for the flanking force to appear in the enemy rear. But, with a wide gap between the columns, Enslin's troops had run into heavy resistance and were driven back to the start point. The situation was not critical, but Brits now ordered a reluctant Beves to rejoin Enslin. The next day, Nussey was still unaware of Brits' presence, and attacked the fully alert Germans. He too was driven back with loss and retired to the north. Despite Smuts' ludicrous claim that Nussey 'severely punished the enemy', it was a double defeat in detail and ended any hopes of trapping the enemy.[52]

Second Division had struggled to reach Kidodi on 10 September, following the destruction of its supply dump and withdrawal of its garrison. It was still short of the River Ruaha, but the rain and physical exhaustion meant that its advance had ended. Further east, Hoskins' First Division was having similar problems as it hacked through dense tropical forest crossed by numerous fast-flowing rivers and aided by a few primitive tracks. Much of its effort had to be devoted into bridge-building and road-making in the pouring rain. By enormous exertions it reached the village of Tulo, on the River Ruwu, on 9 September at the same time as news of Brits' reverse at Kissaki.[53]

Hoskins was now ordered to press on towards the River Dutumi which was held by the 900 men of Abt Stemmermann which exerted a strong resistance with well-sited machine guns. Fighting continued on 11 September, with the first guns moving forward on the newly constructed road. However, Lettow had moved up substantial reinforcements in the form of Abt von Liebermann, bringing the defenders up to 2,200 rifles, now outnumbering the attackers. Several heavy counter-attacks ensued, with both sides unsuccessfully trying to outflank the other. This continued throughout 12 September, but the next morning the enemy had again slipped away undetected.[54]

Smuts had planned for Brits to push on from Kissaki to the Rufiji where he would link-up with Hoskins from the east. However, on realising that his move had failed and that Lettow seemed likely to retire on the lower Rufiji about Utete, he ordered a landing at Kilwa where a force of 2,000 to 3,000 could operate against them. Elsewhere, van Deventer was to drive Kraut south of the River Ruaha in order to determine his direction of retreat.[55] Such plans ignored the reality; all three divisions were badly under-strength, exhausted and suffering badly from illness.

Smuts now ordered Brits' exiguous mounted troops forward again, but Brits demurred from another attack. Fearing a repeat of Kissaki, he waited for more infantry before moving on 14 September. Now with 1,200 men in two brigades, he found Kissaki was abandoned by the enemy and occupied the place. At the same time patrols from First Division linked up with Brits' weary troops and the main body was finally reunited.[56]

The Germans were established on the line of the River Mgeta where they took up strong positions. It was a very difficult place to fight as the almost impassable vegetation and network of streams made movement slow and difficult. The movement of wheeled vehicles was very slow and with no artillery, an attack was unpromising. More importantly, Third Division was absolutely incapable of further effort and First Division was only slightly stronger. Smuts made one last attempt to outflank the Germans by crossing east of Dutumi, but the falling of very heavy rain on 20 September ended the advance. The troops had done all that was humanly possible, but they had reached their limit. For the remainder of the month, the roads became impassable and food stocks dwindled.

STRATEGY FOR LATE 1916

In late September, Smuts unveiled his plans to London. He proposed to keep the bulk of Second Division between the Great Ruaha River and Kilimatinde to protect his lines of communication and to prevent Wahle from linking up with Kraut. In the east, Kilwa would receive a second brigade that would move north-eastwards towards Utete on the lower Rufiji. A single brigade would remain on the Mgeta to push towards the Rufiji. In the south, Norforce would advance east from Iringa and reach Mahenge within a few days. In the far south, Smuts left offensive operations to the newly-arrived Portuguese Expeditionary Force, although he expected no practical assistance from them.[57]

The ground would be very difficult. The land south of the Uluguru Mountains was swampy and low-lying with the Mgeta and Rufiji rivers running broadly west to east. These lowlands were hot, humid and pestilential with no roads or centres of population. Furthermore, they were covered in dense bush, high grass and swamp. The valleys flooded extensively during the rains with the Rufiji expanding from its 400-metre width in the dry season to over 9 km of swamps on either bank. The physical difficulties were compounded by the presence of vast quantities of malarial mosquitoes and the dangerous tropical diseases that were so prevalent throughout their area.

On the coast and north-west of Kilwa were the dominating Mtumbei Hills that led to the lower Rufiji Valley. From there, the land dipped back into the massive basin of the Mgeta, Rufiji and Ruaha rivers until it met the northern tip of the Utschungwe Mountains, a wide spur of highland that extended from Iringa in the north to Lake Nyasa in the south. Almost in the centre of this broad central plain was the Mahenge plateau which towered above the steaming forest below. The highlands, particularly around Iringa, were wild and thickly forested although the climate was much less trying than in the valleys below. If the roads were poor and communications difficult, they were still much easier than those through the Rufiji basin. German-held Mahenge was known to be a population centre based on fertile uplands and a relatively healthy climate, but any approaches would have to cross either the Ulanga River from the west or the Ruaha River from the north.[58]

The severity of his situation was reflected by his decision to evacuate medically all those troops who had been chronically ill or who were judged unlikely to be fit for further operations. Given the fact that so many soldiers were seriously debilitated by disease, Smuts decided on medical grounds to reduce numbers and to repatriate the worst affected. By sending these men back to South Africa, he hoped to have a smaller cadre of fit men.[59] However, the same sense of urgency was not applied to the many British and Indian troops who were in a similar or worse plight. On the other hand, it was the indigenous, but still small, KAR that was deemed capable of surviving the rigours of future fighting.[60]

Brits' exiguous Third Division was the first to be disbanded, as it had withered to an ineffective shell. Van Deventer's battered Second Division was retained, but its two weak brigades had to be reinforced by the survivors of Brits' force. Only Hoskins' First Division was retained as a striking force, although it too was drastically under strength, with two brigades sent to Kilwa and a third remaining on the Mgeta. By the end of October, some 12,000 South Africans would be ordered home, representing two-thirds of the force that had arrived only in March and April of the same year. Even this was muddled, as Smuts ordered the withdrawal before an evacuation plan had been drawn up or the various staff branches had been consulted. The result was disorder and it took some time for the organisation of routes, transport and camps to be organised.[61]

Discontent was rising at home as harrowing stories of administrative and medical failure were in the press while the Nationalists were continuing to attack the Botha government. His troops were increasingly unhappy and a formal complaint by a commanding officer into allegations of negligence could not be ignored. Smuts had little option but to set up a court of enquiry. Fortunately for him, it was conducted by his own staff and would take a number of months to report.[62]

Although the Germans had been pushed into as unhealthy and low-lying ground as the British, reaching them and then beating them in battle would be a very difficult process. Despite his hopes of surrender, Smuts was well aware of Lettow's likely intentions:

> I wonder if the Germans are going to fight it out there [Central Railway] so that we can go home soon, or whether they will retire southwards and prolong the war for months. It looks very much as if they will do the second. My hope is that many Askaris will refuse to go south and that Lettow will therefore flee with only a small part of his force.[63]

Lacking the resources to advance further, he tried bluff, writing to Governor Schnee at the end of September and calling on him to surrender. However, with an undefeated army and high morale, this stratagem was seen for what it was and ignored.[64] Smuts now had to face the reality of a prolonged campaign in some of the worst country of the world and being unable to start before January. This meant that it would be up to Northey to maintain the pressure. The latter's troops were suffering from the climate, but his well-organised supply and medical arrangements were now paying off.[65]

While the high command pondered the future, the troops had to remain in close contact with the Germans, separated by the swampy and unhealthy Mgeta River. Neither side relished the unpleasant living conditions, nor the dense bush that made it ideal for raids and ambushes. In fact, it was singularly ill-chosen as a forward line with swamps extending for some distance on either side of the river and being distinctly malarial. Even by East African standards, the lines of communication were exceptionally difficult and the long-suffering porters bore the main burden. Simply feeding the troops was a major problem, let alone supplying the rest of their needs.

This is illustrated by the state of supplies as the columns had already passed nearly 80–160 km beyond their original destination on the Central Railway and there had been no opportunity to stockpile supplies. Despite glib talk of the supply and transport system having reached 'its extreme radius of action', it had been near collapse since the end of May. Apart from a few days in the period June to August, it had never delivered more than half the needs of the troops.[66] The Central Railway required extensive repairs and many locomotives had been destroyed. As a stopgap, it was planned to run modified Reo lorries and trailers on the tracks as soon as they could be repaired. While not ideal, each pair could carry between 7,200 and 9,000 kg of capacity although very slowly. However, the first such vehicle only arrived in Dodoma on 6 October and it was not until early December before a full service of locomotives drawing railway freight cars could be restored. It was also very far short of the daily divisional requirements of over 54,000 kg.[67]

Even then, the railheads at Mikesse and Kilossa were still a considerable distance from the forward areas. The final legs were rough in the extreme with many river crossings and difficult stretches to overcome. There was also the problem of passing through 'fly belts' and the ubiquitous malarial mosquito. For instance, First Division was carrying its supplies 120 km forward from its refilling point and living on half rations whereas the reduced Third Division had just enough to live on, but no reserves. Further west, Second Division was now operating 420 km from its refilling point and moving further away. Total lift had fallen considerably in the past month to about 113,000 kg of which nearly half was broken down or in workshops being repaired. The weather continued to hinder supply operations as the combination of rain and mud made movement very difficult. A month later, First Division was in a worse plight as it had not received full rations since 27 May, some four and a half months ago, while a third of its lorries were too heavy for the appalling roads to the forward areas.[68]

The ravages of the tsetse fly and horse sickness ruled out any sustained use of animal transport despite the arrival of over 600 new wagons since June; animals could not be kept alive long enough. An additional 300 light Fords reached the forward areas at the end of September, but there were insufficient drivers who also fell sick in large numbers.[69] The only alternative was human porterage, but apart from its inherent inefficiency, carriers themselves were becoming increasingly difficult to recruit (or coerce) in sufficient numbers.

By the end of November, Smuts had plenty to deal with, politically and militarily. He estimated that Lettow had about 4,000 rifles on the Rufiji, while Kraut's 2,000 men had been joined by a maximum of 500 or 600 of Wahle's force. With the Schutztruppe having a maximum of 7,000 effectives, he proposed to add the newly-arriving Nigerian Brigade to cut the enemy off on the lower Rufiji. In the west, he expected van Deventer and Northey to drive the enemy into the Ulanga and Rufiji basins. They would then leave Indian and African battalions to hold the line while the white troops were pulled back to the railway. He discounted any need for further Belgian assistance and considered that the expanded KAR would be capable of dealing with any forces beyond February 1917.[70]

The Belgians had been quite prepared to halt, having captured Ruanda and Urundi, but at British request they agreed to continue advancing further east to Tabora. Having taken that place ahead of Crewe's Lake Force, they rather surprisingly offered to vacate that place to British troops prior to the October rains. While this was politically acceptable to the British, the War Office had to ask the Belgians to remain in Tabora owing to lack of troops. This, plus the prolonged internal departmental debate over future policy, meant that the rainy season overtook events. In the meantime, the Belgians established their own administration and exerted political control over the African population.

Smuts was unhappy with the Belgians, who he believed to be both unwilling and unable to pursue Wahle's force south from Tabora. This was hardly surprising as he had done little to encourage them and was actively scheming against them. His own troops in the area, the Lake Force, were unable to move further south owing to lack of sufficient transport and were isolated at the end of a very precarious supply system. With the Westtruppen believed to be moving eastward to rejoin Lettow, probably via the Great Ruaha or Ulanga river valleys, this posed a threat to Northey's vulnerable lines of communication running south from Iringa. The gap between Second Division and Norforce was still more than sufficient to allow the Westtruppen an uninterrupted passage to the east.[71]

The Belgians now made further military assistance dependent on payment for the captured territories either if returned to the Germans or retained by Britain. It was a steep price, but the War Office wanted them to pursue the escaping Tabora garrison and recommended that the requested 2,500 troops be provided. Bonar Law disagreed and, caught between political ambitions and military necessity, he sought Smuts' advice who conveniently reported that he could now do without them. There were other factors behind the decision, notably the 'grave disorders' alleged to have been committed by the Belgian troops, but these were not officially communicated to the Belgian Government over fears that it would worsen negotiations over the evacuation of Tabora.[72]

In the circumstances, the Belgians suspended further military operations, although they did not rule out future co-operation. In fact, they quickly revived negotiations in mid-November, when they offered eventually to leave Tabora and possibly provide troops. This change was welcomed, but the British remained firm on the question of Tabora and insisted on its early evacuation.[73]

The CIGS pointed out to Smuts that the Belgians could probably be induced to help if necessary. In response, Smuts stated that he did not believe that further Belgian assistance would be needed, even if the campaign were to go into 1917, although he would be happy to have a reserve column of 1,500 rifles available at Tabora. This seems complacent given the desperate state of his own forces and the need for manpower. Further disagreements about recruiting and Tabora ensued and by late December GHQ was officially informed that all negotiations with the Belgians had been dropped.[74] It was an unhappy episode that reflected little credit on Smuts or Bonar Law. The breakthrough of the Westtruppen and threat to Norforce were the direct consequence of the breakdown in military co-operation. Thus, the first phase of Anglo-Belgian co-operation came to an ungracious end in mid-November 1916, with both sides seemingly more interested in arguing over territory rather than beating the common foe.[75]

THE FIGHT IN THE SOUTH-WEST

Colonel Lettow was concerned with his vulnerable western flank and ordered the reinforcement of Mahenge. He realised that Second Division was incapable of further immediate action and despatched Major Kraut to take charge of the defences. Mahenge itself was very weakly held, with less than eighty rifles, although Abt Braunschweig, with five companies of 1,150 rifles and twelve machine guns, provided some security. However, in the south, barely thirty soldiers and a number of auxiliaries held the rich farming area between Wiedhafen to Songea to the Portuguese border. Kraut brought important reinforcements south with him, some ten companies, twelve machine guns and six guns, totalling about 1,200 rifles; by the beginning of September, the total force amounted to about seventeen companies of 2,450 rifles, twenty-four machine guns and six guns. The force was now strong enough to prevent a further advance and offered the chance to deal a sharp blow to any isolated column.

Kraut was a dependable and aggressive officer who would not give up ground without a fight. His aims were twofold; the first was to block any movement eastward from Iringa and the second was to prevent a link-up between Northey and van Deventer at Kidatu. He recognised that the former posed the greater threat and left only a rearguard at Kidatu to hold the enfeebled Second Division. He then began to move his powerful force south-west of Iringa and took Abt Braunschweig under command. As ever, the supply situation was a major concern as food was short and there were insufficient carriers to move it.[76]

This shift was detected by the British, and Northey was growing increasingly concerned about having to deal with Kraut in the east at the same time as Wahle was moving in the west. He wanted van Deventer to push south to Iringa in order to concentrate Norforce to meet the new threat, but the former could not move until his shrunken units were reorganised. Furthermore, Smuts remained anxious to continue the advance on Mahenge. Norforce was widely stretched between Rodger's and Murray's columns near Iringa, with Hawthorn around Mkapira and with a subsidiary column around Songea. On the German side, Lettow was pressing for Kraut to attack both Songea in the south and Mkapira in the centre, while Wahle's position remained unknown. Lettow was concerned with what he considered his subordinates' propensity to disperse their forces unwontedly and he wanted to strike a blow against what he considered a vulnerable forward column. Accordingly, he issued orders for Kraut to attack Hawthorn's column at Mkapira on 1 October, although the latter had only six companies in the immediate area and required reinforcement from Abt Falkenstein.[77] Despite Lettow's impatience, it was impossible to regroup so quickly in the difficult conditions of the Ruhudje Valley and Kraut would require several weeks to make adequate preparations for the attack.

While these moves were taking place, Northey was given yet another task for his stretched forces. He had been concerned about the rich farming district of Songea, but had left it untouched owing to lack of troops. Now, he was instructed to occupy that region and had to send his only reserve, a newly raised African police battalion. Using his command of Lake Nyasa, he sent this force to Wiedhafen by steamer where it landed on 12 September. Immediately marching inland, the column forced out the tiny German garrison and occupied Songea on 20 September. Kraut only learned of the landing five days later and immediately ordered Falkenstein to secure Songea. It was too late, and Abt Falkenstein was ordered to cover the road to Liwale.[78]

A further British advance to Mkuju on 5 October led Lettow to order Major Grawert to attack on 12 October, with three companies to move south as reinforcements. Ominously, the mood of the African population had changed for the worse as they provided the British with information and also began to attack isolated posts and their lines of communication. This further delayed Grawert's move and forced him to detach security forces.[79]

If the main bodies of both forces were at a standstill, the Westtruppen under General Wahle were still some 480 km to the west, but moving eastward. From wireless intercepts, he learned that Lettow and the main body were now south of Morogoro and that Iringa was only lightly held. He resolved to march on the latter place in order to disrupt the British advance and break through to Lettow. Smuts showed little concern for this force, which was deemed to be only 1,500 strong and ready to surrender. In fact, it exceeded 2,500 and was fully determined to fight its way through to Mahenge.[80] Even taking the lower estimate of 1,500 at face value, it was still sufficiently large to inflict serious damage on Northey's dispersed command, not to mention his virtually defenceless lines of communication. Despite Northey's repeated representations to Smuts on this issue, the commander-in-chief minimised the danger and provided little practical assistance. He seems to have given only half-hearted consideration to asking for a sustained Belgian pursuit of the Westtruppen as he was more concerned about denying them any territorial spoils.[81]

After evacuating Tabora on 19 September, the Westtruppen had withdrawn southwards to Sikonge where they regrouped and the companies were reorganised. They now had the daunting task of crossing some 480 km of virtually foodless and arid land to Iringa. Despite careful preparations, the march began badly as over 5,000 locally-conscripted carriers deserted at the onset and over 60,000 kg of food, plus spare clothing, tobacco, alcohol and private belongings were burnt. Even worse, much of the ammunition had to be abandoned owing to the death of the pack animals from the effects of the tsetse fly. The loss of so much food and the need to forage widely forced Wahle to split his troops across three routes, each some distance apart. The columns were to link-up by 24 September, when the reunited force would deliver a converging attack on Iringa four days later. The main march began on 29 September and with the Belgians remaining static a few kilometres to the north, the Westtruppen disappeared from view.[82]

Northey remained concerned about Iringa and the dispersion of his force. He continued to press for assistance from Second Division, but had to be content with the despatch of a mounted squadron to Nyukwa's along the Ruaha River, that duly arrived on 27 September. It was the best that van Deventer could do, but it still left some 112 rugged kilometres of forest and mountain between it and Iringa and was too far away to be of any real use in blocking the enemy. Despite this, Northey was unwilling to withdraw south as he saw the holding of Iringa as important, for the local population had been very helpful to him and it offered a vital link to the main body. Smuts also wanted Northey to carry on to Mahenge and Iringa was a useful base.[83]

However, Iringa was too distant to support major operations and Northey planned to use Lupembe to support his next major move. He left Rodger's small column at Iringa and ordered Murray to link-up with Hawthorn at Mkapira on the Ruhudje River, from where the combined column would advance north-east through the lowlands towards Mahenge. Hawthorn had arrived at Mkapira on 10 September, and discovered a strong enemy position held by Abt Krüger on the west bank. After careful reconnaissance, his column forded the river and manoeuvred the Germans out of their defences on 27 September. The next day Krüger led a strong counter-attack that failed to dislodge the British column and had to withdraw. In the meantime, Murray was moving forward from Iringa through Muhanga on the eastern edge of the escarpment some 1,500 metres above the Ulanga Valley. Brushing aside minor resistance from Abt Braunschweig, he began the arduous descent into the sweltering and steamy valley before joining up with Hawthorn on 29 September.[84]

Despite this promising start, Hawthorn had to alter his plans for the advance on Mahenge. He learned that van Deventer would not even be able to move for at least a fortnight, which meant that the forward column would have to face the full weight of Abt Kraut. As his link to Lupembe was limited to a narrow bush path, he decided to dig a strong defensive position on the west bank of the Ruhudje and await news of van Deventer's advance. At the same time, he attempted to bring forward and stockpile as many supplies as possible.[85]

In the north, the leading elements of Wahle's force contacted Rodgers' patrols on 12 October. It was clear that another six to seven companies were en route for Iringa and Northey was in trouble. If Smuts could no longer ignore the danger, Second Division was only capable of limited assistance. One battalion and a section of mountain guns marched from Kilossa on the Central Railway to Iringa via Nyukwa's while another was despatched on a lengthy and tortuous journey to Nyasaland. Leaving Morogoro on 15 October, it moved by foot, rail, ship via South Africa, and river steamer to Wiedhafen before finally going ashore and marching forward to Songea. It did not arrive until 27 November after an epic journey.[86]

In the meantime, the marching battalion, now only 380 strong, was struggling southward, but could not reach Nyukwa's until 17 October. The combined Hawthorn-Murray column was over 160 km or a week's march away and could not be supplied around Iringa. That town had less than 100 defenders, while to the south the vital supply dumps at Ngominyi, Malangali and Ubena that formed Norforce's lifeline were even weaker. Northey deployed his last available reserve, a half battalion of African police, to Buhora and could do little else but wait for the expected onslaught.

On 19 October, Wahle's main body was moving around Iringa, but suffering from poor inter-communications. Neither Abt Wintgens nor Hübener were in touch and the latter's howitzer would be important in any attack. Unfortunately, thick bush had made progress very slow and Hübener was still far away. Matters were worse for Northey as, with the telegraph cut, he had to leave the battle to his subordinates. However, the sudden arrival of Wintgens on 22 October made an assault possible.[87]

It was the last-minute arrival of the South African relief battalion, now only 290 strong and suffering badly, and the completely unexpected arrival of a mounted regiment from Dodoma on 25 October that tipped the balance. They launched a pre-emptive attack that disrupted Wahle's preparations. It also convinced him that Iringa was too strong and he cancelled the planned assault and decided to move south. A rearguard was left to mask the move while the main body took the road south.[88]

Ngominyi had already been under siege for nearly a week when Abt Wintgens attacked on 28 October. Despite a determined fight, the outnumbered and surrounded defenders were forced to surrender, yielding the Germans a much-needed quantity of food and supplies. More importantly, Norforce had been cut in half and it seemed certain that the larger base at Malangali would be next. It was also clear that the Westtruppen were much stronger and more aggressive than previously thought. Smuts' earlier complacency had been shattered and he now had to face the prospect of a major defeat.[89]

At the same time, Kraut was preparing to deal with Hawthorn and Murray in the south. On 22 October, he started to encircle the British, driving in outposts and seizing and fortifying a feature to the west of their position. The envelopment was completed on 23 October and the track leading to Lupembe was cut. Despite firm orders to attack the British, Kraut resolved to starve them into submission. What he did not know was that Hawthorn had stockpiled a large quantity of supplies and was in wireless communication with General Northey at Neu Langenburg.[90]

After a week of isolation, with food running short and hearing of the enemy move on Ngominyi, Hawthorn decided to break the German siege. He realised that it would be impossible to escape with his baggage column and precious wireless set, without first driving the enemy off completely. Laborious reconnaissance had found several routes through the swamps and a plan was devised. Surprise was of the essence, and he determined that the Germans would be unprepared for a simultaneous attack from north and south. The night of 28/29 October was chosen for the breakout, with Murray striking to the south-east and Hawthorn attacking to the north-west. The action was a complete success and Kraut was driven back to the eastern bank of the Ruhudje.

The victory at Mkapira enabled Northey to regain the initiative as he instructed Murray to march back to Lupembe where he arrived in the first week of November. One company was immediately sent forward to reinforce the 100 recruits holding Malangali while the rest of the battalion was sent forward on 8 November by motor cars to defend Lupembe. Apart from being a major road junction that lead to Iringa and Mkapira, it was the main advanced supply base.[91]

At the same time, van Deventer had managed to get his division moving south, being given command of the Iringa area on 30 October. His troops were weak; the 3rd SA Infantry Brigade was a shell of its former self as nearly 75% of the troops had gone down with sickness and its four battalions were amalgamated into a single unit. The 1st SA Mounted Brigade was little better with just 705 men and 245 horses in early October; only by pooling horses and equipment could a single mounted regiment be organised. Once reinforced by the remnants of the 2nd SA Mounted Brigade, a total strength of about 900 rifles could be raised. This was to diminish even more drastically as they marched through the tsetse fly-infested bush towards Iringa, losing over 500 horses en route. In the meantime, a column under Colonel Taylor prepared to follow-up shortly from

Dodoma while the composite infantry battalion held Nyukwa's and the ground to the east at Kidodi.[92]

The German advance guard reached Malangali, which was encircled on 8 November. The next day they opened fire with artillery followed by three bayonet attacks that could not break the defences. The outnumbered defenders held on, but their situation was very precarious. Fortunately for Northey, his foresight in constructing motor roads paid off. He now decided to risk fifty of his precious light cars in a daring relief move to Malangali, despatching Murray there with 130 men and four machine guns. The remaining 125 men and six machine guns marched off cross-country with the aim of linking up there subsequently. At the same time, receiving word that Abt Wintgens was headed south-west towards Lupembe, Northey told Hawthorn to be ready to march back there.[93]

Murray and his troops arrived to within 3 km of Malangali unmolested, having travelled 190 km over some of the roughest roads possible. Debussing safely, Murray sent the vehicles back to Buhora for supplies. A reconnaissance on the morning of 10 November showed that the Germans were too strong for him to attack and he decided to keep his position and maintain contact. Wahle's efforts against Malangali had already cost him heavily and the arrival of the Rhodesians coincided with news of Kraut's defeat further south. He decided to lift the siege and move off south-east towards the Lupembe road to join Wintgens. A two-company rearguard was detailed to maintain the blockade of Malangali and to link-up with Hübener's detachment, still not yet arrived from the west. As the Westtruppen slipped away on the night of 11/12 November, Murray took the advantage to attack and overwhelm this force, causing it serious casualties.[94]

While these events were taking place, Wintgens had reached Lupembe and had put in an attack on 13 November, sending a detachment to cut the road to Ubena. This effectively cut off the garrison, which was well stocked with food and ammunition but also contained 300 wives and children of the mainly KAR recruits. An outwork was taken, the wireless masts destroyed, but the garrison grimly held on. Heavy firing was kept up throughout the day and another determined, but ultimately unsuccessful attack was put in before dawn on 14 November. Following a ceasefire to deal with the wounded, no further attacks were pressed and Wintgens withdrew the next day.[95]

In the meantime, with Hawthorn still some distance to the east, Northey decided to redeploy Murray by vehicle. His column drove back to Ubena on 14 November from where foot patrols were sent out. They located the enemy roadblock about 48 km west of Lupembe and the column moved forward for action, spending the better part of two days in reconnaissance. Striking on the evening of 16 November, he overwhelmed the two-company block, clearing the road to Lupembe. The beleaguered garrison was relieved by the arrival of Hawthorn's column on 15 November, after Wintgens' departure, and following a slow and difficult journey from Mkapira. This was timely, for Wahle's main body appeared from the north-east the next day. Knowing that Kraut had been moving westward, the British feared that he would combine with Wahle for an attack on Lupembe. Now that Ubena appeared to be safe, Northey ordered Murray to move forward and rejoin Hawthorn at Lupembe.[96]

The link-up duly took place on 18 November, with the two columns united for the first time since the end of October. Together they mustered an effective marching force of about 1,100 rifles and had shown themselves well able to give the enemy a sharp blow. However, Wahle had no intention of lingering as he realised that the British would reinforce Lupembe strongly. His main body moved unopposed to the north of Lupembe from 17 to 19 November, moving towards the Ulanga lowlands. The march of the Westtruppen was finally completed on 22 November, when Wahle met up with Kraut and assumed control of all forces on this front with headquarters at Tanganika.[97]

Freed from the main command, Kraut ultimately advanced up the eastern edge of the plateau, seizing the village of Mfrika, 9 km east of Lupembe, and standing at an altitude of 1,800 m, with the Mahenge plains at 450 metres above sea level. Too weak to attack, he constructed a strong forward position there, with a second being built some 9 km west at Msalala. These fortifications, together with the thick bush and broken ground, made a British attack a difficult proposition. Furthermore, both sides were exhausted after the arduous marching of the past few months and neither had sufficient supplies or carriers to sustain further offensive operations, particularly in light of the coming rains.[98] An operational pause ensued and reorganisation was set in train.

Almost unnoticed under the strain of the battle was the loss of Northey's independence as a field force commander on 14 November. General Smuts had requested that Norforce be placed under his operational command (although without responsibility for supply) on 7 November, citing the need to co-ordinate the fighting in the Iringa-Mahenge area. After over two years' fighting, the British forces in East Africa were finally united under War Office control and a single commander-in-chief.[99]

While these actions were taking place in the north, Grawert had been prodded by Lettow to deal with the enemy around Songea on 23 October. Advancing on 31 October, he sent orders to Falkenstein to advance on Songea and join him in the attack on 5 November. However, owing to delays and confusion he did not join up with Grawert until 11 November. Finally, with time short, Falkenstein moved on the British force early on 12 November and without Grawert's troops, part of whom had been left behind as security detachments. Despite a promising start, Falkenstein was killed leading the attack and ammunition began to run short. Unable to make further progress, the Germans broke off the battle, retiring to a position about 3 km north-east of the boma. By 17 November more reinforcements were marching forward to reinforce the threatened position. This force was too strong for Grawert, who then prudently retired.[100]

While these events were underway, the almost forgotten rearguard under Lieutenant Colonel Hübener remained at large. With some 300 rifles and a howitzer, it had made very slow eastward progress. It was located at Ilembule on 20 November, and, with Lupembe secure and Wahle safely to the east, Northey decided to eliminate this last threat to his columns. Again, using his superior wireless communications and mobility, he sent Murray with 450 men to Ubena by vehicle, whence it marched off to deal with Hübener the next day. The German officer was not a great tactician nor overly energetic and allowed the British to surround his position and secure the vital waterholes by 26 November. Despite heavy firing by the howitzer, British casualties were slight and the lack of water made further defence hopeless. He duly surrendered, with seven officers, forty-eight Germans and 249 Askaris going into captivity together with one 10.5-cm howitzer and three machine guns.[101]

There were now no German forces west of the line Neu Langenburg-Iringa. Despite considerable local superiority of numbers, Wahle had failed to inflict any significant damage on Norforce and had himself lost over 500 soldiers, although he had successfully brought his force across 480 km of desolate territory. Both Murray and Hawthorn had shown themselves to be determined and effective leaders who had given Wahle's troops some rough handling. Indeed, much more could have been achieved had Second Division exerted any sort of pressure from the north, but the opportunity was missed. The threat to General Northey's force had passed. Indeed, a relieved General Smuts reported to London that some seventy-one German and 370 Askaris had been killed or captured during the withdrawal of the Westtruppen.[102]

THE SWITCH OF EMPHASIS TO KILWA

As General Smuts began to appreciate the difficulties of the Mgeta line, he decided to redeploy the bulk of First Division to the coast using the harbour of Kilwa as its base.[103] This offered the opportunity to strike west along the line of the Matandu River before northward to the Rufiji as well as cutting off the main route to the south. However, while Kilwa Kisiwani had an excellent anchorage, it possessed no port facilities and it would be necessary to build-up the base before any advance in strength could be attempted. The leading troops landed there on 8 September and the remainder of the month was spent in developing its facilities and building up numbers. The first formation to be deployed was Brigadier General Hannyngton's newly established 3rd EA Brigade and it was complete by the first week in October.[104]

Hannyngton was instructed to push rapidly inland in the hopes of cutting off the enemy forces further north. Hannyngton decided to act quickly. Early reconnaissance revealed that the village of Njinjo, some 68 km inland along the Matandu Valley, provided a jumping-off point for either a move north towards the Rufiji, or alternatively, south towards the food-producing areas of Liwale. However, a second and more direct route was found. Instead of following the Matandu inland, it was possible to cross that river following the track north-west to the Mtumbei Hills. The key to the area was the junction at the hilltop station of Kibata that dominated the local region. From there, a route ran through the hills straight to the major German supply centre of Utete. An advance through the Mtumbei Hills promised to be much shorter than the Matandu route, while they were also cooler and healthier than the coastal plain.[105]

For the Germans, the food situation remained critical and the growing of crops on the lower Rufiji was essential to their continued survival. Initially, the local commander, Captain Looff, decided to concentrate at

Utete, leaving the area north of the Rufiji virtually bare of forces. Lettow immediately countermanded the order and appointed a new commander, Major von Boemken, while Looff was packed off to the south to counter the growing Portuguese threat. The Mtumbei Hills were also rich in food and Boemken and his four companies were ordered to march for Kilwa on the evening of 12/13 September. After a lengthy journey by river steamer and much marching, they reached Kimbarabara on the southern slopes of the Mtumbei Hills on 25 September.[106]

Further west was Njinjo, key to the Matandu Valley and an important magazine. Lettow had ordered the evacuation of the contents, but owing to faulty dispositions, a British patrol had reached it and destroyed the supplies. In response, a reluctant Boemken launched a half-hearted assault that was easily repulsed and then returned to Kimbarabara. This left the Matandu Valley open and Hannyngton's troops occupied Njinjo without opposition on 7 October. The misfortunes were capped two days later, when reinforcements sent from Liwale were ambushed and scattered near Njinjo. Boemken now shifted his defensive positions to the west of Njinjo in order to block the road to Mpotora.[107]

Lettow now wanted Kibata to be properly protected and instructed Boemken to garrison it. However, through a mix-up, his troops went to the wrong location, leaving the main route from Kilwa to the Rufiji River open. Unaware of this, Hannyngton sent two battalions to occupy Kibata and the surrounding hills on 10 October, taking the unoccupied fort four days later. One battalion left to garrison Kibata while the other was withdrawn back to Kilwa. At the same time, the brigade pushed one of its units to a position 6 km west of Njinjo, at Mchemera, and a screen of outposts to the north and west was established. Lettow was furious with this blunder and relieved Boemken of command, sending Captain Schulz to take over on 17 October.[108] Nevertheless, the damage had been done.

With his main body immobile, Smuts made a personal visit to Kilwa at the end of October. He believed that by pushing one column westward along the Matandu Valley and the other striking north-westwards from the Mtumbei Hills, he could cut off Lettow. He decided to send another brigade to the area and to place Major General Hoskins in command. These deployments were put into effect shortly after Smuts' visit, with First Division assuming command of the Kilwa area on 15 November and the units of the 2nd EA Brigade complete by 29 November.[109]

North of the Rufiji, the German presence was not detected until the end of September. Despite the gravity of his own supply situation, Smuts ordered the IGC to clear the area. He was concerned about the possibility of raids against the railway and seems not to have realised that the enemy was there to protect the crops until they ripened in March. With neither an operational headquarters nor much in the way of fighting troops, an attempt in early October to clear the area failed miserably with heavy losses. This setback spurred Smuts to send reinforcements that were in position by 21 October.[110] But, they arrived too late as Lettow had sent Abt Stemmermann there to reinforce the defences.

As the rain fell, and operations wound down, much effort was expended in trying to disrupt the other side's supply chain by small-scale patrols. No significant advantage was achieved, while morale dropped owing to the sense of isolation and weather. Smuts continued his withdrawal of forward troops leaving the 1st EA Infantry Brigade holding the Mgeta while the remnants of 2nd SA Infantry Brigade was along the Ruaha at Kidete further west. The southern bank was soon abandoned and only piquets held the northern shore with the main body on higher ground. As the front remained static, large labour gangs of Africans were engaged in the cutting of roads while the engineers worked on improving the bridges across the numerous rivers and streams. Unfortunately for them, the continuing rain in October and November undid much of this valiant effort and large sections of the road dissolved into mud.[111]

THE PORTUGUESE INVADE FROM THE SOUTH

Anglo-Portuguese relations were worsening as Gil correctly saw that Smuts intended to limit him to holding the Rovuma Valley and limited local thrusts. This was immensely frustrating to the ambitious officer, who saw it as a deliberate attempt to keep the Portuguese in the unhealthy lowlands, rather than attacking the Germans. In contrast, Northey's genuine requests throughout September for the occupation of Songea were unfulfilled, owing to Portuguese inability to advance. In light of this, Bonar Law instructed Northey to occupy it himself with his own over-stretched force. It also had the politically attractive advantage of forestalling the planned Portuguese occupation of Mtengula, which was then abandoned.[112]

At the same time, Smuts also ordered a landing at Mikindani Bay followed by a move north to Lindi. While part of his overall plan, these movements were aimed at denying the area to the Portuguese and preventing territorial claims. Faced by the arid and barren Makonde plateau to his immediate north, Gil decided to move further inland to Newala, which lay on the western edge of the upland. On 1 October, with the lower Rovuma held in force, he received renewed instructions to proceed in the direction of Mahenge, seizing territory as he went.[113]

These grand plans were unbalanced by the news that a major African rebellion had broken out in the Zambezi districts to the south. This forced the withdrawal of a number of troops, weakening the planned invasion force. Smuts now considered their role as preventing German foraging parties from gathering food in the area.[114] Gil had greater ambitions and his troops pushed back the tiny Abt Sprockhoff, with its barely 120 rifles. Even then the advanced guard of four companies was ambushed and forced to pull back until reinforcements arrived. For their part, the Germans had an unpleasant surprise as they found the Makonde people actively hostile and provided the Portuguese with guides and local intelligence. Schnee's fears had finally come true.

The Portuguese made for the village of Newala and the neighbouring waterholes of Muata, taking them both on 26 October. They now placed 400 in Newala itself with a further 1,100 in outlying positions around Muata. Lettow reacted quickly, for while his opinion of the Portuguese was low, they posed an unmistakable threat to the food-growing area of the south. He despatched Captain Looff with Abt Rothe and Abt Hinrichs, both two companies strong, to reinforce Sprockhoff. Ordered firstly to eliminate the Portuguese and then to crush the Makonde rebellion, Looff had just over 520 rifles and several guns to deal with nearly 1,500 Portuguese.[115]

As the Portuguese were moving forward, Smuts had not given up on his aim of having a British officer administer the newly captured territory. This attempt to supervise Portuguese administration naturally caused resentment and did little to improve relations between the armies. Gil simply refused to receive any political officer and subsequently offered to provide one to the British. Finally, the War Office stepped in and organised the exchange of military liaison officers, a far more productive exercise. In the end, the fiasco at Newala put paid to further questions of administration and the matter was quietly dropped.[116] Nevertheless, it was a needless irritant and confirmed Smuts' readiness to place politics over military necessity.

After a month's movement and preparation, Looff was ready and moved to Newala on 19 November. Pinning the troops in Newala, he launched a surprise attack that captured the waterholes. The garrison was too strong to attack, so for the next six days the Germans bombarded it heavily. Looff attacked on 28 November and the dehydrated defenders fled, leaving behind large amounts of ammunition and equipment and streamed back to the Rovuma in disorder. It was a humiliating defeat as all of their territorial gains were lost within two days. In the meantime, the Germans followed up slowly, eliminating all their posts north of the Rovuma and capturing the bulk of their equipment. Gil, who like many of his soldiers was unwell, lost his nerve completely, and wild rumours abounded about an enemy advance on Palma despite the river's rising waters.[117]

Gil was hospitalised with dysentery, but this failed to save him as he was removed from command and recalled to Lisbon. It was not to be a happy return, for he was lambasted in the legislature for his poor performance and failure to take adequate precautions during the advance to Newala.[118] The governor general now took command, pressing for British assistance. But with Smuts about to launch his major offensive in the north, there were no troops to be spared; the Portuguese had to be content with the visit of a cruiser. They had lost any shred of credibility as 500 Germans had overwhelmed a force three times their size. This was amplified by the Consul-General's damning report that showed failures in their administrative and medical systems had led to the deaths of over 800 men together with literal starvation in the forward areas while tons of food remained at the ports. A completely new expeditionary force would be required to replace Gil's exhausted force.[119]

Quietly, Smuts now sought the permission of the Portuguese Government to enable the landing of a British force in case of future emergencies. Although a sensible precaution, the combination of offensive operations and the coming monsoon meant that activity died down on the southern front.[120]

THE BATTLE OF KIBATA

As the British advance halted in the mud of the Mgeta Valley, Colonel Lettow was considering his options. He too thinned out the forward areas, leaving only Abt Otto with eight companies of 950 rifles in the line. The remainder were drawn back in echelon up to 32 km south of the river, where they could react to any moves from Kissaki or Dutumi. The pressing need for food, now in very short supply, forced him to disperse his Abteilungen, while rampant sickness reduced their effectiveness. On the other hand, he was aware that his opponents had suffered badly from lack of feeding and chronic malaria. It seemed clear that the Mgeta front would be quiet until after the short rains ended in November.[121]

As ever, Lettow was keen to force a decisive battle, but conditions on the Mgeta were very unfavourable and Wahle was still out of touch. Norforce had proved a hard nut to crack and Kraut had an enormous area to cover, while the troops north of the Rufiji were protecting the ripening harvest. On the coast, matters seemed different as the growing lodgement at Kilwa threatened both German food supplies and their rear area. Despite his later protestations of unconcern, Lettow clearly took the threat very seriously, ordering half of the main body to move there a day after Kibata's loss. In all, eight companies plus the bulk of his artillery marched south-east, leaving nine companies and a gun to hold the line of the Mgeta under the command of Otto. The heavy rain and poor state of the tracks, meant that it would take nearly three weeks to arrive.[122]

The British noted this redeployment and continued their build-up at Kilwa as well as attacking the German supply system. At the end of October, successful raids were launched on the magazines at Mpotora and Ngarambi Chini that destroyed supplies and forced the enemy away from the coast. General Hoskins understood the threat in such wild and mountainous country and pushed his forces forward, with Hannyngton's 3rd EA Brigade in the north holding Kibata and the Mtumbei Hills, and the newly-arrived 2nd EA Brigade under Brigadier General O'Grady south along the Matandu Valley. A small reserve, consisting chiefly of the immobile artillery, was held at Kilwa.[123]

By early November, British intelligence was aware that ten German companies were moving on, information that was confirmed by the capture of documents and the interrogation of prisoners. The first probe on Kibata was launched on 7 November, with a two-company reconnaissance-in-force led by Captain Schulz. It was repulsed by the British by 9 November and spurred of their defensive measures. Despite the rebuff, Schulz informed Lettow that, with artillery, Kibata could be taken without heavy losses.[124]

The position at Kibata, although strong, was far from an ideal defensive position and the fort itself, with high walls on a prominent hilltop, was obsolete for modern warfare. It was almost completely surrounded by a ring of small hills about 1,000 metres distant with prominent river valleys running to the west and east. The most important was Picquet Hill, a long and narrow ridge to the north-west of the fort. Originally covered with thorn bush, it had been cleared by the defenders to improve the fields of fire. It was actually higher than the fort and, in recognition of its importance, had two major positions known as No 1 and No 2 Redoubts – although they lacked dug-outs and sufficient depth. These features were in turn dominated from the north by a large ridge running west to east. The loss of any of that high ground would make the possession of Kibata fort difficult, but the retention of Picquet Hill was vital as it commanded the roads leading in and out of Kibata as well as two of the three water sources.[125]

In the first week of December, the British garrison consisted of about a battalion around the fort, and a series of company positions on surrounding hills, including each of the redoubts on Picquet Hill. For supply reasons, the nearest reserve battalion was some 58 km away, with the rest of the brigade further to the south-west. It was on the afternoon of 6 December that the defenders first sighted columns advancing from the north before their outposts were driven in. Lettow now brought up his trump card: artillery. Hundreds of African labourers had hacked paths and dragged a 4.1' *Königsberg* gun, a field howitzer and two mountain guns from the Rufiji Valley. Now, with the advantage of range and firepower, he hoped to overwhelm his opponents who had only two mountain guns.[126]

The Germans now numbered nine companies against the defender's six and two Abteilungen were pushed forward while a company was ordered to infiltrate around the defenders to cut the track leading back to Kilwa. The battle began the next day with a severe artillery bombardment that culminated in a successful dusk attack on Piquet Hill. In close proximity, the two sides now held on a few metres apart. The British now rushed their reserve battalion forward, making a gruelling forced march of some 58 km in thirty-four hours in pouring rain.

In the meantime, Lettow pressed the assault again early on 8 December. Supported by artillery, the troops in the lodgement attempted to rush the redoubts that narrowly failed. Thereafter, in heavy rain, the Germans bombarded the positions with heavy and accurate fire from the *Königsberg*.[127] This was followed by an unsuccessful British counter-attack against the German lodgement. Back at Kilwa, Hoskins was now seriously concerned, ordering the remainder of 3rd EA Brigade to move forward on 10 December.

Now roughly equal in numbers, Hoskins determined to push the Germans back. He planned a move against the enemy right flank with two reinforcing battalions for 15 December, but things quickly went wrong as Lettow attacked first. After ordering a heavy artillery bombardment, he sent his reserves in with a strong infantry attack that was only held with great difficulty and heavy casualties. By the end of the day, the relieving force could only think of extrication rather than any advance.[128]

While this fight was raging to the west, General O'Grady was planning his own attack. Using the new Mills bombs (heretofore unknown in East Africa), he ordered a night attack on Piquet Hill, after the artillery had spent the day registering the German positions. Lettow had already committed his reserve to the west, and the weakened position was overrun.[129] With its loss went his chances for victory at Kibata.

Both sides now needed to regroup and make good their losses. Lettow's biggest attack since Kondoa Irangi had failed. While he drew in the bulk of First Division and seriously damaged one battalion, the battle was tactically inconclusive and consumed a great deal of ammunition. Once again, instead of encircling an isolated garrison and starving it out, Lettow had chosen a set-piece attack against dug-in troops. However, it had delayed any move on the Rufiji and revealed that the new KAR battalions were still not up to the Schutztruppe's standard in battle. The situation at Kibata would remain largely unchanged until the end of the year.

SMUTS' LAST THROW: THE FINAL PUSH TO RUFIJI

On 22 December, General Smuts was ready for an advance on all fronts and left for Duthami the next day. On the Mgeta front, Sheppard's reduced 1st EA Infantry Brigade was preparing for a move with Beves' 2nd SA Infantry Brigade echeloned behind. The first elements of the Nigerian Brigade were in the process of arrival at Dar-es-Salaam, but they lacked any transport. On the Kilwa axis, Hoskins' First Division remained tired and under-strength, with Second Division in a similar state at Iringa. Norforce was still recovering from the exertions during the recent operations against the Westtruppen, but was still fit to fight. The whole force was woefully short of porters and suffering from undernourishment and disease.

Smuts planned a three-pronged operation that would outflank the weak forces along the Mgeta coupled with several others that would seize a crossing of the Rufiji. Once across, the reunited force would turn eastwards and push along its southern banks to Utete in conjunction with an advance by First Division towards Utete. Finally, a small column would clear the area north of the Rufiji of any remaining enemy. Optimistically, Smuts hoped that this would compel Lettow to seek surrender. In the west, Second Division was ordered to clear the Iringa escarpment and push eastwards to Ifakara while Norforce was to take Mfrika and drive Kraut's troops behind the Ulanga River.[130]

On the Mgeta front, a total of four columns would operate against the forward positions. The newly arrived Nigerian Brigade was ordered to launch a holding attack from Dutumi into the centre of the Mgeta line, while Sheppard's 1st EA Infantry Brigade would turn its flank by moving from Dakawa to Wiransi in the west. Concurrently, a small, two-battalion column would make a similar march from Tulo to Tshimbe in the east. Sheppard would also detach a single battalion to conduct a deep-flanking move against the enemy's lines of communication stretching south-eastwards to Behobeho. Key to the plan, however, would be Beves' 2nd SA Infantry Brigade. It would start from Kissaki in the west, making a wide sweep around all known enemy concentrations to emerge on the north bank of the Rufiji, near the village of Mkalinso. From there, it would march cross-country south of the river and astride the road running south from Kimbambawe. Once the defenders had been rounded up, the columns would unite and start the second-stage move on Utete. At the same time, Hoskins' First Division was to prevent the eastward or southward move of the German main body, should it try to escape in those directions.[131]

It was a bold plan that relied on rapid movement and good co-ordination. However, despite the recent pause, his troops remained underfed and in poor health, while food reserves were low and transport inadequate. It was a race, and in many ways a gamble, to outmanoeuvre the Schutztruppe, before the onset of the main rainy season. Furthermore, rain had not stopped falling across the battle area and the ground was very soggy. Second Division's transport had been unable to move for ten days and its troops were again on half rations as food stocks were non-existent. For his part, Northey had less than 72 out of the 560 km of motor roads still usable, forcing supplies to be carried by porter from Lake Nyasa over

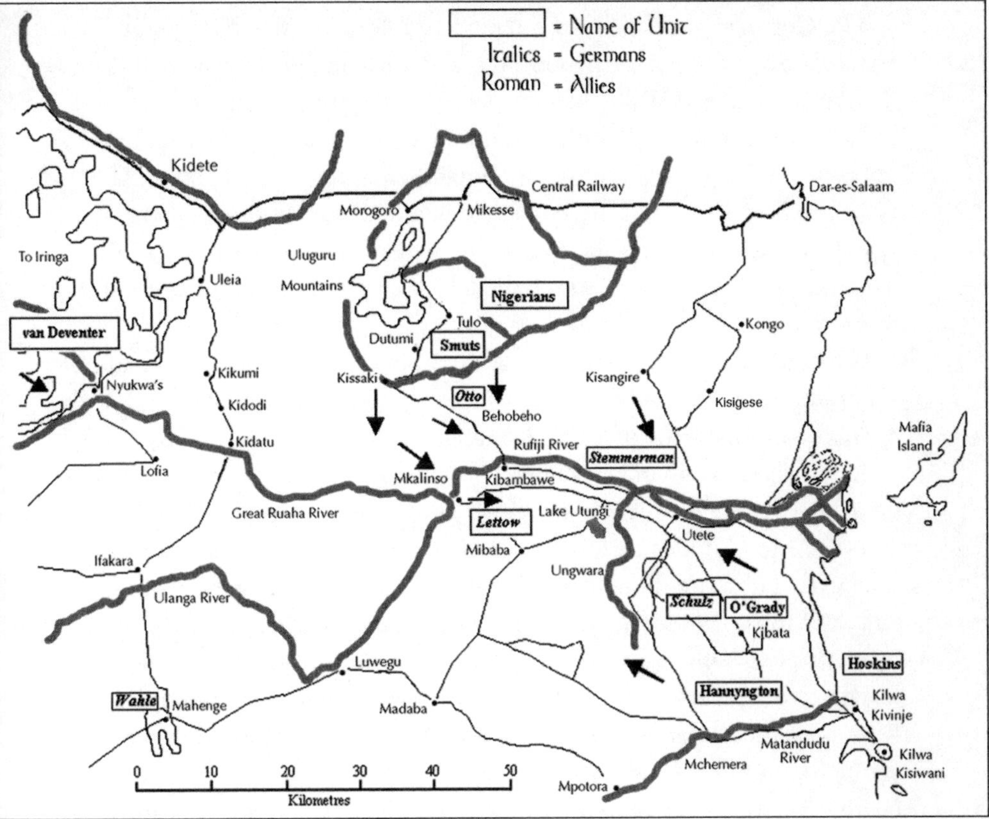

The Rufiji area, December 1916-February 1917

the Livingstone Mountains.[132] Nevertheless, despite the continuing rain, both Northey and van Deventer began their advance as planned on 23 and 24 December respectively. The main advance started a week later, as the weather did not clear until the end of the month.

FIGHTING IN THE WEST

Smuts hoped that van Deventer and Northey would be able to draw off German strength, but they were widely separated and incapable of close co-operation. Second Division was now only equivalent to a brigade, being barely able to muster a squadron of mounted troops or move more than two of its twelve guns.[133] Norforce was actually stronger, but it was tired after its strenuous exertions of the preceding three months.

The Germans also faced considerable problems, as their forces were suffering badly from lack of food and ill-health in the low-lying Ulanga flood plain. General Wahle had to spread his six Abteilungen across a wide arc to cover the likely British lines of approach. Three were in the north opposite van Deventer and the remainder were further south facing Northey. Despite its fertility, Mahenge had had two disastrously dry years which forced the Germans to remain widely scattered so as to forage. This, plus poor communications and a lack of carriers, were major limitations on their tactical flexibility.[134]

Whatever van Deventer's reservations about Smuts' plan, he was a loyal subordinate. He divided his force into three columns, lettered A to C, with approximate strengths of 1,450, 1,150 and 790 respectively. He planned a series of flanking marches against Abt Lincke, while Column A under General Nussey leading the mounted troops on a southern flank march and Column C under Colonel Taylor making a similar envelopment from the north. He wanted the flanking columns to converge on Muhanga and cut off Lincke before Column B under General Berrangé launched a frontal attack from Dabaga on 25 December. Little was known about the terrain to be traversed except that it was mountainous and difficult.[135]

Good, sunny weather on 20-21 December soon gave way to heavy rain and cold. Column C suffered terribly from this weather, particularly the nearly naked carriers brought up from the plains. A combination of sickness and desertion rapidly reduced the carrying capacity of the column and all tents and heavy stores had to be left behind. The driving rain and slippery conditions soon exhausted the column and, on 25 December, Colonel Taylor with a battalion pushed on alone to Muhanga. A short fight drove out the small German detachment there and the road from Dabaga was effectively closed. During the day the remainder of the column made its way forward and prepared its defences.[136]

On the southern flank, Column A concentrated on the eastern bank of the Little Ruaha River. On 22 December, the flanking move was seriously delayed by heavy rain with two units unable to arrive there until the next day. After two days of climbing mountains and crossing thick swamps, it had reached its intermediate objective and prepared to set up its block. Two regiments were ordered to press on to the north and east to link-up with Taylor's column, with one holding Makungwa's and the fourth in reserve. This plan required the whole column, not more than 1,200 strong, to be spread out over a frontage of some 16 km of the worst country possible, with tracks so difficult that passage on foot was almost impossible. Lack of accurate maps and guides reduced this plan to confusion as the link-up force spent much of 25 December in a fruitless march looking for Muhanga, not arriving there until the following day. Headquarters was established on the high ground between that place and Makungwa's, but communications were limited to runners owing to the rain. By 26 December, the trap appeared to be shut.[137]

In the meantime, the frontal attack planned for Berrangé's Column B was underway on 25 December. Despite the lack of guns, which had been delayed by flooding rivers, the attack was reasonably successful and the troops dug-in within 250 metres of the German line with few losses. The next day was spent in an intensive fire-fight between the two forces and was followed by a night infiltration, but, when patrols went forward early on 27 December, the trenches were empty, with the defenders having withdrawn to the south-east and the Germans having escaped through the bush.[138]

Although Muhanga had been captured, Abt Lincke had escaped largely unscathed. Orders for a further advance were countermanded as the transport system had nearly collapsed under the strain of submerged roads and swollen rivers. By 30 December, Second Division had just four days' rations for the European troops and none for the Indians. There was a choice: either to evacuate the troops or face starvation. Accordingly, van Deventer ordered most of his South Africans back to the railway while leaving two battalions, one Indian and one African, to hold the line. On 2 January 1917, he informed the commander-in-chief of the desperation of his situation and that he was forced to abandon the advance through lack of rations. This was virtually the last action of that formation, for five days later GHQ announced that owing to the supply situation it would be withdrawing it to Dodoma as a preliminary to returning van Deventer and his South African whites back to the Union.[139]

Colonel Taylor was left in command of the remaining two battalions and took up positions on the high ground opposite Lincke's force. The Iringa highland overlooked the flooded valleys of the Ulanga Valley that stretched for many kilometres below. As the month ran on, decreasing patrol encounters and skirmishes soon made it clear that the enemy had begun to thin out their forward positions in this area and were transferring troops to the still militarily active areas further south.

Further south, Norforce advanced on Kraut at Mfrika on 24 December only to find the position evacuated the next day. While the supply situation was becoming increasingly difficult and one column had to be temporarily withdrawn, the British remained on the attack. An intermediate position at Msalala, some 9 km east, was surrounded before again being forced out. Much hard marching ensued, and by 9 January the escarpment was clear and Abt Kraut was heading south. Northey now shifted Murray's column in pursuit, while Hawthorn cleared to the Ruhudje River, now beginning to flood. Kraut was now trying to move south towards Songea, which was being reinforced by Abt Grawert.[140] On 19 January, the British were in a strong position with Ifinga occupied and Grawert's troops surrounded near Songea. Cut off and out of food, the latter, with over 230 soldiers and a gun, surrendered on 22 January; a major blow to Kraut's planned assault. The rain continued to fall and by the end of the month the rising rivers forced Northey to pull back from the Ruhudje Valley and onto the high ground.[141] It had been an excellent achievement as Norforce had fully carried out its orders to drive the enemy into the unhealthy lowlands while capturing an entire Abteilung intact. It was in stark contrast to events further north.

FIGHTING ON THE MIDDLE RUJIFI FRONT

On the middle Rufiji, Colonel Lettow had echeloned his troops; the first behind the Mgeta and the second behind the Rufiji. He placed Abt Otto, with five companies, in the forward area, with Abt von Chappuis, with another three companies, positioned back along the lines of communication. Although outnumbered, he enjoyed two major advantages. The first was the difficulty of crossing the River Rufiji as the current was strong and the waters were rising. The second was superior tactical mobility in that he was falling back on prepared routes towards his magazines whereas the British had to advance over two river lines.[142]

Operations began on 31 December with Beves' wide-flanking move some 16 km to the west of the main body. He was to cross the Rufiji near Mkalinso, some 32 km south-west of Kibambawe before turning east. Initially, he made excellent progress, covering 35 km by nightfall on 2 January. Undetected by the enemy, and after thirty hours' continuous marching, the lead unit crossed the river by the next morning. The rest of the day was spent building and ferrying the remainder of the column on rafts; Beves was now well placed to strike towards Kibambawe and was ahead of schedule. He also realised that the sole enemy company at Mkalinso was completely unaware of the South Africans' presence.

Sheppard's flanking battalion, moving about 8 km west of the main body, also started on 31 December from Kissaki. It was to reach Behobeho and then set up a roadblock behind the forward German troops while the main body pushed them south. The next day, Abt von Chappuis collided with the block and nearly overwhelmed it before breaking off to the south. This left 1st EA Brigade to continue south, struggling in the intense heat and difficult terrain for the next two days.

Some 19 km to the east, Lyall's column was marching south from Tulo to set up another roadblock on the Kiderengwa-Behobeho road as well as linking up with 1st EA Infantry Brigade, further to the west. Leaving on 31 December, the column was south of the Mgeta and at its objective by early afternoon the next day. Just as trenches had been dug, they were hit by part of Chappuis's troops and a fierce battle ensued. After a determined defence and strong counter-attack, Lyall's troops held firm, having captured a howitzer. They now awaited the arrival of the Nigerian Brigade, unaware that the rest of the enemy had bypassed them, having marched off into the bush the night before.[143]

The Nigerians, heavily supported by artillery and aerial observation, made their holding attack on the forward positions south of Dutumi, clearing the line without difficulty and linking up with Lyall on 2 January. Here, the acute lack of carriers made itself felt and forced the brigade to return to the Mgeta where they could be more easily fed.

Early on 4 January, Smuts had one column across the Rufiji near Mkalinso with the other three converging on Behobeho. They had failed to trap Abt Otto as planned, but they were pushing steadily to the Rufiji. Success now hinged on Beves making his move north-eastwards to Kibambawe and cutting the Germans in two. He seized Mkalinso the same day, but a warning was passed to Otto, who immediately despatched a company to there. But, the strength of the advance and worries about the western flank convinced him to withdraw his entire Abteilung to the south bank of the Rufiji and to destroy the crossing site at Kimbambawe.[144]

Now Beves inexplicably failed to move. If his troops were exhausted by their formidable exertions, the urgency of the situation was clear and the enemy was unbalanced. Beves now squandered his advantage and remained static until 6 January, when he was ordered to attack north-east of Mkalinso, which was conducted half-heartedly the following day. A very real chance of catching Otto out at Kibambawe was lost through inaction and insufficient initiative.[145]

In the centre, Sheppard and Lyall had continued their drive south, reaching Kibambawe on 5 January. Despite their strenuous exertions, Otto had outpaced them and had destroyed the sole bridge. Now it would be necessary to make an opposed crossing across a major river that was between 400–700 metres wide. On the night of 5/6 January, Sheppard's troops found a crossing site about 2.5 km from the bridge site. With only seven Berthon boats, the task was to be both slow and difficult and only a company managed to cross before daylight. Too weak to hold against attack, these troops had to spend the following day hiding amongst reeds, suffering intensely from the heat and lack of food. That evening, Sheppard sent across another three companies, giving him 400 rifles and four machine guns on the south bank by first light on 7 January.[146]

Otto's troops detected the lodgement early that morning and a single company was sent to attack it. This attempt failed and Otto, realising the threat, brought up three companies from reserve. In the meantime, a daylight re-supply attempt from the north bank was broken up by German shellfire. Now, the British attacked in succession from their bridgehead, but these were beaten back by the arriving enemy reinforcements. With ammunition very short by afternoon, more was rowed across the river at great risk and the British bridgehead was stabilised.[147]

Otto refrained from further counter-attack, having lost heavily the previous day. Sheppard used the night of 7/8 January to ferry across another three companies, while also bringing up two naval guns on the north bank of the river. This enabled him to break-up another counter-attack, but he still lacked sufficient strength to break out. In the meantime, Smuts was anxious to reactivate his western flank and sent two Nigerian battalions to take over from Beves. But, it took time to find carriers and they did not arrive until 15 January, twelve days after the original crossing and too late. The pause had certainly helped the Germans, as Lettow now ordered Otto to cover the supply lines running south in order to permit the evacuation of supplies. He was concerned about maintaining the route from the Rufiji to Luwegu and thence to Mahenge open.[148]

On 8 January, Smuts received two important pieces of news. The first was from his own staff, informing him that his force had received less than 10% of its essential supplies in the preceding two weeks; unless the forward troops were reduced, starvation might ensue. The second was the official notification that he had been waiting for; he was to hand over command to Hoskins and proceed to London to take part in the forthcoming

Imperial Conference. The conference presented Smuts with the honourable exit that he had sought.[149] Despite the urgency of the battle, he found time to draft a lengthy press release, justifying his recall in terms of a military success:

> The military situation in East Africa, is fortunately, such as to make a change in command, and some reorganisation comparatively simple, and indeed the steps that are now contemplated in consequence of the sudden demand for General Smuts' services elsewhere are those which would have been taken in any case very shortly… His [enemy] forces in consequence of casualties and desertion are much reduced in strength and morale.[150]

Beves' brigade was now recalled to the Central Railway prior to repatriation, leaving the Nigerians to carry on the link-up with 1st EA Brigade who were to push south of Kibambawe. By 18 January, all was in readiness for the breakout from the bridgehead. After a clever feint operation, assisted by massed gunfire, 1st EA Brigade advanced easily, pushing back a small rearguard. Kibambawe was cleared the next day, the rearguard putting up only light resistance, while Beves' force made slow, if unimpeded, progress towards Mpanga's. The Nigerians had left the Mkalinso crossing site on 17 January and promptly turned out the defenders from Mkindu the next day. Otto was now being pressed back on two sides, but continued to keep the lines of communication open. Fearing an attempt to cut his forces in two, Lettow had moved his headquarters eastwards to Lake Utungi to maintain links with Otto and Schulz. But the line was simply too large to be held continuously and gaps had to be accepted.

On 20 January, the Nigerian Brigade attacked Otto's positions and forced him south. Outnumbered, he executed a fighting withdrawal to new positions further south near Mkwembe. Deployed in depth, he faced renewed attacks on 24 January that were held off with difficulty and skill. It was a heavy battle and a fine performance by Otto who had held off much superior forces in difficult conditions.[151]

On the lower Rufiji, operations began badly as the IGC was expected to push out 800 defenders with barely 1,100 rifles himself. An initial attack on Kibesa on 3 January had failed and the commander replaced. By the time the next attack was launched on 9 January, Abt Tafel had withdrawn south, leaving the blow to fall on empty positions. A series of flanking moves and a naval landing forced an evacuation of Kissengire on

18 January, which had anyway been earlier ordered by Lettow. With the Rufiji now in full flood and the current strong, there was no follow-up and the British were content to declare the area north of the river clear.[152]

FIGHTING ON THE KILWA FRONT

Following the Kibata battle, Lettow had left only Abt Schulz with four companies to deal with First Division. Smuts had wanted it to advance west towards Utete and, in conjunction with Beves, cutting off Lettow on the lower Rufiji. But, the plan was hamstrung by a severe shortage of carriers and only one brigade could be used. Hoskins opened his advance on 5 January, when 3rd EA Brigade moved forward to clear the Mtumbei Hills as a preliminary operation. During the next week, the area around Kibata was cleared and Schulz was slowly pushed back. Lettow ordered Schulz to conduct a vigorous opposition, but his troops were outnumbered and increasingly exhausted. The key magazine at Utete was now under direct threat and he despatched Abt von Haxthausen and von Lieberman to reinforce Schulz on 7 January.[153]

The supply situation in the area was becoming critical, with the main stocks of food being moved south of Lake Utungi. The security of the lines of communication was vital as the outlines of the British converging movement were becoming clear. Abt Tafel had been ordered south of the Rufiji on 12 January and the main body was to concentrate around Lake Utungi. Haxthausen was soon under pressure from 3rd EA Brigade at Ngarambi Juu the next day with Ungwara falling four days later. The British were also using a new tactic, with KAR mounted infantry being sent out to destroy ripening crops.[154]

First Division now had both brigades in action and continued to press hard. 3rd EA Brigade reached Mohoro along the Rufiji on 18 January while 2nd EA Brigade cleared the country west of the Mtumbei Hills. Lettow was now worried about the security of Mpotora and the links to the south, but was soon aided by the rain that began to fall heavily on 25 January. The situation continued to worsen as the British finally occupied Utete on 31 January and the north bank of the Rufiji was cleared by the beginning of February.[155]

Lieutenant General Hoskins assumed the chief command on 20 January, leaving his own First Division to carry on its own offensive. Taking over in the middle of a battle, he had little choice but to carry on the plans of his predecessor. He faced an unpleasant and difficult situation. In the middle Rufiji, the 1st EA Brigade held both banks of the river around Kibambawe while Cunliffe's Nigerian Brigade had pushed south and east to Mkindu. On the lower part of the river, Hannyngton, now commanding First Division, had his 2nd EA Brigade at Mohoro on the edge of the delta, with 3rd EA Brigade at Ngarambi on the fringe of the Mtumbei Hills.[156] Second Division had effectively collapsed several weeks earlier and was completely ineffective. Norforce had successfully pushed Kraut back into the lowlands although further advances were questionable owing to the weather.

He was further hamstrung by demands for manpower elsewhere. After three days in command, the CIGS instructed Hoskins to make significant reductions in his British and Indian forces so as to release shipping. This meant the departure of eight infantry battalions, five artillery batteries, three armoured car batteries, the RFC squadron and various smaller units. Such a loss would seriously weaken Hoskins' offensive capability and he replied that it would reduce his numbers to below the bare minimum needed to conduct operations. This convinced Robertson and he agreed to let Hoskins keep as many troops as he considered essential to fight the campaign.[157]

These reductions had been ordered largely because London believed that the Germans were considerably weaker than they were, estimating that they had a maximum of 600 whites and 6,000 Askari whereas Hoskins' figure of 8,450 was rather more accurate. But a greater blow was the weather, for on 25 January the rains struck even harder and the entire area became a swamp. By mid-February 1917, the end could be put off no further and Hoskins was forced to signal Robertson that the offensive was over and that it could not be resumed until May.[158] Smuts' pronouncements of victory were certainly premature.

Both sides were exhausted and very short of supplies. With the torrential rain, it became impossible to use motor vehicles and with two of the bridges over the River Matandu washed away, the advance was over. Hannyngton was forced to move his troops back to Kibata, while O'Grady also began to pull back towards Kilwa. The Germans held their positions around Lake Utungi and began to move to high ground to avoid the worst of the flooding. Everywhere, the rations for the forward troops were of the most meagre amount.[159]

Despite the valiant efforts of the troops and administrative services, Smuts' grand plan had failed. It would have been an enormous challenge to the fittest and healthiest forces and the distances were simply too great for the resources available. The great pincer movements that looked so clear on the map had been thwarted by difficult terrain, lack of transport and the exhaustion of his force. The Schutztruppe had fought well and had once again evaded Smuts' attempts to pin them down in tropical jungle. They, too, were suffering heavily from the climate and sickness, but Lettow had preserved his force for another campaigning season.

However, from a political viewpoint, Smuts had conducted a rare campaign of genius, advancing more in a day than the BEF had managed in months. Apart from capturing large swathes of enemy territory and the major centres of population, he appeared to be a daring and decisive leader.[160] This impression had been reinforced by Smuts' own upbeat communiqués that emphasised his successes and gave little hint that the achievements had been attained at a huge cost in disease and suffering. In reality, it represented the last gasp of an exhausted and gravely weakened force that was incapable of further offensive efforts without both substantial rest and reinforcement.

This unsatisfactory situation was worsened by Botha's and Smuts' public pronouncements that the campaign was more or less finished with only mopping up left.[161] In fact, nothing could have been further from the truth as the Germans had yet to be defeated in a defensive battle and they had plenty of fight left in them. The damage from Smuts' untrue assertions was to be considerable, as to politicians and senior generals it appeared that East Africa could be removed from the list of theatres requiring resources and manpower. Unfortunately, these were precisely what Hoskins required if the fighting was truly to be brought to a successful end. It also caused a great deal of anger and dismay amongst his former troops and many South Africans.[162]

The campaign had been marred by personality clashes between commanders and differing national goals. Practical military co-operation ended on a sour note in the autumn of 1916, partly because the Belgians had achieved their immediate political goals and partly over a prolonged dispute about the division of the spoils. Above all, their government wanted the complete return of occupied Belgium and by seizing sufficient German territory they had strengthened their hand in any peace settlement. They were well aware of German designs on the Congo colony and the possession of Ruanda-Urundi gave them additional security. Ultimately, they wished to add the captured territories to their Congo colony, an approach which clashed with the British desire to leave such settlements to the end of the war.[163]

6
Reorganisation: January–May 1917

STRATEGY OF THE SECOND COALITION GOVERNMENT

As General Smuts had been making the final preparations for his offensive, greater political events were underway in London. December had witnessed a major crisis in the British Government that had resulted in the fall of the Asquith administration. Although long-standing in cause, it had been precipitated by violent disagreement over conscription, Ireland and the conduct of the war. The result was a new coalition, under David Lloyd George, who quickly instituted a smaller and more vigorous War Cabinet to direct the policy of the war.[1]

The new government retained its predecessor's broad strategic goals of retaining Britain's status as a great power, together with enhanced security at the end of the war. More than anything else it realised the need for continued public support if these ambitious aims were to be achieved. This meant achieving real victories, not the bloody and inconclusive fighting that the Western Front seemed to offer. In practical terms, this led Lloyd

George and others to support operations on the strategic periphery that offered a chance of success and hence a real boost to public morale.[2] While East Africa was still below Italy, Palestine and Mesopotamia in strategic importance, Smuts seemed upon the verge of a useful victory.

Imperial German strategy for 1917 continued along the same lines as the earlier stages of the war. While Solf and his colleagues continued to argue for a greatly expanded African empire largely at Belgian and Portuguese expense, they still lacked any means of directly influencing events there since the loss of the coastline and the cancellation of the two planned relief ships in late 1916. Schnee had not lost hope and after a tortuous journey, his plea for help reached Berlin early in January 1917. Captain Looff proposed that a supply ship together with a U-boat be sent to the remote Aldaraba Islands, north of Madagascar. Once a base had been established, the submarine would attack and disrupt the British blockading ships, enabling the freighter to land its supplies at a convenient point along the coast. Despite the urgency of the situation, the request was mired in bureaucracy for several months. It was not until late April that Solf wrote to both the heads of the naval and military staffs, asking for such assistance, justifying it on the need to retain bargaining power for the peace negotiations. He had no success, as Ludendorff rejected it on both technical and strategic grounds.[3] While the journey was probably beyond the submarines of the day, it was clear that the colony could make great use of another supply ship. In the end, nothing was sent and East Africa's future remained dependant on a military victory in Europe.[4]

THE CRISIS ON THE RUFIJI

The reality for General Hoskins was rather different. He had to wind-up his predecessor's hopeless offensive in the worst possible climatic conditions without giving up its meagre gains. His force was in tatters and on the verge of collapse, yet Smuts was declaring that the campaign was all but finished. The loss of nearly 12,000 South Africans had only been partially offset by the arrival of the Nigerian Brigade, some 4,500 strong, and the expansion of the indigenous KAR. But with only eight battalions, and two of them brand new, the KAR was too small a force to be decisive, especially as the recruiting, equipping and training of these new units would take many months. A particular problem was finding sufficient British officers and NCOs who could actually speak the local languages.[5]

On the other hand, Hoskins' experienced British and Indian troops were worn out and needed replacement.

The practical problems were immense. If the rains had forced a halt in operations, they also increased the sick-rate dramatically while the transport network either dissolved into mud or was submerged under water. There were three distinct, but related problems. The first and most pressing was the need to reduce the numbers of the troops in the forward areas to the minimum level necessary for security and that could be physically fed. With thousands of troops and carriers suffering from acute tropical illnesses and the effects of prolonged under-nourishment, he had to prevent his army from collapsing.

The next challenge was to rest and reorganise the entire force so that it would be strong enough to resume the offensive in the next dry season. Nothing less than a complete overhaul of the supply, transport and medical services together with full replacement of previous losses was needed. Hoskins also recognised that far-reaching changes in the system of command and control, both tactical and administrative, were essential as most of the previous year's failures were linked to deficiencies in this area [6].

The third and, from London's point of view, most important question was the need to devise and put into place a strategy that would wrap-up the campaign as quickly as possible in 1917. This called for a decisive and well-executed plan based on sufficient numbers of fit and well-supplied troops. This was more problematic given the shortage of troops and resources to carry out these wishes.

The situation was not helped by one of the wettest seasons known in East Africa for many years. If December and early January had been bad, as the wet season progressed, it got much worse throughout the Rufiji-Ulanga-Ruaha basin. Roads simply ceased to exist and carriers were often the only alternative, with the troops sometimes having to wade through waist-deep water for kilometres. In the west, the Dodoma-Iringa line of communications crossed the Great Ruaha River by an easy ford in dry weather. During the rains, there was not just a flooded river to cross but a swamp 2 metres deep and 9 km beyond either bank. Elsewhere Kilwa and the lower Rufiji suffered heavily from flooding and raging torrents. Only in the Iringa highlands, so far above the river basins, was movement possible, but even then it was made very difficult by the heavy rain and the loss of most roads. Animals could only survive a few weeks and their condition deteriorated badly before death.[7]

If the Germans still had a formidable number of opponent veteran troops that had not been beaten in battle, they had immense problems of their own. The carefully built-up supply and manufacturing infrastructure based along the Central Railway was gone and the Schutztruppe faced severe shortages of transport, food and medical supplies. The loss of the lower Rufiji had been a major blow and food stocks were under great pressure. Stocks had been consumed far faster than expected, with levels held on the lines of communication some 125,000 kg less than the forecast 300,000. As the forward force consumed over 10,000 kg daily, this was serious.[8] Lettow realised that he had to protect the key mtama and rice-growing areas from the British whilst they ripened. In the meantime, he reduced ration scales drastically and discharged hundreds of followers so as to reduce consumption. It would hamper his own mobility, but there was little choice. Health was a serious concern, with large numbers suffering badly from malaria and dysentery in particular.

Lettow remained the undisputed director of war policy and resolved to continue his mission of surviving for as long as possible in the face of superior enemy forces. This would be achieved through the use of delaying tactics while being ready to give any weak or isolated detachments a hard knock as the opportunity presented. This policy was aided by the advantages of operating on interior lines and being able to retire on routes of their own choosing. Lettow also realised that he need not restrict himself to the colony, if only to rid himself of the governor's authority. Apart from exploiting Portuguese military weakness, their territory offered an attractive and friendly refuge. Less positively, the country south of the Rufiji was little known and covered in low-lying tropical forest. Population and food supplies were scarce, while signs of African resistance were beginning to appear. Finally, regardless of the excellence of the doctors, the Schutztruppe would be confined to the unhealthiest part of the colony at the worst time of year.

HOSKINS REORGANISES HIS FORCE

Realising the urgency of his requirements, General Hoskins bombarded the War Office with requests for more materiel and specialist manpower. He had appreciated that failure to organise sufficient transport had undermined Smuts' plans and that future offensives would require vast numbers of carriers. Preliminary plans in February called for 160,000 carriers, together with the provision of 16,000 replacements per month. By comparison, out of the 160,000 porters that had been recruited up the end of 1916, only some 62,000 remained and many were in poor health.[9] Hoskins directed his first efforts towards colonial governments on 6 February with requests to Uganda and Nigeria for 5,000 additional carriers each. The Governor of British East Africa was also approached and demurred on the need to sustain recruiting. West Africa was also asked for 5,000 carriers, which were eventually provided.[10] The main problem was that the neglect and poor working conditions had made service in the Carrier Corps extremely unattractive regardless of the rates of pay, and recruiting was becoming very difficult.

Carriers, although important, were far from the only demand on African manpower. The existing lines of communication had to be maintained, new roads had to be cut and improved, while defensive positions and camps had to be built along their length. Ports and bases needed labourers, while many worked as personal servants to the military and civil adminstrations. Part of the problem was that the Germans had already swept the occupied areas for their own needs, while the difficult conditions under which the carriers served was a powerful disincentive to volunteer. Furthermore, many men suffered from a poor physique and were not up to the demands of the job regardless of its urgency.[11] This became a major area of contention between the civil and military authorities as officials rightly feared that, with the African population pressed to the limit for labour and farming purposes, further coercion might lead to a revolt. It was a fine line between providing maximum strength to support the war effort and the need to maintain law and order.

Under heavy military pressure, the solution of a levée en masse of all available African manpower for service with the forces was adopted. However, it was easier said than done, as many fled into the bush to avoid the recruiters and those working on European farms were often exempted. Even with coercion and the subsequent passing of a Compulsory Service Act in March 1917, in which the mass conscription of Africans for carrier or labour service was authorised, it was impossible to reach anything like the levels required. Special appeals were sent to the various colonial governments for more African manpower, but the pool of healthy labour was simply insufficient. Despite the best efforts of the civilian administration, numbers never approached the required levels; by the end of March 1917, some 76,000 Africans were in the field with the number rising to 100,000 by May when some 208,000 had considered necessary.[12]

There was also little success in recruiting either soldiers or labourers in Belgian-occupied territory. The Belgians had not forgotten Smuts' previous tactless attempt to enlist Belgian Askaris, while rejecting their Belgian officers, but were also highly sensitive to the situation in occupied Belgium, where forced labour deportations had already begun. Citing the Hague Convention, whereby occupants of an occupied territory could not be forced to take up arms against their former country, they rebuffed British attempts at recruitment.[13] They did not wish to provide any pretext for German retaliation in Belgium and the project foundered. In reality, they could not even raise carriers for their own needs and the British ultimately had to supply them with 5,000 men. For their part, the Portuguese resisted efforts to open up their territory to British recruiters, especially in the face of competition for manpower from South African mining interests.

Reorganisation had left only the First Division, plus a number of independent formations directly under the control of the commander-in-chief. Smuts' tendency to ignore his staff and existing command structures had exposed the limitations of the divisional system in the African bush. While it functioned effectively elsewhere, it relied upon the constituent brigades operating in relative close proximity to one another. This enabled the commander to support his fighting formations with artillery and engineers as required, while divisional supply and transport units maintained the link between them and the lines of communication troops. The system ran best with the combination of a centralised rear area supporting a number of similarly organised formations, all backed up by an efficient rail and road network. To be really effective, it also required a large and well-trained administrative staff under the control of a single officer. Unfortunately, none of these conditions was present in East Africa.

Quite simply, the system could not cope with the problems of supplying widely spread brigades at great distances from their railheads together with insufficient transport. Transport units had been designed to support a brigade of fixed composition and could not easily cope with increases in numbers or distances. The answer was the expanded use of the independent column. This was nothing new, as it had been the mainstay of colonial operations, most notably Norforce. In this system, each column was based on a varying number of fighting troops, usually about three to four battalions strong, depending on the task. The solution was to centralise all transport resources and then allocate them to the columns as necessary. By pooling junior commanders as well as vehicles, the system could become much more flexible.

A force headquarters, its size also dependent on the mission at hand, supported a varying number of columns and maintained the lines of communications. The system was more flexible and could be adjusted according to the supply or tactical situation. While it could not resolve the problems of acquiring sufficient transport or moving supplies over difficult terrain, it did give tactical commanders greater operational freedom. It also made it easier to ensure that the number of troops sent forward was equivalent to the local supply capability; the haunting memories of semi-starved divisions littered around the Rufiji were not forgotten. However, it was not possible to overhaul the entire command apparatus at once and the decision to move to columns, taken in late February, would not be fully implemented for several months to come.[14]

Another vital task was to sort out the administrative chaos that resulted from Smuts' repeated failure to consult his staff properly.[15] A major problem was establishing new sea bases in occupied territory as Mombasa was too far distant. Dar-es-Salaam was the new base, but its harbour had to be cleared of the sunken dock and scuttled ships while additional wharves and steam cranes had to be installed.[16] Further south, Kilwa Kisiwani had an excellent natural anchorage, but was almost totally undeveloped and unloading had to be carried out with lighters. Finally, Lindi in the far south had only the most basic facilities and would require substantial development. These problems were magnified by the acute shortage of trained technical troops and the time it took to send material out to East Africa.

Attempts to use the Rufiji as a supply line were defeated by the strength of the floodwaters which simply overwhelmed the motor boat engines.[17] The Central Railway was in increasing use, but the biggest challenge was to reach the forward troops. Animal transport was impracticable as the huge mortality of draught animals had already shown. Mechanical transport was by far the best solution, for a single Ford car of 135 kg cargo capacity could match the efforts of 300 carriers. However, this was offset by the almost complete lack of roads and their vulnerability to wet weather as well as insufficient numbers. This meant that considerable reliance on human transport would be essential, particularly in areas of difficult terrain or where roads had not yet been constructed. Even where vehicles could still be used, sickness amongst the drivers meant that they operated well below capacity.

This led to resolving the major deficiencies in the medical services which remained severely overstretched. The lack of integral transport meant that medical units could not move themselves and they had often fallen behind the advance. Evacuation of patients had been badly organised and, though newly arriving motor ambulance convoys were welcomed, their usefulness was limited to the dry season. Thought was put into making equipment easier to carry and stretcher-bearers were added to establishments. Two extra field ambulances were brought out from India, and the system of evacuation and treatment was rationalised. Instead of the previous ad hoc arrangements, columns were now allocated their own medical detachments and transport resources were centralised.[18] Behind the lines, hospital trains and ships were formalised with sailings between India and South Africa.

However, as important as these measures were, it would take much more than simply withdrawing the bulk of the force to the Central Railway, which itself was far from healthy or comfortable. They needed complete rest in a dry climate with a proper diet and replacement of their ragged uniforms. This was difficult to achieve during the height of the rains and the need to continue military operations. Apart from South African units expected to return, a British battalion had been sent out of the country for recovery, while the four longest-serving Indian units were rotated to India in exchange for fresh units as shipping became available. The measures were limited and slow in effect.

PLANS FOR THE OFFENSIVE

Apart from the essential reorganisation of the force, Hoskins began to consider his plans for the dry season of 1917, which would begin in May. The difficulties of trying to advance and sustain operations across the Mgeta and Rufiji rivers had already been amply demonstrated. Fighting at the end of elongated lines of communication in primeval jungle magnified the British weakness in transport while giving few tangible advantages in return. However, by using Kilwa as a base of operations, the British could utilize their maritime supremacy to much better advantage while also shortening the overland supply lines. Movement by ship also made possible the rapid and large-scale redeployment of troops, if only along the littoral.

These factors, coupled with the realisation that Lettow was likely to retreat into southern German East Africa, led Hoskins to select Lindi as a future base of operations. However, the landings in September had left only the immediate area of the town and anchorage in British hands, with the enemy holding the dominating high ground to the west. Before any serious development of the port and base could take place, it would be necessary to clear the area from direct observation and to establish secure forward positions. To ensure this vital task was carried out, Hoskins selected Brigadier General O'Grady, an aggressive and energetic officer, to assume the command there. He and his brigade were to reinforce the small garrison with the initial task of removing the threat to Lindi and then preparing for a subsequent advance.[19]

Hoskins then proposed to launch a four-pronged advance from widely separated positions converging into the heartland of the German colony. In the north, a column would push south from the Rufiji River towards Madaba and Luwegu, supported in the west by another column advancing from Iringa to Mahenge; from the coast, a third column would move westwards from Kilwa towards Liwale and a fourth would move north-westwards from Lindi in an attempt to cut off any escape to the south. Norforce was to move east, blocking any German attempts to move into either Rhodesia or Nyasaland. Fundamental to the success of this plan was the provision of substantial replacements, particularly signallers and drivers, as well as many more porters. Hoskins warned that without them, the campaign could not be wound up.[20] This seemed to precipitate a deterioration in relations between Hoskins and Robertson, as the CIGS began to lose confidence in the former's judgement. This seems to have originated in the rather vague operational plans and unco-ordinated nature of Hoskins' demands.[21] It seems that poor staff work and badly phrased telegrams had damaged Hoskins' credibility.

Relations between the British and Portuguese had not been eased by the complete failure of General Gil's expedition in late 1916 and the panic that it had subsequently induced in the latter. With the planned sending of another expeditionary force in early 1917, the governor general, Dr Alvaro de Castro, assumed the temporary role of commander-in-chief. Whatever his qualities, the governor general was not the man to direct operations and wanted to speak to the commander-in-chief personally.[22] Owing to the offensive Hoskins was unable to travel and, in his place, the homeward-bound General Smuts met with de Castro on 25 January.

Smuts pressed the Portuguese to clear a line 80 km south of the Rovuma of all food and to prevent the inhabitants from sowing any crops in January or February, forcing the Germans to surrender. He also advocated that a light line of observation posts be placed along the river, with any garrisons strong enough to withstand heavy German attacks. For his part, de Castro announced that he was in the process of raising the troops and carriers necessary to make a simultaneous advance with the British at the beginning of the dry season.[23]

The meeting was adjudged a success, but the clearance of the Rovuma was completely beyond Portuguese capabilities. The most tangible outcome was the agreement to swap liaison officers in the near future and regular communications between the two commander-in-chiefs. Even with improved relations, the British still maintained severe reservations about the quality of the Portuguese forces and placed little reliance on their promises.

Portuguese strength was suddenly weakened in March, when a revolt by the Makombe people erupted, chiefly in protest against excessive and brutal tax collection together with the conscription of labour for the war effort. It began in the remote frontier region of Barue and quickly spread throughout the Zambezi region. By May, Portuguese control of the area was severely threatened and reinforcements were badly needed.[24] Ordinarily, when white rule was threatened by black rebellion, the colonial powers could expect immediate support from their neighbours, such as had occurred in January 1915 in Nyasaland. Regardless of the fact that Portugal was a co-belligerent, the local British authorities in Southern Rhodesia and Nyasaland declined to provide that assistance, mainly because of their disgust and contempt for Portuguese rule and methods.[25] Apart from sending a very limited supply of obsolete arms and ammunition, the British declined to offer any military assistance and indeed offered asylum to many thousands of refugees fleeing the inevitable Portuguese reprisals. Unsurprisingly, this went down badly with the Portuguese who suspected duplicity.

As attention increasingly focused on the south of the German colony, the possibility of having to continue operations in Portuguese territory became more and more likely. As the British held no faith in the ability of the Portuguese to defend themselves, diplomatic overtures to the

Portuguese Government aimed to determine a joint strategy in the event of invasion. Finally, a meeting between General Hoskins and Dr de Castro was held at Dar-es-Salaam on 9 April. To the former's dismay, de Castro proposed to send a force of over 700 rifles from the coast to Chinde, thence up the Zambezi River into southern Nyasaland and into Lake Nyasa where it would land at Mtengula which was believed to be Abt von Stuemer's objective. He suggested that it would be completed in late May, but this was hopelessly optimistic given Portuguese transport facilities. More importantly, it was unwelcome as the force would get in Northey's way and cause major supply problems. From the British perspective, it would be far more useful for the Portuguese to establish a strong blocking force along the Rovuma as well as protecting the vulnerable line of communication running up the Zambesi River. This would ease the pressure on Northey, already weakened by the pursuit of Wintgens, and would prevent the intermingling of forces. Hoskins put his suggestions as tactfully as possible, and, unable to change de Castro's mind, he left the matter unresolved.[26]

In contrast, the British needed Belgian assistance. The War Office was beginning to realise that the campaign in East Africa was far from over and there were no spare troops in either Britain or India. The merchant fleet was being devastated by the U-boats, making shipping increasingly scarce. The use of the tried Belgian colonial troops was an attractive solution to the problem of finding reinforcements and moving them to the theatre of operations. But, relations remained formal as the British government continued to press the Belgians to evacuate Tabora, despite the considerable ill-feeling that this generated.[27] Matters had not been helped by Smuts' ambivalent attitude to his allies and his attempts to keep them from the spoils of victory. The new colonial secretary, Walter Long, supported the anti-Belgian line, but necessity soon dictated otherwise as the Foreign Office asked the Belgians to consider the provision of more troops in mid-January.

This was easier said than done as the demobilisation of the Belgian colonial forces was well underway and only four battalions remained in occupied German East Africa. The remainder of the force was either disbanding or in the process of travelling tc their permanent garrison locations, many of which were far in the interior of the Congo. Discussions were hastened in early March, with the approach of Abt Wintgens towards Bismarckburg while Hoskins was desperately trying to find the

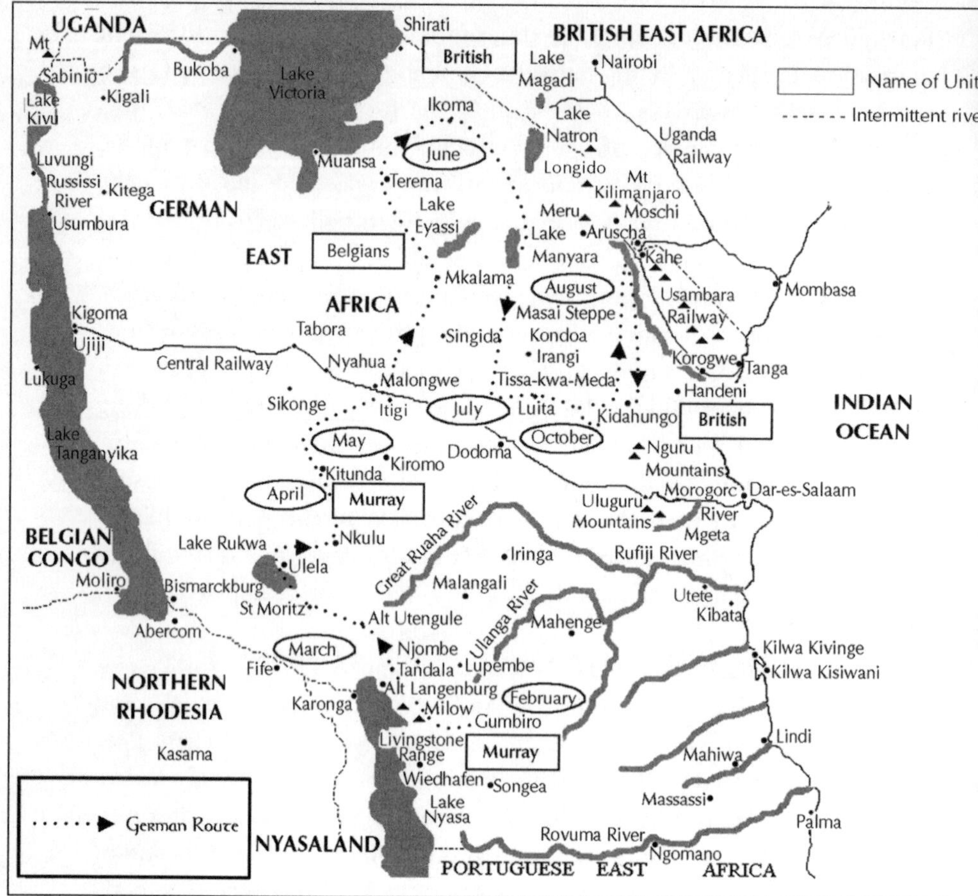

The Wintgens-Naumann raid, February-October 1917

carriers for his offensive.[28] In the circumstances, the Belgians responded generously, as they not only took over Bismarckburg, but also deployed several other units near Lake Tanganyika and ordered another five battalions to concentrate around Kigoma. They then agreed to the British being given access to their section of the Central Railway and lake steamers in any emergency. Whatever the new-found spirit of co-operation, it would take some time to rebuild and redeploy forces back into the main theatre of operations.[29]

The continued raid by Abt Wintgens added to the urgency as it had sapped Norforce of much of its manpower and threatened to delay the dry season offensive. A conference in London was hurriedly convened on

11 April as more troops were needed for the pursuit as well as covering the gap in the Iringa-Mahenge area. It was a success as the two governments agreed to resume combined operations with two main priorities: the first being the rounding up of Abt Wintgens, and the second being part of the encirclement and destruction of the German main body in the south-east of the colony. It was provisionally agreed that three Belgian columns, totalling some 2,000 rifles with supporting services and carriers, would be provided, although the exact details were left to the military commanders on the spot.[30]

Hoskins and Colonel Huyghé, his opposite number, subsequently met at the Belgian headquarters at Ujiji on 18/19 April to finalise matters. They agreed that the Belgians would provide a total of 3,000 soldiers divided into two mobile columns of 1,200 rifles, each supported by an operational reserve battalion of 600 rifles, plus a further two battalions of 500 men each to provide individual replacements for casualties. Numbers were capped at 4,000 soldiers and the national contingents were to remain operationally distinct, although both would be under the overall direction of the British commander-in-chief who would set out both the objectives and the respective zones of operations for each. Within those constraints, the Belgian commander-in-chief was free to execute his missions as he saw fit although he would be dependent on the British to provide supplies and equipment. Importantly, the Belgians reserved their right to decide on any extension of the campaign, should it move into Portuguese East Africa.[31]

The first Belgian column was to be ready immediately to take up the pursuit of Wintgens while the second was to be organised and equipped for the main offensive. Once the raiders were dealt with, the two columns were to unite in the Iringa area preparatory for an advance across the Ulanga River towards Mahenge. They would operate between Norforce in the Songea-Ubena area and the British detachment at Iringa. Liaison officers were exchanged at both general headquarters as well as with the various column headquarters, while the Belgian base was fixed at Dodoma on the Central Railway.[32]

A major consideration was time; for if the conquest of East Africa was to be made before the start of the rainy season (mid-November to early December), it was vital that the offensive commenced by the end of July or mid-August at the latest. Failing that, a new campaign in 1918 would be necessary under even less favourable conditions. It would expose the pursuers to all the problems encountered in the past rainy season and would allow the Germans a chance to regroup and, more importantly, cultivate new food supplies.[33] At the same time, the rapid elimination of Abt Wintgens was essential, although the re-mobilisation and re-deployment of Belgians meant that it would take time.

The military plan of operations was divided into two distinct phases that reflected both the exigencies of the moment and the difficulties of remobilisation. The first phase was the most pressing and involved despatching all the available troops in occupied German East Africa, some 1,200 rifles, against Abt Wintgens in co-operation with Colonel Murray's column in the south. The aim of this force was to encircle and destroy the raiders as quickly as possible. The second and subsequent phase envisaged a reinforced Belgian contingent of some 2,000 to 3,000 rifles working with General Northey's troops in the west and south. Together, they would help to drive the Germans into the general operational encirclement planned for June and July.[34] These arrangements were presented back to the national governments for approval, with the Belgians signalling their assent on 26 April. Despite the irritations of previous disputes, the Belgians were back in the campaign.

By early April, Hoskins was clear about the scale and arrival dates of his reinforcements. At the end of the month he issued his plan, having assessed that the Germans had reduced their troops along the Rufiji, with detachments opposite Kibata, Kilwa and Lindi. Their main body had moved south and was likely to put up the greatest resistance in the Kilwa and Lindi areas. In the west, Kraut's main body remained opposite Norforce in the Tunduru area while the Wintgens column was still moving west and north. To counter this, the British would concentrate on firstly destroying the fighting power of the enemy and secondly on eliminating his sources of food. This would be achieved through a multi-column concentric advance, with the Nigerian Brigade advancing south from the River Rufiji towards Madaba, with the Kilwa force of two brigades moving south-west to Liwale, and the Lindi brigade moving either westwards toward Massassi or north-east to the Mbemkuru River as necessary. The Iringa column would clear the area between the Ruaha and Ulanga rivers while the newly-arriving Belgians would take on responsibility for containing any attempted breakouts to the west and moving on Mahenge. This would enable Northey to concentrate further south and to be prepared to move on either Liwale or Tunduru or both as required. Finally, a general reserve would be kept back at Morogoro. The Portuguese forces were considered valueless and were more likely to provide supplies to the enemy than effective opposition.[35]

Fighting troops remained in short supply, for, despite Robertson's calculations that with planned reinforcements Hoskins would have some 50,000 troops to counter 8,000 Germans, the latter disagreed strongly. He placed his 'effective' infantry at 16,000, with the rotation of tired units and the new South Africans adding another 3,700 and the Belgians a further 3,000. He calculated his effectives at being 23,000, of whom at least 20% would be unable to participate owing to sickness. The new KAR battalions promised to bring another 2,500 men, but the quality of these units would be low for many months to come. This meant that after deducting 1,200 for the lines of communications, only 8,600 were assessed as being efficient for operations. Northey had some 4,000 rifles, of whom about 1,900 could be placed in the field, making a total striking force of 10,500. He also expected the return of three South African infantry battalions that would add about 2,000 rifles. It was hardly an overwhelming force to deal with the assessed 8,000 enemy.[36] In fact the Schutztruppe still numbered over 9,000 effectives. These consisted of some 6,534 (1,423 Germans and 5,111 Askari) of whom 4,419 were considered able to fight in the Osttruppen and 2,854 (535 Germans and 2,319 Askari) in the Westtruppen. To this must be added the 554 soldiers in Abt Wintgens in the British rear areas. Of course, Lettow was finding supply and health even more difficult than his opponents, as was Wahle in the west.[37]

The commander-in-chief also informed the War Office that he considered it impossible to stop the Germans from entering Portuguese East Africa if they wished to do so. More ominously, he noted that should he be required to continue the campaign in Portuguese territory, then operations would be very lengthy. A few days later, the CIGS accepted Hoskins' assessment and ordered him to concentrate on the most dangerous or vulnerable enemy columns first, defeating them one at a time. He also announced that the War Cabinet had considered the potential for a campaign in Portuguese East Africa and had decided that if the Germans were to break into that colony in force, then they were to be pursued until they surrendered or were defeated.[38]

In the south, Northey was hard-pressed as he believed that Wintgens was making for Tabora and that, with German foraging parties already in Portuguese territory, he expected to commit forces to the southern end of

Lake Nyasa before long. Even for a force accustomed to being widely spread, this was simply too much. For his part, Hoskins was astonished to learn that Northey had not been informed that the Belgian forces had ceased active operations some months before. Finally, he outlined his strategy into its essentials: beating the Germans in the field and depriving them of their food centres.[39]

OPERATIONS ON THE RUFIJI AND THE EAST

On the British side, the withdrawal of the South Africans had been largely completed by mid-January and a small two-battalion column of Indians and KAR had replaced the Second Division.[40] It was nearly a month later before the remaining troops could thin out the forward areas; on the coast, First Division had pulled its two brigades back towards Kibata and Ngarambi-Namatewa areas by 19 February. Further west, the 1st EA Brigade retained the miserable task of holding the Rufiji line until the now fully-arrived Nigerian Brigade could move forward to assist it. In the west, the planned concentration of Norforce around Lupembe and Songea was taking place although hindered by the extremely wet conditions.[41]

For their part, the Germans were suffering heavily too and were forced to make similar changes. On the middle Rufiji, the forward troops were thinned out considerably, leaving only major concentrations opposite the Nigerian Brigade at Mkindu and at Utenge. Even then, conditions were perilous as a hospital containing 200 soldiers was cut off by the rising waters and had to surrender. On the lower Rufiji, the rain kept the main detachments concentrated around Utete and Lake Utungi. In the west, the rise of the Ulanga River forced an evacuation of the west bank and a climb to drier ground. Sickness there was tremendous; Abt Braunschweig reported that over 75% of the Europeans were unfit for duty.[42] Elsewhere in the Schutztruppe, life was equally miserable through lack of food and illness.

Lettow's continued main concern was the survival of his force and he ordered a drastic reduction in numbers, dismissing many carriers and personal servants. He ordered severe cuts in the rations and that units should live off the land as much as possible. The threat of starvation was never far away while physical conditions were miserable in the extreme, with pouring rain and clouds of mosquitoes and tsetse fly.[43] A participant and later historian was to note:

> The German forces found themselves in a more critical situation than the British, the most critical that troops can face, that of existence or non-existence. The spectre of starvation threatened for the second time and it would not be easily overcome by the reoccupation of the southern portion of the Dar-es-Salaam district.[44]

On 1 February, the German position along the lower Rufiji was becoming precarious with Abt Tafel, of five companies, around Mpanganja, Abt Göring, also with five companies, securing the approaches to Ungwara while Headquarters remained at Lake Utungi with a reserve of two companies. Further to the south, holding 2nd EA Brigade at bay, was Abt Rothe with three companies at Mpotora.[45] The British held the general line Njinjo-Ngarambi Chini-Kiwambe-Utete with 3rd EA Brigade holding the centre, while 2nd EA Brigade was spread between Utete and Kibata.

Severe under-feeding was the norm during these conditions and starvation was a very real threat. The lack of transport and difficulty of movement meant that survival took priority over major operations. For example, the Nigerian Brigade was put on half rations on 30 January as all of their porters were withdrawn to keep the lines of communication open. This rendered the brigade virtually immobile and dependent on the vulnerable lifeline to the north. Remaining in the area into early February, its sick rate duly mounted, aggravated by the paucity of rations. This was reflected in the casualties from disease; the Brigade had twenty-eight officers and 500 men unfit for duty, or approximately 22% of the officers and 21% of the African ranks that had started at the end of December.[46] These sufferings were not unique to the Nigerian Brigade, as others endured similar shortages. The Gold Coast Regiment, serving in First Division and stationed south of Utete, had the misfortune not only to be on half rations for most of the period January-February, but also a great deal of the supplies that arrived had rotted and were unfit for human consumption. Many of the soldiers were very emaciated and eighty had to be hospitalised for starvation.[47]

The carriers, on who so much depended, had been badly neglected and had suffered vastly higher death rates than the soldiers. Now numbering over 150,000 strong, they were allocated the use of some twenty-eight mixed rest stations, five casualty clearing hospitals and seven carrier hospitals. However, these changes, overdue as they were, were too late to ease the immediate problems caused by the tropical monsoon. In the period 8 January to 5 May, 33,133 were admitted to hospital, with malaria accounting for 9,629 cases and pneumonia 2,342. Of the total, some 15,845 were invalided, 4,435 deserted and 4,168 died. In comparison to the followers, 38,333 soldiers were admitted with 23,349 having malaria and 2,684 having dysentery. The cost was high with 10,436 being invalided overseas, forty-three being discharged from military service, and 642 dying.[48] These figures may be an understatement, as it is clear that many remained with their units despite suffering bouts of illness.

Despite a brief improvement in the food situation in early March, it was decided to withdraw the remainder of 1st EA Brigade for rest and recuperation. This left only the Nigerian Brigade along the middle Rufiji position, and by 17 March it held a line of nearly 80 km, running from Nyangandu to Nyakisiku. However, the Rufiji continued to rise and the supply situation worsened appreciably. From 28 March to 1 May all ranks were on half rations, supplemented only by shooting of game. However, even this source became depleted through flooding and constant depredations by hungry soldiers. To cap things off, the flying bridge was swept away and the entire force was cut off for three complete days.[49]

The extent of difficulty may be judged from a single measurement: a level gauge had been established on the normal dry season high water mark at Kibambawe on the River Rufiji. By 1 April, the river was 147 inches (3.7 m) over the mark, nine days later the excess had risen to 175 inches (4.4 m), with the peak of 201 inches (5.1 m) being reached on 14 April. Thereafter, the level stayed around 180 inches (4.5 m) above the gauge until the end of the month, when it again peaked at 201 inches before diminishing in May. Considering that the valleys were generally broad and shallow, the volume of extra water was simply enormous.[50]

Finally, despite all human efforts, on 8 April the Nigerian Brigade was compelled to send half its troops back to the railway line owing to lack of food and clothing. Within a week, the food situation was getting worse even with half the brigade back at Morogoro. The returning units were so weakened with hunger that during the ten-day march to Mikesse, large numbers fell out, incapable of completing the trek. To call it a 'road' was a loose description, as in many places it was waist-deep in water, and littered with the bodies of dead animals and even porters as well as broken-down vehicles and carts. It was a depressing sight – even the patrols had to be conducted in canoes. Finally, in mid-May the rains began to abate and the supply situation improved slowly, although active operations would not be possible until the Mikesse Road had been made fit for use by vehicles.[51]

Operations on the middle and lower Rufiji during the period February to May 1917 largely consisted of thinning out the forward positions and patrol actions owing to the rain and flooding of the countryside. Sporadic fighting and occasional raids took place, although, with both sides seriously weakened by sickness and insufficient food, such encounters were usually indecisive. The withdrawal of the main body of the Osttruppe began in early March as soon as it became clear that the First Division had pulled back from its forward positions towards Kibata and Kilwa. Leaving only a relatively weak force on the Rufiji, Lettow moved south on 12 March, establishing his new headquarters at Mpotora five days later. In the meantime, he also strengthened the forces of the southern commander in order to meet the increasing enemy strength in Sudi and Lindi. Abt Rothe, with three companies, arrived there in mid-March, strengthening the defending forces considerably.[52]

South of the Rufiji, Lettow was determined to hold Lake Utungi and the Ligonya River Valley, which was now a formidable obstacle to movement. A number of small battalion-level operations in the second half of April near Utete resulted in local British successes, but fighting petered out by early May as both sides were now in the process of shifting their forces southward towards Kilwa and Lindi. These moves enabled First Division to move both its brigades south to the Matandu River. The brigade structure was now dropped, and on 2 April Colonel Grant (the former 2nd EA Brigade) was given command of all troops north of the Matandu and Colonel Rose (the former 3rd EA Brigade) was given command of all troops south of the river. In early April, patrols noted activity in the area of Kimamba Hill and Rumbo. A camp was set up in the bush around Makangaga; on 12 April it was estimated that some eight to ten companies were coming up the main road with a further three companies moving further east towards Kimamba via Mchakama. General Hannyngton, the GOC First Division, was concerned that the presence of this force would disrupt his preparations for the general advance and decided to take pre-emptive action. In mid-April, he instructed Rose to drive the enemy out of its positions. Accordingly, a column consisting of a reinforced battalion, numbering some 540 rifles, left Rumbo on the morning of 18 April to attack Abt von Liebermann, which was over 300 strong.[53]

The journey was not easy as the column had to cross the steeply-sided and swollen Ngaura River before reaching the enemy defences, and it poured with rain throughout the day. The going was slow and difficult with the column soon running into heavy fire. Faced by three companies in good positions surrounded by tall elephant grass and dense bush, visibility was very poor and communications difficult for the attackers. A flanking move was unable to make sufficient progress and it was decided that the enemy was too strong to defeat and a withdrawal was ordered. However, Liebermann reacted vigorously and threw in a strong counterattack that nearly overwhelmed the column's rearguard, losing three machine guns after their teams had been killed. Furthermore, a panic amongst the carriers resulted in the loss of a great deal of ammunition and baggage. The situation was saved by a courageous and determined effort by the rearguard, but it was a stinging defeat that did little to improve morale.[54]

The whole point of the raid was highly questionable from the outset, as the sending of the equivalent of five companies against a detachment estimated to have eight to thirteen companies, with at least 300 in the forward defences, was almost certain to fail. As it was, the attack merely re-emphasised the dangers of sending weak and unsupported columns against unreconnoitred defences. This event marked the end of serious offensive efforts by First Division for the remainder of the rainy season. The heavy losses, particularly in British officers, and the drop in morale were serious, but it was the lack of carriers that precluded any resumption of the offensive. It also showed that the new KAR battalions still had a long way to go in terms of training and tactics before they were able to take on the more experienced Schutztruppe on equal terms.[55]

The Germans had noted the British redeployment and the reductions on the Rufiji line. Suffering from similar problems to his opponents, Lettow decided to reduce his forward forces and to begin the slow withdrawal to the south. He wanted to be ready to fend off any subsequent British moves against his lines of communication as well as reinforce his troops along the coast. Concerns about rear area security and the loyalty of the African population were also apparent, especially in the area of the Makonde highlands. The British had been trying to induce the inhabitants to rebel against German rule since the previous autumn and had provided some material support. The disaffected tribes began to disrupt food gathering and made the links to the west much more dangerous than previously.[56]

The Germans remained effective as, on 5 May, they opened fire with a captured Portuguese mountain gun at the ships lying off Kilwa Kisiwani harbour from the mangrove swamps to the west. While it had little effect, it was a reminder of the enemy's ingenuity. Generally, though, they continued to pull back from the Matandu River and reinforce their existing positions on the Ngaura River. By 20 May, Mpotora had been completely evacuated with the garrison splitting between Liwale and Likawage.

As First Division moved south of the Matandu, it was transformed into Hanforce after the name of its commander, Major General Hannyngton. It comprised two columns, No 1 Column, now led by Colonel G.M. Orr in place of Rose and No 2 Column, led by Colonel H.F.L. Grant. No 1 Column was deployed in an approximately 40 km-long arc, covering the approaches to Kilwa port. Its front followed the line of the River Ngaura to the coast with a total of five forward posts being held. No 2 Column was more concentrated and occupied Mchemera, on the Matandu River, less a few detachments to the north. It was poised on the main route leading west from Kilwa towards Mpotora and the interior. However, heavy rain continued in the coastal areas until the middle of May and it then required a drying out period followed by intensive repairs on damaged roads and tracks before the supply system could become fully operational and effective.[57]

OPERATIONS IN THE SOUTH AND WEST

Although the heavy rains had brought operations in the Rufiji area to a complete halt, the precipitation further south was not as severe, or at least initially. If the main force was suffering badly from the climate, Norforce, although better off, needed a rest after the long advance to Iringa and the subsequent fight against the Westtruppen. The columns were tired and required reorganisation while wet weather had seriously impeded the effectiveness of the long lines of communication. However, further unexpected events would shortly make this requirement even more troublesome.

As has already been described, the bulk of the Westtruppen had broken through Northey's slender forces and had linked up with Abt Kraut in the Ulanga Valley. Although they had suffered a significant number of casualties, the now-united force was much stronger than Norforce. While the low ground was flooding heavily, two enemy groups remained on the edge of the great escarpment and in close proximity to Northey's troops. Abt Kraut remained in its strong defensive position at Mfrika watched by Hawthorn's column, but Abt Wintgens was at large. In the meantime, Wahle had to contend with severe supplies problems around Mahenge and ordered Kraut and Wintgens to operate in the Wiedhafen-Songea area for as long as possible.[58]

Norforce was widely stretched over a vast area of country, the distance from his headquarters in Ubena to the forward troops being 210 km alone. The columns were split between Likuyu, Songea, Kitanda, Alt-Langenburg and Lupembe. As the month progressed, the rains became increasingly heavy and the broad lowlands east of the escarpment continued to flood. Although on higher and healthier ground than Hoskins' main body, the troops of Norforce were still suffering from the climate and disease with the South African units particularly hard-hit.[59]

The threat to Norforce was very real, for on 3 February both Abteilungen arrived at Gumbiro and surrounded its garrison. On receiving Wahle's orders of 29 January, the two commanders had a major dispute. Kraut, the senior officer, insisted that they move south in accordance with their instructions, but Wintgens, a strong-willed and difficult personality, wanted to go north. It is unclear why he disobeyed such explicit orders, although it has been suggested that his Askaris wanted to return home to Tabora and that he did not get on well with Lettow. Whatever the reason, on 6 February he lifted the unsuccessful siege and moved north while Kraut took his troops south.[60] It was to be the start of an epic movement that would only end some eight months and several thousand kilometres later.

On 8 February, intelligence indicated that Kraut was moving southwards and this was confirmed two days later when he appeared on the Wiedhafen-Songea road making several unsuccessful attacks on isolated British posts. He continued south the next day with Hawthorn now in hot pursuit. Reportedly in a discontented state from lack of supplies, Kraut's Askaris moved quickly and, despite some heavy knocks by Hawthorn's column, they managed to make the Portuguese border. On 24 February, Northey was informed that a large enemy force was assembling at Likuyu and he recalled Hawthorn back to Songea. No longer being pursued, Kraut was now to forage in the southern portion of German East Africa and posed a potential threat to the Portuguese. Lettow was eager to exploit their territory and ordered Major von Stuemer with about 200 troops to move south towards Mwembe, some 128 km south of the Rovuma River in a fertile tract of land between the Lujenda River and Lake Nyasa in late March. There it was welcomed by the African population and soon obtained large quantities of food. Kraut's force was still on the move and unlocated, but it was presumed to be heading south for the Rovuma.[61]

Whilst Portuguese East Africa had relatively little strategic value in itself, the presence of a German force there was important. Firstly, it could plunder the relatively rich food areas for the supplies so badly needed by the main force further north more or less at will. Secondly, the extreme antipathy felt by the indigenous Africans for their Portuguese colonial overlords meant that recruiting for the German force was both possible and likely. Thirdly, Northey's long and vulnerable lines of communication along the Zambezi River to the Indian Ocean would be at serious risk from such a move. If these were interrupted, then his entire force would no longer be capable of serious offensive operations as the land links through the Rhodesias were too undeveloped to be of practical use.

Whatever the consternation that Wintgen's actions were causing the British, Lettow considered it an unnecessary dissipation of his force. He had more pressing worries as the combination of the Makonde rising and the British build-up at Lindi threatened his supplies in the south. In mid-March, he ordered Abt Krüger, three companies strong, to leave Tunduru for the port of Mikandini. Initially given orders to crush the rebellion in the Makonde plateau, Krüger was soon drawn into Looff's operations against the lodgement in Lindi. Indeed, Lettow believed it was time to strike before the British could reinforce further and to drive them 'out of the continent'.[62]

Meanwhile, O'Grady's brigade launched an attack on Abt Rothe, taking a forward company position at Njangwani, some 12 km north-west of the town. Eager to redress the loss and to use his newly arrived reinforcements, Looff decided to strike a week later. Leaving Abt Krüger opposite Lindi, he sent Abt Hinrichs, with three companies, to take the small port of Sudi. The position was a strong one, with the defenders protected by wire and stake obstacles. Launched on 24 April, the attackers, who lacked artillery, were unable to break through the defences and suffered a number of casualties. The battle was broken off and a single company was left to contain the British. The next day Abt Rothe gained its revenge for its earlier setback and seized the lost forward position, driving the Indian defenders back into Lindi.[63]

Despite Lettow's stated aim of destroying the British coastal enclaves, the attack at Sudi was an expensive waste of scarce soldiers on an operationally and tactically unimportant position. A few days later, on 3 May, he declared that the time for decisive measures at Lindi had run out and he ordered two companies to march north to face the growing threat from Kilwa. Dissatisfied with the conduct of operations there and having clashed repeatedly with Captain Looff, he dismissed him as southern commander on 5 May, leaving him in command of an Abteilung. Major Kraut took his place and quickly reorganised the defences with four companies placed in the strong Ngurumahamba position west of Lindi; and with another two positioned to the south and west at Majani. Apart from chasing Wintgens, the wet weather in March prevented Northey from doing little else than maintaining the defensive and preparing for the offensive. From his headquarters in Ubena, his force was strung out south-eastwards on the line Likuyu-Kitanda-Lupembe, roughly paralleling Lake Nyasa. The detachment of Murray's column, some three battalions strong, was only partially counterbalanced by Hoskins' decision to send a KAR battalion south from Iringa in March. He remained vulnerable in the south, as Abt Kraut could either attack Songea or move into Portuguese East Africa.[64]

THE WINTGENS RAID

Wintgens was an ambitious and able commander, who seems not to have been entirely happy under Lettow's command. He was also concerned about his increasingly constricted area of operations and the need to obtain food. Against orders and on his own initiative, he decided to make a feint on the line Songea-Lupembe and then to break north-westwards towards the northern end of Lake Nyasa, to Tandala. Leaving his sick and wounded behind at Milow Mission on 15 February, he ran into a combined South African and KAR column the next day. The British column was forced back that night, having lost its commander, and a number of others were killed. This fight confirmed the renewed threat to Northey's lines of communication running between Alt-Langenburg and Ubena, while his forces were too small to prevent a breakthrough to the west. Acting rapidly, he recalled Murray's Column from the Ruhudje, and it promptly marched back to Tandala, at the northern head of Lake Nyasa.

Two days later, a KAR company near Tandala was nearly surrounded and cut off by the Germans who then besieged the garrison. Murray's column's timely arrival on 22 February forced Wintgens to abandon the siege, leaving behind a destroyed 3.7-cm gun. Heading northwards, Wintgens had about 520 soldiers, eleven machine guns and two field guns. As soon as the relieved garrison was sorted out, Murray set off in hot pursuit on 25 February.[65] Now faced by serious opposition, Wintgens intended to use his head start and superior mobility to best advantage. He planned to make a series of short marches in a north-westerly direction until he reached the old British lines of communication leading from Neu Langenburg to Iringa. From there, he would feint towards the Rhodesian border while actually moving towards Lake Rukwa. He succeeded in losing his pursuers until British aircraft located his camp on 26 February, although Murray's patrols were not able to restore contact until 11 March as he headed for St Moritz.[66]

Murray was also a determined and capable officer, but he had to bring his food forward while Abt Wintgens stripped the countryside bare. He remained in hot pursuit, heading for St Moritz where he believed that Wintgens was trapped behind two swollen rivers. After a number of encounters, the Germans reached their objective on 26 March where they began to build rafts out of packing crates. Murray, delayed by supply problems, arrived on 3 May just as the enemy completed its escape. He was unable to cross and the follow-up was again broken.[67]

The emergence of these five companies into the previously secure rear areas caused disruption out of proportion to their fighting strength. The thickness of the bush, the sheer size of the country being traversed and the lack of any infrastructure meant that substantial pursuing forces were required. In order to support Murray, at the end of March Hoskins had reinforced Bismarckburg, while a partly trained KAR battalion was sent to block the approaches to Tabora.[68] The raiders occupied Kitunda Mission on 4 May and a halt was called as Wintgens and many of the Europeans were critically ill with typhus. Norforce was also under severe strain, as the brigade-sized force was spread out over 720 km of wild bush, mountain and swamp. It risked defeat in detail and the lengthy supply lines were unsustainable. Northey asked General Hoskins for the return of his detached troops, but he was turned down and was ordered to keep his main body in its existing locations. Help was on the way, for the Belgians took over responsibility for Bismarckburg and Tabora while British reinforcements moved up the Central Railway. In the meantime, Murray kept pushing from the south, but remained some distance away.[69]

In the meantime, Wintgens' condition had worsened seriously and he handed command to Lieutenant Naumann on 21 May, who was enjoined to link-up with the Westtruppen back in the Mahenge area. With Murray pressing hard from the south and the Belgians on the move, Naumann decided to march north-east across the Central Railway. Marching hard, they narrowly escaped being intercepted by a British column, and continued north. The Belgians launched three battalion-sized columns in pursuit, but with several days' lead and no lines of communication, the Germans were an extremely elusive prey. Now, moving towards Lake Victoria, Abt Naumann posed a threat on an incursion into British East Africa, and Huyghé ordered his mobile columns to prevent a breakthrough.[70]

Fortunately, he had taken a number of precautions beforehand that were now to pay useful dividends. Despite not being required to raise extra forces in the April agreement, he had ordered the re-mobilisation of three additional battalions in case they were needed in the new circumstances. In May, he had organised his available forces into two major columns, one based on the old Brigade Sud, armed with the Mauser rifle, and the other based on the Brigade Nord, armed with the Gras rifle. An operational reserve (RO) of two battalions' strength was formed while two others provided security for the lines of communication. This meant that the diversion of troops in chasing Naumann would not upset van Deventer's more important plans for a general offensive.

SOUTHERN OPERATIONS

There was also Abt von Langenn, on the Ruhudje to the east of Lupembe, and Abt Lincke at Likuyu (the crossing of the Likuyu River on the Songea-Liwale road) to consider, especially the latter which was 80 km north-east of Songea. Colonel Hawthorn was sent from Songea in March to drive Lincke away. He arrived near the Likuyu River on 7 April and, after an inconclusive skirmish four days later, he attempted to cross the flooded river. This took some time and Hawthorn's force was successfully over the obstacle on 23 April and was some 9 km north of the suspected German encampment. He occupied it unopposed on 27 April, with Lincke having evacuated some days beforehand and moved further east.[71]

While Hawthorn was struggling through the sodden bush, Kraut's force had reached Tunduru and was believed to be making enquiries about access to the Rovuma River and the areas to its south. There was considerable doubt as to the veracity of these reports, but these were dispelled on 20 April, when a captured document revealed that Kraut had split his force into two columns, one under himself and the other under Major von Stuemer who had the mission of raiding Portuguese territory.[72] This was unpleasant news for Northey, who now faced yet another demand on his much diminished force.

Northey reacted at once and sent his only available troops, a newly raised South African battalion, to Fort Johnston on 30 April. This unit, which had been badly affected by illness and were recuperating while carrying out security duties between Wiedhafen and Songea, was his only formed reserve. Even so, it was far from fully trained and barely equalled the numbers of Germans in the area; it could only be supplemented by KAR recruits diverted from essential training in Zomba.[73]

While these deliberations were taking place, the threat to Northey's southern flank continued to increase. Stuemer was now believed to have over 400 soldiers plus a substantial ruga-ruga contingent. Furthermore, it was clear that the local population welcomed the German presence and were actively supporting their activities. An advance party from his column had already reached as far south as Mtonia, a village only 24 km from Lake Nyasa and the British border. His main body was believed to be heading for Mtengula which lay north-west of Mtonia on the lake shore. Abt Kraut was also identified in Portuguese territory, about 125 km to the east of Stuemer, and in Mwiriti on the Msalu River. Apart from the above-mentioned supply and recruiting opportunities that this offered, Mwiriti lay on a motorable road (with telegraph line) that led to the coast and Porto Amelia.[74]

Having been denied the return of Murray's column, General Northey made several changes to counter the mounting threat to Nyasaland. On 6 May, he moved his new KAR battalion to Fort Johnston while one of the detached battalions was marching back to rejoin the main body. At the same time, he shifted his headquarters from Ubena (north and east of Lake Nyasa) to Zomba (south of Lake Nyasa and Fort Johnston) in order to be near the greatest threat.[75]

Whilst these further deployments were getting underway, the South Africans had arrived at Fort Johnston with barely 270 effective soldiers. Promptly reinforced by several hundred KAR soldiers from the depot, the unit left immediately for Mangoche, a few kilometres to the north and east, where they arrived on 8 May. Their speed was needed, for on the same evening an advanced detachment of Stuemer's force took the Portuguese boma at Mandimba, only 9 km from the border and close to Mangoche.

The Germans actually crossed into Nyasaland the next day, but were deterred from a further advance by the presence of the newly arrived battalion and withdrew to Mandimba. The British force then shifted to Namwera, a few kilometres north-east of Mangoche, where it commanded the main road between Nyasaland and Portuguese East Africa. Neither side was strong enough to force the other and a local stalemate prevailed.[76]

Despite the difficulties in obtaining detailed information on each other's forces, by May 1917 liaison was improving between the British and Portuguese. This was helped by the positive impression Hoskins had made on the governor general. Similarly, Northey had done his best to encourage co-operation. The problem lay with the Portuguese inability to translate good intentions into positive military action. Fortunately British assistance was at hand.[77]

This was as well, for the Portuguese troops only reached Chinde, at the head of the Zambezi, on 25 May and Stuemer's move on Mtengula forestalled their further advance. Instead, it was agreed that the local Portuguese commander would meet Northey in Zomba to arrange a revised deployment. This was ultimately decided as the reinforcement of the existing Portuguese boma at Mlanje, on the other side of the British-Portuguese border, and was forward of both the railway line and the River Zambezi. It provided much-needed protection of each force's lines of communications and, as the British desired, kept the two armies separated.[78] With the revolt in the districts of Tete and Barue and the need to reinforce the beleaguered garrisons there, it was probably as much as could be obtained. This would remain a major consideration for the Portuguese until the rebellion came under control at the beginning of June. Hostility to colonial rule was high elsewhere too, as when Abt Stuemer arrived in the Yao region east of Lake Nyasa, in April both they and the Macua tribes rose and provided the Germans with considerable assistance.[79]

Events continued to move rapidly. General Northey reached Zomba on 14 May and on the same day half of the KAR battalion arrived in Fort Johnston. Given the seriousness of the situation in the south and the fact that the Songea operations were now halted owing to rain, Northey decided to bring Colonel Hawthorn down to command the force in Nyasaland. Three days later, on 17 May, the Germans occupied Mtengula on Lake Nyasa while intelligence showed that they might shift their attentions further to the south and towards the key port of Quelimane. This would be a direct threat to Portuguese operations as well as Northey's communications, and needed to be neutralised.[80]

However, it soon appeared that Stuemer had encountered more opposition than he had expected and was unlikely to press into Nyasaland, given the relative balance of forces. A detachment occupied Mtonia on 26 May, but patrols and scouts were unable to locate any Germans south of that place. However, presence of any enemy was both a threat and a drain on available resources. Accordingly, Northey resolved to drive them out of Portuguese territory and north of the Rovuma into the developing envelopment being led by the main forces.[81]

On 25 May, the remaining half-battalion of the KAR arrived at Fort Johnston, giving Northey a local numerical advantage. This enabled him to order patrols into Mtonia the next day, followed by its capture on 1 June. The Germans appeared to be thinning out and it was decided to reinforce the advantage south of Lake Nyasa. On 3 June, Northey moved his KAR battalion forward to support the South Africans, while withdrawing his details of trained KAR soldiers back to Zomba where they resumed the vital task of instructing the new recruits for the forthcoming operations.[82]

By the last week of May, Norforce was stretched out over an enormous distance as the pursuit of Naumann, together with the countering of Stuemer's threat to Nyasaland, had drawn off all its available reserves. However, on 29 May, as dry season approached and the Belgians came into the campaign, van Deventer ordered Murray's column, now only 80 km south of the Central Railway, to return to Northey's command. This determined force, which had been on the march since February, now had to turn about and retrace its steps to Neu Langenburg, some two weeks' distant. From there, it would then have to march forward to reach the forward areas in order to participate in the general advance.[83]

HOSKINS' DISMISSAL AND THE APPOINTMENT OF VAN DEVENTER

By the third week of April, General Hoskins' efforts were beginning to pay off as a total of 484 light lorries with over 1,100 drivers and artificers were en route. As well, 300 signals personnel, 400 Lewis guns, twelve of the new 2.75' mountain guns, and twenty Stokes mortars were arriving.[84] Although the numbers were relatively small, they added substantially to East Africa's resources. Furthermore, he had taken over a force in the worst of condition and had done much to restore its fighting effectiveness. Much remained to be done, but in the circumstances of an exceptionally wet season, the prevalence of disease and the physical weakness of the troops under his command, he had been successful. His plans for an offensive were set and the troops largely in position.

But, unbeknownst to him, his greatest problem was in London. Although he was clearly an energetic and efficient officer, he had failed to impress the CIGS who began to doubt his suitability as an independent commander-in-chief. Hoskins had issued a number of rather unco-ordinated demands and his operational plans were highly conditional on the level of support that the War Office could provide. His position was not helped by the breakout of Abt Wintgens to the west, nor by his continual demands for more manpower. As a former commander-in-chief and prominent politician, Smuts was also involved. He had been supportive of Hoskins in mid-April, but that had changed dramatically by early May: 'The progress of Wintgens in the direction of Tabora makes it clear to me that there is no firm handling of the situation at present in that theatre'.[85]

Whatever the exact machinations, Robertson had made up his mind and on 23 April the War Cabinet decided to dismiss Hoskins.

> The Chief of the Imperial General Staff stated that for some time he had not felt that the British operations in East Africa were being carried out as satisfactorily as could be desired. He had discussed the matter on more than one occasion with General Smuts, who, while holding a high opinion of the officer in command, Major-General A.R. Hoskins, had agreed that apparently he had lost grip of the operations and had perhaps become tired.[86]

It is clear that Smuts had his successor firmly in mind, for his old protégé, van Deventer, was quickly suggested. Indeed, no other candidates appear to have been mentioned and after brief negotiations with South Africa, the War Cabinet confirmed his appointment on 1 May.[87] It seems that Smuts' popularity with his British colleagues as well as the need to maintain South Africa's active support for the campaign played an important part in the decision. Predictably, the change caused considerable resentment as many believed that Smuts had hatched an unsavoury political deal with his British counterparts, especially as the bulk of the South Africans had long departed.[88] Furthermore, many officers were well aware that Hoskins had done much to clean up the mess left by Smuts and that he was to be replaced by another 'political' South African general. Of course, they were unaware of Robertson's personal dissatisfaction and political pressure to wind up the campaign quickly.

7

The Clearance of German East Africa

BRITISH STRATEGY FOR 1917 AND EAST AFRICA

By Spring 1917 Britain was running out of money to fund the war and the unrestricted U-boat campaign was increasingly successful in throttling its seaborne trade. In the first four months of 1917, British losses to submarines had risen from 109,954 tons (thirty-five ships) in January to 516,394 tons (155 ships) in April.[1] At this rate, the country would soon be starved into submission, as replacement ships could not be built fast enough to offset the losses. Given the gravity of the situation, it was decided to concentrate shipping on the North Atlantic routes at the cost of reductions in Indian and Australian waters. At the same time, the Russian military defeat and the mutinies in the French Army meant that Britain would have to carry the strain of military operations in Europe, leaving little for peripheral theatres.[2] At home, declining civilian morale was becoming a major problem and Lloyd George continued to look for a striking victory that would sustain faith in the war effort. With all the important parts of German East Africa in Allied hands, there seemed little prospect of further achievements in that theatre, while the continued existence of the Schutztruppe meant that the campaign had to carry on. The War Cabinet now appreciated that Lettow had to be defeated militarily and as quickly as possible.

On his arrival in East Africa on 29 May, the new commander-in-chief was given his instructions. The CIGS came immediately to the point:

> In view of requirements other theatres and of the fact that it is essential to release at earliest possible moment vessels absorbed by supply and maintenance of your force, His Majesty's Government attach great importance to early termination of campaign. I must also impress upon you importance during remainder of campaign of limiting demands for tonnage to minimum.[3]

Van Deventer was instructed to try to prevent the enemy from leaving German East Africa and entering Portuguese East Africa. He was authorised to operate in the latter territory if necessary, although the Portuguese themselves were expected to give little useful assistance. In contrast, considerable hopes were placed on the Belgians, who would provide a column in the continued pursuit of Abt Naumann as well as building up their main striking force in the Iringa-Kidatu area. There was no explicit mention of any other campaign objectives, but it was clear that they implied the destruction of the enemy force and its ability to fight.[4]

The new commander-in-chief was very different to his predecessors. Now a lieutenant general, van Deventer had been a loyal member of the Botha/Smuts axis since the second Anglo-Boer war. He had begun his military career as a gunner in the Transvaal Artillery in 1896, rising rapidly through the ranks, reaching battery commander by the outbreak of war in 1899. He fought with distinction throughout the conflict and showed himself to be an able independent commander. Promoted to combat general in 1902, he served as Smuts' second-in-command in the Cape Colony. He was recalled to service as a colonel in 1914 to participate in the South-West Africa expedition, but helped to suppress the Afrikaner rebellion first. Having completed that mission, he was promoted brigadier in general command of the Upington column in the advance against German South-West Africa, finishing as a divisional commander.[5]

After a few months at home, he followed Smuts to East Africa where he rapidly rose from brigade to divisional commander. Van Deventer returned with the bulk of the South African troops in January 1917 and resumed farming until being asked to assume the chief command in May. If the new commander-in-chief was a Smuts loyalist, he was very different in outlook and character. He was renowned for his sense of discipline, a quality often lacking in Boer formations, and did not shrink from battle. Although he was most at home leading mounted columns, he realised that the infantry would be the mainstay of the campaign. This did not preclude the use of mounted troops, but only in areas where the tsetse fly was not present.

He had learned from bitter experience the futility of trying to outmanoeuvre the Germans in such difficult terrain and grasped that they had to be defeated in battle. Equally important was his understanding that operational plans had to be based on sound planning and administration. This meant that his place was at GHQ, where he could plan and direct operations without becoming drawn into the details of the tactical battle. It also ensured that the various staff branches could co-ordinate their work much more effectively. Finally, he kept on the talented and highly professional Brigadier General S.H. Sheppard as his Chief of General Staff. Together, they were to form a close-knit team.

Both men understood that the Schutztruppe had two major vulnerabilities; its dependence on European officers and NCOs, all of whom were irreplaceable, and its need to live off the land. This led to a policy of hard-hitting wherever possible, with the aim of inflicting the maximum casualties while lowering morale and the will to continue. While the firepower of the machine gun and German mobility meant that the attacker would generally suffer higher casualties than the defender, this was not a decisive disadvantage. For restricted as British manpower and equipment reserves were, they were still vastly superior to their opponents and could be replaced, albeit with difficulty. But this aggressive approach would be complemented by a campaign against the enemy lines of communication, and in particular eliminating their food-growing areas.

Nevertheless, van Deventer appreciated the formidable difficulties facing him. Although Hoskins had done much to reorganise and re-equip the force, the exertions and overwork of the preceding year had taken a very heavy toll. Furthermore, the Germans still retained interior lines in a territory some 480 km square and difficult to penetrate. For example,

Mahenge to Liwale was seven days' march for the Germans while for the British to have moved a force from Mahenge to either Kilwa or Lindi, still some distance from Liwale, would have taken the same number of weeks. None of this was eased by the lack of accurate maps and lack of roads or railways in the area of operations. Equally, the problems of disease remained enormous and could only be minimised through careful planning and strict attention to health.[6]

PLANS FOR THE GENERAL OFFENSIVE OF 1917

The general offensive for 1917 could not begin before the end of the rains and the subsequent drying out of the countryside, which would not occur until late June at the earliest. Van Deventer had very little time to settle into his new command, but Hoskins had set the necessary planning, reorganisation and regrouping in train. Five possible lines of advance had been identified. The first was the Dodoma-Iringa-Mahenge route in the west. While it was the healthiest, it was also the longest and passed through the Ulanga and Great Ruaha valleys which were unsuitable for motor transport and highly vulnerable to flooding in the wet season. The second option was slightly further east along the line Kilossa-Kidatu-Mahenge. It was shorter and more practical for vehicles than the first approach, but it too suffered from its vulnerability to the rains. The third approach followed Smuts' route across the middle Rufiji going via Mikesse-Kibambawe-Mahenge. Plunging as it did through the Mgeta and Rufiji valleys, it was by far the most physically difficult to support. The nightmarish conditions of the last rainy season were still all too evident, while the country south of Kibambawe was a wild tangle of bush and almost totally impracticable for motors. The fourth option was an advance on the line Kilwa-Liwale. It had the unhappy reputation of having the unhealthiest climate of all, although it did offer the advantages of being close to a large proportion of the enemy's forces and to a first-class harbour. The final choice was the approach Lindi-Massassi. Its chief advantage was that it offered a direct line of advance that could potentially cut off any retreat towards the Portuguese border, although the country was very difficult. Health, too, was a problem, while Lindi harbour had considerable limitations and could only be used by a proportion of the available shipping.[7]

The attractiveness of operations launched across the river basins, which had never been high, now waned significantly. Apart from the unhealthiness of the climate, the difficulty of the countryside made supply very difficult and there was insufficient transport – either human or vehicular – to support concurrent major advances from the interior and the coast.[8] As well, Lettow's gradual redeployment to the south near Kilwa made the coastal operations more attractive as they were easier to supply and reinforce.

General Northey considered that the Germans would only move into Portuguese East Africa if pushed there, and, until the situation east of Mahenge was cleared up, there was the potential for another raiding force to break westward. He proposed converging simultaneous thrusts against the enemy, but, conscious of the time needed to get Murray's column back and suitably rested, he expected that his advance would start after the others. Van Deventer agreed, realising the importance of having Northey attack Mpepo and Mtarika as it would draw off enemy forces on the Ruipa line prior to the arrival of the Belgians. Once they were ready, Northey could then shorten his line by handing over the Ruhuje sector to them. By that stage, Murray's column would be rested and ready to participate in the general offensive.[9]

This would leave the Songea column at about 1,000 rifles with sixteen machine guns and two mountain guns, and the Fort Johnston column with a similar amount. While these columns would be ready to start at the end of June, Murray's column would need extra time to reach Songea and would not be ready to advance before 7 July. This would provide another 1,000 rifles, giving him over 3,000 men advancing on two axes. He also noted that two battalions' worth of reinforcements would be arriving in July, but neither would be ready for the field before August.[10] Likuju would also form an important staging base, as both a wireless station and small airfield were established there.

The Portuguese were given a small role to play in these plans. Co-operation and the exchange of information had been greatly improved by the appointment of the former consul general, Errol MacDonell, as military liaison officer to the Portuguese Headquarters in mid-March 1917. This was reciprocated several weeks later with a Portuguese officer, Major Azumbuju Martins, being attached to the British GHQ.[11] He had East African experience, having been chief of staff to the ill-fated General Gil. Hitherto, neither side had any detailed information on each other's forces, intentions or capabilities and Major MacDonell's first task was to ascertain where the Portuguese troops were located and whether they intended to defend the Rovuma River boundary.[12]

However, MacDonell had spent many years in Moçambique and knew that his job would not be an easy one in light of Portuguese sensitivities and pride:

> A very large number of Portuguese Officers and men are fully alive to the fact that they have up to the present made a hopeless fiasco of the German East campaign, and though this has been stated to me in private, if any foreigner were to make a similar statement he would incur the obloquy of the Military, Press and public…I shall be looked upon with suspicion by the military authorities.[13]

The change of command also changed some anxiety with the Portuguese, as they had heard rumours that van Deventer was taking over from Hoskins. They had enjoyed working with Hoskins and feared that the South Africans harboured anti-Portuguese sentiments.[14] Furthermore, they had a major task in the suppression of the Barue rebellion and were not pleased by the lack of British support.

On 10 June 1917, van Deventer signalled his plan back to London. It reflected the changed strategic situation as well as the imperatives given in his own instructions during the previous month. It was as follows: first he wanted to catch and destroy Abt Naumann as quickly as possible in order to rest and redeploy the forces involved; secondly a preliminary and limited assault would be launched at Lindi to secure the high ground surrounding the town and to secure a better water supply. At the same time, he would attack the Ruipa River position from Iringa in order to deny its rich food-growing area to the Germans. Finally, he would push southward from Kilwa as soon as sufficient reinforcements could be brought up. Concurrently, Northey was to concentrate his force at Songea, having got Colonel Murray's column back, and then to advance eastwards as soon as he was ready. The commander-in-chief understood that Lettow would attempt to avoid encirclement and escape south:

> The establishment of considerable food depots in the MASSASSI (GGF.F.8.c.) area, together with the presence of a considerable enemy force in PORTUGUESE EAST AFRICA, appears to point to his eventual retirement by this line. One of my chief aims must therefore to be to prevent his main force breaking through into PORTUGUESE EAST AFRICA, as that might necessitate a new campaign.[15]

Van Deventer and Huyghé met at the Belgian Grand Quartier Général (GQG) at Dodoma on 18 June to agree final details. However, before the main operational objectives could be reached, there were several preliminary operations that had to be completed beforehand. The most important of which was the clearance of Tafel's forward troops from the Ulanga Valley between those two settlements between Mpepo and Malinje which would also cover the move forward of the Belgian main body from Kilossa. Anxious to get going, van Deventer had already asked Huyghé to provide a column of 1,200 rifles by mid-June, but this could not be readied until the end of July owing to lack of transport. However, Huyghé showed some flexibility over British concerns that another German raiding force might break out to the west. He agreed to send 500 rifles to fill the gap around Mpanga, despite breaking the agreed principles of a concentrated Belgian deployment.[16]

For the main push, the Belgians were to drive Abt Tafel out of the Mahenge area with the Brigade Sud establishing itself between Colonel Tytler's column at Iringa and Norforce at Lupembe. The Brigade Nord would assume sole responsibility for the pursuit and destruction of Abt Naumann with all British columns being withdrawn into reserve. Two of its battalions would continue the chase while the remainder continued their concentration on the railway. Once the brigade came into action in late July it would advance on Mahenge while the detached troops to the north would take over more of the British sector as soon as Naumann had been dealt with. Effectively, this would turn the whole of the Mahenge operations over to the Belgians. Lastly, in the vital matter of supplies, it was agreed that the British would provide carriers and vehicles to bring Belgian provisions to their supply base at Dodoma. Equally, the Belgian pioneers would be responsible for road and bridge building in the forward areas.[17]

General van Deventer issued his final timetable for the offensive on 27 June. A preliminary operation in Portuguese East Africa would begin on the same day with Norforce sending a column against Mwembe. The main phase would commence on 2 July, with the Iringa Column attacking the Ruipa position supported by 250 rifles from Norforce moving from Lupembe against Mpepo. The principal attack would follow on 4 July when Linforce moved on Mtua, with an assault planned there on the following morning. Also on 5 July, Hanforce would assault the Nguara River position and Norforce would advance Likuju towards Liwale. Finally, on the middle Rufiji, a battalion-sized force from the Nigerian Brigade would leave Kibambawe for an attack on Msswega on 9 or 10 July. Furthermore, the Belgians would send a column of 500 rifles from Kilossa towards Kidodi on 8 July, although the remainder of their forces would take some time to get into position. [18]

THE OPPOSING FORCES AT THE END OF JUNE 1917

The Allied forces had used most of June to prepare themselves for the coming offensive. As ever, the question of effective numbers remained a major concern, for despite the improvements to supply and hygiene, sickness constantly depleted the units and many of those in the forward units were still weak. Reinforcements in the form of two newly raised KAR battalions were due to be fielded by the end of June, with a number of other battalions in various stages of formation, but it would be a considerable period before they could be considered remotely ready for operations. Further help was also due from South Africa with two new reformed battalions scheduled to arrive at the end of the same month. Although these units had fought through the 1916 campaign, in reality they were brand new and only partially trained. It is interesting to note that these battalions could not be raised for Hoskins, but were made available to van Deventer.[19]

Only the Nigerian Brigade remained on the Rufiji front, based on Kibambawe, while further east at Iringa there was a small two-battalion column commanded by Colonel Tytler who was to prevent any breakouts and hold the line until the arrival of the Belgians who were still concentrating. Their GQG moved from Ujiji to Dodoma on 29 June, but Brigade Sud remained at Kigoma, on Lake Tanganyika. Brigade Nord had two battalions chasing Abt Naumann, with another still guarding the rear areas south-west of Tabora and the fourth en route for Iringa.[20] The artillery was moving forward to join the brigades while the pioneers were preparing to start work on the new base at Dodoma. The rear services operated on the existing line Stanleyville-Albertville with new stages of Dodoma-Iringa and Kilossa-Ruaha. Slowly but surely, the Belgians were moving into position for the next phase of the campaign.[21]

To the south, Norforce had moved its headquarters from Fort Johnston to Songea on 24 June, arriving a week later. In the north, the main body of Northey's troops were in their jumping-off positions around Kitanda and Likuju ready to strike north-east. Further to the west, the 1,000-strong

Murray column was continuing its long and wearying journey back while a separate striking force of 500 under Colonel Shorthose prepared itself to clear Abt von Stuemer from Portuguese East Africa.[22] In principle General Northey had nearly 3,400 soldiers, but many of these were insufficiently trained recruits and sickness forced him to relegate a number of units to the lines of communication.

On the coast at Kilwa, Hanforce disposed of two substantial columns that numbered 1,100 and 500 strong respectively, although they too were short of officers and trained troops. In light of the potential opposition, the commander-in-chief had already agreed to reinforce them with one South African and up to two KAR battalions before beginning the advance. Finally, in the south, Linforce had about 2,500 rifles concentrated in the immediate area of Lindi although a considerable proportion were not fit for field duties.[23]

Overall, the situation was hardly good. The Indian Army battalions were largely worn out with average strengths being less than 400 men and two barely able to muster 100 men each. Despite the less demanding duties on lines of communications, the Imperial Service troops were also suffering heavily from disease. The pursuit of Naumann had drawn off many troops, leaving only a single battalion in general reserve, although the eventual return of Murray would help. More than ever, the Belgians were needed to help fill the gaps in the centre of the line.[24] They were arriving in the Kilossa area, with several battalions moving forward to Kidodi, although it would be several weeks before the planned brigade was complete. Far to the west and north, the equivalent of a brigade of Belgians was pursuing Naumann and there was a small central reserve at Morogoro. The Portuguese had landed their latest expeditionary force of 4,500 at the port of Palma, but it was far from being ready to take the field.[25]

On the German side, their troops remained in two major groupings, with the Osttruppen under Lettow, based at Liwale, and the Westtruppen commanded by Tafel from Mahenge. They numbered an estimated 6,200 and 2,500 respectively, giving effective combat strengths of 4,100 and 1,500. Lettow's force was split into four main detachments; in the far south, Abt Looff had six companies and two guns between Lindi and the Portuguese border; Abt Göring, with seven companies and a gun, held the ground near Mpotora against Hanforce; Abt Otto had seven companies and a gun on the Rufiji; while Lettow retained direct control of six companies and four guns under his direct control, chiefly in the Mpotora-Liwale area.[26]

Tafel had three substantial Abteilungen radiating some 112 km west, north and east of Mahenge down to Likuju; Abt von Brandis with three companies was near Kidodi; Abt Aumann with three companies was along the Ruhudje River; Abt Lincke with five companies was facing the main body of Norforce. The marauding Abt Naumann of six companies had been long out of contact and was effectively an independent force.

PRELIMINARIES IN JUNE

As June progressed, the country began to dry up rapidly, which aided mobility but also caused many water sources to disappear. At Lindi, General O'Grady faced a difficult situation, as events of the previous month had shown that the enemy remained in good condition and full of fight. Equally, the new KAR battalions were short of experienced officers and NCOs, while the soldiers were largely newly trained recruits, untested in battle. Yet, they were expected to push the Germans some 8-10 km to the west, in a preliminary move to gain space as Lindi was an unhealthy coastal town ringed by high ground to the west and its creek to the east and south. His options were limited: there was the northern approach through the Ngurumahamba position or an advance up the Mohambika and Lukuledi valleys. The unsuccessful attack in April demonstrated the strength of the former's defences while the approach to the latter was hindered by the nearly 25 km of swamp that lined the rivers. To achieve this, he had about 2,000 effectives to face an estimated six companies of approximately 600 rifles which were believed to be mainly in the Ngurumahamba area.[27]

O'Grady was an aggressive leader and devised a bold scheme to resolve this difficulty. He proposed to launch a pincer movement with simultaneous advances by land and sea. One column would move out from the northern edges of the Lindi defences and march west for the Lutende Hills before turning south and heading for Naitiwi, thereby cutting off the Ngurumahamba position. At the same time, an amphibious force would sail 10 km up the Lindi Creek, landing two battalions east of Mingoyo. Once ashore, they would then march south-west before turning north-east towards the Mohambika River in order to cut the trolley line and link-up with the northern column.[28]

Key to the plan was the plantation trolley line that served the village of Mingoyo and inland. The water there was deep enough for ships to come within 2.5 km and lighters could then be used to offload supplies. The chief obstacles were the enemy positions on both banks of Lindi Creek supported a rail-mounted *Königsberg* gun. If spotted, it could easily destroy a landing force although the deep water also meant that British warships could provide direct fire support. In consultation with the Royal Navy, a night landing was ordered; a blacked-out force of boats and lighters would move past the German outposts at high tide before moonrise to land at the Kenjengehe pier. Once landed, two battalions would move initially south-west towards Mkwaya and then make the decisive turn north towards Mwreka.[29]

Detailed operational planning was backed up by extensive and realistic joint rehearsals. It was as well, for the Germans were considerably stronger than estimated; Abt Wahle actually had seven companies totalling over 900 rifles, sixteen machine guns and two guns. They were deployed as follows: Abt Looff with two companies was nearly 8 km south of the mouth of the Lukuledi near Namunda while Abt Kraut, with five companies, had three at the Ngurumahamba position and the remaining two companies at Majani in depth.[30]

Under strict secrecy, the operation commenced on the night of 10/11 June and the boats moved past the forward German posts without coming under serious fire. However, the movement was eventually detected and Wahle decided to converge on the river to meet the landing. Abt Looff was to march north and rejoin the main body while Kraut was to do the same, leaving only a single company on the Ngurumahamba position. The aim was to hit the British from two sides and to drive them back into the water.[31] By early evening the landings were underway, with O'Grady and Admiral Charlton in the lead motor boat. With the rising of the moon early on 11 June, the *Königsberg* gun had a lively engagement with HMS *Thistle* leading to a lively naval engagement.[32] Now sure that the landings were in earnest, Wahle ordered Kraut to attack the landing site with two companies.

However, by this time O'Grady's troops had pushed nearly 8 km inland with one regiment holding Tandamuti Hill, well to the south-west of Mrweka and another moving to the latter place. Both sides collided there after daybreak and a heavy engagement followed with the British being held on the south side of the Mohambika Valley. Unable to advance, each brought up reinforcements and attempted local flanking movements.[33] Wahle was handicapped by the non-appearance of Abt Looff from the

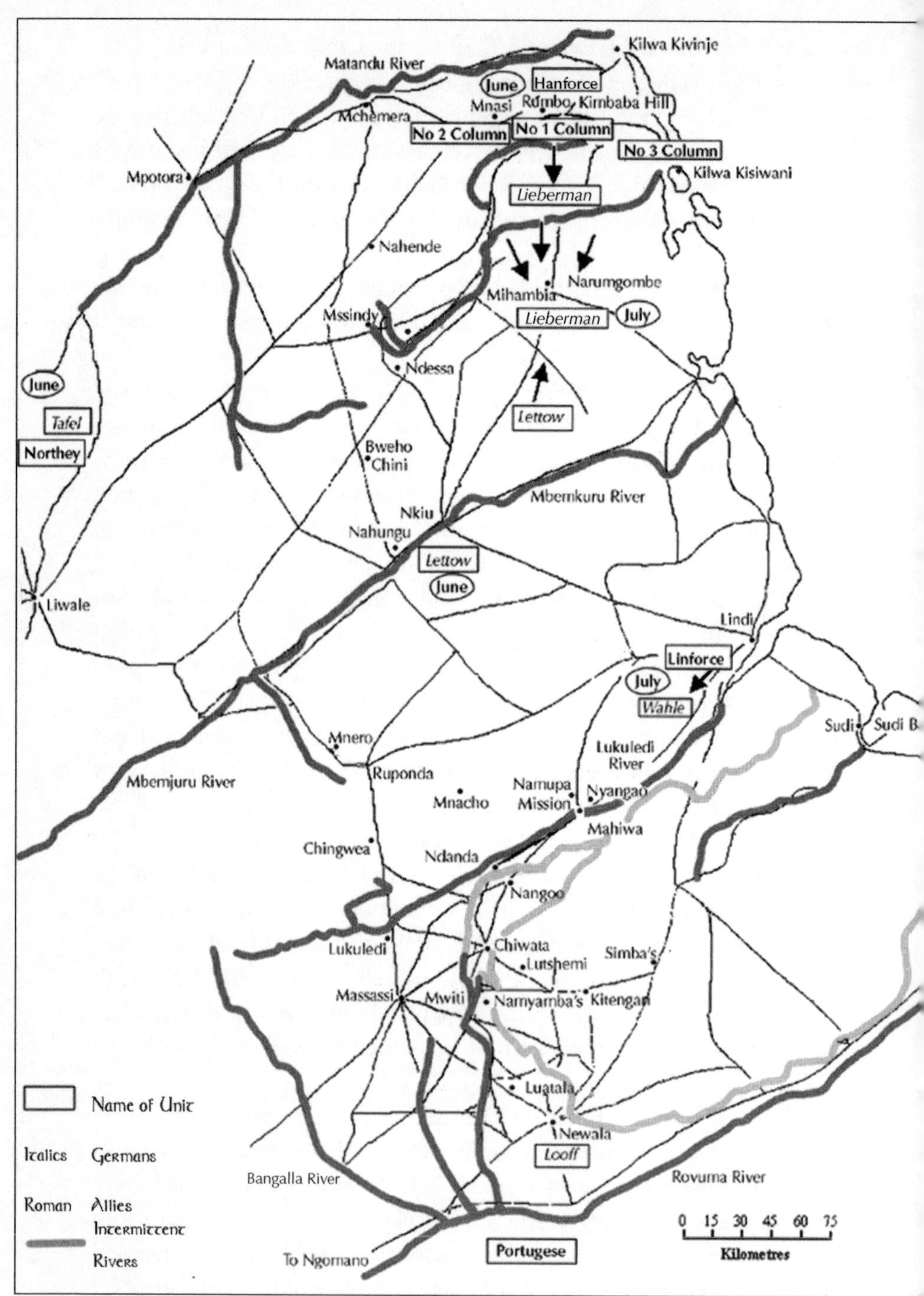

Van Deventer's initial advance from Kilwa and Lindi, June–July 1917

south, and in late afternoon he received the unwelcome news of the second, and hitherto undetected, British column in the north. After reaching the Lutende Hills, it had moved south and was now in possession of the key junction at Naitiwi. This immediately rendered the Ngurumahamba position untenable as well as threatening his forward forces concentrated at Mwreka. Wahle immediately ordered the evacuation of the position, sending his troops and baggage another 10 km back to Narunyu.

In turn, the British were surprised by the late appearance of Abt Looff near Tandamuti Hill. Their attack was thrown into disorder, but the damage had been done and the Germans continued their withdrawal. The Linforce now controlled the key approaches to Lindi and at relatively low cost although it was not decisive. The enemy had lost a great deal of stores and supplies, but had escaped while the new KAR battalions remained brittle. The British line was now established well inland and the Germans occupied the line Tandamuti Hill-Mohambika Valley-Schaedel's Farm, while the British faced them from positions along Mkwaya-Mrweka-Majani-Naitiwi. Both sides needed to regroup and operations in the Lindi area wound down.[34]

Elsewhere, British efforts to destabilise German rule were bearing fruit. Agents had supplied the Makonde people with arms and ammunition for use against their nominal overlords. This erupted into open revolt across the Makonde plateau as German food-gathering parties were attacked and harassed. Lettow now had to deal with the uprising that he had long dismissed. Two companies were sent to re-assert German rule there while another six companies were despatched to reinforce Wahle from the Kilwa front. Lettow himself set up his headquarters at Nahungo on 24 June with the intention of preventing a breakout from Lindi as well as attacking any detachment that that came into range. Moving to Lutende, he reconnoitred the forward area, hoping to find a chance of driving the British back to the sea. In this, he was aided by O'Grady's impatience at waiting for reinforcements. British patrols had detected activity around Lutende, but not its strength. On 30 June, O'Grady decided to send a half-battalion of Indian troops there, where they pushed out the defenders. But, this was quickly followed by a fierce counter-attack on the outnumbered Indians that drove them back in disorder and the German line was re-established. The reverse was sharp and salutary; several unsupported companies without artillery were always vulnerable and could achieve nothing substantial. After this minor success, Lettow concluded that a surprise attack on Linforce was impossible and that better chances were offered north in support of Abt von Liebermann. Marching with five companies and two batteries, he left on 9 July leaving Wahle to hold the Lindi area.[35]

Further north at Kilwa, General Beves, temporarily in command, recognised that the Germans might be forced to withdraw further inland before a decisive battle could be fought. Accordingly, he decided to launch a pre-emptive attack whilst the enemy was still in easy range of his own supply bases. He proposed to attack as soon as reinforcements had arrived, but without waiting for more transport. He saw the advantages in fighting close to his own base and trying to inflict heavy casualties as greater than the disadvantages of an immediate, prolonged advance thereafter. To that end, on 13 June, he asked GHQ for permission to divert a battalion from Lindi as O'Grady had already achieved his initial objectives and his own reinforcements were still in pursuit of Naumann. The commander-in-chief agreed and the latter increased the reinforcement to include a battery of the highly effective Stokes mortars.[36]

Beves' assessment proved to be correct as the Germans had begun to evacuate their forward positions at the end of June. Patrols located them in the Kiturika Hills, still within range of the force's logistical and operational range. As the South African reinforcements began to arrive earlier than anticipated, he organised three columns for the advance. No 1 had four battalions, eight guns and eight Stokes mortars; No 2 had three battalions, six guns and four Stokes mortars; and No 3, under Colonel Taylor, had about a battalion. His plan was to converge on the enemy's positions near Mchakama, and bring him to battle while attempting to cut off his retreat to the west. He faced a substantial force, as Lettow had left Abt von Liebermann some ten companies and two guns to hold the area.[37]

General Hannyngton, now out of hospital, decided to use the main columns in a converging movement from the north, while the third, smaller column under Colonel Taylor would march south-west from Kilwa, cutting off the southern escape route. Leaving its jumping-off point after dark on 6 July, No 1 Column marched south-west for 11 km, before linking up with its forward reconnaissance elements. While these troops attacked the next morning in the thickly wooded positions, No 2 Column was engaged in an arduous approach march from the north-west. The attack was successful and a flanking movement by No 1 Column forced the Germans to retire to Mtshikama and the two columns linked up the next day.[38]

For their part, the Belgian Brigade Nord was doggedly pursuing Abt Naumann but was hindered by difficulties in obtaining supplies and lack of intelligence. The small and mobile German column was living off the land and had a sufficient start to elude its pursuers. Finally, as the enemy reached the southern shores of Lake Victoria, the Belgians caught up. On 29 June, in conjunction with a small British column from the north, they brought the Germans to battle at Ikoma. The attackers ran into well-sited defences and lacked the numbers to break through, suffering a large number of casualties in the process. This gave Naumann his chance to escape and he immediately turned south, headed towards Kondoa Irangi and the Central Railway. After the setback, and at the end of very long supply lines, the Belgians had to pause for a few days before resuming the chase.[39]

THE ADVANCE BEGINS

With forward positions established, Hannyngton then spent a few days preparing for the main effort and reconnoitring the ground. An initial move forward by No 3 Column on 17 July persuaded the Germans to move some 16 km further south to Narungombe which had an important set of water holes. Securing water was essential to Hannyngton's plans as the intermediate sources at Kihumburo, about 10 km to the north, were less certain. The next day the main move began with Colonel Orr commanding Nos 1 and 3 Columns for the planned fight at Narungombe; he had to win or be faced with returning to Kihumburo, and, if its water proved to be insufficient, then a move even further back might be necessary.

Late in the day, the leading troops bivouacked about 3.2 km short of Narungombe, which was believed to have eight companies and two guns around the water pool with the possibility of reinforcements arriving from the south. Now given No 2 Column as well, Orr planned to use No 1 Column to engage the enemy from the front while No 2 moved against the enemy's left flank and No 3 on his right flank. A bombardment by mountain guns and Stokes mortars would commence as soon as daylight permitted. He was unaware that Abt von Liebermann had positioned itself across the road with its right flank secured by a substantial swamp and the left by a hill covered in virtually impenetrable bamboo and bush. The approaches had been carefully cleared and were backed by three sets of trenches and rifle pits over an 1,800-metre frontage.[40]

Early on 19 July, the attack went in, but progress was slow. The two flanking columns were more successful than the frontal one, with No 3 Column making good progress on the right. After several heavy counter-attacks, Orr made an all-out effort to break through the defences. But a crisis emerged when a newly raised KAR battalion in No 3 broke and the column was nearly overwhelmed. After much bitter fighting, a final push on the left by No 2 Column broke into the defences and relieved the pressure. Unable to progress further and unwilling to give up their gains, the British dug in for the night preparatory for another attempt in the morning.[41]

Liebermann had suffered heavy casualties and was very short of ammunition. Believing himself unable to hold further, he used the cover of darkness to evacuate the position and fall back to Mihambia. There, he met an irate Lettow, who had arrived with reinforcements and was indignant at the loss of the most important position for many kilometres. It was too late, for Orr had occupied Narungombe in strength at first light. He too had incurred many losses and now had to clear the battlefield of wounded. Water continued to be a concern and No 2 Column had to be sent back 19 km to a more plentiful source of water. Nevertheless, it was a victory for Hanforce.

Narungombe was one of the hardest fights of the campaign and one of the first in which the Germans had been fought rather than manoeuvred out of position. It underlined the importance of water sources as tactical objectives as well as the Schutztruppe's weaknesses in ammunition and manpower. It also underlined the fragility of the new KAR battalions as they still lacked experienced troops and leaders.[42]

With Narungombe secure, Hannyngton took the next week in readying for his next move, which would be on Mssindy, some 16 km further south-west. On 28 July, No 2 Column moved towards that place and, despite a number of encounters, occupied it. This meant that he had a second well-watered jumping-off point from which to conduct a further move. The rate of advance was tempered by the need for patrols to locate water sources and roads, as well as finding the enemy and disrupt his supply system. A flight of aircraft set up base at Mssindy and were joined by an Indian cavalry regiment, who immediately began raiding the enemy lines of communication, often with considerable success. Another method was the deliberate setting of bush fires, so as to clear the vegetation concealing the German defences.[43]

In the meantime, O'Grady proposed that Linforce advance along the road running from Lindi to Massassi, in order to cut off Lettow's escape route. Believing that the Germans would not hold Liwale but would fall back to Massassi and thence into Portuguese East Africa, he pushed for an initial advance along the road as far as Mahiwa, with a subsequent move onward to Massassi. This proposal fit in well with van Deventer's own plans and would complement Hanforce's push south. He sent substantial reinforcements in the form of three infantry battalions, a mountain battery and the Stokes mortar battery to join Linforce. Nonetheless, it took until the end of July to ferry all the troops and the vital carriers from Dar-es-Salaam into Lindi while reconnaissance was underway.[44]

NORFORCE

Norforce used most of June to prepare itself for the arduous moves ahead. Colonel Murray's column had completed its epic march back to Nyasaland, and after a week's rest, it moved by steamer to Wiedhafen on 25 June. Murray then moved up to Songea where he assumed command of the reserve force there, reinforced by a Rhodesian battalion. Furthermore, with his South African battalions almost ineffective through sickness, Northey disbanded them and converted the remaining personnel into Lewis gunners. They were then distributed amongst the new African battalions to provide additional firepower and experience. With the return of Murray's troops Norforce was stronger, but the advancing columns were hardly overwhelming. The Likuju column under Colonel Stevens had about 900 rifles as compared to Lincke's 600, while Carbutt's 650 men faced 350 of Aumann's Mpepo and Shorthose's 700 were ranged against Stuemer's 400.[45]

In the centre, Stevens' preparations were nearly upset by the enemy. Abt Lincke, with four companies and a battery near Likuju, was unaware of the scale of the British build-up. Ordered to attack the British camp on 28 June, Lincke launched a strong assault that surprised Stevens. The defenders held their ground and the Germans broke off the attack just in time to escape encirclement from two nearby British columns that were preparing for their own advance. Once the danger was over, all converged on Likuju for rest and final preparations.[46]

While these preparations were underway, Tafel was trying to increase his own reserves at Mahenge. Supply problems had forced him to disperse his forces and this meant that it took two to three days for a message to reach him with a similar period required to pass the information back to headquarters.[47] With an offensive expected daily, he needed to be able to react to the enemy's main thrust quickly and he could not afford to wait a week to receive instructions. A stronger reserve would weaken the forward fighting strength, but would allow him to reinforce threatened sectors. He was faced by a difficult situation and would have to rely on his subordinate commanders.

Norforce began its advance on 2 July with the aim of locating and destroying Abt Lincke. It was located the next day, some 37 km from Likuju, at the important track junction linking Songea-Liwale and Songea-Mahenge. A KAR battalion was ordered to attack, while the remainder of Murray's Rhodesians arrived at Songea, completing the arduous return march. The enveloping move took a few days to develop as the deep ravines and densely vegetated valleys were difficult to negotiate. Finally, with the encirclement complete on the night of 6/7 July, the Germans hastily evacuated their very strong position, leaving behind a considerable amount of equipment. Escaping with a number of casualties, they made good use of darkness and some newly cut bush paths. Lincke himself was evacuated sick to Mahenge and command devolved onto Poppe.[48]

The advance continued although Poppe moved unexpectedly north rather than towards Liwale. He was short of food and was engaged in delaying tactics, taking care not to become decisively engaged. Already the leading troops were beginning to outpace the supply columns, as previously ordered motor vehicles had still not arrived. In the meantime, much further south, Shorthose's battalion was closing in on Mwembe, some 240 km north-west of Fort Johnston, preparatory to attacking Abt von Stuemer there. After ambushing a German patrol on 5 July, the battalion attacked Mwembe the next day and drove out the defenders.[49]

On his northern flank, a smaller force under Colonel Carbutt of about 650 was preparing to move on Mpepo against Abt Aumann, which was estimated to have 350 rifles and five machine guns. This move was intended to draw off any German reinforcements for Mahenge and thereby assist the Belgian advance further north from Iringa. Norforce also made maximum use of the slender air resources available. With one aircraft based at Likuju and another pushed forward to Mwembe, they were constantly engaged in reconnoitring and bombing enemy positions. Supply dumps, usually based in highly flammable grass huts, were a favoured target and several successes were achieved. With the advance going well, Northey convinced van Deventer that he should abandon the advance on Liwale in favour of Mpondas, so as to concentrate on destroying the enemy rather than seizing ground. Although the Belgian build-up was going slowly, Northey's request to continue the simultaneous drives against Abt Aumann in the north and Abt von Stuemer in the south were approved.[50]

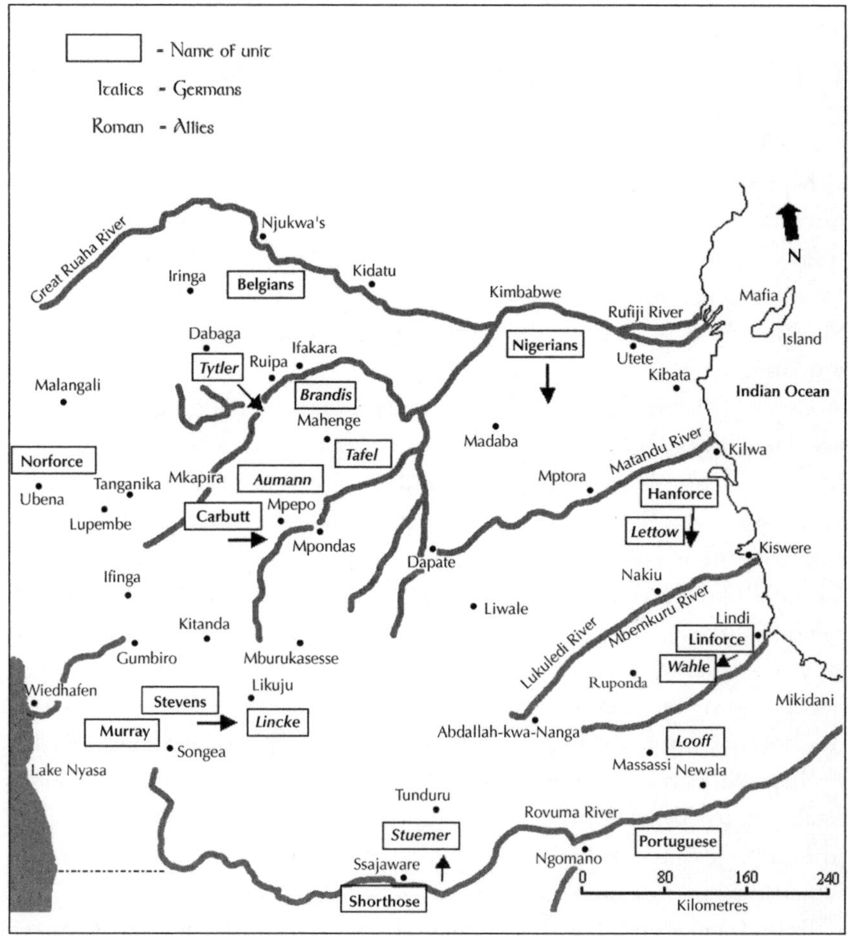

Norforce pushes east, July 1917

By the middle of the month, Norforce was fully engaged in all three areas, pushing back the various enemy detachments. On 15 July, the welcome news of the arrival of the first Belgian contingent at Iringa was received although tempered ten days later by learning that they would not take over the Lupembe-Mpepo sector as previously agreed. As recompense, van Deventer promised to send another KAR battalion from Iringa to Northey although this was little comfort to the widely-spread Norforce. Further to the north, the column now commanded by Colonel Fair had forced back Abt Aumann between Mpepo and Mkapira on the right bank of the River Ruhudje by 26 July, but lacked the strength for an all-out attack.[51]

At the beginning of August, General Northey remained highly concerned about the dispersion of his force which, despite having nearly 4,000 effectives, was split in five columns over a front of 480 km. This, and the need to cover Mpepo, meant that he was unable to concentrate on Tunduru in the south. In the north, Fair's troops had invested Abt Aumann at Mpepo with heavy, but indecisive firing occurring. The main column under Stevens had advanced steadily and fought a number of minor, but time-consuming, rearguard actions to bring it within 5 km from Mpondas, where Abt Lincke was heavily fortified. More positively, Shorthose's column was making good progress moving north against Abt von Stuemer.[52]

Unhappy with events, Northey arranged for a meeting with Sheppard, van Deventer's CGS, on 16 August in order to discuss future operations face to face. There, they resolved a number of issues and agreed that a rapid advance by Hanforce and Linforce would be necessary to end the campaign. In the meantime, the resolution of the crisis in Nyasaland enabled Colonel Hawthorn to return north and assume command of the column opposite Lincke. There was more good news as Shorthose had cleared almost 400 km of Portuguese territory, having outmanoeuvred his opponent, crossing the rapidly flowing and crocodile-infested Rovuma without boats by improvising rafts and ropes out of tree bark and grass. Finally, he held Murray's column and the lines of communicationn in reserve, unable to use them as intended on Tunduru. He also retained three battalions in Nyasaland partly for security, but mainly to continue their training which was still not highly advanced.[53]

Both Lincke and Aumann launched counter-attacks at Mpondas and Mpepo respectively on 22 August. Both were easily held, but it was apparent that the stubborn resistance there was being used to cover the withdrawal of the forces north of Mahenge. Northey was now instructed to attack both places until they had fallen while also denying the enemy the Tunduru district and any attempted re-entry of Portuguese East Africa. Shorthose duly took Tunduru in a daring move the next day while Fair continued to tighten the encirclement at Mpepo. Aumann decided to evacuate during the night of 27/28 August, but a hot pursuit followed in which the Germans suffered heavily, with nearly a third of their force as casualties. By the end of the month, Norforce had inflicted significant losses on the Westtruppen, with twenty-two Germans and 241 Askaris being confirmed casualties and three guns taken.[54] August had brought success at relatively low cost.

STRATEGIC POLICY

As van Deventer's offensive rolled on, the shipping crisis continued to mount. The War Cabinet was urgently reviewing the tonnage needed to sustain the overseas theatres and the possibility of making reductions. By early July, of the 328 ships employed in these duties, East Africa took up thirty-five representing about 11% of the total. However, its need represented 34% of troop and horse-carrying ships and 22% of hospital ships. With an estimated shortfall of 8 million tons for the year, every ship was needed.[55] The War Cabinet noted:

> The urgent necessity of clearing up the position in East Africa once and for all, and the fact that the conduct of operations by us in that quarter was monopolising the carrying power of thirty-five ships, were [sic] pointed out. It was agreed that, in order that the campaign in this quarter might be brought to a close at the earliest possible moment, every reinforcement that it was found possible to send to General Van Deventer should be sent to enable him to do this.[56]

However, as long as East Africa remained an active theatre, its demands could not be reduced below a minimum level. Equally, van Deventer's plea for more artillery and other reinforcements was only met by the sending of a single mounted regiment and, while useful, it could hardly transform the situation in East Africa.[57] The government faced a dilemma; it could not cut shipping without finishing the campaign and it could not finish the campaign without adequate shipping. East Africa was a drain on resources, but not important enough to justify substantial additional effort.

Anglo-Belgian relations also began to fray as July progressed. The chief reason was the lack of British troops in the Iringa area and the slow arrival of planned Belgian reinforcements. In the interests of expediency, one battalion was under direct British command and the various columns were interposed.[58] This violated the earlier agreement that the British would allocate the Belgians a distinct zone of operations in which their commander-in-chief would have full operational responsibility. Now under pressure from his government, Colonel Huyghé sought to resolve this dispute as well as details of supply and transport. A conference was arranged at the British GHQ in Dar-es-Salaam from 20-23 July 1917.

It was finally agreed that Mahenge would remain the immediate Belgian objective. To that end, the Colonne Hubert, presently en route from Iringa to the Ulanga Valley, was instructed to reinforce Colonel Tytler's column along the line of the River Ruipa. The Brigade Sud, having concentrated at Uleia was then to advance to Kidatu and start preparations to cross the River Ruaha. Once in position, Tytler was to withdraw his column and Hubert was to come under Belgian orders once again. It was also agreed that the British-installed telegraph line would be turned over to the Belgians.[59]

As ever the question of transport loomed large, with the British agreeing to supply foodstuffs and that their mechanical transport would move supplies forward from the railheads at Dodoma and Kilossa to the forward line of the Ruipa. From there, the supplies would be moved forward by British carriers and mules. Owing to a shortage of Belgian personnel, the British agreed also to provide overseers to supervise Belgian-recruited carriers. For their part, the Belgians agreed to take responsibility for the roads in the forward area as well as bridging the many rivers en route, with the greatest being the requirement to allow eight-tonne vehicles to cross the Ruaha and Ulanga rivers. As these were, respectively, 21 metres wide and 3 metres deep and 91 metres wide and 6 metres deep, they represented a major task.[60]

THE ADVANCE IN AUGUST 1917

In the east, Lettow kept a strong force at Mihambia where it could easily reinforce either Liwale or Massassi, with strong columns opposite both

Hanforce and Linforce. The British were still unsure as to his ultimate intentions; whereas he had initially appeared to be headed for Portuguese East Africa, he now appeared to be staying in the Mahenge-Liwale area. Furthermore, they believed that the reinforced and aggressive operations from Lindi would draw him in and that resistance would be substantial. Norforce would impede any escape to the south, as it had cleared Abt von Stuemer from Portuguese territory before occupying Tunduru. He also planned to reintroduce a reformed South African mounted regiment into the tsetse fly-free areas in the south.[61]

Van Deventer paid a personal visit to Lindi in early August, conferring at length with O'Grady and setting out his policy for a further advance. O'Grady was a good commander, but inclined to be impetuous. On 4 August, he had launched an attack that had been violently thrown back with heavy casualties, with one Indian regiment losing over 250 men. The commander-in-chief ordered that he carry out detailed reconnaissances of the enemy positions and to avoid frontal attack on the well-defended positions at Tandamuti Hill. He wanted to ford the Lukuledi River so as to turn the defences, before hitting them hard. For this mission, O'Grady was given substantial reinforcements together with a large number of individual replacement officers and NCOs and eight new Lewis guns per battalion.[62]

O'Grady decided to concentrate his troops into two mobile columns of 1,200 each with only a weak garrison left in Lindi. Colonel Taylor's column would assemble at Mkwaya to make the outflanking march and to seize a position on the German line of retreat while O'Grady would launch the main attack. Scheduled for 9 August, the offensive began with aerial bombing of Tandamuti Hill as a diversion while Taylor crossed the Lukuledi near Mkwaya, halting overnight. The next morning all the available guns, including the two monitors, opened up on Tandamuti Hill as O'Grady's column marched west, hoping to cut off the retreat of the defenders. Opposition was slight, but the dense bush made for slow going and it was not until dusk on 10 August that the leading battalion reached the trolley line before digging in for the night. In the meantime, Taylor's column had continued on to its objective, a point 1.6 km east of Narunyu, and began to entrench itself. Now they waited for the Germans to break out. But, only one probe was launched and the remainder of the defenders had moved back to the trolley line at Narunyu.[63]

The first phase a success, O'Grady now had to operate outside of the ships' gun range and sickness was beginning to rise. The Narunyu position now had to be taken, but it was formidable with the southern side protected by wide and impassable swamps and the eastern face largely covered in a dense sisal plantation. It offered a small stretch of open ground, but the Germans had placed a sisal abattis in front of the trenches. A steep escarpment and thick bush added to the strength of the defences. Only in the north was the country was more open and held the possibility of a flank approach. O'Grady decided to take this option and issued orders for the move on 13 August. However, continuous heavy rainfall forced the postponement of the attack until the evening of 17 August.

Lettow had been active and had left Mihambia with five companies on 3 August once he had heard of the attack on Tandamuti Hill. He had: 'decided to join General Wahle with some of the companies from Ndessa and perhaps bring off the operation that had failed at Narungombe; a decisive success by an unexpected reinforcement'.[64] Marching hard, he had linked up with Wahle and was in position by 18 August. The dispositions were: Abt Kraut on the right with three companies; Abt Rothe on the left with two companies; and Abt von Chappuis with two more in reserve. Further back, Lettow kept two companies under his own control.

O'Grady's plan involved making a feint towards the marshes to the south coupled with an artillery bombardment of the main position to cover the move of the main body to the north.[65] He detached a single battalion to hold the line and make the demonstration against the marshes while the two columns made their flanking move. Taylor left before dark on 17 August, followed by O'Grady. After halting for the night, the advance was resumed before dawn the next day along a compass bearing. Emerging onto a newly made road, the lead battalion pushed back a series of outposts. Using the road as a new axis, progress was impeded by the surrounding bush which became almost impassably thick. Moving slowly now, the lead elements reached a small collection of huts held by elements of Abt Kraut that afternoon. A brisk fire-fight secured the position, but increased firing from the bush induced the battalion to halt and dig-in until reinforcements arrived. This proved to be a wise precaution as German reinforcements continued to arrive through the afternoon. Wahle, having already committed one company in the morning, sent in his last reserve at 1500 hours but it was unable to make significant headway owing to the heavy fire. Taylor pushed his troops forward as quickly as possible and by 1600 both his battalions were facing an enemy outflanking movement. Owing to the ground, he pulled back about 600 yards, just as

Lettow arrived with his two companies. A heavy close-range battle raged through the night and each side held their own. Finally, Lettow broke off the firing and ordered Wahle to hold his existing positions and to reform an adequate reserve.[66]

While this confused fighting was underway, O'Grady's column was still following Taylor's, but encountering numerous enemy patrols. He pushed through early on 19 August, to find that Abt Wahle had withdrawn less than a kilometre to the west and was strongly entrenched, supported by the fire of a *Königsberg* gun. It was clear that Lettow and substantial reinforcements had arrived. The balance of forces had changed materially and Linforce was continually losing troops from sickness. For the time being, a further advance was out of the question. O'Grady pulled back Taylor's column from its exposed forward position and established defences with a strong reserve back on the Lukuledi River. Linforce now went over to the defensive until support could be obtained from Hanforce, still further north.[67]

Meanwhile, in the north Abt Naumann remained a threat although it was gradually losing strength. It had reached the Kilimanjaro area in late August and threatened to enter British East Africa. Finally, faced by reinforcements moved hastily by rail, it turned south again. Van Deventer had reinforced the Belgians with a battalion plus mounted infantry who began to outpace the raiders. Wishing to speed up the Belgian concentration further south, on 12 August he made the elimination of the Germans a solely British responsibility.[68]

VAN DEVENTER DRIVES SOUTH

In early September, General van Deventer issued instructions to his principal commanders. He believed that the Schutztruppe's powers of resistance were weakening and that one or two serious reverses would bring the end of the campaign nearer. He wanted to avoid frontal attacks as they were usually slow, costly and indecisive. Instead, he expected columns to seize positions in the enemy's flanks and rear and to defend them so as to force the Germans to counter-attack under unfavourable conditions. These methods were to be supplemented by extensive reconnaissance through long-range patrols, aerial observation and the Intelligence Scouts. He recognised that transport would be the critical limiting factor, but wanted operations to be continuous and place relentless pressure on the enemy. By making great sacrifices now, he hoped to draw the campaign to an end within two or three months.[69]

With the various columns having to pause briefly, van Deventer and Hugyhé met at Dar-es-Salaam from 6-9 September to discuss the next phase of operations. The good news was that, after much dogged pursuit and effort, a significant element of Abt Naumann had surrendered on 2 September. The use of mounted troops had helped to trap the tired force which was also faced with a serious lack of supplies.[70] The main limitation was the coming rainy season in December that would make communications between Kilossa and Mahenge virtually impossible. Van Deventer proposed to reduce the garrison of the latter to a minimum and to return the bulk of the Belgian forces to the railway. Huyghé was opposed to this idea as his forces were now at maximum strength and the carriers recruited in the Belgian Congo were moving forward to the front. Faced with such opposition, the plan was shelved and a modified directive issued.

It was agreed that the Belgians would take Mahenge in conjunction with Hanforce moving south on Nahungu, Linforce advancing towards Massassi and Norforce pushing towards Mpondas and Liwale. Once the Belgians had taken Mahenge, they would establish a blocking position from Mpondas to the River Luwegu in order to prevent any enemy breakout to the west. Concurrently, they would prepare to send a substantial force to occupy the rich food-growing area around Liwale. Should the combined actions prove insufficient to wind-up the fighting before December, then Huyghé was to be ready for a further campaign operating either from Ifakara on the Central Railway or possibly from Liwale or Kilwa. Van Deventer ended by urging them to bring the Germans to battle as speedily as possible.[71]

To that end, Tytler's column would only remain in the area of the River Ruipa until the Brigade Sud could move forward from Kilossa and start preparations for the crossing of the River Ruaha. The Colonne Hubert, which was presently en route from Iringa towards Makuas-Mpanga to reinforce Tytler, would remain in the area and rejoin the Belgian main body on arrival.[72]

These plans were also influenced by the arrival of the fourth commander-in-chief of the Portuguese forces, Colonel Thomas de Sousa Rosa, on 12 September. Like his predecessors, Rosa was a newcomer to colonial campaigning and seems to have been selected on account of his political leanings.[73] He faced a number of serious problems, the most immediate of which was the unhealthiness of the main base at Mocimboa da Praia. Sanitation was woefully inadequate and the newly landed troops quickly went ill. He had insufficient transport to sustain an advance and many soldiers lacked adequate training. The inland road network was much improved, but still needed work in many parts. The continuing Makombe rebellion in the south and the support given to Stuemer's troops showed that the African population was strongly hostile to the Portuguese presence.

The British had no faith in Portuguese capabilities as their liaison officer had sent a series of warnings about their allies' lack of effective leadership, low morale and weakness in defensive preparations. Van Deventer wanted them to remain strictly on the defensive along the Rovuma line. While sensible, it offended Rosa's pride as he wanted to take the offensive and strike into German territory. He was deeply unhappy about having to remain in the unhealthy valley of the Rovuma as he saw it both inglorious and detrimental to the spirit for his troops. But, as his own government had subordinated him to the British, there was little that he could do. Indeed, the possibility of moving Belgian troops into Portuguese East Africa was quietly examined by Colonel Huyghé. A covert reconnaissance of the harbour and facilities of Mocimboa da Praia was carried out by the naval authorities, but the project died quietly.[74]

Portuguese dissatisfaction was reflected in their pressure for Northey's troops to be withdrawn from Mwembe as soon as the enemy had been pushed out.[75] Well aware of the unhappy relations between the two headquarters, the British GHQ decided to send its French liaison officer, Colonel Viala, on a mission to the Portuguese commander-in-chief. Van Deventer hoped that, as a representative of an Allied power, Viala might be able to build bridges and gain information. Informally, his aim was to divine Rosa's plans and the intentions of the Portuguese as well the extent of his transport problems. Importantly, he was also to ascertain whether the direct support of British or Belgian troops would be acceptable. It was a highly unusual method of liaison, but as General Sheppard stated:

> The Portuguese are probably less suspicious of the French than ourselves, and I think VIALA's visit will have excellent results, for he is a first class fellow, and very keen on helping on the campaign in any way possible.[76]

The initiative proved to be a success and Viala's visit, together with the professionalism of the British Intelligence Scouts operating south of the Rovuma, had made a favourable impression on Colonel Rosa. But, this was double-edged as he now proposed to lead a three-pronged advance into German East Africa towards Newala. These ambitions worried both van Deventer and Northey as they were highly pessimistic about the chances of success.[77] The former officer appealed to London for help in quashing such ideas:

> I think that the Portuguese proposals if carried out will be fatal. The Portuguese troops well entrenched on the line of the ROVUMA may possibly be able to prevent a thrust on the left between them on the part of the enemy but in the open field they have no chance whatever against the Germans… I shall be most grateful therefore for any assistance you can give in this matter. The Portuguese are most touchy and I cannot force my opinions for fear of giving offence.[78]

The tactlessness of the Portuguese liaison officer at GHQ, who was thought to be ill-disposed towards Rosa, did not help and Viala had to smooth matters over. For his part, Rosa used Viala as a conduit for trying to convince van Deventer of the need for a Portuguese offensive as well as raising the African tribes in revolt.[79]

HANFORCE PUSHES SOUTH TO THE LUKULEDI

By the middle of September the time was ripe again for the advance; both the Kilwa and Lindi forces had been substantially reinforced and motor transport was now available to the entire force. Van Deventer wished to push Hanforce south with a concurrent move south-westerly by Linforce; his aim was to catch the German main body whatever course of action it took. The western troops, both British and Belgian, were to carry on aggressively in order to contain the troops in the Mahenge area.[80]

While the advancing columns were pushing hard against the Schutztruppe in German East Africa, British intelligence had gathered much useful information about the strength and state of morale from the Portuguese side of the border. Captured prisoners revealed that at the end of July some 1,800 Europeans remained in the field, of whom some 300 were sick and another 600 were employed on the lines of communication,

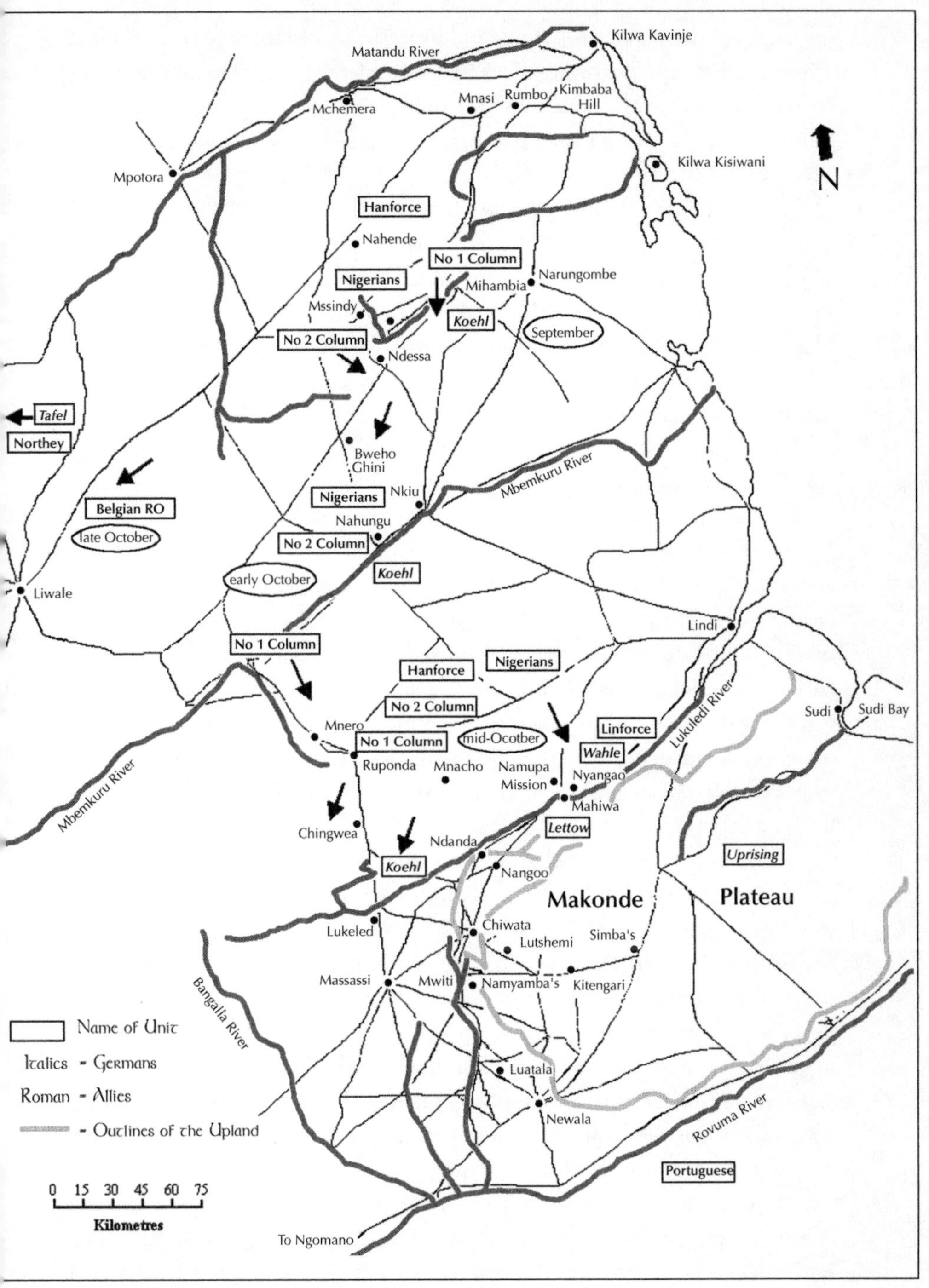

Van Deventer's advance to the Lukuledi, September–October 1917

leaving less than 1,000 in the front-line units; morale remained good.[81] This information was supplemented a week later by intelligence showing that resistance would continue and that German morale was being sustained by the reports of the enormous Allied shipping losses and Lettow's own personality.[82]

Reinforced with the Nigerian Brigade and Colonel Dyke's reserve brigade, Force HQ was well forward, co-located at Mssindy with the bulk of its units. It faced two enemy groupings, with the larger at Ndessa facing No 2 Column and the weaker at Mihambia opposite No 1 Column. The plan was to use the two columns to turn out the defenders from their strong positions, while the Nigerians were used to make a deep outflanking move to cut off their retreat to the River Mbemkuru. The greatest problem was the lack of water and the need to find, secure and develop suitable sources – as ever the best positions were usually defended.

The Nigerian Brigade had been moving forward for some time, reaching Kilwa in September and then marching the 130 km to Mssindy. Leaving the latter place on 18 September, it was given the intermediate task of developing water sources some 32 km to the south-west. The rest of Hanforce started the next day with No 1 Column moving towards Mihambia and a small flanking force making for Nitshi, some 19 km south-west. No 1 Column reached its objective and, despite the presence of unexpected depth defences, it outflanked the defenders and the all-important waterholes were secured. The next day was less successful and as it appeared unlikely that Nitshi and its water supply could be reached, Orr was ordered to return to Mihambia on 21 September.

The Nigerians continued to press south, trying to find the track that led to the Mbemkuru River before the opposition arrived.[83] On 22 September, the small village of Bweho Chini was reached, and after a short, sharp fight, was hastily occupied. As this lay directly on the most probable escape route to Nahungu, the brigade closed up and began preparing its defences. A strong reconnaissance force of two companies was sent out to the north-east, but hardly had it left Bweho Chini than it was heavily engaged and nearly cut off. At the same time, a strong attack was launched against the eastern side of the hastily dug perimeter. The advanced force managed to fight its way back to the boma, having suffered heavy losses, while the German attack intensified. Charges were led against the northern and eastern faces of the defences and patrols were probing the other sides. By 1700 hours, the brigade was encircled and heavily engaged on all sides. Fighting was fierce and, just before sundown, a very strong attack, supported by heavy machine gun and rifle fire, crashed into the defences. The defenders just held and then a company counter-attack with fixed bayonets drove back the Germans. During the night a lull developed, and the time was used to collect the wounded, improve the trenches and to coral the frightened carriers. Ammunition was beginning to run short and there was no sign of the other columns.

The battle was resumed at 2130 hours by moonlight and continued throughout the evening. A number of attacks followed and firing continued, but the main impetus had been lost so that by midnight the action had been reduced to sniping while the attackers collected their dead and wounded. At dawn, it became clear that the battle was over and the Germans had broken up into small parties, moving toward Nahungu. Considerable stores and ammunition were left behind while patrols later rounded up a number of stragglers. Pursuit was impossible owing to the lack of food and water, while the remaining porters were insufficient to carry either the wounded or first line supplies. Finally, the dead had to be collected and buried; a task that lasted all day.

In the meantime, No 2 Column and Dyke's reserve column were moving on Ndessa. In order to avoid a full-frontal assault, Dyke and elements of No 2 Column would attack from the north, while the bulk of No 2 Column would move around the position to cut off escape to the west and south-west. With only 1,400 rifles and four guns to cover a frontage of over 6 km, it was not an easy task against a well-prepared enemy. Colonel Ridgway decided to use new tactics to force the enemy into counter-attacks on the ground of his choosing. This entailed cutting a new road about 5 km west of Ndessa by a flanking force. Protected by a small garrison, the remainder of the column marched up this track and then fanned out in the direction of the enemy. The battalions then began constructing a thorn boma as silently as possible. Finally, after four and a half hours of marching and construction, the defences were ready and artillery opened up on the defences. The frontal fixing attack had the desired effect and the Germans attempted to withdraw to the west where they soon ran into the newly made boma. They launched a series of heavy assaults throughout the night of 21/22 September, but were repeatedly repulsed. Finally, they moved past No 2 Column, having had to abandon a large number of stores and equipment. Ndessa was now in British hands and the Germans continued to move south-east.[84]

Elsewhere, No 1 Column was experiencing difficulties in developing water supplies and getting sufficient rations forward. Nevertheless, it pressed on with two days of hard marching in hot sun with little food. By 24 September, the whole of No 1 Column was in Bweho Chini and had linked up with the battered Nigerians. The wounded were evacuated up the road to Mihambia and the troops marched off to Bweho Juu and rejoined the rest of the brigade. It had been a severe test for both sides, but the Nigerians had retained the field of battle.[85]

The loss of Ndessa and Mihambia forced the Abt Köhl to fall back rapidly on Nahungu, leaving behind ammunition and food stores. With the momentum firmly with Hanforce, on 25 September No 2 Column went was sent south towards Nakiu on the Mbemkuru while No 1 Column and the Nigerian Brigade pressed south-west to Nahungu. At the same time, a cavalry regiment was sent off to attack and destroy various food depots along the enemy lines of communication, linked only by wireless and aircraft. On 27 September, Nahungu was reached and surrounded by the columns. It was attacked and fell into Hanforce's hands two days later. The line of the Mbemkuru had been reached and now it was time to push south to the Lukuledi and join up with Linforce.[86] Van Deventer had reason to be pleased, as Hanforce had advanced rapidly and retained good morale while a great deal of food-producing areas had been denied to the opposition. He now decided to send the Nigerians south on a flanking move to Ruponda and the Lukuledi in order to reinforce O'Grady while maintaining direct pressure on Köhl.

By 1 October, Köhl had retired to a strong position at Ngambururu, some 24 km to the south-west of Nahungu. With increasing problems of communication and looking for a success, Lettow marched five companies north from Massassi to reinforce his beleaguered subordinate. This was timely as both No 1 and 2 Columns continued to push south, with the former reaching Ruponda on 11 October and the latter engaging the Ngambururu position. Repeating its road-building tactics and supplemented by aircraft reconnaissance, No 2 Column forced Köhl to abandon his position and withdraw again. He was also hampered by Lettow's decision to return to the Lukuledi in search of the decisive victory that he continually sought.[87]

By 10 October, Hanforce was forced to halt, as it had outrun its lines of supply. Both columns had to be recalled to Ruponda and Ruangwa respectively so as to build-up sufficient stocks of food. Sickness, particularly of drivers, was taking its toll, while the shortage of water was a major constraint to the next phase of the advance.[88] The Belgians had taken Mahenge and were now in the process of advancing towards Liwale, while one battalion had landed at Kilwa and cut a road from Mssindy to Liwale before joining its comrades. The Portuguese, too, resolved to help, through the despatch of three columns across the Rovuma towards Newala.[89] On 17 October, No 2 Column had driven Abt Köhl back to Mkoe while No 1 Column had reached Chingwea, en route for Lukuledi Mission.

LINFORCE ADVANCES UP THE LUKULEDI

If Hanforce was making good progress, the same was not true of Linforce. It had been on the defensive since 21 August, using the time to rest and reorganise. However, van Deventer was anxious to take Narunyu and decided to send reinforcements in early September. Major General Beves was appointed commander and arrived at Lindi on 9 September. His retained a main striking force of two brigade-sized columns, commanded by Brigadier General O'Grady and Colonel Taylor, to be known as No 3 and 4 Columns respectively. O'Grady had three battalions totalling 1,300 rifles, seventeen machine guns, eighteen Lewis guns, two mountain guns and four Stokes mortars, while Taylor commanded four battalions and a machine-gun company with 1,250 rifles, twenty-nine machine guns, twenty-nine Lewis guns, four mountain guns, and four Stokes mortars. He created a Force Reserve of two battalions, numbering 800 rifles, twelve machine guns, sixteen Lewis guns and six guns.[90]

He planned to strike on 23 September with a move on Narunyu against Abt Rothe. Moving by night and hiding by day, No 3 Column set off on a flanking move, while No 4 Column remained firm. After two nights' marching, O'Grady reached his objective, the crossing of the Lukuledi, and pressed on to the enemy positions. Initially deceived into thinking that this was merely a patrol, Rothe was warned of the danger by heavy firing. Sending his reserves forward, he was able to halt No 3 Column, which promptly began digging in and bringing down heavy artillery fire. By midday on 25 September, it was apparent that the British were too strong to dislodge easily and General Wahle decided to abandon the Narunyu position. He ordered a withdrawal to Nambalika's with Rothe acting as rearguard.[91]

Concurrently, No 4 Column had been cutting paths through the dense sisal plantations in front of Narunyu so as to aid the subsequent attack once No 3 was in position. However, by the evening of 26 September Wahle's troops had already slipped away and had to be located again. No 3 Column soon found them and ran into a series of strong positions on Chirumaka Hill. Soon, the column became entirely committed and ,despite heavy casualties, the ridge was cleared and a final counter-attack was successfully beaten off.[92]

After a brief rest, Beves ordered the advance to resume on 30 September. No 3 Column moved forward through dense bush to take Chirumaka Hill, which provided excellent observation for many kilometres. A tough fight ensued, but by the end of the day it was in O'Grady's hands. Once again, casualties had not been light and Wahle's troops had been able to escape encirclement. In the circumstances, General Beves now decided to delay further advance until Hanforce was in closer proximity.[93]

MAHIWA

One of the reasons for the advance on Mahiwa was logistical; Kilwa was too distant to be effective as a supply centre and it was intended to switch Hanforce to the Lindi lines of communication as soon as the road to Massassi was cleared. Water was also a problem as sources were scarce and still diminishing. Van Deventer wanted to make rapid progress in destroying the Schutztruppe and a combined offensive made sense, provided that it could be adequately co-ordinated. Hanforce had the advantage in the north while the Nigerian Brigade had shown its determination at Bweho Chini. Linforce had been less successful, but was ready to advance again after a pause to reorganise and bring up supplies.[94]

The construction of roads and rail links continued at top speed with the railhead reaching some 9 km south-west of Mtua by late October. With the main body pushing hard, it was up to Norforce and the Belgians to maintain the pressure. This was consistently applied, although the approaching rainy season in the Mahenge area forced the phased withdrawal of the bulk of the Belgians from there. By 30 October, Norforce had taken Liwale and the Belgians were still attacking near Ligombazi. Importantly, the motor road between Mssindy and Liwale was nearing completion and a Belgian column was approaching the latter place.[95]

Van Deventer's campaign plan depended on catching the enemy main body in battle and destroying it. Finally, Abt Naumann had been cornered at Luita, north of the Central Railway, and forced to surrender on 2 October.[96] This was extremely welcome news, for, after nearly eight months of dogged pursuit, the troublesome raiders had finally been eliminated. They had caused disruption far out of proportion to their size and delayed the offensive against the main body of the Schutztruppe.

With Hanforce progressing well, the Lindi-Massassi road seemed to offer the most favourable opportunity for cornering Lettow. Massassi was an important supply centre and communication node that linked Songea to the west and Newala in the south. The difficulty of the terrain and lack of alternative routes made the road of considerable operational importance to both sides.

Beves now had wireless communications with the Nigerian Brigade which was now at Nahungu. He believed that Wahle had eight to nine companies between the Nengedi River and Mahiwa, of which six were around Mtama. His plan was to have No 3 Column make a frontal push from the east, while No 4 Column advanced up the north bank of the Lukuledi River, crossing at Mputo and then engaging Mtama from the south. In the meantime, the Nigerians in the north were to cut the Lindi-Massassi road at Mahiwa and then move north-eastwards into the German rear. They were to prevent the enemy from withdrawing, while Nos 1 and 2 Columns moved south on Massassi. Concurrently, cavalry patrols would range freely to find and destroy as many food supplies and supply depots as possible.[97] The plan was a bold one, but required a speedy advance, close co-operation between widely-spread columns, and aggressiveness.

In the first week of October, a large number of patrols had been sent out to locate the enemy positions. By 7 October, O'Grady had gained a foothold on the far bank of the Nengedi River, launching a reinforced battalion onto the high ground overlooking the river. Supported by artillery fire, the infantry reached their objective, but were hit by a strong counter-attack. Sensing the situation's importance, another unit was pushed forward. This was hit by a strong German counter-attack and the high ground was lost. Fighting stabilised with the arrival of further British reinforcements and the bridgehead on the western side of the Nengedi River was retained. This was followed by a resumption of the advance on Mtama the next day. While O'Grady's troops continued to progress, the resistance was increasingly stiff and it was becoming clear that the Germans intended to fight hard and cause delay.[98]

In light of the strong defences, Beves now decided not to press a direct attack on Mtama and to encircle it instead. On 12 October, he sent No 4 Column, now under the command of Colonel Tytler, marching west and crossing the Lukuledi below the confluence with the Nengedi River. After an arduous march lasting several days, the river was crossed and Mtama was entered in the afternoon of 15 October, but the defenders had withdrawn. At the same time, No 3 Column had been moving west along the road, pushing back the German rearguards until they linked up with No 4 Column near Mtama. Van Deventer was anxious to give his opponents no rest and kept pressing Beves to maintain unrelenting pressure.[99]

On 13 October, Beves made a major alteration to the plan, ordering the Nigerian Brigade to send one battalion to cut the main road south-west of Mahiwa with the remaining units to attack that village on 15 October. At the same time, No 3 and No 4 Columns would continue their convergence on Mtama. Unknown to the British, Lettow was marching hard to the Lukuledi, hoping to achieve a major victory through surprise. Both sides were looking for a major battle and neither was to be disappointed.[100]

But, General Beves had greatly underestimated the time required for the Nigerian Brigade to reach its objectives. They had only reached Namupa Mission by late on 14 October and lost direction in the thick bush and darkness. Exhausted, the column dug-in for the night unaware of the exact location of the enemy. Colonel Mann, now in temporary command, was concerned about the vulnerability of his baggage train, and decided to leave it at Namupa Mission. He also had serious misgivings about his role as his own intelligence pointed to a much stronger enemy at Mahiwa than that assumed by General Beves.[101]

Early on 15 October, the Nigerians moved from Namupa Mission on its assigned tasks. The detached battalion went off to block the Lindi-Massassi road, while the other two advanced on Mahiwa. The roadblock was set up, but the main body ran into increasing resistance as it approached the Mahiwa River. Beves ordered the Nigerians on despite their running into heavy opposition. To Colonel Mann, it was clear that they had hit a substantially strong position that could not be bypassed. The leading unit was forced to halt and dig-in under heavy German fire from Mrembe Hill.

The Nigerians were now in a difficult situation as the newly-arrived Abt von Ruckteschell immediately launched a heavy attack onto the exposed positions. The lead battalion desperately clung to its ground and fended off the attacks well into the night. Both sides had suffered heavy losses, but the Nigerians were in trouble as it was clear that further enemy reinforcements were being brought forward for the attack. With his brigade strung out between Nyangao and Namupa, Mann was also running short of ammunition. He decided to concentrate all of his forces together on a hill overlooking the Mahiwa River. He informed Beves of the situation and was permitted to make the adjustments early the next day.[102]

Matters worsened, however, with Abt Göring encircling the defenders as well as cutting communications. Late on 16 October, two guns were brought onto to Mremba Hill and began bombarding the trenches. Heavy fire raked the trenches, before Abt von Ruckteschell reached to within 100 metres of the forward trenches. Unable to break in, the attackers withdrew after an hour.[103] The situation was becoming desperate.

Linforce was doing its best to link-up with the Nigerians. By midday on 16 October, No 3 Column had pushed to Mahiwa, but found no sign of the brigade. Hearing the distant sounds of battle, O'Grady marched off to join in before learning of an enemy detachment on the main road. He immediately ordered No 4 Column to attack these troops while his column marched off on the flank. Despite good initial progress, it was halted by a counter-attack sent in by Wahle. Beves was now well aware of the Nigerians' plight, who had too little ammunition and physical strength to put in a counter-attack.[104]

Mann's planned concentration was not going well either, as the returning battalion had returned to Namupa Mission, where it took control of nearly 3,000 non-combatants in the brigade train. Marching to relieve the forward troops, it was hit by Abt Göring and driven back. Matters were worsened by the appearance of Abt Köhl, which joined in the fray. Close range and bitter fighting threatened the loss of the ammunition reserve which was saved by the discipline of the Nigerian defenders. Losses had been very heavy and the main body remained isolated.[105]

O'Grady's columns were still straining to reach the beleaguered Nigerians. They had marched through the night while great teams of carriers had dragged two 5' howitzers forward. By mid-morning on 17 October, No 4 Column was heavily engaged with Abt Wahle and unable to progress. O'Grady sent in No 3 Column on the flank, but was hampered by the thick bush and German redeployment. With both columns fully committed, there was nothing he could do to relieve the pressure on the Nigerians.[106]

Lettow continued his efforts to destroy the Nigerian Brigade, directing heavy fire onto the trenches and eventually destroying the vital wireless mast. The firing of Linforce could be heard, but the troops were still too far away to be of assistance. A breakout was out of the question and the only option was for Linforce to continue its drive through the encircling force. However, with Force HQ still far in the rear at Mtua, Beves was unable to exert detailed control of the operations and O'Grady was again given local tactical control. He then issued instructions for an attack at dawn the next morning by all units of No 3 and No 4 Columns.[107]

Early on 18 October, O'Grady launched an all-out assault with his columns. However, both came up against heavy resistance and were unable to make any significant gains against Wahle's troops. A series of attacks and counter-attacks, supported by heavy artillery fire, ensued with mutual exhaustion setting in. Finally, the two sides took up hasty defensive positions. Casualties had been heavy and neither side was fit to attack further.[108] If Linforce had failed to relieve the Nigerian Brigade, it had extricated itself. Patrols had detected a gap in the Germans' encirclement and Mann had ordered a breakout when the battalion Namupa Mission linked up. The Germans were unable to prevent the relief and the crisis was over.

Mahiwa had been the bloodiest battle of the campaign, with the British fighting units suffering 1,455 casualties, making over 40% of their strength, while ammunition supplies were nearly exhausted. The Germans did not get off lightly with a total of 611 losses; Abt Wahle lost 30% of its strength, while Abt Göring, Köhl, and von Ruckteschell all lost about 16%. The evacuation of casualties, reorganisation and resupply of material would take some time, and for the immediate future the advance of Linforce had halted. Beves himself arrived at the forward positions on 19 October, but his position had been seriously weakened by the failure of the offensive. He was recalled the same day to Dar-es-Salaam in order to make a personal report to the commander-in-chief and was subsequently sacked.[109]

Mahiwa had been an opportunity for both sides to achieve a great success, but neither attained it. It was tactically indecisive and losses were very heavy, with each side losing nearly a third of its fighting strength. Lettow had his long-awaited chance to defeat the British in detail, as they had fought with insufficient co-ordination and were too far apart for mutual support. Beves had ignored the dangers of too hasty an advance without knowledge of the enemy positions and blundered into a trap. But, the Germans had suffered major losses and had consumed a great deal of their ammunition. Lettow's desire to inflict a heavy defeat had drawn him into an attritional slugging match that the British desired and that he could ill-afford. He did bring van Deventer's advance to a halt, gaining three weeks of vital time, but at a very high cost.

THE PUSH TO THE PORTUGUESE BORDER

While the Schutztruppe were steadily being driven back, an unusual proposal was being considered in Germany. It was to send an airship loaded with supplies and medicine into the heart of the colony. The distance was formidable, but the Admiralty agreed that the journey was feasible and obtained approval for the expedition. Preparations were begun in the autumn of 1917 with the L57, a naval airship capable of carrying 15 tons of cargo. Its departure was planned for the middle of October, but was set back when the craft was destroyed by fire during a test flight. With a new airship having to be found and prepared, Schnee was informed by wireless that expedition would be delayed until 14 November, when it would now land on the Makonde plateau.

Despite security measures, the British had been aware of the scheme before it started, with a warning being issued on 8 October. The source of their information is unclear, but they clearly knew the wireless frequencies and callsign of the airship, as well as its destination. All wireless stations between Salonika, Egypt and East Africa were put on alert and ordered to report any traffic immediately. Almost immediately after the loss of the L57, another signal informed van Deventer that the attempt would be delayed a month, although no reason was given.[110]

Oblivious to these activities, the Germans arranged for a specially modified dirigible, the 226-m-long L59 to make the long journey. After several false starts for technical reasons, it left Jamboli, in Bulgaria, on 21 November with 10 tons of ammunition and a further five of medicine, equipment and food.[111] On the same day, the RKA had received worrying news about the advance of the British towards the Makonde and advised the Admiralty to cancel the mission. However, it was too late as storms disrupted communications and it could only report that the airship was west of Khartoum on 23 November, having travelled some 3,500 km.

There it received a signal, ostensibly from the Schutztruppe, that the military situation was hopeless and to return to base. This it did, returning to Jamboli on 25 November, having travelled over 6,000 km. If the RKA had lost heart, the signal to return was controversial as later information indicated that the L59 could have landed its cargo. The Germans later suspected treason, but the British had intercepted their wireless traffic and may have sent the recall message themselves.[112]

At the same time, and against General van Deventer's wishes, the new Portuguese Expeditionary Force was beginning a preliminary move north of the Rovuma, with the aim of taking Newala, Matua and Nangyadi. The move was unwelcome because of his complete lack of confidence in the ability of the Portuguese, viewing their plans as hopeless. Nonetheless, he was aware of their sensitivity to criticism and sought London's assistance in tempering their plans.[113]

Throughout October, General Northey in the south and west had maintained steady pressure as ordered. Colonel Shorthose moved his column north-east from Tunduru, reaching Abdallah-Kwa-Nanga by mid-month. The remaining 80 km to Liwale were covered in the next two weeks, putting the fertile district in British hands. In the west, Colonel Hawthorn continued to push along the Luwegu River, establishing his troops on the north bank and east of the enemy's position on 5 October. He attacked on 16 October, but the enemy was forewarned and withdrew down the Luwegu River, having first destroyed his two remaining field guns. Hawthorn followed up relentlessly and by the end of the month both sides were along the river at a point south of Liganduka's.[114]

Unbeknownst to the fighting troops, a diplomatic row was brewing in London. Since the capture of Tabora, there had been a number of reports about outrages and atrocities commited by the Belgian forces against the inhabitants of German East Africa. From the range of evidence, it seems doubtless that a number of incidents ranging from murder, rape to plundering did occur. However, despite vocal protests by a number of British clerics, the problem was largely swept under the carpet and ignored in the interests of prosecuting the war efficiently. These protests arose in renewed form in October and caused a minor diplomatic furore.[115] Apart from military considerations, this may have done more to prevent the renewal of Belgian co-operation in the campaign of 1918 as it strained the relationship.

In the centre, the Belgians had pressed on, capturing Mahenge on 9 October. This, and the pressure by Norforce, had forced Tafel to withdraw his forces south-eastward towards Kahambu. This was accompanied by a large number of desertions and individuals surrendering to the advancing Belgians. The German western front was now giving way rapidly, but the long lines of communication prevented the Allies from exploiting their advantage to the full. Hawthorn's troops were at their extreme radius, while Huyghé's columns were unable to move fast enough to trap Abt Otto.[116]

However, van Deventer wanted to employ the Belgian RO in the east. It had been reinforced to a strength of about 2,000 rifles with artillery and had sailed from Dar-es-Salaam to Kilwa, where it landed on 13 October. Commanded by Commandant Hérion, the RO then moved forward to Mitondo where it cleared the local area, before moving on towards Liwale to co-operate in the defeat of Abt Tafel. Colonel Huyghé and General van Deventer met at Kilwa on 27 October to discuss future operations. The Belgian advance had stalled 40 km south of Mahenge owing to supply problems that had been exacerbated by the lack of food in the local area. With the rains coming shortly and the Belgian administrative services generally weak, they agreed to abandon the advance from Mahenge to Liwale and to withdraw the bulk of the Belgian forces back to the Central Railway before the roads became impassable. Thus, by the end of November, there would only be two Belgian battalions left in Mahenge whose role would be purely defensive. In order to enable the RO in the east, the motor transport used to maintain the Kilossa-Mahenge line would be transferred to the Kilwa-Liwale route.[117]

The retirement began swiftly and by mid-November, only a small force of 2,100 was left in and around Mahenge. On 25 November, with heavy rainfall, these remaining troops were recalled to Kilossa and the area handed over to British control. By 2 December, the bulk of the Belgain troops had reached the railway where they would shelter for the wet season.[118]

THE SITUATION IN NOVEMBER 1917

By early November, the situation was as follows. Abt Otto, with about six companies, was facing Norforce and a Belgian column in the area of Liganduka's. Tafel remained in overall command of the forces in the northern area, controlling some fifteen companies. In the south, Lettow disposed of about twenty-five companies, with seven holding the Mahiwa area, one to two at Mnacho, two mainly convalescent companies at Newala and the main body of twelve to thirteen held centrally between Nangoo and Lukuledi.[119] He was faced by the combined Hanforce and Linforce in the east with Shorthose's column at Liwale and the Portuguese along the Rovuma.

The German situation was not good as they had less than six weeks' supply of food and the earliest harvest was in March. Furthermore, ammunition was also limited to 400,000 rounds and the artillery was now virtually non-existent. The rich area around Chiwata was key to survival and Lettow still hoped that Tafel would be able to link-up there. As ever, Lettow wanted to fight a major battle, but in the circumstances was too weak to do so.[120]

With Tafel apparently moving southwards to join Lettow, van Deventer also ordered Norforce to concentrate on preventing any move towards Portuguese territory. He wanted Linforce to fix Lettow around Mahiwa while using Hanforce and the newly-formed Mounted Column to cut off the enemy retreat at Chiwata. The Portuguese were to hold the Germans north of the Rovuma and to prevent Tafel from linking up with the main body under Lettow. To this end, they made several demonstrations north of the river, but seemingly to little effect.[121] The Belgians had the RO operating out of Kilwa, but Huyghé was under political pressure to maintain a distinct sphere of operations. This was now becoming increasingly difficult and the Foreign Office had to ask the Belgian Government to be more flexible so as to wind-up the campaign as quickly as possible.[122]

In the north, the Belgian RO had reached Liwale on 30 October after two weeks' marching under the blistering sun, where it joined up with elements of Shorthose's column, who had arrived the day previously. The British handed over control of the village and then returned towards Abdallah-Kwa-Nanga on 2 November.[123] At the same time, the transfer of a second Belgian battalion together with mountain guns was underway, with the troops arriving in Kilwa on 30 October; a third had been planned, but its participation had been cancelled after its abortive march from Mahenge.

On the night of 1/2 November, Hawthorn attacked and seized the position at Liganduka's, taking twenty-four prisoners and a machine gun. The remaining enemy on the Luwegu retired to the east; the British followed, with Hawthorn moving to Kabati Mzee and Fair towards Kabati

Moro. They maintained the pressure, with Hawthorn having driven the enemy rearguards from both banks of the Luwegu by the evening of 5 November and to within 2 km of Kabati Mzee. Fair reached Kabati Moro the next day receiving the surrender of some 142 Germans and 140 Askaris as well as finding three machine guns and some hundreds of damaged rifles.[124] On the same day, eighty-two more Askaris surrendered to the Belgian column; over the next day or two more sick soldiers surrendered at Kahambu and Mlembwe. Apart from this, it was clear that the Germans were now moving south through Dapate. Hawthorn turned to the south-east while Murray, with 250 rifles, pushed east along the Songea-Liwale road.

The main British advance resumed on 6 November with Hanforce marching southward to its former positions around Lukuledi Mission, arriving there two days later. Further east, Linforce, now suitably reorganised and brought up to strength, began pushing Wahle's rearguard south-

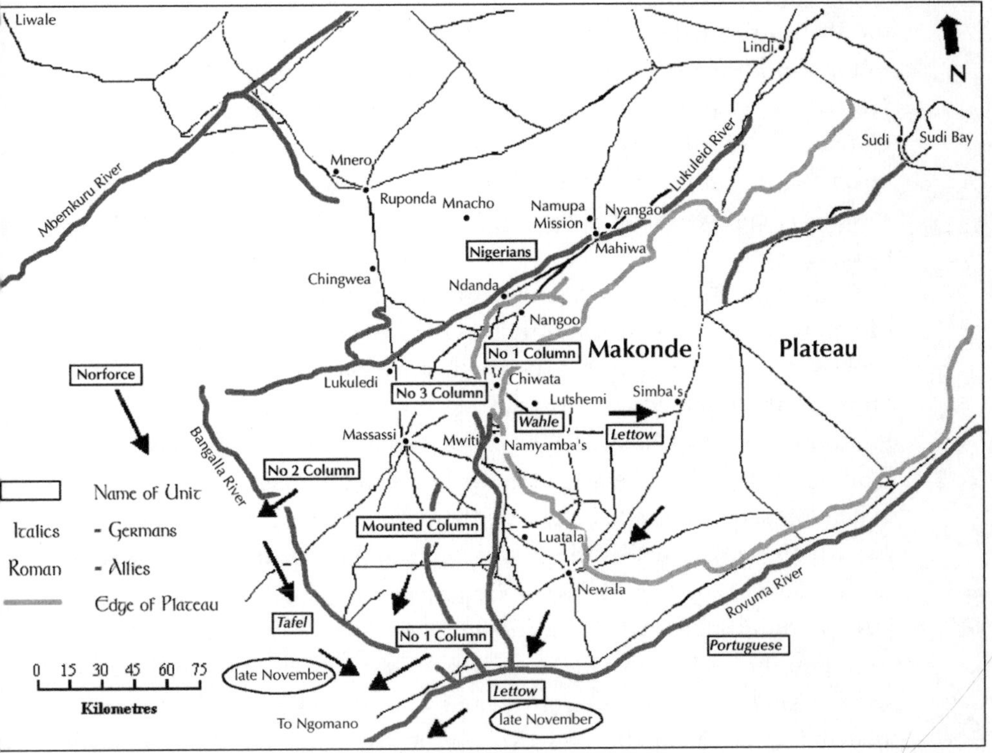

The clearance of German East Africa, November 1917

west the following day and making good initial progress. On the flank, the Mounted column was ordered to seize Mwiti about 8 km south of Chiwata with the aims of cutting the tracks leading south to the Rovuma and destroying food stocks.[125]

There was no water between Mahiwa and Nangoo and Linforce was now encountering stiff resistance from Abt Wahle. Hanforce was then ordered to send No 1 Column north-east to Ndanda, where it was believed that the rearguard would have to pass through. With the bulk of the enemy between Nangoo and Ndanda, van Deventer wanted to Hanforce and Linforce to link-up quickly with the Mounted Column securing the south. In reality, while Abt von Lieberman held No 1 Column from Ndanda, Abt Wahle was actually moving to the south along an undetected track from Nangoo to Chiwata. At the same time, Abt Tafel was concentrating at Dapate, 240 km to the north-west, preparatory to moving south to join the main body. Norforce and the RO were to converge on it and prevent a breakthough.[126]

By 12 November, the desired link-up had taken place at Nangoo, but the British realised that the enemy had escaped using bush paths to the south. Van Deventer now ordered No 3 Column from Ndanda and the Nigerian Brigade from Nangoo to drive south on Chiwata while No 2 Column of Hanforce pushed east from Lukuledi Mission. In a daring move, No 1 and the Mounted Columns were to sweep south-eastwards towards Kitangari, deep in the enemy's rear and believed to be Lettow's next objective.

At the same time, considerable effort was put into improving the lines of communication, with the Lindi-Massassi route taking the strain. This enabled the closure of the 320-km link between Hanforce and Kilwa. Similarly, the Lukuledi-Mwiti road was much improved, while the tramline now reached Mtama. All available sappers and miners, plus several fighting columns, were engaged in further road building.

The pressure on the Schutztruppe continued as late on 14 November, No 1 Column had seized the Mwiti defile and blocked any escape route to the south-west. The Mounted Column had reached Mkunde and was pushing on to Kitangari. No 2 and 3 Columns and the Nigerian Brigade were just outside of Chiwata, ready to assault the position there.[127] Lettow was determined not to be trapped and had ordered Chiwata to be evacuated and it was taken after a sharp fight by No 2 and 3 Columns. Nearly 500 prisoners were taken and some seventy prisoners of war were released. The loss of Chiwata with its stores and hospital had been a major blow to the Germans who continued south to Nambindinga, which they gradually reached between 15 and 17 November.

Now faced with starvation or annihilation, Lettow made the fateful decision to reduce his force drastically. He could maintain a force of no more than 2,000 rifles and the remainder were left behind to surrender. Only the best soldiers were retained, while those whose enthusiasm for fighting had dimmed were to be left behind. Lettow also had to recognise that the Schutztruppe was no longer the force it had been, as it had lost 473 Germans and 1,072 Askari in the first two weeks of November.[128]

Tafel's move south through the loose Anglo-Belgian cordon was marked by a number of losses from desertion. By the second week of November, his troops were close to the half-battalion of KAR troops at Abdallah-kwa-Nanga who were anxiously awaiting the arrival of reinforcements with Colonel Shorthose from Tunduru, while Murray with 400 rifles was also moving south-east in support. The numerically superior Westtruppen fell on the outpost on 14 November, which was quickly cut off and attacked. A desperate situation was saved by the resourcefulness of the Belgian battalion at Liwale, which immediately sent a company to its assistance. Arriving early on 16 November, it learned that seven enemy companies were attacking the KAR; despite the disparity in numbers they moved forward, hitting the German main body in the rear and scattering them and taking a number of prisoners. This timely attack saved the British from destruction, but also resulted in the capture of documents that revealed Abt Tafel's routes and order of march.[129] This was to be an important piece of intelligence.

At the Makonde plateau, it was becoming apparent that the Germans were moving south-eastwards. Another attempt at encirclement was made with the Nigerian Brigade sent west of Mwiti Hill, while No 1 Column was sent on towards Lutshemi. No 2 Column was placed in reserve at Mwiti and No 4 Column was ordered to improve a track between the east edge of the Makonde and the sea. Wahle was moving along the high ground, while the main body was moving just below the plateau and ahead of the Nigerians towards Nambindinga. By nightfall on 17 November No 1 Column had occupied Lutshemi, after a very difficult march, and secured its vital water source. Again, under cover of darkness, the Germans slipped away to Nambindinga that evening, but leaving over 300 Germans and 700 Askaris there for capture. Lettow now led his troops neatly out of the closely-drawn net and made his way east towards Simba's, about 24 km north-east of Kitangari.[130]

Van Deventer was well forward at Ndanda, when he met Huyghé on 18 November to discuss the future use of the RO. They agreed that it would move to Massassi where it would assist in the reduction of the German main body while the remainder of the Belgian forces would remain at Dodoma and Kilossa. However, two additional battalions were already marching to join the RO, reaching Mnero at the end of November and subsequently Liwale a few days later.[131]

The elimination of the Westtruppen remained a difficult task, as it was now known to be double that previously estimated, with over 1,700 rifles. Good fortune appeared on 18 November when a liaison officer sent by Tafel to von Lettow was captured by the British. His papers revealed that Abt Tafel had left Abdallah-kwa-Nanga on 16 November and that it was now headed towards the Makonde.[132] Van Deventer now ordered No 2 Column and the Nigerian Brigade to prepare, ready to deal with this new threat.

Concurrently, No 3 Column was pursuing Lettow down the track to Simba's, with No 1 Column moving towards the junction at Lulindi and the Mounted Column was reconnoitring north-east and east. On reaching Simba's on 18 November, for only a brief pause, Lettow continued his march reaching Newala, on the south-western corner of the plateau, two days later. He was acutely aware of the precariousness of his supply situation and conducted a last regrouping of his bedraggled force. He had to replenish his supplies and rest his force away from the enemy; Portuguese East Africa offered the only opportunity. All the sick, infirm and uncommitted were left behind as the remaining 300 Germans, 1,700 Askaris and 3,000 porters marched south-west to Mpili on the north bank of the River Rovuma, arriving there early on 21 November.

The British were in hot pursuit and No 1 Column entered Newala on 21 November, a day behind the Germans whose morale was reported to be very low and the troops much tired although Lettow was still holding his force together with a combination of exhortation and threats. The chase was not helped by the difficulty of the ground and the rough road from Ndanda to Newala made resupply very arduous.[133] The Mounted Column had reached Luatala, some 16 km north of the Rovuma, but as the chances of capturing Lettow were fading rapidly, attention turned to Tafel.

On 23 November, Abt Tafel was located moving south along the Bangala River towards the confluence with the Rovuma although intelligence indicated that it was unaware of Lettow's move south. With Murray's column following from the west, it was time to unleash the reserve columns from the east. The next day, No 1 Column move south from Luatala to the River Rovuma while No 2 Column marched south-west from Massassi and No 1 Column left Luatala. Despite enormous difficulties of terrain and supply, the trap was closing as Norforce was manoeuvring to prevent any move northward towards Tunduru.[134]

The weather was very hot and trying, but the British columns were now at both ends of the river. It was here that the efforts of Major Pretorius, the chief scout, paid off in big measure. Having captured a letter from Tafel to Lettow, Pretorius moved to the nominated junction, and cleared all food and inhabitants from the area. On 27 November Tafel reached his destination, and, unbeknownst to either party, Lettow marched north-westwards less than 2 km away. Lettow retained his head start and, after a huge effort by his exhausted troops, he was able to carry up the Rovuma Valley towards Ngomano. Contact had been broken and it would be up to the Portuguese to stop the Germans from entering their territory.[135]

No 1 Column then hit the Westtruppen in the front while No 2 Column ran into their rear. Now surrounded and very short of food, Tafel decided to surrender. On 27 November some twenty-seven Germans and 178 Askaris, with 1,112 porters of the rearguard, surrendered, while that evening Tafel's offer of capitulation was received. The next day, he and the remaining thirteen companies surrendered, comprising some 1,115 Europeans, 3,382 Askaris, forty-three machine guns and four guns. At a stroke, the Schutztruppe had been halved, while Tafel had also destroyed 1,200–1,400 rifles, twenty-five to thirty machine guns and two guns.[136]

By the end of November, the whole of German East Africa had been cleared of enemy and the Schutztruppe's fighting power had been broken. The failure to catch Lettow was a major disappointment for it meant a campaign in 1918, although the surrender of the Westtruppen had been a great success. The British reaction was immediate; the size of the force was to be reduced as soon as possible with the East African Force reduced in size and all of the Indian units were to be sent to other theatres. The West African units were to be returned to their homes while further Belgian co-operation was seen as being desirable, political considerations began to arise. Norforce would become the main striking force, with operations based on the Moçambique coast to be avoided if possible owing to the shipping shortage. Finally, reductions in numbers of troops were agreed and the campaign was to become largely an African one supported by Imperial technical troops.[137]

General van Deventer had not lost his drive, informing the CIGS on 5 December that he proposed to take vigorous action to round-up Lettow before the rains started. Estimating that two months of campaigning weather remained, he wanted to hold the southern border along the Rovuma strongly, pushing the Nigerian Brigade as far south as supplies would permit, while General Northey would make the main advance from Nyasaland towards Mwembe. However, he recognised that if the Germans moved south of the Lujenda River towards the Medo district, that they would effectively place themselves out of reach in the period before the rains.[138]

The Belgians had similar feelings about the conquest of the German colony. The RO was soon sent marching to Lindi where it embarked for Dar-es-Salaam. The Belgian Government had reserved its right to consider continuing the fight in Portuguese territory while the British now saw the campaign as largely over. Faced with the difficulties of working with the Portuguese, it saw the negotiations for a continued Belgian presence as being too time consuming, in terms of both necessary reorganisation and political decision-making. In the end, the two nations ended on a much more amicable note than the year previously. By early 1918 all Belgian forces were ready to return to the Congo or the Belgian zone of occupation.[139]

The question of Anglo-Portuguese co-operation was much different as the dangers of letting even the rump of the Schutztruppe roaming around Portuguese East Africa outweighed the need to wind-up the campaign. The Portuguese forces were considered too inept to stop Lettow and the British would have to conduct the real fighting. This was a blow, but unavoidable in the circumstances. Henceforth, the campaign would be conducted by the British and Portuguese only.

8

The Fight for Portuguese East Africa

As they trudged along the Rovuma, Lettow's troops had little time to reflect on the narrowness of their escape or the whereabouts of Tafel. The most immediate problem was survival, as there was only enough food to last until 1 December. Ammunition was also in very short supply and urgent action was required.[1] Lettow realised that the imminent rainy season would halt any major British offensive operations and the Rovuma would rise substantially. Furthermore, the almost totally undeveloped nature of Portuguese East Africa would force them to build-up the infrastructure and stockpiles needed to support a campaign. This would give him time to deal with the Portuguese and resolve the critical supply issue.[2]

The Germans assessed the Portuguese as having some 6,500 rifles, forty-two machine guns and fourteen guns with which to guard their 400-km border along the Rovuma River.[3] Of these, they believed that nearly 3,000 were deployed in posts between the coast and the major boma at Ngomano, which commanded the confluence of the Lugenda and Rovuma rivers.[4] Its garrison was estimated as being between 1,800 to 2,000 rifles, although likely to be poorly laid out and carelessly guarded.[5] From past experience, Lettow had only contempt for the Portuguese forces and viewed their camps more as potential supply bases rather than serious opposition. Furthermore, Ngomano was in marching range as well as some distance away from the British bases on the coast.

Although weakened by hunger, the greatly reduced Schutztruppe was still very capable as it retained the most experienced and determined soldiers. Abt Göring, with three companies, formed the advance guard, followed by the main body of fifteen companies and the support elements, with a single company bringing up the rear. The total strength was nineteen companies, comprising 268 Europeans, 1,700 Askari, and about 3,900 carriers and 370 'boys'. Despite his concern for reducing ration strengths to the absolute minimum, not even a disciplinarian like Lettow could induce the Askari to leave their wives and children behind. This added over 600 wives and children, plus a further 700 Askari 'boys' who had to find their own rations while keeping up with the march.[6]

News of a small Portuguese boma south of the river led to Abt Göring being detached to deal with it while the main body continued towards Ngomano.[7] It was reached early on 25 November and, after running into patrols, Lettow decided to attack off the line of march. The Portuguese were driven back into the fort and opened a lively fire. The Germans replied with fire from a mountain gun while Abt von Ruckteschell launched a fixing attack from the north-west. In the meantime, Abt Köhl was sent on a southerly march to hit the Portuguese flank and storm the positions. The attack succeeded completely as 187 Portuguese were killed and another 500 taken prisoner, with many running away. The seizure also yielded six heavy machine guns, 600 rifles and a quarter of a million rounds of ammunition. At a stroke, German fighting power was restored, although African rations remained in very short supply. Once again the Portuguese had failed and although Colonel Rosa later tried to blame the British for failing to send reinforcements, Ngomano did not even have trenches dug.[8]

After a brief halt to treat casualties and collect their booty, the main column set off down the Lugenda Valley on 27 November. Stuemer's raid earlier in the year had shown it to be very sparse in food, but the area further south was much more promising.[9] However, it was some distance away, and conscious of the precariousness of his stocks, Lettow split up the force to forage independently. Fortune, and poor Portuguese dispositions, led to the discovery by Abt Köhl of a small platoon-sized boma at Nanguare that was duly taken on 2 December. It seized seventy rifles plus 300,000 rounds of ammunition, but also eight days' rations in carrier loads that would be essential for the coming journey through the barren stretch ahead. Despite the find, Köhl's carriers were surviving on half rations and his Askaris were having to spend a great deal of effort in local foraging.[10]

In the meantime, Abt Göring was isolated and out of touch with the main body. It had captured some Portuguese papers showing the existence of a magazine at Nampakesho. Marching rapidly, the garrison was able to burn the fort with the petrol stocks held there and only a few supplies were saved. Concerned about his own survival, Göring then marched to Ngomano where he expected to find the rearguard. Arriving on 1 December to find the British there, he waited in concealment for two days before setting south down the Lugenda Valley. It was not until 12 December that he was able to catch up with the rearguard, although Lettow did not learn about the link-up for another six days.[11]

Fortified by these successes, the main body set off for the south on 4 December, trying to pass the foodless belt as quickly as possible. It reached the post at Chirumba on 11 December, surprising the occupants and taking it without a fight. This was another major coup as 800 loads of African food and another eighty of flour were seized, easing the food situation considerably. More success followed as a patrol seized another 15,000 rounds of small arms ammunition and 300 mountain-gun shells. Finally, Abt Wahle, which had been moving slowly as it foraged, came across a dug-in Portuguese position in the Mkula Hills. Despite the near parity of numbers, the position was easily overrun and a large quantity of supplies, including valuable quinine and eighteen days' food, was taken on 8 December. This was followed by minor captures of food and weapons at another post in the Oizulo Hills on 27 December, in which thirty-four Portuguese and Askaris were killed.[12]

Lettow now had the resources to complete his march to the fertile areas in the area of Mwembe-Chirumba-Lusinje-Medo, which, apart from food, also put him at the maximum distance from the various British detachments. While headed south, an emissary under the white flag reached his rearguard at Ngomano, bearing General van Deventer's call to surrender on 4 December. It finally reached Lettow on 8 January and formally informed him of Tafel's surrender, although it appears he had

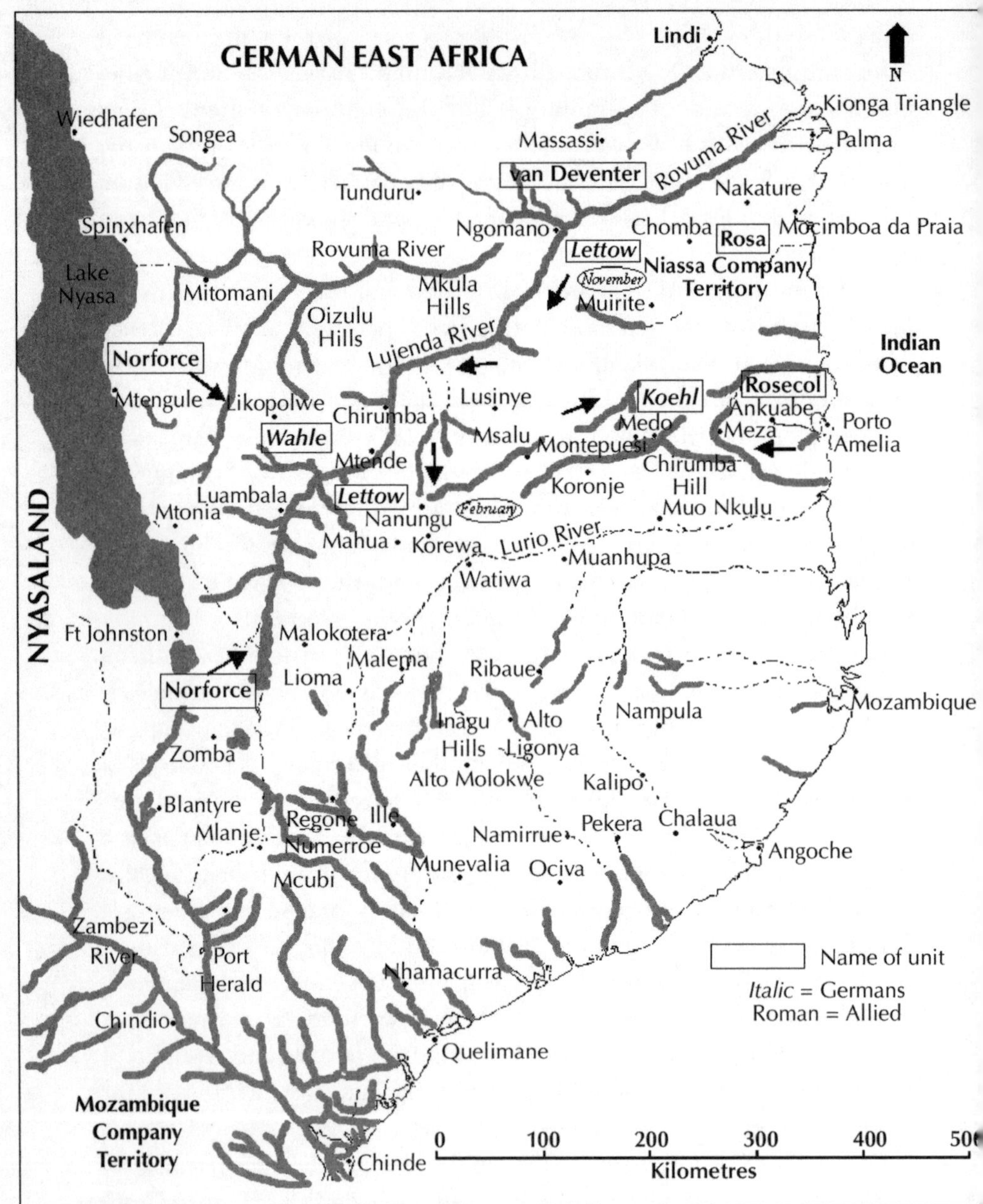

Operations in Portuguese East Africa, November 1917–April 1918

learned of that fact following the capture of Ngomano on 29 November. It had never had much chance of success, and with the Germans buoyed by success it was ignored. The first two weeks in Portuguese territory had been extremely fruitful, as the threat of imminent starvation had passed while the munitions problem had been solved by the capture of 750 rifles, twelve machine guns and 680,000 rounds of ammunition.[13]

The Schutztruppe's escape was a bitter blow for General van Deventer, as he had come very close to eliminating the enemy, only for the incapacity of his Portuguese allies to undo all his strenuous efforts. He was hardly surprised at such a dismal performance, but it was infuriating, especially as he would be unable to deploy substantial forces south of the Rovuma for several months. The reduction in forces was underway and columns had to be refitted and reorganised for the next phase. The rainy season would make campaigning difficult while the swollen Rovuma would be virtually unpassable for several months.

The German move south forced a decision as Lettow despatched Abt Köhl towards Montepuesi, a village not far from the Portuguese base at Porto Amelia. Colonel Rosa requested assistance and on 12 December British troops sailed south from Lindi. A new force known as Rosecol, under Colonel Rose, was formed and the Gold Coast Regiment landed the next day. Its mission was to secure the port and be ready to move inland by the end of December, but much depended on the water supply and the state of the port, which was reported to be primitive. Further north, intensive patrols reaching as far as 175 km south of the Rovuma had failed to locate the enemy.[14]

Van Deventer understood the dangers of the wet season and reduced the forward troops with only the Nigerian Brigade along the Rovuma, holding Ngomano with a battalion in reserve at Massassi, and the remainder moved back to the railhead at Mtama. The new KAR battalions were concentrated for rest and training in preparation for the dry season offensive. By the end of December 1917, the military situation was largely quiet, apart from near the Nyasaland border where Northey's troops were in contact and were pushing east and north from Mtengula and Namwera. Rosecol had completed its build-up at Porto Amelia and with the river starting to reach dangerously high levels, the Nigerian Brigade was pulled back to the north bank. Everywhere, the rain was beginning to fall and the roads started to dissolve.[15]

PLANS FOR 1918

With the turning of the year, British politicians were concerned about three major areas: manpower, casualties and Ireland. The heavy fighting in Flanders had drained the BEF of its offensive power and the prime minister, Lloyd George, looked for a success in Palestine to sustain public morale. With the slow build-up of American forces and the collapse of Russia, the war seemed unlikely to end before 1919. The need to conserve manpower for the perceived final effort meant that reinforcements were unavailable for East Africa, even had the shipping been available. For a while the U-boat threat had been contained, it was far from being eliminated, with merchant shipping losses in the latter part of 1917 running at 241,260 tons or seventy-five ships per month.[16]

Another area concerning policy-makers was that of the fate of the captured colonies. From the beginning of the war, the British Government had been careful not to declare any annexations or make formal claims on captured territory. Initially, it had not wanted to add to the size of the Empire and had rebuffed attempts by South Africa and Belgium to proclaim their suzerainty over South-West Africa and Ruanda/Urundi respectively. However, as the war progressed and the complexion of government had changed, attitudes began to harden. Imperialists, such as Curzon, Milner and Amery, and sub-imperialists, such as Botha and Smuts, continued to demand the permanent retention of Germany's overseas possessions.[17]

An influential report in April 1917, presented by a committee chaired by Lord Curzon, looked for substantial gains in Africa and elsewhere. Supported by the Imperial War Cabinet, although not binding on the British Government, it showed the strength of feeling on the issue.[18] The prolonged resistance in East Africa played its part, as lack of resources had impelled the British to make widespread use of the indigenous Africans, and former German subjects, in their war machine. In German eyes, this constituted treason, and widespread retribution was threatened against perceived collaborators. Smuts noted that: 'The Germans also asserted that… any native who had deserted during the war would be hanged by the order of the German Government when that war was over.' This view was certainly shared by General van Deventer, who said:

> No German deserter will return to the enemy lines as he knows that he will be forthwith shot or hung… Last and most important is the question of a guarantee and protection… The Germans assiduously assert even granting they lose German East Africa now it will assuredly be given back to them at the end of the war, and that every man who has deserted or who has helped us in any way will infallibly be hung. And this certainly would be the case unless we can authoritatively refute the statement.[19]

At a local level, the British realised that the Schutztruppe was vulnerable although it still had considerable power and resilience left in it. However, there were a number of important factors to consider for the campaign of 1918. The first was the perennial problem of manpower and health. Many units were now worn out and heavily depleted by sickness. This was by no means restricted to the British and South Africans, as the Indians and West Africans were also suffering badly. Believing that the native East Africans were better able to withstand both the rigours of the climate and the ravages of disease, the bulk of non-KAR fighting troops were sent to other theatres or returned home. However, substantial numbers of white technical and administrative soldiers were retained to support the new campaign.[20]

Shipping was a major limitation as heavy losses from submarines continued to constrain both the numbers and quantities of supplies that could be sent to East Africa as well as the intra-theatre movement of supplies. Because of limitations of vessels, port capacities and unloading facilities, all arrivals into theatre had to come through Dar-es-Salaam. It was uneconomical and virtually impractical to send personnel and stores direct to the sea-base of destination. Instead, a complicated process of unloading at Dar-es-Salaam, waiting and then loading before sailing to Kilwa, Lindi or Mombasa had to be followed. If major operations south of the Rovuma River were to be undertaken, then it would be necessary to set-up and operate one or more ports in Portuguese East Africa, with all the extra effort and delay that that implied.

The commander-in-chief was aware on the lack of resources south of the Rovuma, but also that, from the previous year's operations against Abt von Stuemer, the central districts of the Niassa Company's holdings were both fertile and healthy. This, and its distance from both the coast and Nyasaland, made an ideal resting place for the Germans. Roads were virtually non-existent and the British had no bases south of Lindi. If left undisturbed, the Germans could gather food and possibly recruit more

Askari, potentially regaining strength. On the other hand, a British advance could disrupt and possibly destroy the enemy, but at the cost of immense difficulties in supply and reinforcement. With firm instructions and little option of remaining inactive, van Deventer decided to clear Portuguese East Africa as quickly as possible.[21]

He now had three aims: the first was to fight the enemy wherever and whenever possible in order to cause maximum losses; the second was to prevent the invasion of Nyasaland; and the third was to prevent the enemy from re-entering German East Africa.[22] In the short term, the approaching rains would make it difficult to achieve the first goal although the others would be helped by the impasse. Once the dry season returned, an aggressive and offensive policy would be needed.

Regrouping of his force was still underway, while scarce shipping resources were occupied with the withdrawal of the Belgians, the removal of the numerous prisoners of war, plus the evacuation of the many sick and wounded back to the base at Dar-es-Salaam. This meant that the bulk of British forces would have to remain in the German colony. For the wet weather, the Nigerian Brigade would be retained north of the Rovuma with the remainder of the force concentrated at Ndanda for ease of supply and training.[23] His new striking force would have two major elements. The first was largely East African, with two brigade-sized columns each of three battalions. These were based on the 2nd and 3rd Regiments KAR and known as Kartucol and Kartrecol respectively. The other element was Norforce based on Songea and southern Nyasaland. Colonel Murray and the Rhodesian elements and two battalions of 4 KAR were garrisoning the Wiedhafen-Songea-Tunduru line and its vital food supplies, while Colonel Hawthorn with three battalions of 1 KAR and the Cape Corps were operating out of Nyasaland into Portuguese territory.[24]

Maintaining these widely separated forces in the field was a major challenge. Northey's lines of communications would use those established during its earlier clearance of Portuguese East Africa. The troops operating from the coast had greater problems. The Rovuma and the lands to its south offered few advantages as supplies would have to come from Lindi to Massassi to Ngomano before going into the largely roadless south. The coast was more promising as large ships could easily supply the good harbour at Porto Amelia. A base there offered a direct approach to the German positions and, almost uniquely for the coast, it was virtually malaria-free.[25]

Van Deventer was determined to bring the Schutztruppe to battle as quickly as possible and, with delays caused by the rain and a lack of carriers, he ordered General Northey to start pressuring the Germans from the west. His intention was to drive in the German outposts in order to restrict the enemy's foraging and to harass his tired units. He was equally sure that operations with the Portuguese would be unsuccessful without a unified command and on 1 January he requested the War Office to seek their subordination to him.[26]

The disaster at Ngomano had changed matters completely. The Portuguese authorities, now in a state of great concern, had consented to the main British force operating in their territory.[27] The need to build-up a new base at Porto Amelia precipitated the first major clash; within a few days, the British found it difficult to recruit labour as the local Niassa Company officials were obstructive and unwilling to help. This led to the British Ambassador in Lisbon being formally instructed to seek:

> Entire control of everything connected with movements of troops and stores at Porto Amelia, including hiring and management of dhows. Control, by arrangement with local Portuguese Authorities of the Base and lines of communication inland...It is important that Portuguese Government should agree that actual engagement and payment of carriers &c. should be done by British Authorities, experience having shown danger and inefficiency of Portuguese methods.[28]

These wide-ranging demands were accompanied by private information for the Ambassador that General van Deventer suspected the local Portuguese military authorities of colluding with the Germans and that the Niassa Company was actively hindering his attempts to recruit carriers.[29]

This was followed by a demand for further control: now the War Office was asking for the Portuguese to place their military forces under General van Deventer's command. Again the language was notable for its directness and lack of diplomacy:

> The course of events since the crossing of the frontier by Major-General Von Lettow with a small and exhausted force about 27 November last has shown that the Portuguese command is incapable of conducting military operations, or is unwilling to offer effective opposition to the Germans. Detachments have been left in advanced and isolated posts, despite the rep-

> resentations of the British Headquarters, and have surrendered after a feeble resistance with their arms ammunition and stores of supplies, on which the German troops have mainly subsisted.[30]

The pressure and a concurrent change of government in Lisbon soon achieved the desired results: the Portuguese acceded to a joint command provided that it was under the highest ranking officer and that a 'mixed' headquarters was formed.[31] Colonel Rosa had his own priorities and was concerned about the security of their line Mocimboa-do-Rovuma to Chomba that secured the area between the Rovuma and Porto Amelia.[32] He still fielded substantial forces of one European battalion and ten Askari companies and a battery of mountain guns. They were deployed with the battalion and three companies near Nampula, three companies in the south moving towards Alto Molokwe, and the remaining four companies dispersed amongst a number of stations. The mountain battery was due to move to Nakature, but was immobile owing to a lack of carriers.[33]

The uneasy relationship between the British and Portuguese had to be kept on track, for, despite their private misgivings, the British needed close co-operation if there was to be any chance of ending the fighting in 1918. Accordingly, a conference between van Deventer and the acting governor general was held at Lourenco Marques on 29 January. The national governments had agreed that military operations in the Portuguese colony should be under unified command with the British taking the lead.[34] This was absolutely essential as the disasters of January had shown, but it involved a more tactful and sensitive approach to Portuguese national pride. Van Deventer then met Northey in Beira, before travelling north to Mocimboa-da-Praia, where he met Colonel Rosa on 12 February. There they agreed that both Northey's and Rosa's forces would co-operate in trying to defeat the Germans in their present locations, or, if necessary, to drive them south of the River Lurio in the hopes that their Askari would desert. Further south, the Portuguese were asked to provide a mobile column at Chomba of some 1,500 rifles to attack the enemy from the north in conjunction with the British. KAR battalions were sent to hold Moçambique and the fertile Namule district (107 km east of Lake Shirwa), while other Portuguese forces were asked to secure the line Ribaue-Inagu lying between those units.[35]

For his part, Rosa agreed unwillingly, but had to comply with his government's decision to make Porto Amelia freely available to the British and even worse, to the physical separation of the two contingents. Van Deventer left with a very low opinion of the main body of Portuguese troops he inspected at Mocimboa. He considered them militarily worthless; an opinion to be vindicated during the course of the campaign.[36] Furthermore, Rosa was unhappy with British requests to move columns back and forth around Muirite as he regarded this as a trick to occupy his troops unnecessarily. In March, the British arrived at Nampula where they did serve alongside the Portuguese, although friction soon developed and separate sectors were assigned.[37]

By January 1918, Lettow had achieved his immediate goal of positioning his force in the more fertile portions between the Rovuma and Lurio rivers. His efforts were now set on obtaining further supplies of food while sheltering the troops from the effects of the wet season. He expected the enemy to resume their technique of concentric movements as soon as the rains stopped and the country had dried out.[38] He planned to occupy the area between the River Lurio and the line Montepuesi-Msalu-Mtende for as long as possible, and at least until the new crop could be harvested sometime in March-April. The protection of these supplies was a high priority while he also knew that the longer his troops stayed in an area, stripping it of supplies, the more it denied support to the British. In order to reduce the pressure on local resources, he divided his forces into five groups: Abt Wahle, with three companies, occupied the area Likopolwe-Mwembe; Abt Göring, also with three companies, around Muabala; Abt Otto, with two companies, en route from Chirumba to Luambala; GHQ and a single company, at Chirumba; and Abt Köhl of five companies stretching from Muo to Namunyo opposite Porto Amelia. This layout also maximised the length of the enemy's lines of communications with a concomitant weakening of forward fighting power. Thereafter, he would have to react to the actions of his opponents.[39]

OPERATIONS: JANUARY-APRIL 1918

Norforce was the best positioned to continue harrying the Germans and Hawthorn's column was sent north on 3 January to dislodge Abt Wahle which was now gathering food around the River Lugenda. Arriving there on 7 January, he had two battalions with him, as the others were further west, unable to move further owing to a shortage of transport. Lettow received word of this two days later, and despatched Abt Otto as reinforcements. Wahle met Hawthorn's troops above Luambala, causing some delay, but he fell back east on the night of 11/12 to protect his magazines. In the meantime, Abt Otto had been instructed to reinforce Wahle's threatened position and marched from Chirumba on 12 January.[40] However, difficult going and the rising river meant that he was only able to cross the Lugenda River on 15 and 16 January; too late to effect a junction and increasingly short on supplies, Wahle abandoned the boma on the night of 16/17 and withdrew east. The British occupied Likopolwe on 14 January and Luambala four days later, thus achieving their immediate goal, but now hampered by the increasingly heavy rainfall.[41]

As these actions were underway, the rains continued to fall with their customary violence. Further north, Colonel Fitzgerald's Kartrecol had taken over the task of securing the border with German East Africa along the line Ndanda-Massassi. It had the secondary aim of being ready to raze crops along the banks of the Rovuma River and of moving the population northward should the enemy re-emerge. Finally, it was given the unglamorous, but vital, job of building roads up the Lugenda Valley to Nanguare and also west to Tunduru.[42]

Lettow also learned of the British activity in the Mkula Hills, further north. This and Hawthorn's advance meant that an expansion of food-growing areas was impossible and the expected stocks of food in Mwembe-Chirumba-Luambala would only last a few days. Faced by shortages, von Lettow decided to move the main body back to Nanungu, via Mtende, while reinforcing Chirumba with a company from each of Wahle and Köhl. Norforce's advance had also come as a distinct surprise to Lettow, coming as it did from the least expected direction.[43] He decided to intensify his food-gathering operations while trying to hold off the enemy columns. Abt Wahle was despatched to Chirumba to oversee the transportation of food stocks there while Abt Otto maintained a barrier to the west. However, the local African population was now struggling to feed itself and began to hide food supplies from the Askari. The rising waters and deteriorating tracks meant that transport was considerably more difficult and slow than previously. Operationally, the German commander was hamstrung until he could collect enough food to carry on elsewhere.[44]

Matters were not helped by a clever British campaign against his African troops. Leaflets and rumours were spread about the hopelessness of the German cause and offering good treatment to deserters. It was effective, as

112 Askaris and 150 carriers deserted in the month of January; since this represented 10% of the nine western companies it could be ill-afforded. The effects of success against the Portuguese had been offset by the unexpected speed of the follow-up and growing war-weariness. By Lettow's order of 2 February, the commanders read out and publicly dismissed the British arguments while some deserters were caught and executed.[45]

These actions, coupled with Hawthorn's advance, led Lettow to move his forces further east, starting on 27 January. Abt Wahle was ordered to act as rearguard in the west while Abt Köhl fulfilled the same function in the east, with the main body heading for the large supply depot at Nanungu. At the same time, Rosecol had pushed inland nearly 80 km from Porto Amelia, reaching the village of Pamune on 24 January, where it drove back the defenders and captured 5,000 kg of food. As supplies began to run out, Abt Köhl was forced back at Montepuesi.[46] Despite the rain, Rosecol was able to occupy Ankuabe by the end of January and maintained contact with Abt Köhl some 37 km further west. With the harvest due in mid-February, Köhl had to remain in place and prevented any withdrawal to help relieve the pressure in the west.[47]

This pressure was maintained throughout the rest of January and well into February 1918. Operations were heavily constrained by the rain as many bridges were washed away with a number of Wahle's Askaris and carriers being drowned. In the west, Hawthorn had cleared the left bank of the Lujenda River and was forcing the German rearguard east, while Northey conferred with the commander-in-chief about future strategy at Beira on 4 February. By early February, the British had four battalions facing the five enemy companies on the road Chirumba-Mtende-Nanungu. On 7 February, Köhl and Otto were ordered to give up a company each to support the threatened area.[48] The exhaustion of supplies around Mtende forced a contraction on Nanungu with Abt Göring retiring on the latter place by 14 February. Abt Wahle, in turn, was sent off to reconnoitre and to gather as many supplies as possible. By 22 February, Hawthorn was at Mtende, some 120 km to the east of Luambala while Rosecol occupied Meza a week later, it having been abandoned by Köhl owing to lack of food.[49]

This renewed pressure was worrisome and, late in February, Lettow made the protection of his food supplies the highest priority. He assessed that he faced three columns of some twenty to thirty companies in the west with at least thirty in the east. He believed that these forces would encounter major difficulties in maintaining sufficient supplies and that he could counter them by concentrating the maximum number of companies to hit a single British column. There were two possibilities: either to march north to the Lujenda towards Luambala or to go south to Hawella-Malema.[50]

The continuing Barue rebellion along the Zambezi kept van Deventer concerned about the security of Norforce's lines of communication leading to Nyasaland. He urged Rosa to divert any reinforcements at Beira rather than bringing them forward to Moçambique. While it made sound sense to secure the Portuguese base of operations, it also had the added value of keeping their troops away from contact with the Germans. Of course, Rosa was quick to note this, correctly perceiving it as another slight on his forces.[51]

By early March, the British converging movement was progressing well, with Northey reporting the area north-east of Luambala clear for 160 km and Malokotera occupied. On 5 March, Rosecol clashed with a German detachment some 43 km to the east of Medo Boma, which was clearly held in some strength. As it was a key road junction and led to the main body of the Schutztruppe, van Deventer correctly surmised that it would be strongly defended. He decided to reinforce Rose with another column of two battalions of 2 KAR and half a mountain battery under Lieutenant Colonel Giffard. Both columns were placed under the overall command of Brigadier-General Edwards and known collectively as the Porto Amelia Force or Pamforce. The third KAR battalion was sent on to Moçambique to protect the local area and stiffen Portuguese resolve.[52]

At the end of March, the Schutztruppe were deployed in three main areas: GHQ and six companies were south-east of Chizona; Abt Wahle with two companies at Nanungu; and Abt Köhl with six companies and the mountain guns around Montepuesi. With the British closing in on the new German positions, Lettow had been ensured that the newly ripe crops were harvested, diverting a considerable number of Askari for the task. After several weeks, sufficient food was collected to last until the end of May. The Germans now had their freedom of action restored, at least for several months.[53]

On the British side, van Deventer was having less success with his idea of creating a foodless barrier along the Rovuma. The Colonial Office was strongly opposed and had lodged a strong complaint with the War Office.

Although the commander-in-chief was given sanction for his plans, the practicalities of such a project were immense and the project quietly withered away.[54]

THE BATTLE FOR CHIRUMBA HILL

Despite the continuing rain and sodden conditions, van Deventer kept pushing as hard as possible. He had Pamforce with its two columns, Rosecol and Kartucol, pushing westwards on the Medo-Mwalia road against Abt Köhl, while in the west Hawthorn was closed up with Abt Otto. It was Pamforce that had the first opportunity to attack when it ran into a strong German position of about six companies around Chirumba Hill, a long rocky outcrop that paralleled the road running from Medo to Mwalia. General Edwards determined to seize the hill and to press on to Medo as quickly as possible.

The defenders had placed only two companies on the eastern edge of the hill, where they could block the road. The remainder, under Köhl, were echeloned south-east of the defences, ready to counter-attack or conduct an ambush. This was unknown to Rosecol who reached and seized the eastern end of the position by the evening of 10 April. The next day, Kartucol was sent on a flanking movement to the south of Chirumba Hill with the aim of cutting off the Medo-Mloco road and thence to Medo on 12 April, while Rosecol launched a holding attack along the Chirumba Hill to cover the move.

Giffard's column moved off successfully at dawn on 11 April and made reasonable progress bypassing the hill despite encountering a large swamp. However, it was here that he would meet Abt Köhl in its depth positions.[55] By mid-morning, the lead battalion was halted by heavy machine-gun fire that continued past midday, when Köhl launched all four companies into the counter-attack. In the meantime, Rosecol had been pushing slowly westwards along the road towards Medo with two battalions. They did well and began to push back the defenders. As the counter-attack was beginning to threaten Kartucol, Köhl noticed that Rosecol had occupied the high ground to his flank. Despite trying to push them off, he was unsuccessful and with the main position astride the road lost, he decided to break off the battle. The fighting continued until dark when Abt Spangenberg with two companies was left to form the rearguard while the remainder went on to rejoin the main body.[56]

This battle, the first major encounter in Portuguese East Africa, cost both sides a number of casualties and forced Köhl to expend some 53,000 of his precious rounds. As well, food was becoming short and he had to live off the land as much as possible in order to conserve stocks. The loss of Chirumba Hill threatened his stores and he had them evacuated from Namunyo to Mdalamia, but was forced to fight another action on 16/17 April to cover that move. This action inflicted over 100 casualties on the British, but cost him another 46,000 rounds and he continued to withdraw under pressure, while using fighting patrols to try and disrupt the British supply system.[57]

The British advance continued slowly against a series of small-scale ambushes that were greatly enhanced by the very difficult country and thick bush in the area. Mwalia was reached on 20 April, with the columns having averaged about 6 km per day since leaving Medo. Abt Köhl continued its move toward Nanungu, taking up a position around Mblama on 24/25 April. Despite the difficulty of the advance and the unfavourable conditions, the British scored a minor coup as Kartucol attacked a German convoy and seized all the spare rifles, ammunition and documents for Köhl's six companies.[58]

Pamforce ran into heavy opposition on 1 May when a German counter-attack nearly led to the loss of a mountain battery near Koronje. A flank attack onto Kartucol caused a high number of British casualties including forty-two dead and the loss of two mountain guns. Despite the losses, the advance was pushed on against stiff resistance, maintaining the pressure on the rearguards.[59]

In the meantime, van Deventer had grasped Lettow's intentions and ordered his forces to converge on Nanungu. Northey was instructed to advance from his position at Mahua while maintaining forces to the north to prevent a breakthrough in that direction. Edwards was told to carry on driving along the Mwalia-Nanungu road while Colonel Rosa was asked to use his troops to cover the gap between the two forces. Norforce occupied Mahua on 5 May, having overrun and dispersed a German company the day previously. This move worried Lettow, who had moved westward with five companies to block the advance. The British columns reacted to the German response by digging in near Makoti, less than 40 km southwest of Nanungu.

On arrival, Lettow launched a ferocious attack, using two flanking movements. Despite the strength of the blow, it was unable to dislodge the defenders and Lettow had to regroup under cover of darkness. Casualties were heavy on both sides, with the Germans having over 100, and they had to amalgamate two companies, reducing their overall strength to thirteen. For their part, the British suffered over 200 losses and were forced to halt to sort out the casualties.[60]

This sharp action led the British to believe that Lettow still considered a move north, a fact apparently confirmed by the statements of prisoners. To that end, van Deventer ordered one column to hold the north along the Msalu River while the remainder of Edwards's and Northey's troops would close in on Nanungu in an attempt to bring the Germans to a decisive battle. The advance resumed on 17 May with Kartucol entering Nanungu unopposed two days later. Finding that place abandoned except for a hospital full of sick soldiers, Edwards despatched Kartucol down the Mahua road in pursuit of the withdrawing Germans. Rosecol and Grifcol were sent off on flanking marches to the north and south of the road respectively on 20 May. Lettow had already left in a south-westerly direction along the Mahua Road going in the direction that the British were least prepared and least able to deal with. He had organised his force into four Abteilungen with the customary advance and rearguards ready for a move south of the River Lurio.[61] The first major stop was at Korewa, some 38 km south-west of Nanungu while he kept alert for an opportunity to strike at an isolated column.

The next day, Kartucol ran into Abt Köhl, now the rearguard, and quickly started working around its position. This forced the Germans to pull back further through the dense bush and out of British clutches. Despite the break south, the situation was beginning to look favourable for van Deventer as the bulk of the Schutztruppe were being concentrated into a fairly tight area, albeit rocky and thickly vegetated, while the flanking columns were pressing in. However, he was unaware that Lettow was now preparing to strike back at his pursuers.

Having first sent off the baggage train to a safe distance, Lettow instructed Abt Köhl to launch a spoiling attack on the morning of 22 May. It was not intended to be decisive, just enough to disrupt the advance and enable the rearguard to break clear and slowly move back. At 0900, Kartucol came into battle as the road went into a narrow gorge flanked by impassable hills. The lead battalion engaged Köhl's troops with its mountain guns and Stokes mortars to good effect while the flanking columns moved on. Grifcol emerged from the south onto the Mahua road to the rear of Köhl's main body, surprising a company at its midday meal and driving it off. Moving on, it then captured Abt Köhl's baggage, while cutting the German force in half. Lettow was not far behind, with both Abt Poppe and Göring, and immediately advanced on hearing the firing. In danger of being trapped, Köhl had begun withdrawing through the gorge when Lettow arrived. He launched a furious eight company counter-attack onto Grifcol, but it failed to dislodge the now-surrounded column. Further east, Kartucol kept pressing hard and Lettow was compelled to despatch two companies and later a third to protect this flank. His blow had failed, and, in considerable danger of being destroyed in place, he ordered the battle broken off. The night provided an opportunity for the weakened Schutztruppe to escape through the dense bush and regroup to the south.[62]

The two-day battle cost both sides heavily, but especially the Germans. They had suffered heavy casualties, losing over 100 troops and 300 carriers. Four companies were effectively destroyed, with the governor, both artillery batteries and Abt Köhl losing their baggage. Over 30,000 rounds had been expended while the British had captured a further 70,000; this left only 613,000 for the entire force. Furthermore, food was running short and the whole situation had a distinct resemblance to November 1917 when the force had barely escaped from a similar scrape. This setback forced Lettow to break contact and march south slowly in order to evacuate the seriously wounded and sick.[63]

From the British point of view, the battle had represented a chance to end the campaign. Had Rosecol been able to join the battle, it might have made the difference. As it was, the Germans were mauled heavily, although at some cost to the advancing columns and a significant reduction in their fighting strength. Nevertheless, they were still not beaten and the British had once again run into the limits of their supplies. Nanungu marked a turning point in the campaign as the Germans were under severe pressure to gain both food supplies and ammunition.

THE MOVE SOUTH TO MOÇAMBIQUE

Reorganising on the spot, Rosecol was broken-up while Kartrecol deployed a battalion to secure the road along the line Malema-Moçambique while another was sent to stiffen the Portuguese detachment along the Ribane-Maleme road. It was left to Kartucol and Grifcol to carry on the pursuit of Lettow in parallel columns. Rearguard actions were the norm and were only broken up by the capture of another hospital left behind by the Germans.[64]

Lettow remained as wily as ever and quickly moved his reduced force south gaining a day and a half's head start on his now-halted opponents. His aim was to replenish his diminished stocks and to secure enough food to live off; going south offered the best opportunities while putting more strain on his opponents' supply lines. By 27 May, the advance guard had reached the River Lurio and had reconnoitered a suitable crossing site near Watiwa.[65]

By 1 June, the Germans had almost completely crossed the River Lurio at Watiwa and now threatened to break through the difficult area between the river and Inagu and into the more settled areas around Moçambique. The land was exceptionally difficult with numerous hills, very thick bush, little cultivation and few paths. The indigenous population was also strongly anti-Portuguese and willing to assist the incoming Germans. Given the past weakness of the Portuguese forces, van Deventer had to assume that they would be incapable of serious resistance and therefore had to deploy his own troops to support them. He asked Colonel Rosa to move some of his troops from their positions just south of the Rovuma to the port of Quelimane and to be prepared to move them inland from there. The final arrangements were agreed at a meeting in Dar-es-Salaam on 8 June, although subsequently the Portuguese commander's enthusiasm for attacking had to be curbed by van Deventer. Instead, Rosa was instructed to await reinforcement and was to ensure the fortification of the supply base at Nhamacurra, at the end of a small railway line north of Quelimane.[66]

The German push south forced van Deventer to reconsider the ever-lengthening lines of communication. As things stood, Porto Amelia was too distant, but the shifting of the entire base by sea to the port of Moçambique was out of the question owing to shortages of shipping. Consequently, a motor road was cut from Medo down to Nanripo, where the Lurio was crossed, and then south to Mcuburi and finally on to Nampula. Van Deventer was particularly concerned about the ability of the Portuguese to defend themselves, and decided to reinforce their key garrisons with his own troops. A new column under Colonel Fitzgerald, named Fitzcol, was formed from two KAR battalions at Muo Nluku.[67] Hoping to box the enemy in the Malema area, he sent a unit to Inagu

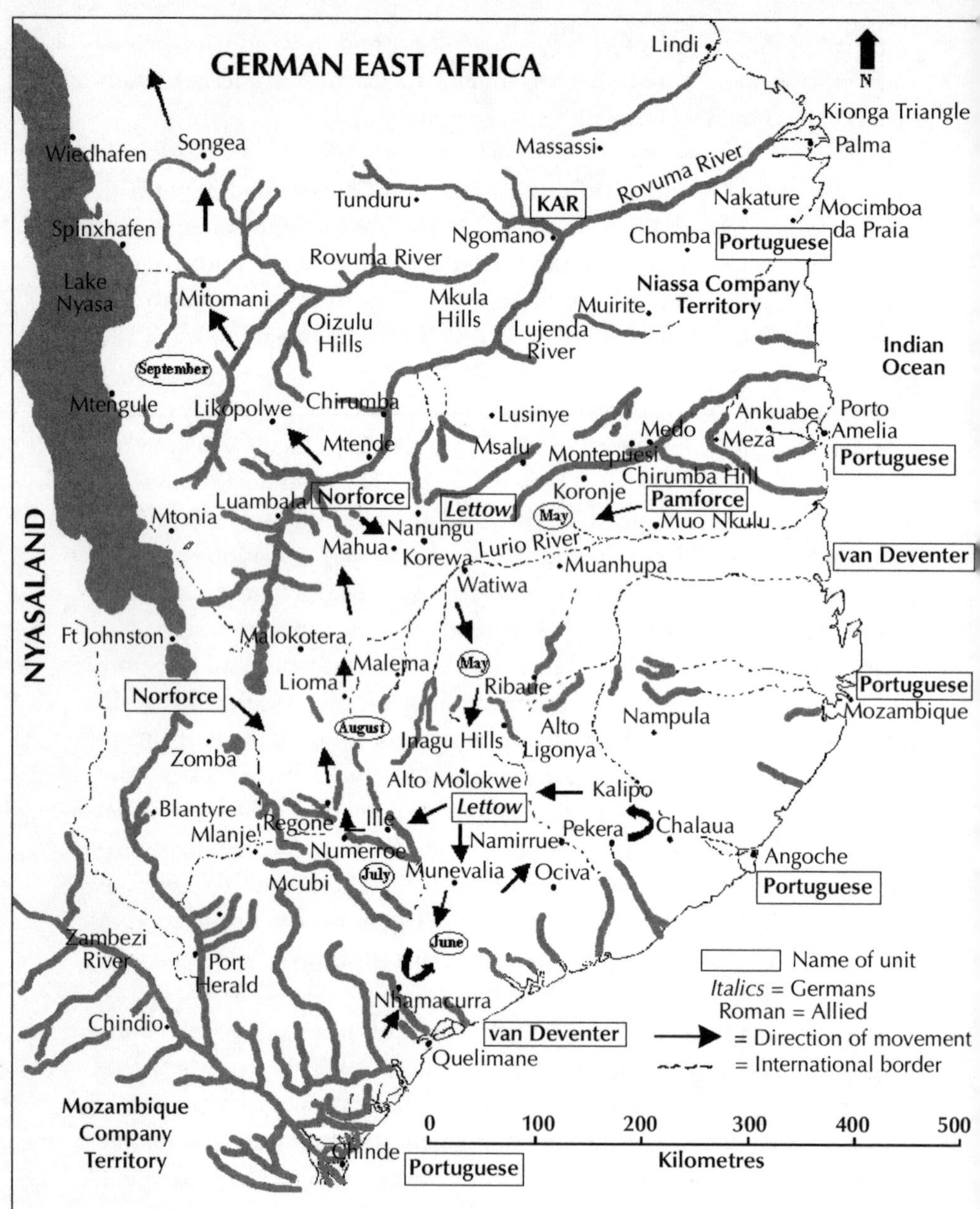
GERMAN EAST AFRICA
N
Lindi
Kionga Triangle
Palma
Massassi
Rovuma River
Wiedhafen
Songea
Tunduru
KAR
Nakature
Mocimboa da Praia
Spinxhafen
Ngomano
Chomba
Portuguese
Rovuma River
Lake Nyasa
Mitomani
Niassa Company Territory
Mkula Hills
Muirite
Oizulu Hills
Lujenda River
Indian Ocean
September
Mtengule
Likopolwe
Chirumba
Lusinye
Ankuabe
Porto Amelia
Medo
Meza
Mtende
Msalu
Montepuesi
Portuguese
Chirumba Hill
Luambala
Norforce
Koronje
Pamforce
Mtonia
Lettow
May
Muo Nkulu
Nanungu
NYASALAND
Mahua
Korewa
Lurio River
van Deventer
Muanhupa
Watiwa
Ft Johnston
Malokotera
Malema
May
Portuguese
Lioma
Ribaue
Mozambique
Norforce
Alto Ligonya
Nampula
August
Inagu Hills
Zomba
Alto Molokwe
Kalipo
Blantyre
Lettow
Regone
Ille
Mlanje
Pekera
Chalaua
Namirrue
Numerroe
Angoche
Munevalia
Ociva
July
Mcubi
Portuguese
June
Zambezi River
Port Herald
Name of unit
Italics = Germans
Roman = Allied
Nhamacurra
Chindio
van Deventer
= Direction of movement
= International border
Quelimane
Mozambique Company Territory
0
100
200
300
400
500
Kilometres
Chinde
Portuguese

Operations in Portuguese East Africa, May–September 1918

while another moved into Malokotera with an Anglo-Portuguese column concentrated at Ribaue. Further north, both Grifcol and Kartucol were still struggling to cross the Lurio in the face of German rearguards, finally making the crossing by 5 June.[68]

The Germans were wasting little time and managed to evade the converging columns on the Malema line. The advance guard, Abt Müller with three companies, attacked the Portuguese boma at Malema that had been reinforced by several companies of KAR on 31 May. For once, the attack was unsuccessful and the defenders held firm.[69] Müller remained there for a few days and then marched off, rejoining the main body on 8 June. Lettow then decided to march in the direction of least resistance and sent off Müller towards Alto Molokwe. Arriving there on 12 June, the boma was found empty, its garrison of two Portuguese companies having fled without a shot, and a rich haul of food and documents were taken. Most importantly, the captured papers mentioned an incoming ammunition column. Müller immediately followed up this lead and went off searching the local area for its whereabouts. Occupying Ille, Alto Ligonye, Nampave and Muyeba in turn, he seized 2,200 loads of food and various materials. Furthermore, the tracks of a column were found and Müller captured 150,000 kg of food and numerous other supplies on 23 June. A subsequent attack on a lone Portuguese company yielded several machine guns, some food and 13,000 rounds of ammunition. Despite these considerable successes, the supply column could not be located and ammunition remained scarce.[70]

After halting on the Malema line to sort out the supply situation, on 16 June van Deventer ordered the three mobile columns to move south, with General Edwards assuming command of the Moçambique theatre. The new base at the port of Moçambique opened up the next day, while the lead units of Colonel Rosa's northern troops landed at neighbouring Quelimane on 20 June. It was van Deventer's intention to trap and hammer the Schutztruppe between the villages of Ille and Alto Molokwe, and then to drive it towards the coast. General Hawthorn, now having taken over Norforce, brought the bulk of his troops to Ille while Philcol moved to Nakwa and Alto Ligonye; Fitzcol was due to link-up with them near Ribaue, while the Portuguese were relegated to securing the coastal towns.[71] But, van Deventer miscalculated, as his opponent had already determined to continue south-east and just beat the British to Ille. On 25 June, the lead unit ran into the German advance guard, Abt Spangenberg, but was unable to push through. While fighting was underway, the enemy main body and rearguard bypassed the fighting and slipped away.[72] More troops were now brought into the fighting as Kartrecol was taken off its duties along the Rovuma and brought south. Fitzcol left Mbalama and, after a long and exhausting march, joined General Edwards at Nampula on 30 June.

ANGLO-PORTUGUESE DIFFERENCES

Portuguese suspicion of British intentions remained high with matters reaching a head in late June 1918 when van Deventer felt obliged formally to reassure the local administration that British forces would withdraw from the colony after defeating the Germans. After obtaining Cabinet approval for the statement, he then informed the Portuguese of Britain's adherence to past treaties and agreements.[73] However, even explicit assurances were not enough and differences continued to rankle on both sides. Only a few days later, fed up with the continuing Portuguese practice of leaving small detachments scattered throughout the country without adequate support or proper defences, the commander-in-chief sent a withering critique to the War Office. Instead of adding to his military power, such outposts acted merely as a supply of food, weapons and ammunition for Lettow, and neutralised many of the successes gained in battle. He was equally exasperated from constantly pressing Colonel Rosa to draw up a more concentrated and workable plan of defence.

The time had come for drastic measures and van Deventer now proposed to relegate all of the Portuguese military forces to rear areas or coastal protection, while all elements of the civil administration were to be withdrawn from the area of operations owing to their obstructiveness. For the sake of good relations, he praised Colonel Rosa's efforts as well as the civilian governor of Niassa although the governor of Moçambique was directly accused of being obstructive and unhelpful to the military effort.

> I think the time has come when the Portuguese authorities must be told the truth, namely that their troops in Portuguese East Africa are totally unreliable and a source of grave danger to their allies. The personnel, both European and African, is of the poorest possible quality, and the natives of Portuguese East Africa detest Portuguese to such an extent that when we

> act in conjunction with Portuguese troops we can get no help from them. When acting alone removed from Portuguese sphere of influence natives help us freely.[74]

The British Ambassador was instructed to deliver this highly undiplomatic message; it was a measure of the desire to conclude the campaign in East Africa that the government assented to such drastic terms. For good measure, the Portuguese Government was to be informed that their colonial authorities were incapable of ruling effectively and were opposed by their African subjects.[75] Events would soon underline the unpalatable truth of the charges. For his part, Colonel Rosa suspected that van Deventer was continuing Smuts' policy of forcing his troops to operate in the most difficult and dangerous area of the Rovuma, to save British troops.[76] It was partially true, but for very different reasons.

DISASTER IN JULY

As July opened, the Germans posed a distinct threat to the port of Quelimane. This also placed the major supply base at Nhamacurra and its railway to the port in jeopardy. Nhamacurra was essential for the support of any columns operating north of that port and had a large stockpile of food and essential stores. Van Deventer was especially concerned about its security and he ordered Colonel Rosa to reinforce it while also providing a half battalion of KAR. On at least two occasions, he sent explicit instructions for its defence, charging Rosa with responsibility for the execution of his orders. This was important as the British were short of information owing to the hostility of the local population, but they did realise that Lettow was in the area.[77]

On paper the garrison was formidable, with three Portuguese infantry companies and one artillery, together with the two KAR companies. The defences were laid out over a distance of 3,000 metres with three sectors, the western and central being allocated to the Portuguese and the eastern to the British. The railway station formed the right of the position and was held by the KAR. The Nhamacurra River marked the left before swinging around the rear of the defences.[78]

On 27 June, von Lettow sent off his advance guard, Abt Müller, with orders to obtain more ammunition and intelligence with the main body remaining a day's march behind it. Africans informed Müller of the position at Nhamacurra and he promptly decided to march on it. Emerging from the bush only 30 metres from the Portuguese positions around the sisal factory in the western sector, he was surprised to run into the enemy. However, they fled at literally the first shots and the position quickly collapsed, with substantial quantities of weapons and ammunition being captured. Moving toward the centre of the position, Müller's troops ran into further Portuguese and some British troops, who put up some resistance but were eventually forced out.

Consolidating on the objective, he awaited the arrival of the main body who duly arrived on 2 July. Patrols had located the KAR positions at the railway station and Köhl now resolved to attack it. Well dug-in and disciplined, the KAR held their positions and inflicted heavy losses on the attackers. Heavy machine gun and rifle fire continued throughout the day as well as most of 3 July. At 1500 hours, one of the captured Portuguese mountain guns was made serviceable again and began firing. The first round hit the railway station building and drove out a number of Portuguese Askaris and carriers in a blind panic. They stampeded through the KAR positions causing chaos while the Germans took advantage of the confusion to infiltrate. Now overwhelmed and being overrun from the rear, the position began to collapse. The defenders tried to withdraw over the deep Nhamacurra River to their rear and many drowned or were shot down as they tried to escape.[79]

The result was a disaster. The Portuguese garrison had been largely wiped out as well as the KAR companies. More importantly, vast quantities of food, weapons, ammunition and stores fell into the Germans' hands, relieving their supply worries at once. It gave them the ability to fight on for some considerable time. They seized some five heavy machine guns, three light machine guns, 484 rifles, 327,000 rounds, 300,000 kg of food, and, critically, 3.75 kg of quinine.[80]

This disaster also caused considerable panic to the Portuguese administration as Quelimane was now directly threatened. On 4 July, Colonel Rosa ordered the families evacuated and the bullion stores placed on ships as a precaution, while there was wild talk of abandoning the town. However, the British resolved to hold it and Lettow had other ideas. He realised that the Zambesi was in flood and therefore impassable while the British strength lay in their ability to move by sea. He decided to reverse his steps and to head north-east with the secondary aim of disrupting their newly created lines of communication. Marching in five groups with the standard advance guard of Abt Müller and rearguard of Abt Köhl, the Germans set off on 5 July.[81] However, owing to the loss of contact and active deception by the local population, the British lost track of these movements for a few days.

The failure at Nhamacurra was the final straw for van Deventer. He had tried to give Rosa another chance and it had been a complete disaster. A major breach now ensued. As he told the CIGS:

> I now intend to inform the Portuguese Commander-in-Chief frankly, that I cannot consent, under any circumstances, to allow Portuguese troops to co-operate with mine in the field. I propose to ask him to take over the coast line from Quelimane to Angoche, inclusive, and to hold it with the troops at his disposal as he considers best. British troops alone will carry out all active operations.[82]

For Rosa's part, he blamed the disaster on van Deventer's decision to land reinforcements elsewhere, forgetting the poor performance of his troops in the battle and the failure to secure supplies in the area. This was the end of his command as he was relieved on 9 July and ordered to return to Lisbon. Leaving in mid-August, he returned home in October to be arrested by the Government and thrown into jail, where he spent nearly two months in confinement. Ironically, the British Government, sensitive to future good relations, awarded him a Companionship of the Order of the Bath (CB), a startling contrast to the disgrace meted out by his own country.[83]

Finally, Philcol ran into the leading elements of the Schutztruppe near Ociva on 11 July. Thus warned, General Edwards sent Fitzcol north from Nhamacurra towards Ociva while the redoubtable Kartucol was ordered to try and head off the Germans at Murrau. Van Deventer released the last of his battalions along the border of German East Africa, sending two KAR battalions from Fort Johnston to Moçambique.[84] The chase was now in full flight. A Portuguese post at Mtiba fell easily, but Philcol and Kartucol were now closing hard, and Köhl had to hold them off as the main body slipped off north towards the small post of Namirrue, held by two companies of KAR. Fitzcol reached the Namirrue River about 40 km west of the boma on 20 July. Setting off the next day, it could hear the sounds of battle from the direction of the garrison; the column marched as quickly as it could through the heavy bush. Pausing only briefly on the night of 21/22 July, Fitzcol emerged onto the Alto Ligonha-Namirrue road to find the boma was already under attack by the six companies of Lettow's main body while the three companies of advance guard secured the flank.

Fitzgerald was well aware of the potential seriousness of the situation and his lead battalion pressed on towards the beleaguered garrison. By 1600 hours, the leading German outposts had been driven in, but an hour later a strong attack checked the column's progress. The enemy withdrew at nightfall and both battalions dug-in in line. Lettow had been informed about the threat to his rear and had launched a night flanking attack. At 1900 hours, it hit the right flank of the forward position that was still under construction. The Schutztruppe managed to break into the defences and routed the battalion completely. The shock was so complete that the commanding officer and his headquarters staff were taken prisoner. Stragglers quickly reached the second battalion and alerted Fitzgerald to the impending threat. A desperate fight ensued until 2100 hours, when the battle was broken off by the attackers. A much-weakened column then withdrew to protect its baggage train. The next day revealed that one battalion had practically ceased to exist and the other was reduced to less than 200 effectives. Against the main body of the enemy, the column was now helpless and could do little more than defend itself.[85]

The defeat of Fitzcol sealed the fate of the unlucky garrison holding the boma at Namirrue. Cut off from its water supply and overwhelmingly outnumbered, the post fell on 23 July after several assaults and surrendered. However it did cost the attackers dear, as one company commander was killed in the attack and another severely wounded.[86] During this time, Kartucol had been far from idle as it had left Munevalia on the night of 2/3 July. It had spent some considerable time chasing rumours of the Germans heading south towards Quelimane when news was received about the disaster at Nhamacurra. The column returned to Munevalia on 14 July, having marched 300 km or an average of 27 km per day through heavy bush. Despite their considerable fatigue, there was no opportunity for rest and they marched straight off towards Tipe in an attempt to head off the Schutztruppe before it could cross the River Molocque.

Kartucol reached its objective on 20 July only to find Abt Köhl holding the crossings. Showing great determination, crossings were forced and the column pushed up against the Germans until 22 July when firing could be heard from the direction of Namirrue. The enemy's camp was located on 24 July, but the column did not attack until the arrival of reinforcements and a much needed food resupply.[87] It then advanced to the site of the camp to find it evacuated and burnt out. On hearing that the Germans had turned east, Giffard ordered a forced march to Calipo, north-east of Namirrue, where he then halted to link-up with the remnants of Fitzcol. A brief rest ensued as Kartucol had marched 530 km in a month with little food, no blankets or personal kit. It was a remarkable achievement.[88]

The unsatisfactory military situation led to another meeting between General van Deventer and the governor general at Quelimane on 22 July. It was decided to give each nation separate zones of operation, with the Portuguese being allocated the defence of the sea ports from Quelimane to Angoche together with local inland operations. The British took upon themselves the task of maintaining forces south of the line Moçambique-Malema and with it all active operations.

A week later, on 29 July, van Deventer met with Edwards at Nampula to decide future operations. The Germans were now known to have turned again and this time headed east to the area of Chalaua, which was fertile land between the Ligonha and Meluli rivers. The local population was in a state of near revolt and was actively assisting the invaders against the hated colonial power and its allies. Notable too, was the virtual cessation of desertions since the crossing of the Malema line on 10 June which may have been attributed to the great distances between the Askaris' homes and the location of the fighting forces.[89]

Lettow's calculations had been influenced by documents captured at Namirrue that indicated that the area to its north had few supplies of food. The area east of Ligonye had a number of Portuguese posts, mostly abandoned, and, although over 13,000 loads of food were discovered, the lack of porters meant that most had to be destroyed. He decided to go east and marched to Pekera, arriving on 24 July, before moving on to Chalaua two days later.[90] The force managed to spend a week in the area and the lack of a close pursuit gave the force time to consider some essential measures regarding manpower. It had been possible to make up the diminished numbers of Askaris through the promotion of the best carriers, but in the eight months in Portuguese territory over a third had been lost (1,190 from 1,790) while 310 good porters had been enlisted to replace them and began immediate training. However, more serious was the dimunition of the irreplaceable German officers and non-commissioned officers who had dwindled by nearly 30% in the same time (197 remaining out of 281). The loss rate of ten-eleven per month was increasingly serious, particularly when the need for good leaders was especially acute.[91] Pitched battles were becoming too expensive and were working in favour of the British.

While these operations were underway, the British continued their work on improving the communications in Portuguese East Africa. The extension of the motor road from Medo to Nampula was completed quickly and large numbers of vehicles were moved via this route to the Moçambique line rather than by sea. The road leading from Mnapo to Chinga was extended to Ribaue and Malema, while General Hawthorn's engineers continued the road from Nyasaland to Malokotera. Similarly, the Portuguese built a road from Ngomano through Chomba to Medo. The net effect of this activity was that, by the end of August, it was possible to drive from the Rovuma to Medo, through Nampula and Malema and on to Zomba in Nyasaland.[92] It was a major achievement and greatly aided the movement of supplies and troops. A number of smaller tracks were also constructed, as were improved telegraphic links from Nyasaland and the major ports of Quelimane and Moçambique.

These efforts were to have beneficial effects in the next stage of events. With a brief rest being granted to the most tired units, a number of smaller columns were sent out to protect the vulnerable lines of communication. Then, on 9 August, van Deventer initiated a converging movement on Chalaua with the aim of trapping Lettow. The latter, of course, had no intention of being caught and had already started to collect his dispersed force, with a preliminary move on 7 August toward Namatil as a feint towards Moçambique. His real aim was the British magazine in the rich area around Regone. The rapidly closing British forced him to halt on 10 August and then he turned south followed by west and then north-west, in a successful attempt to confuse the scent.[93] However, a captured telegram was to have fateful consequences as Lettow learnt that the supply centre at Mukubi was being evacuated to Regone. This tipped the balance and he now ordered his columns to make for Regone.

The threat to Nyasaland was never far from van Deventer's mind and the latest move by the Schutztruppe led him to order the reinforcement of his western flank. General Hawthorn was ordered to hold Regone while Kartucol was sent rapidly to Alto Molokwe; the remaining troops were instructed to follow the Germans as closely as possible. On 24 August, Numarroe had been reached and Abt Müller ran into a battalion of KAR. A heavy fight ensued with the battalion being forced back to the boma at Regone.[94] It was an important advanced supply base, containing 10,000 loads of food, 500 cases of small arms ammunition and 200 of Stokes mortar bombs; its loss would have severely hindered British operations in the area apart from providing the Germans with a large augmentation to their resources.[95]

Lettow wanted to take Regone by the use of small side paths, thereby avoiding the main defences. However, his plan miscarried through heavy fog, rain and difficult going. He reached the boma on 26 August to find it well defended and recently reinforced. In view of its strength and the approaching columns, he made the decision not to attack and to move off to the north instead.[96]

While these movements were underway, Hawthorn's troops had dug themselves in south of Lioma while Kartucol had its three battalions spread between Inagu and Muanhupa having arrived there from Alto Molokwe. A hastily reinforced Fitzcol also went to Muanhupa to add to the defences. On 30 August, the Schutztruppe located and attacked the Norforce in its entrenched positions, with eleven of its twelve companies being committed to the assault. Despite being hit from all sides, the battalion held on tightly and was relieved by the arrival of Fitzcol on the same day. That unit sent in a counter-attack that was followed by another battalion arriving from Muanhupa early on 31 August. This resulted in the taking of Abt Müller's baggage column and the loss of 50,000 sorely needed rounds. Realising that he had stumbled into a strong position, Lettow changed his plans and headed north.[97] Kartucol followed up with its usual vigour as it located the enemy crossing the Muanhupa River on the next day; its lead battalion launched an attack from the west supported by another from the east. Although able to deflect these blows, the Germans lost two of the governor's key staff officers, a medical officer and the field hospital.[98]

Lioma-Regone was probably Lettow's narrowest escape. Trying to defeat the British in detail, he had very nearly been caught in a trap. Casualties were heavy and the losses of military equipment and medical stores were marked. Sixty-three were killed with a further seventy wounded, while some 250 valuable carriers were captured by the British.[99] Equally, he had inflicted major losses on the enemy between Nhamacurra and Namirrue with about three battalions being put out of action. But such battles were unsustainable and the losses were irreplaceable.

Prisoners taken by the Schutztruppe indicated that yet another KAR battalion was now to the east coming from Alto Molokwe and Malema. Increasingly desperate to escape the British trap, Lettow decided to move north and recross the River Lurio, which was now a trickle. Forced marches between 1 and 3 September were interrupted only by attacks on the rearguard by the persistent British columns.[100] On 5 September, the Germans had their first rest day in twenty-five, but could only pause briefly as the pursuers were close at hand. Supplies were again growing very short, and the country was devastated from previous incursions and the German columns had to separate widely in order to seek food.

Shortcol was sent ahead to try and prevent the crossing of the Lurio, but collided with the rearguard on 5 September. Kartucol left its camp on the same day and made for the Germans' expected position. But a German detour into the bush quickly confused matters; Kartucol thought that the enemy was some way to its north (and front) when it came under contact. Quite unexpectedly, it had hit the main body while in column of march. This unexpected collision caused great confusion in both opposing columns as the rear battalion of Kartucol clashed with the middle of the German line, that of Abt Müller. The engagement was fought in terrain with very limited visibility and it took several hours for reinforcements to arrive on both sides, owing to the dispersed nature of the respective columns. The confusion was exacerbated by the Germans running into the British transport. They believed that they had chanced upon a supply convoy and initiated a rapid attack. The KAR were placed under heavy pressure as it had to react quickly, while the rest of the column was some 3 and 6 km ahead respectively. It took several hours for the second unit to come into action and block the German attack. Finally, the lead battalion reached the battle in late afternoon and launched a final counter-attack. This was successful, and the battle was broken off and the Germans moved off into the bush. Kartucol had suffered heavily in the encounter and was unable to continue the advance which was given over to Shortcol. Again, the Germans lost heavily in officers and suffered against the good British defences.[101]

The inevitable reorganisation after battle included the collection, treatment and evacuation of the wounded. Kartucol had to deal with over 200 stretcher cases, including the enemy's, and deliver them to the Lurio for evacuation by motor ambulance. This was completed on 8 September, while it was not until 13 September that the battered KAR battalion was able to rejoin the column.

The battles at the end of August and early September were painful to both sides. The Germans had suffered thirty-nine soldiers killed, 133 wounded and fifty-one captured, as well as 437 carriers lost. Telling was the impact on the command structure as two Abteilung leaders and three company commanders had been either killed or seriously wounded. The force was reduced to twelve companies that had lost a great deal of baggage together with forty packs of crucial medical supplies. The weather was also hurting the Germans' health as the intense heat of the days was followed by severe cold at nights, coupled with little food or water. An epidemic of lung influenza broke out in early September.[102] For their part, the British had lost eight soldiers killed and seventy-one wounded from one unit alone on 6 September.

THE BREAK TO THE NORTH-WEST

By now, Lettow was anxious to avoid another series of battles and did his best to break free; Mwembe was reached on 17 September after another exhausting march only for the Germans to find all its stores burnt or removed.[103] Shortcol could only support one battalion in the pursuit owing to supply difficulties. Durcol reached Inagu and Malema in early September, only to be disbanded once the enemy crossed the River Lurio. Kartucol lost one of its battalions which went into reserve near Tabora, while the remaining two crossed the Rovuma on 28 September.

The break northwards gave rise to concerns about the safety of both Mahenge and Songea, which were fertile areas and well known to the Germans. The newly developed road system came in extremely handy as units were re-deployed throughout September. Kartucol was broken up, having marched an incredible 2,500 km, crossed twenty-nine large rivers and fought thirty-two engagements. Its well-worn troops were sent into reserve to secure the southern portion of German East Africa in the area Massassi-Ndanda. Fitzcol was disbanded and the bulk of units transferred to a new formation, Cenforce. It was commanded by Colonel Fitzgerald and based along the Central Railway between Morogoro and Dodoma with columns extended south to Mahenge and Iringa. Van Deventer's aim was to use his strategic mobility to reinforce threatened areas as required while keeping up the close pursuit by Shortcol. Hawthorn recalled his forward units to Fort Johnston, preparatory to a move by steamer north along Lake Nyasa and thence to Sphinxhafen. He wanted to catch the Schutztruppe in the flank before they could reach the Rhodesia-Nyasaland border. Orders were given by GHQ to send Norforce to Songea and Ubena, with battalions sent to garrison Mahenge and Iringa while the remaining infantry battalions were concentrated around Massassi.[104]

However, the age and decrepitude of the vessels on Lake Nyasa meant that frequent breakdowns impeded the speed of deployment. Hawthorn's lead battalion left Fort Johnston on 18 September and concentrated at Sphinxhafen by the end of the month. It too was tired, having been marching and fighting continually since the previous March. The Rhodesian police units followed up as quickly as resources permitted, but the enemy lead was still too great.[105]

While the reasons for this loss of momentum were quite clear to General Hawthorn, the commnder-in-chief was very displeased. A sharp telegram accused Norforce of having lost its drive and determination. While Hawthorn's angry rebuttal had some justification, it verged on the insubordinate. There was truth in both views, as some of the column commanders had let opportunities slip, but equally it was clear that the overall strategy had not been a great success either. Firmly rebuked, Hawthorn was given the task of pursuing Lettow northwards and of bringing him to battle at any cost.[106]

If the Germans had made good their escape from the clutches of General Edwards, they were not having an easy time of it. Health worries impinged in a major way as influenza and pneumonia hit the force. Weakened by the continual marching and poor rations, all members of the Schutztruppe and its followers were suffering from serious weight loss and weakened resistance to disease. At times, 50% had influenza and each company had six to eight pneumonia cases. Only ninety of the worst cases could be carried and the rest had to walk. Between 1 and 22 September, twelve Askaris and twenty carriers had to be abandoned due to exhaustion, while twenty-four Askaris and sixty-seven carriers had deserted. The main Abteilung of five weak companies could muster only three officers. Matters came to a head on 20 September when Governor Schnee sent a letter to General Lettow stating that the carrying along of the seriously ill was an unjustifiable sacrifice of lives and that they should be abandoned as advised by the doctors. This went down poorly and he retorted that to do so would irretrievably weaken his combat power and many of the sick would recover in time. The situation was not helped by the continued reports of the unfavourable military situation in Europe from the remaining wireless receiver and captured newspapers.[107]

Having rebuffed the governor, Lettow then called in all of his Abteilung leaders and emphasised their mission of tying up as many Allied troops as possible and telling them not to be depressed by the apparently bad news from Europe. It was a crisis of confidence that appears to have been staunched for the time being. However, the pressure was beginning to show in the columns as they had had only had one day's rest out of thirty-five marching. Desertions amongst the African troops were increasing - Abt Kraut lost 300 of its experienced carriers in two days while over 200 prisoners of war managed to escape.[108]

Having kept his force together with the strength of his personality, Lettow's next move was to cross the Rovuma some 30 km east of Mitomani on 29 September and re-enter German territory after an absence of some ten months. It had been a difficult time, particularly from British pressure in the latter months, and the German force had shrunk from 278 to 168 Europeans, from 1,600-1,700 Askaris to just over 1,000, and the experienced carriers from 4,000 to about 2,000. While the fighting power of the Schutztruppe remained formidable, the constant sufferings and losses were taking a toll on morale. Abt Wahle was broken up on 2 October and the force became even more concentrated than ever.[109]

Patrols soon found that the British were holding Mitomani and captured documents indicated that two further companies were en route from Sphinxhafen to Songea. This resulted in an action on 4 October as Abt Spangenberg blocked the progress of these companies along the Wiedhafen-Songea road, while the remainder of the force bypassed to the west and continued their march north. Although successful, this action cost another thirty-forty casualties while both Askaris and carriers were deserting in greater numbers.[110]

The options facing the Germans at this stage were manifold, as the British could not move troops rapidly enough to go off in the direction of their choice. Furthermore, the rains were due in December and this would make the roads from the Central Railway to Iringa and Mahenge unusable. Therefore, if either place could be seized prior to then, it would be almost impossible to dislodge them until the following May. With the bulk of the British forces in the long process of redeploying from the heart of Portuguese East Africa, it would be some time before a suitably large formation could be assembled. As a precaution, van Deventer ordered the reinforcement of the Lindi-Tunduru area in the south with additions to the garrisons of both Mahenge and Iringa while roads leading south from the railway were improved. All steps were being take to prevent a thrust back into German East Africa.[111]

Lettow was unaware of all this and, having bypassed the first blocking force, he continued his rapid march north. Hawthorn was anxious to stop him at the northern end of Lake Nyasa and ordered two battalions to move by ship up to Alt Langenburg as quickly as possible. With shortages of carriers and food, it was only possible to keep one battalion in the pursuit. Furthermore, the poor condition of the Lake fleet meant that two of the three available ships broke down in the middle of one move. The battalion was finally complete at Alt Langenburg on 18 October and further reinforcements were still en route.

On 15 October the KAR regained contact with Abt Köhl and maintained it over the course of the next few days. The Germans were also successful in foraging as some ten days' supplies were found and carried off during the engagement. On 17 October, Lettow felt able to have a rest at Ubena, the first in seventeen days. It was here that the redoubtable General Wahle was left behind, too ill to continue. It was a remarkable effort by a sixty-four-year-old man, who had previously retired from the Saxon Army and who had suffered a double hernia and much malaria during the arduous campaign. He was left behind with a number of sick and wounded troops and their followers. [112]

On 19 October, the columns moved onto Gambawano where a quantity of food was collected over the next two days, while the British were unable to pursue and remained static in Ubena. Here, Lettow decided to turn west and enter Northern Rhodesia instead of carrying on to Tabora as expected by van Deventer. His troops had largely recovered from the epidemic in September, but badly needed rest, while the low stocks of ammunition constrained their ability to fight battles. They had averaged nearly 29 km per day since 12 August with only three rest days. The core of the Schutztruppe had kept up a gruelling programme.

Northern Rhodesia had not been touched heavily by the war since late 1915 and there were few defences to slow down an invader. Lettow considered going on to the west coast and Angola in particular, as neither the Portuguese nor the Belgians could do anything meaningful to stop his movements. The British would have to redraw their extensive lines of communication and commence another campaign. All of this time would enable a new harvest to be gathered and the Schutztruppe would be able to continue their actions, suitably refreshed.[113] On the other hand, the dire situation in Europe was apparent to the German element and the desertion of carriers continued unabated. As the governor recorded in his diary:

> Everyone hopes for peace… deliverance from our situation, which grows ever more unbearable and which consciously or unconsciously will leave its mark permanently on us… The terrible privations and hardships, the constant danger to health from unhygienic and other causes, the perpetual sickness, frequent periods of insufficient nourishment, the uncertainty of the final result, and the very unpleasant conditions, all have told unfavourably on the health and spirits of the Europeans and our good blacks have worked in vain (one wonders?).[114]

THE END OF THE CAMPAIGN

As the Schutztruppe moved on, van Deventer was informed that his command would shortly be downgraded to that of a division and substantial reductions made in the force. Now aware of the changed enemy direction, van Deventer was taking no chances sending troops to Bismarckburg as well as getting the Belgians to stand by. All the major centres were occupied and strong forces were being positioned to cut off any move north. Thus, it was a surprise when Lettow continued south into the relatively foodless areas of Northern Rhodesia. Fife was occupied only hours before the Germans arrived on 1 November; an attack the following day was held off by the defenders. Unable to secure the vital stores there, they decided to make further south to Kasama which was the major supply depot from the south. It was a rich source, but carriers continued to desert in large numbers and valuable machine guns had to be abandoned.[115] The main body arrived in Kasama on 12 November, while Köhl's rearguard collected supplies back in Brandt. In the meantime, von Spangenberg's advance guard was reconnoitring crossing sites on the Zambesi.

Desperate to catch the Germans before they moved off again, Hawkins with the KAR left his supplies far behind and attacked the main body with only his 750 men on 12 November. A number of casualties were inflicted, but he could not move further until his baggage train caught up with him. This was to be the last engagement of the war as the armistice had been already signed in Europe although it was not until 13 November that Lettow received formal notification of it from van Deventer.

It was the end to an extremely arduous and hard-fought campaign in which both sides had marched incredible distances in virgin bush and on very short rations with almost no creature comforts. The force that surrendered consisted of twenty German officers, six medical officers, the governor and thirty-two officials, three subordinate officials and 122 German NCOs, 1,168 Askari, 1,522 carriers, 130 prisoners of war, 428 agricultural carriers/workers, 282 'boys' for the Europeans, 427 wives, and 392 'boys' for the Africans. An overall total of 155 Germans and 4,416 Africans remained together until the end.[116] As a mark of respect for the Schutztruppe, van Deventer gave orders that the officers and German NCOs could retain their arms until reaching their final destination; the War Office agreed to this, adding that Lettow and his officers should have their swords returned on a ceremonial parade 'in recognition of their gallant efforts' and his Askari should be dismissed to their homes.[117] It was an unusual ending to a decidedly unusual campaign.

9
Summary and Conclusions

The campaign fought in East Africa was unique in many respects. In some ways it reflected the priorities and methods of nineteenth-century colonial warfare with its reliance on largely infantry columns marching through trackless bush, supplied and supported by carriers. Manoeuvre was often as much about obtaining food or water as it was with tactical advantage. Yet, it also introduced the industrialised warfare of the twentieth century with the use of aircraft, motor vehicles, mortars, light machine guns and wireless. In contrast to other theatres, casualties from battle were relatively light, although those from disease were enormous.

The extremes of climate and terrain found in East Africa meant that campaign conditions were usually very difficult. Given the dependence on subsistence farming and food imports, a well-organised system of transport and supply was absolutely essential to success or even survival. This was a considerable problem that had a major influence on the course of military operations throughout the war. Both sides relied heavily on human porterage and suffered heavily for it; in late 1916 and early 1917, both the Germans and British faced starvation on several occasions. In the end, the British with their superior resources partly overcame this limitation, although there was never an overabundance for the hard marching columns deep in the virgin bush. All participants suffered severely from insufficient rations, medicine and equipment at one or more times. Extreme physical exertion and discomfort were the norm.

The other dominating factor was the prevalence of disease. Malaria was the greatest plague for soldier and follower alike, with no one – regardless of rank or position – being immune. It caused enormous problems and disabled thousands for long periods, often permanently. Dysentery was second in seriousness followed by pneumonia. Apart from the extremes of precipitation and aridity, human life was made miserable by the swarms of biting insects, parasites and dangers of wild animals. For domestic animals, the effects of the tsetse fly were even more devastating and scarcely a beast survived the rigours of the campaign. Put simply, East Africa was an extremely unhealthy and uncomfortable place in which to fight a war.

The war caused enormous human suffering, directly and indirectly. If deaths in battle were proportionately much lower than in Europe, the opposite was true of sickness. The life of a soldier was hard, with few of the comforts or distractions provided elsewhere. But, the burden fell even more heavily on the African carriers and followers, who accompanied the soldiers into battle, as at least 40,000 are known to have died in British service alone and many others never returned home. These men were expected to carry heavy loads in all weathers and for very long periods with meagre food supplies. Both sides exploited indigenous manpower ruthlessly and many perished from exhaustion, illness or battle. The exact numbers will never be known, but several hundred thousand people served in a formal capacity and hundreds of thousands more informally.

Less well documented, but probably even more severe was the suffering of the indigenous civilian population in the war zones. Requisitions and the need to move food to depots were an imposition in 1914-15, but by the following year they were a major threat to survival. Smuts' failure to provide sufficient food for his underfed troops led to widespread foraging and looting of food, whereas Lettow made such methods the basis of his supply system. Chits of paper were offered for payment, but in many areas this counted for little when there was neither money nor goods to purchase. It must also be said that Lettow was quite ruthless in devastating districts for food, both for his own supplies as well as denying his pursuers sustenance. He was quite prepared to leave a district absolutely destitute regardless of the consequences for the African population. But all participants caused major upheaval wherever they passed, and the full consequences have yet to be uncovered.

Military capability varied considerably. The war began with small but high-quality colonial forces in the KAR and Schutztruppe, with the Force Publique developing quite rapidly. The Indian troops of 1914 were nowhere near the standard of those of 1916-17 who had been hardened in battle elsewhere. This was also reflected in the calibre of leadership, as the pre-war senior officers were not prepared for modern war. The result was poor morale and setbacks until mid-1915, when things slowly began to improve with the building of the railway and the raid on Bukoba. However, it was the arrival of Smuts and the South Africans that marked the greatest difference. He tried to fight a tropical war in bush and jungle without adequate preparation or training. He seized the best part of the German colony, but at a huge cost to his own troops. Smuts' operational aims were reasonable, but he failed to reconcile them with the reality on the ground, be it terrain or supply. As an ambitious politician, he did not want the casualties from bloody battle, hoping to outmanoeuvre his opponent into surrender. The result was that his army effectively disintegrated while his opponent was weakened, but still intact.

Hoskins was left with a very difficult hand and did much to rebuild the shattered force left by Smuts. He instigated an aggressive policy of hitting the Germans hard whenever possible and destroying their food supplies. But, he fell foul of London and was soon replaced by van Deventer, a man of very different outlook. The South African had learned from the mistakes of the past year, particularly regarding the need for an adequate supply and transport system. He adopted Hoskins' plans and carried them out vigorously. Now with a largely Indo-African force, he benefited from the arrival of better weaponry and a rising generation of aggressive young column commanders. Despite setbacks and the inevitable supply problems, 1917 was the year that the fighting power of the Schutztruppe was effectively broken and it was only the sheer incompetence of the Portuguese forces that enabled the enemy to survive. Now with a mainly African army, he spent most of 1918 trying hard to bring the enemy to bay, although never quite attaining that goal.

The Germans were fortunate in having an exceptional leader in Lettow, who displayed remarkable drive and energy in shaping the Schutztruppe. He was instrumental in creating a large and highly capable force despite many old and less vigorous officers. His personality and unshakeable will to win kept his troops going throughout the entire war, although by the end of 1917 it was reduced to a hard core of the most experienced and determined troops. Lettow was best at the conduct of defensive and delaying operations in the bush, and he was a master of the timely counter-attack. He was a bush fighter rather than guerrilla leader and was always impatient for decisive results that were often beyond his limited means. This resulted in a number of fruitless attacks that inflicted irreplaceable casualties and expended scarce ammunition. Jassini, Kondoa Irangi, Kibata and Mahiwa were the major examples of this, while he often pressed distant subordinates into attacks with inadequate resources that often failed. He was keener on victory in pitched battle rather than to inflicting steady losses or popular support.

His clashes with others, notably the governor, were intemperate and bitter, which did not always help the war effort. Lettow treated the campaign in East Africa as strictly a military problem and considered that everything else should be subordinated to its achievement. He was ruthless and remarkably single-minded; qualities that the British admired, but also helped to ensure that the captured colony would never be returned to Germany.

Lettow succeeded in surviving until the armistice. Had he achieved his self-imposed task of diverting large numbers of enemy troops from the decisive battle in Europe? To some extent he did, mainly in terms of the Indian troops, although many of those brought in from 1915 onwards were being rotated out of heavier fighting. Despite the large number of South Africans, most had enlisted specifically for service in East Africa and not in Europe. Black African troops were initially raised for local operations only and the subsequent question of their potential use elsewhere was dependent on the campaign in East Africa being concluded. The greatest inconvenience caused was the diversion of scarce shipping resources to a minor theatre followed by the cost in gold.

If the East African campaign was of limited strategic value and only a minor part of the First World War, it was nevertheless of overwhelming importance to those who lived and fought there. It brought large-scale devastation and suffering to an enormous region, yet conversely it also introduced modern technology on a major scale. It led to the ejection of Germany from Africa as well as other significant changes to the nature of the colonial state. However, it was overshadowed by the greater events elsewhere and remained a forgotten front for many years. It deserves to be better remembered.

Epilogue

As the war ended, the struggle for peace began. The Germans were to lose their entire overseas empire, with the British receiving the bulk of their former East African Protectorate and the Belgians receiving Ruanda and Urundi for their effort. The now-captive Schutztruppe was eventually moved to confinement in Dar-es-Salaam, where it remained until the homeward journey in January 1919. Amidst the chaos of post-war Berlin, they returned in honour, with Schnee, Lettow and Looff riding at the head of the gallant remnants through the Brandenburg Gates. The wartime feud was continued through the written word, with each recording a ringing account of their experiences for the wider public.

On the surface, Britain and Portugal finished the war on amicable turns, with van Deventer lavishing praise in his official despatch. However, he also prepared a supplementary, secret despatch for the government that described his true thoughts about the Portuguese in the strongest possible language. He summarised his thoughts as:

> In fact, the Germans simply looked on the Portuguese forces or posts as convenient ordnance and supply dumps. The effect of these easy conquests on the morale of the enemy's troops was very great; and it can perhaps be conceived what an incredible handicap the Portuguese forces have been to me, ever since the enemy crossed the ROVUMA in November 1917.[118]

It was fortunate for diplomacy and good relations that this document remained secret.

List of Abbreviations

A/GHQ	Advanced GHQ
BEF	British Expeditionary Force
CB	Companionship of the Order of the Bath
CID	Committee of Imperial Defence
CIGS	Chief of the Imperial General Staff
FK or Field Companies	Feldkompagnien
GHQ	General Headquarters
GOC	General Officer Commanding
GQG	Grand Quartier Général
IEF	Indian Expeditionary Force
KAR	King's African Rifles
NCOs	non-commissioned officers
RKA	The Reichskolonialamt (or Colonial Office)
RO	Operational Reserve
Sch K	Schützenkompagnie
SMLE	short-magazine Lee-Enfield rifle
SNO	Senior Naval Officer

Bibliography

UNPUBLISHED PRIMARY SOURCES

Public Record Office (PRO)(formerly the National Archives), London.
ADM Series: 1, 124, 136
CAB Series: 5, 8, 21, 22, 23, 24, 44, 45, 103
CO Series: 534, 551, 619
FO Series: 371
WO Series: 32, 33, 95, 106, 158, 310, 800, 808
Bodliean Library, Oxford
Harcourt Papers
Rhodes House Library, Oxford
British Library, London
Buxton Papers
Barrow Papers
Bundesarchiv, Berlin
Reichskolonialamt R1001 Files
Bundesarchiv/Militärarchiv, Freiburg im Breisgau
Boell Papers
Lettow-Vorbeck Papers
Cambridge University Library
Smuts Papers
Imperial War Museum, London
Charlewood Papers
Duff Papers, Sir H.L.
Ewart Papers
Hammill Papers
Johnston Papers
King Papers
Lyall Papers
Lynden-Bell Papers
Northey Papers
Wapshare Papers
King's College London, Liddell Hart Centre for Military Archives
Robertson Papers
Musée Royal de l'Armée, Brussels
South African National Archives, Pretoria
Governor General Papers
Smuts Papers
South African National Defence Force, Documentation Directorate, Pretoria
Personnel Archives and Records – van Deventer
German South-West Africa (GSWA) – WWI Papers (confusingly the East African campaign papers are classified under this series of files)
AG 1914-1921
Secretary of Defence, Group 2
Wiltshire Record Office
Long Papers
Arquivo Histórico Militor, Lisbon
Arquivo Ministério dos Negócios Estrangerios, Lisbon

PUBLISHED PRIMARY SOURCES AND MEMOIRS

Amery, L.S., *My Political Life Volume 2 War and Peace 1914-1929*, London, 1953

Arning, Wilhelm, *Vier Jahre Weltkrieg in Deutsch-Ostafrika*, Hannover, Gebrüder Jänecke, n.d.

Brett-Young, Francis, *Marching on Tanga: with General Smuts in East Africa*, London, Collins Sons & Co., 1917

Buchanan, Angus, *Three Years of War in East Africa*, London, John Murray, 1920

Callwell, Maj.-Gen. Sir C.E., *Experiences of a Dug-Out*, London, Constable, 1920

Christiansen, Kapitänleutnant d. R. Carl, *"Durch" Mit Kriegsmaterial zu Lettow-Vorbeck*, Stuttgart, Verlag für Volkskunst, 1918

Churchill, W.S., *The World Crisis: 1911-1914, Volume I*, London, Thomas Butterworth Limited, 1923

Crowe, Brig.-Gen. J.H.V., *General Smuts' Campaign in East Africa*, London, John Murray, 1918

Deppe, Ludwig, *Mit Lettow-Vorbeck durch Afrika*, Berlin, Verlag August Scherl, 1919

Deppe, Charlotte and Ludwig, *Um Deutsch-Ostafrika Erinnerungen von Charlotte und Ludwig Deppe*, Dresden, E. Beutelspacher & Co., 1925

Dolbey, Capt. R.V., *Sketches of the East African Campaign*, London, John Murray, 1918

Downes, W.D., *With the Nigerians in German East Africa*, London, Methuen, 1919

Fendall, Brig.-Gen. C.P., *The East African Force: 1915-1919*, London, H.F. & G. Witherby, 1921

Gibson, Ashley, *Postscript to Adventure*, Toronto, J.M. Dent & Sons, 1930

Göring, Karl Ernst, *Deutsch Ostafrika Kreigserlebnisse 1914-1920*, Erfurt, n.p., 1925-27

Hancock, Sir W.K. and van der Poel, Jean, *Selections from the Smuts Papers: The Fields of Fire: Volume III June 1910-November 1918*, Cambridge, Cambridge University Press, 1966

Hankey, Lord, *The Supreme Command*, 2 Volumes, London, Allen and Unwin, 1961

Hauer, August Dr, *Kumbake: Erlebnisse eines Artze in Deutsch-Ostafrika 1914-1919*, Berlin, Hobbing, 1922

Hoskins, Lt.-Gen. A.R., *Despatch, London Gazette*, 1917

Inhülsen, Otto, *Wir Ritten für Deutsch-Ostafrika*, Leipzig, v. Hase & Koehler, 1941 (Original edition *Abendteur am Kilimanjaro*, 1926)

Kameradschaft Ehem, *Offiziere der Kaiserlichen Schutztruppe für Deutsch-Ostafrika, Mitgliederliste*, Potsdam, n.pub., 1941

King-Hall, Adm. Sir H.G., *Naval Traditions and Memories*, London, 1926

Köhl, Hauptmann Franz, *Der Kampf um Deutsch-Ostafrika*, Berlin, Verlag Kameradschaft, 1919

Langsdorff, Werner von (ed), *Deutsche Flagge über Sand und Palmen*, Gutersloh, Bertelsmann, 1936

Lettow-Vorbeck, General Paul von, *My Reminiscences of East Africa*, London, Hurst and Blackett, 1920 (Reprinted Nashville, Tennessee, The Battery Press, [n.d.].

–, *Meine Erinnerungen aus Ostafrika*, Leipzig, Koehler, 1920

–, *Heia Safari*, Leipzig, v. Hafe & Koehler, 1920

–, *Mein Leben*, (ed./pub.) (Herausgegeben von Ursula von Lettow-Vorbeck), Biberach an der Riss, Koehlers, 1957

Lloyd, A.W., *'Jambo' or with Jannie Smuts in the Jungle: 30 EA Sketches*, Cape Town, Central News Agency, [n.d.].

Lloyd George, D., *War Memoirs*, 2 Volumes, London, Odhams Press, 1938

Looff, Vizadmiral a.D. Max, *Tufani Sturm über Deutsch-Ostafrika*, Berlin, Verlag Berhard und Graefe, 1941

Meinertzhagen, Col. R., *Army Diary 1899-1926*, London, Oliver and Boyd, 1960

Merriman, John X., *Selections from the Correspondence of J. X. Merriman 1905-1924*, Lewson, Phyllis (ed), Cape Town, Van Riebeeck Society, 1969

Methner, Wilhelm, *Unter drei Gouverneuren: 16 Jahre Dienst in den deutschen Tropen*, Breslau: Korn, 1938

Overstraeten, General R. van, *The War Diaries of Albert I King of the Belgians*, London, William Kimber, 1954

Oxford and Asquith, Earl of, *Memories and Reflections*, Volume 2, London, Cassell and Company, 1928

Pearn, Charles Lukey, *Meet Me at Paddington: The Letters and Diary of Charles Lukey Pearn*, Cambridge, Windward Press, 1998

Pretorius, P.J., *Jungle Man: The Autobiography of Maj. P.J. Pretorius CMG, DSO and Bar*, London, Harrap, 1947

Reid, Frank, *Foot-Slogging in East Africa*, Cape Town, Maskew Miller, [n.d.]

Reitz, Denys, *Trekking On*, London, Faber, 1933

Robertson, Field Marshal Sir William, *Soldiers and Statesmen 1914-1918*, London, Cassell and Co., 1926

Ruckteschell, Hauptmann d. Res. von, *Der Feldzug in Ostafrika*, Berlin, Hugo Bermühler Verlag, 1919

Schnee, Ada, *Meine Erlebnisse während der Kriegszeit in Deutsches Ostafrika*, Leipzig, Quelle und Meyer, 1918

Schnee, Dr Heinrich, *Deutsch-Ostafrika im Weltkrieg*, Leipzig, Quelle und Meyer, 1919

–, *Als Letzer Gouverneur in Deutsch-Ostafrika: Erinnerungen*, Heidelberg, Quelle und Meyer, 1964

Schoenfeld, Fregattenkapitän Werner, *Geraubtes Land: Durchs freie Südafrika ins bedrohte Deutsch-Ostafrika*, Dresden, Deutscher Buch-und Kunstverlag, 1942 (reprint of 1925 original)

Selvagem, Carlos, *Tropa d'Africa*, Lisboa, Livrarias Aillaud e Bertrand, 1924

Shorthose, Capt. W.T., *Sport and Adventure in Africa*, London, Seeley Service, 1923

Smith-Dorrien, General Sir H.C., *Memoirs of 48 Years' Service*, London, John Murray, 1925

Smuts, Jan, *Memoirs of the Boer War*, S.P. Spies and Gail Nattrass (eds), Johannesburg, Jonathan Ball, 1999

–, *Despatches, London Gazette*, PC

–, *East Africa: Address to the Royal Geographic Society on 28 January 1918 by General Smuts* (Reprinted from the *Geographical Journal*, March 1918), London: Royal Geographical Society, 1918

–, *Wartime Speeches: A Compilation of Public Utterances in Great Britain by Lieut.-Gen. The Rt. Hon. J.C. Smuts P.C., K.C., M.L.A. In Connection with the Session of the Imperial War Cabinet and Imperial War Conference 1917*, London, Hodder and Stoughton, 1917

Stewart, Sir J.M., *Jimmie Stewart – Frontiersman: The Edited Memoirs of Major General Sir J.M. Stewart*, Robert Maxwell (ed), Edinburgh, Pentland Press, 1992

Schuffenahauer, Ida, *Komm Wieder Bwana Ein deutsches Schicksal*, Berlin, Süßeroff, 1940

Thielemans, Marie-Rose, *Albert 1er: Carnets et Corresonpondance de Guerre 1914-1918*, Paris, Editions Duclot, 1991

Thornhill, C.J., *Taking Tanganyika: Experiences of an Intelligence Officer, 1914-18*, London, Stanley Paul, 1917

Trew, Lt.-Col. H.F., *Botha Treks*, London, Blackie, 1936

Van Deventer, Gen. Sir Jacob, *Despatches, London Gazette*, 13 December 1918

Van Overstraeten, General R., *En ces temps-la. Carnets d'un Officier de Liaison dans l'Est Africain*, Tervuren, Etudes Historiques et Dynastiques, 1961

Viehweg, Rudolph, *Unter Schwarz-Weiß-Rot in fernen Zone Erlebnisse eines Matrosen auf dem Kreuzer "Königsberg"*, Leipzig, Krüger & Co., 1933

Wahle, Generalleutnant, *Erinnerungen an meine Kriegsjahre in Deutsch-Ostafrika 1914-1918*, n.pub., 1920

Wenig, Richard, *In Monsun und Pori*, Berlin, Safari-Verlag, 1922

Wienholt, Arnold, *The Story of the Lion Hunt*, London, Melrose, 1922

Wynn, E., *Ambush*, London, Hutchinson and Co., 1937

PUBLISHED PRIMARY SOURCES – ARTICLES

Anon., 'The Campaign in East Africa, With Special Reference to the Operations from the N.E. Rhodesia-Nyasaland Border, Under Brig.-General Edward Northey, C.B., A.D.C.', *Journal of the Royal United Services Institute*, LXII, (1917), pp. 269-285

Bayot, 'Les Opérations Militaires à la frontière est de la Province Orientale', *Bulletin belge des sciences militaires*, I, No. 6, Jun 1934, pp. 531-542; II, No. 1, Jul 1934, pp. 21-46; I, No. 5, May 1936, pp. 385-408; I, No. 6, Jun 1936, pp. 479-484; II, No. 1. Jul 1936, pp. 19-28; II, No. 2, Aug 1936, pp. 14-152; II, No. 3, Sep 1936, pp. 245-721

Britten, Lt.-Col. W.E., 'Portuguese East Africa 1918', *Royal Engineer Journal*, XXXIX), pp. 430-444

Charlewood, Cdr C.J., 'Naval Actions off the Tanganyika Coast 1914-1917', II, *Tanganyika Notes and Records*, L.V., (September 1960), pp. 154-180

Etat-Major General de l'Armée, 'Opérations Contre la Colonne Wintgens-Naumann au Sud du rail Kigoma-Tabora-Dar-es-Salam (19 au 26 mai 1917)', *Bulletin Belge des Sciences Militaires*, I, No. 5, May 1937, pp. 387-414

G.D.H. (A South African), 'With Smuts in German East Africa', *Journal of the Royal United Services Institute*, LXI, 1916, pp. 820-824

Jadot, Maj. A., 'Une batterie de montagne des troupes coloniales belges dans l'Est Africain Allemand', *Bulletin belge des sciences militaires*, I, No. 2, Feb 1924, pp. 171-186 and I, No. 5, May 1924, pp. 529-551

Jadot, Col. A., 'L'Artillerie dans les Campagnes Coloniales', *Bulletin belge des sciences militaires*, I, No. 3, Mar 1936, pp. 257-272

Keen, Maj. F.S., 'Lecture on the Campaign in East Africa: Delivered at Simla on the 6th October 1916', *Journal of the United Service Institution of India*, XLVI, 1917, pp. 71-91

Orr, Col. G.M., 'The Indian Army in East Africa 1914-1917', *Journal of the United Service Institution of India*, XLVIII, (1919), pp. 244-261

– , 'Some Afterthoughts of the War in East Africa, 1914-1918', *Journal of the Royal United Services Institute*, LXIX, (1924), pp. 692-702

– , 'From Rumbo to the Rovuma The Odyssey of "One" Column in East Africa in 1917', *Army Quarterly*, VII, (1924), pp. 109-129

– , 'Random Recollections of East Africa', *Army Quarterly*, XI, (1928), pp. 282-293

– , 'Von Lettow's Escape into Portuguese East Africa, 1917', *Army Quarterly*, Volume XIII, (1925), pp. 50-59

– , 'Smuts versus Lettow A Critical Phase in East Africa; August to September 1916', *Army Quarterly*, XIII, (1925), pp. 287-300

– , 'Operations on Interior Lines in Bush Warfare', *Journal of the Royal United Services Institute*, LXX, (1925), pp. 125-134

– , '1914-1915 in East Africa', *Journal of the United Service Institution of India*, LVI, (1926), pp. 58-86

– , 'A Remarkable Raid: East Africa 1917', *Journal of the Royal United Services Institute*,

LXXI, (1926), pp. 73-80

– , 'The Winter Campaign of 1916 in East Africa', *Journal of the United Service Institution of India*, LX, (1930), pp. 69-79

Ridgway, Brig.-Gen. R.T., 'With No 2 Column', I, *Army Quarterly*, V, (1922), pp. 12-28

– , 'With No 2 Column German East Africa 1917', II, *Army Quarterly*, VI, (1923), pp. 247-263

Russell, Maj. A, 'The Landings at Tanga, 1914', *Tanganyika Notes and Records*, No. 58, Mar/Sep 1962, p. 103

Sheppard, Brig.-Gen. S.H., 'Some Notes on Tactics in the East African Campaign', *Journal of the United Service Institution of India*, XLVIII, No. 215, (April 1919), pp. 138-157

Taute, Dr M., 'A German Account of the Medical Side of the War in East Africa, 1914-1918', *Tanganyika Notes and Records*, VIII, (December 1939), pp. 1-20

Thompson, E.S., 'A Machine Gunner's Odyssey through German East Africa', Part I, *South African Military History Journal*, VII, No. 3, (June 1987); Part II, VII, No. 4, (June 1987); and Part III, VII, No. 6, (December 1988)

Van Overstraeten, General R., 'L'Epopée africaine pendant la Première Guerre mondiale. Avec le Général Smuts dans l'Est Africain', *Cahiers Léopoldiens*, 1960, No. 12, pp. 33-62; No. 13, pp. 65-85; No. 14, pp. 67-80, No. 15, pp. 59-89

Wéber, Capitaine H., 'L'Effort belge au Lac Tanganika', *Bulletins belges des sciences militaires*, II, No. 5, Nov 1927, pp. 407-425; II, No. 6, Dec 1927, pp. 508-528; I, No. 1, Jan 1928, pp. 17-36

– , 'La Campagne de Mahenge', *La Belgique Militaire*, 37, No. 2402, 10 Oct 1937, pp. 354-372

Woodhouse, Capt. H.L., 'East Africa', *Journal of the United Service Institution of India*, XLVI, (1917), pp. 329-337

– , 'Railway Demolitions and Repairs', *Royal Engineers Journal*, XXIV, No. 2, (1920), pp. 49-54

– , 'Notes on Railway Work in East Africa', *Royal Engineers Journal*, XXVII, No. 1, (1923), pp. 37-46

OFFICIAL PUBLICATIONS

Admiralty, *Review of German Cruiser Warfare 1914-18*, London, HMSO, 1940

Admiralty (NID), *A Manual of the Belgian Congo*, London, HMSO, 1919

Admiralty (NID), *A Handbook of German East Africa*, London, HMSO, 1923

Admiralty (NID), *A Handbook of the Uganda Protectorate*, London, HMSO, 1920

Admiralty (NID), *A Handbook of Portuguese Nyasaland*, London, HMSO, 1920

Admiralty (NID), *A Handbook of Portuguese East Africa*, London, HMSO, 1920

Blenkinsop, Gen. Sir L.J. and Rainey, Lt.-Col. J.W. *History of the Great War: Veterinary Services*, London, HMSO, 1925

Collyer, Brig.-Gen. J.J., *The South Africans with General Smuts in German East Africa 1916*, Pretoria, Government Printer, 1939.

Corbett, Sir Julian S., *History of the Great War: Naval Operations*, Volumes 1-3, London, Longmans, Green and Co., 1920-1924

– , *History of the Great War: Naval Operations*, I, London, Longmans, Green and Co., 1920

Henniker, A.M., *Official History of the Great War: Transportation on the Western Front*, London. HMSO, 1937

Hordern, Lt.-Col. Charles, *Official History of the Great War: Military Operations: East Africa, 1914-1916*, Volume 1, London, HMSO, 1941

– , *Official History of the Great War: Military Operations: East Africa, 1914-1916*, Volume 1, London, HMSO, 1941.

Jones, H.A. and Raleigh, W., *Official History of the Great War: The War in the Air*, 6 Volumes, Oxford, 1922-1937

Lucas, Sir C.P., *The Empire at War: Volume 4 Africa*, Oxford, Oxford University Press, 1925.

– , *The \ at War: Volume 4 Africa*, Oxford, Oxford University Press, 1925

Macpherson, Maj.-Gen. Sir W.G et al, *History of the Great War: Medical Services General History Vol 1: Medical Services in the United Kingdom; in British Garrisons Overseas; and During Operations against Tsingtau; in Togoland, the Cameroons, and South-West Africa*, London, HMSO, 1921

– , *History of the Great War: Medical Services General History Vol 1: Medical Services in the United Kingdom; in British Garrisons Overseas; and During Operations against Tsingtau; in Togoland, the Cameroons, and South-West Africa*, London, HMSO, 1921

Macpherson, Maj.-Gen. Sir W.G. and Mitchell, Maj. T.J., *History of the Great War: Medical Services General History Vol 4: Medical Services During the Operations on the Gallipoli Peninsula; in Macedonia; in Mesopotamia and North-West Persia; in East Africa; in the Aden Protectorate, and in North Russia: Ambulance Transport During the War*, London, HMSO, 1924

Macpherson, Maj.-Gen. Sir W.G., Herringham, Maj.-Gen. Sir W.P., Elliott, Col. T.R., and Balfour, Lt.-Col. A., *History of the Great War: Medical Services: Diseases of War*, Volume 1, London, HMSO, [n.d.]

Marinearchiv, *Der Krieg zur See 1914 – 1918: Die Kämpfe der Kaiserlichen Marine in den Deutschen Kolonien*, Berlin, Verlag E.S. Mittler & Sohn, 1935

– , *Der Krieg zur See 1914-1918, Der Kreuzerkrieg in den ausländischen Gewässern*, I, Berlin, E.S. Mittler & Sohn, 1922

– , *Der Krieg zur See 1914-1918, Der Kreuzerkrieg in den ausländischen Gewässern*, II, Berlin, E.S. Mittler & Sohn, 1923

Mitchell, T.J. and Smith, G.M., *History of the Great War: Medical services: Casualties and Medical Statistics of the Great War*; Nashville, Tenn., The Battery Press, [n.d.] (reprint of 1931 original)

Newbolt, Henry, *History of the Great War: Naval Operations*, Volumes 4 and 5, London, Longmans Green and Co., 1928-1931

Perry, F.W. (comp), *History of the Great War: Orders Of Battle of Divisions: Part 5a The Divisions of Australia, Canada and New Zealand and those in East Africa*, Newport, Gwent, Ray Westlake Military Books, 1992

Reichsarchiv, *Der Weltkrieg 1914 bis 1918: Die Militärischen Operationen zu Lande: 9. Band*, Berlin, E.S. Mittler & Sohn, 1942

– , *Der Weltkrieg 1914 bis 1918: Die Militärischen Operationen zu Lande: 13. Band*, Berlin. E.S. Mittler & Sohn, 1956

Royaume de Belgique, *Campagnes coloniales belges: Tomes 1-3*, Bruxulles, Imprimerie Typographique de l'I.C.M., 1927-1932

War Office, *Infantry Training*, London, HMSO, 1905

War Office, *Training and Manoeuvre Regulations*, London, HMSO, 1913

War Office, *Field Service Regulations, Parts I and II*, London, HMSO, 1909 (Revised 1914)

War Office, *Statistics of the Military Effort of the British Empire During the Great War, 1914-1920*, HMSO, London, 1922

War Office, *'The Battles Nomenclature Committee' The Official Names of the Battles and other Engagements fought by the Military Forces of the British Empire during the Great War, 1914-1919 and the Third Afghan War 1919*, London, HMSO, 1922

SECONDARY SOURCES

Adams, R.Q.E., *Arms and the Wizard: Lloyd George and the Ministry of Munitions 1915-1916*, London, Cassell & Co., 1978

Adler, Brig. F.B., *The South African Field Artillery in German East Africa and Palestine, 1915-1919*, Pretoria: van Schaik, 1958

Anderson, Ross, *The Battle of Tanga 1914*, Stroud, Tempus, 2002

Armstrong, H.C., *Grey Steel: J.C. Smuts, A Study in Arrogance*, London, Barker-Methuen, 1937

Austin, R.A., *Northwest Tanzania under German and British Rule, 1889-1959*, New Haven, Yale University Press, 1968

Bald, Detlef, *Deutsch-Ostafrika 1900-1914, Eine Studie über Verwaltung Interessengruppen und Wirtschäftliche Erschliessung,* Munich, 1970

Beadon, Col. R.H., *Royal Army Service Corps History: Volume 2*, Cambridge, Cambridge University Press, 1931

Beesly, P., *Room 40: British Naval Intelligence 1914-1918*, London, Hamilton, 1982

Berghahn, V.R., *Germany and the Approach of War in 1914*, London, MacMillan, 1973

Beyers, C.J. and Basson, J.L., *Dictionary of South African Biography*, Volume V, Pretoria, Human Sciences Research Council, 1987

Bidwell, Shelford and Graham, Dominick, *Fire-Power: British Army Weapons and Theories of War 1904-1945*, London, George Allen & Unwin, 1982

Biographie Coloniale Belge

Boell, Ludwig, *Die Operationen in Ostafrika*, Hamburg, Walter Dachert, 1951

Bonham-Carter, Victor, *Soldier True: the Life and Times of Field Marshal Sir William Robertson, Bart., GCB, GCMG, KCVO, DSO*, London, 1963

Brelsford, W.V., *The Story of the Northern Rhodesia Regiment*, Lusaka, The Government Printer, 1954

Brose, Eric Dorn, *The Kaiser's Army*, Oxford, Oxford University Press, 1991

Brown, James Ambrose, *They Fought for King and Kaiser: South Africans in German East Africa 1916*: *South Africa at War Volume 6*, Johannesburg, Ashanti Publishing, 1991

Buxton, Earl, *General Botha*, London, John Murray, 1924

Chapman-Huston, W.D.M., *General Sir John Cowans: The Quartermaster General of the Great War*, 2 Volumes, London, Hutchinson, 1924

Chatterton, E. Keble, *The Königsberg Adventure*, London: Hurst and Blackett, 1936

– , *Severn's Saga*, London, Hurst and Blackett, 1938

Clayton, Anthony, *The British Military Presence in East and Central Africa*, Oxford, Oxford Development Reports Project, 1982

Clifford, Sir H.C., *The Gold Coast Regiment in the East Africa Campaign*, Nashvill, Tenn, The Battery Press, 1995 (reprint of 1920 original)

Cocker, Mark, *Richard Meinertzhagen: Soldier, Scientist and Spy*, London, Secker and Warburg, 1989

Craig, Gordon A., *The Politics of the Prussian Army*, New York, Oxford University Press, 1955

Crichton-Harris, Ann, *Seventeen Letters to Tatham*, Toronto, Kennegy West, 2001

Dane, Edmund, *British Campaigns in Africa and the Pacific 1914-1918*, London, Hodder and Stoughton, 1919

Davenport, T.R.H., *South Africa: A Modern History*, London: Macmillan, 4th ed. 1991, pp. 184-191

Davies, W.J.K., *Light Railways of the First World War: A History of Tactical Rail Communications on the British Fronts 1914-1918*, Newton Abbot, David & Charles, 1962

Difford, I.D., *The Story of the 1st Cape Corps, 1915-19*, Cape Town, Hortons Limited, 1921

Eckart, Wolfgang U., *Medezin und Kolonial-Imperialismus Deutschland 1884-1945*, Paderborn, Schoenigh, 1997

Engelenburg, F.V., *General Louis Botha*, Pretoria, van Schaik, 1929

Farndale, Gen. Sir M., *History of the Royal Artillery: The Forgotten Fronts and the Home Front 1914-1918*, London, The Royal Artillery Institute, 1988

Fischer, F., *Germany's Aims in the First World War*, London, Chatto and Windus, 1967

Forbes, Maj.-Gen. A., A *History of the Army Ordnance Services, Volume 3*, London, Medici Society, 1929

French, David, *British Strategy and War Aims 1914-1916*, London, Unwin and Allen, 1986

– , *The Strategy of the Lloyd George Coalition, 1916-1918*, Oxford, Clarendon Press, 1995

Gann, L.H. and Duignan, P., *The Rulers of German Africa 1884-1914*, Stanford, Stanford University Press, 1977

– , *The Rulers of British Africa 1878-1914*, Stanford, Stanford University Press, 1978

Gardner, Brian, *German East Africa: the Story of the First World War in East Africa*, London, Cassell, 1967

Gifford, Prosser and Lewis, William Roger (eds), *Britain and Germany in Africa: Imperial Rivalry and Colonial Rule*, New Haven, Yale University Press, 1967

Gilbert, Martin, *Winston S. Churchill: Volume III 1914-1916*, London, Heinemann, 1971

– , *Winston S. Churchill: Volume III Companion 2 1914-1916*, London, Heinemann, 1971

Gooch, John, *The Plans of War: The General Staff and British Military Strategy* c *1900-1916*, London, Routledge & Kegan Paul, 1974

Graham, Brig. C.A.L., *The History of the Indian Mountain Artillery*, Aldershot, Gale and Polden, 1957

Groener, Erich, *German Warships 1815-1945: Volume I Major Surface Vessels*, Annapolis Md, Naval Institute Press, 1990

Halpern, Paul G., *A Naval History of World War I*, London, UCL Press, 1994

Haupt, Werner, *Deutschlands Schutzgebietes in Übersee 1884-1918*, Friedberg, Podzun-Pallas-Verlag, 1984

Haywood, A. and Clarke, F.A., *The History of the Royal West African Frontier Force*, Aldershot, Gale and Polden, 1964

Heichen, Walter, *Helden der Kolonien: Der Weltkrieg in unseren Schutzgebieten*, Berlin, A Weichert Verlag, [n.d.]

Hodges, Geoffrey, *The Carrier Corps: Military Labour in the East African Campaign*, Westport, Conn, Greenwood Press, 1986

Hoyt, Edwin P., *The Germans Who Never Lost*, New York, Funk & Wagnell's, 1968

Hoyt, E.P., *Guerrilla: Colonel von Lettow-Vorbeck and Germany's East African Empire*, New York, Macmillan, 1981

Henderson, W.O., *Studies in German Colonial History*, London, Frank Cass & Co., 1962

Herwig, Holger, 'Strategic Uncertainties of a Nation-State: Prussia-Germany, 1871-1918', in *The Making of Strategy Rulers States and War*, Williamson Murray (ed.), Macgregor Knox and Alvin Bernstein, Cambridge, Cambridge University Press, 1994

Hofman, H.H. (ed.), *Das Deutsche Offizierkorps, 1860-1960*, Boppard am Rhein, Harold Boldt, 1977

Hubatsch, Walther (ed.), *Die Schutzgebiete des Deutschen Reiches 1884-1920, Band 22: Bundes- und Reichsbehörden*, Marburg/Lahn: J.G. Herder-Institut, 1984

Hyam, Ronald, *The Failure of South African Expansion 1908-1948*, London, Macmillan, 1972

Iliffe, John, *Tanganyika under German Rule 1905-1912*, Cambridge, Cambridge University Press, 1969

Isaacman, *The Tradition of Resistance in Mozambique*, Los Angeles and Berkeley, 1976

Kaponen, Juhani, *German Colonial Policies in Mainland Tanzania 1884-1914*, Studia Historica 49, Helsinki, Finnish Historical Society, 1995

Katzenellenbogen, S.E., 'Southern Africa and the War of 1914-18', in M.R.D. Foot (ed.), *War and Society*, London, Paul Elek, 1973, pp107-122

Kock, H.W., (ed.), The Origins of the First World War: Great Power Rivalry and German War Aims, London, Macmillan, 1984

Kock, Nils, *Blockade and Jungle,* London, Hale, 1941

Lloyd-Jones, *King's African Rifles: Being an Unofficial Account of the Origins and Activities of the KAR*, London, Arrowsmith, 1926

Louis, W.R., *Ruanda-Urundi 1884-1919*, Oxford, Clarendon Press, 1963

– , *Great Britain and Germany's Lost Colonies*, Oxford, Clarendon Press, 1967

Mackay, Ruddock F., *Fisher of Kilverstone*, Oxford, Clarendon Press, 1973

Macpherson, Fergus, *Anatomy of a Conquest: the British Occupation of Zambia, 1884-1924*, London, Longman, pp. 168-175

McLaughlin, Peter, *Ragtime Soldiers*, Bulawayo, Books of Zimbabwe, 1980

Marder, Arthur, *From the Dreadnought to the Scapa Flow: The Royal Navy in the Fisher Era, 1904-1919*, Volumes 1-5, London, Oxford University Press, 1961-1970

– , *Fear God and Dread Nought: the Correspondance of Admiral of the Fleet F Lord Fisher of Kilverstone*, 3 Volumes, London, Cape, 1952-29

Martins, General Ferreira, *Portugal's Co-operation with Great Britain in the Great War 1914-1918*, Lisboa: Servicos de Informacao e Imprensa da Embaixada Britanica, 1943

Meintjes, Johannes, *General Louis Botha*, London, Cassell, 1970

Millais, J.G., *Life of Frederick Courtenay Selous, DSO*, London, Longmans Green, 1919

Millin, Sarah, *General Smuts,* 2 Volumes, London, Faber and Faber, 1936

Mombauer, Annika, *The Origins of the First World War*, London, Longman, 2002

– , *Helmuth von Moltke and the Origins of the First World War*, Cambridge, Cambridge University Press, 2001

Moyse-Bartlett, Lt.-Col. H., *The King's African Rifles*, Aldershot, Gale and Polden, 1956

Mwase, George Simeon, *Strike a Blow and Die: The Story of the John Chilembwe Rising*, London, Heinemann, 1970

Mosley, Leonard, *Duel for Kilimanjaro*, London, Weidenfeld & Nicolson, 1963

Nalder, Maj.-Gen. R.F.H., *The Royal Corps of Signals: A History of its Antecedents and Development*, London, Royal Signals Institution, 1958

Newitt, Malyn, *A History of Mozambique*, London, Hurst & Company, 1995

– , *Portugal in Africa*, London, Hurst & Company, 1981

Osuntokun, Akinjide, *Nigeria in the First World War*, Ibadan History Series, London, Longman, 1979

Pradhan, S.D., *Indian Army in East Africa*, New Delhi, National Book Organisation, 1991

Page, Melvin E. (ed.), *Africa and the First World War*, London, Macmillan, 1987

Perry, F.W., *The Commonwealth Armies; Manpower and Organization in the Two World Wars*, Manchester, Manchester University Press, 1988

Patience, Kevin, *Königsberg A German East African Raider*, Bahrein: Zanzibar Publications, 1997

Ritter, Gerhard, (Transl. by Heinz Norden) *The Sword and the Sceptre The Problem of Militarism in Germany Volume III: The Tragedy of Statesmanship – Bethmann Hollweg as War Chancellor (1914-1917)*, London, Allen Lane, 1973, pp. 611.

– , (Transl. by Heinz Norden) *The Sword and the Sceptre The Problem of Militarism in Germany Volume IV: The Reign of German Militarism and the Disaster of 1918*, London, Allen Lane, 1973

Roskill, Stephen, *Hankey: Man of Secrets*, Volume 1, London, Collins, 1970

Rothwell, V.F., *British War Aims and Peace Diplomacy 1914-1918*, Oxford, Oxford University Press, 1971

Sands, Lt.-Col. E.W.C., *The Indian Sappers and Miners*, Chatham, Institution of Royal Engineers, 1948

Shankland, Peter, *The Phantom Flotilla*, London, Collins, 1968

Smith, Gaddis, 'Disposition of the German Colonies' in Prosser, Gifford and Louis, W. Roger, *Britain and Germany in Africa*, New Haven, Yale University Press, 1967

Smuts, J.C., *Jan Christiaan Smuts*, London, Cassell, 1952

Stevenson, David, *Armaments and the Coming of War*, Oxford, Oxford University Press, 1996

Strachan, H.F.A., *The First World War – To Arms*, Volume I, Oxford, Oxford University Press, 2001

Stoecker, Helmuth (ed.), *German Imperialism in Africa: From the Beginnings until the Second World War*, Bernd Zoellner (trans.), London, C. Hurst & Co. 1986

Taylor, Stephen, *The Mighty Nimrod: a Life of Frederick Courteney Selous: African Hunter and Adventurer*, London, Collins, 1989

Teixeira, Nuno Severiano, *L'Entrée du Portugal dans la Grande Guerre*, Paris, Economica, 1998

Thatcher, W.S., *The Fourth Battalion, Duke of Connaught's Own 10th Baluch Regiment in the Great War*, Cambridge, Cambridge University Press, 1932

Trzebinski, Errol, *The Kenya Pioneers*, London, Mandarin, 1991

Turner, John, *British Politics and the Great War*, New Haven, Yale University Press, 1992

Turner, J., 'Cabinets, Committees and Secretariats: The Higher Direction of War', in K.M. Burk (ed.), *War and State: The Transformation of British Government 1914-1918*, London, George Allen & Unwin, 1982, pp. 57-83

Waley, Daniel, *A Liberal Life: Lord Buxton*, Newtimber, New Timber Publications, 1999

Woodward, David R., *Lloyd George and the Generals*, London, Associated University Presses, 1983

Wylly, H.C., *The Loyal North Lancashire Regiment*, London, Royal United Service Institution, 1933

Zirkel, Kirsten, 'Military Power in German Colonial Policy: the Schutztruppen and their leaders in East and South-West Africa, 1888-1918', in Killingray, David and Omissi, *Guardians of Empire*, Manchester, Manchester University Press, 1999

SECONDARY SOURCES – ARTICLES

Anderson, Ross, 'The Battle for Tanga, 2-5 November 1914', *War in History*, 8, (3), 2001

Body, Capt. O.G., 'Bush and Forest Fighting Against Modern Weapons', *Army Quarterly*, VIII, pp. 314-324

Cann, John, ,Mozambique, German East Africa and the Great War', *Small Wars and Insurgencies*, XII, No. 1, (2001), pp. 110-141

Davenport, T.R.H., 'The South African Rebellion', *English Historical Review*, LXXVIII, (January 1963), pp. 73-94

Eberlie, R.F., 'The German Achievement in East Africa', *Tanganyika Notes and Records*, No. 55, (September 1960), pp. 181-213

Eichstädt, E.J., 'Der Sanitatsdienst in Deutsch-Ostafrika wahrend des ersten Weltkriegs' *Wehrmedizinsche Monatsschrift*, 5, (1983), pp. 207-210

Freeland, J.C. Col., 'The Indian Army Since the Great War', *Journal of the Royal United Services Institute*, LXXIII, (1928), pp. 757-767

Garson, N.G., 'South Africa and World War I', *Journal of Imperial and Commonwealth History*, VIII, No. 1, (1979), pp. 68-85

Gillman, C., 'A Short History of the Tanganyika Railways', *Tanganyika Notes and Records*, XIII, (June 1942), pp. 14-56

Harrison, Mark, 'Medicine and the Culture of Command: the Case of Malaria Control in the British Army during the two World Wars', *Medical History*, XL, (1996), pp. 437-452

Hatchell, G.W., 'The East African Campaign: 1914 to 1919', *Tanganyika Notes and Records*, XXI, (June 1946), pp. 39-45

– , 'The British Occupation of the South-Western Area of Tanganyika Territory 1914-1918', *Tanganyika Notes and Records*, LI, (December 1958), pp. 131-155

Hatton, P.H.S., 'Harcourt and Solf: The search for an Anglo-German Understanding through Africa, 1912-14', *European Studies Review*, Vol. I No. 2 (1971), pp. 123-145

Hazlehurst, Cameron, 'Asquith as Prime Minister, 1908-1916', *English Historical Review*. LXXXV, (1970), pp. 502-531

Hodges, G.W.T., 'African Manpower Statistics for the British Forces in East Africa, 1914-1918', *Journal of African History*, IX, No. 1, (1977), pp. 101-116

Hughes, C. and Nicholson, I.E., 'A Provenance of Proconsuls: British Colonial Governors 1900-1960', *Journal of Imperial and Commonwealth History*, IV, No. 1, (1977), pp. 77-106

Killingray, David, 'Repercussions of World War I in the Gold Coast', *Journal of African History*, XIX, No. 1, (1978), pp. 39-59

– , 'The Idea of British Imperial African Army', *Journal of African History*, XX, No. 3, (1979), pp. 421-436

Killingray, David and Matthews, J., 'Beasts of Burden: British West African Carriers in the First World War', *Canadian Journal of African Studies*, XIII, No. 1, (1979), pp. 5-24

Killingray, David, 'Labour Exploitation for Military Campaigns in British Colonial Africa, 1870-1945', *Journal of Contemporary History*, XXIV, No. 3, (July 1989), pp. 483-502

Kirke, E. St G Maj., 'Notes on Military Railways', *Royal Engineer Journal*, XL, No. 7, pp. 207-219

Langhorne, R.T.B., 'The Anglo-German Negotiations Concerning the Future of the Portuguese Colonies in Africa', *Historical Journal*, XVI, No. 2, (1973), pp. 361-387.

Lotbiniere, Capt. H.A. Joly de, 'Notes on the Re-organization and Training of Indian Sapper and Miner Field Companies for Modern Warfare', *Royal Engineer Journal*, XXIV, pp. 55-64

Louis, W.R., 'The United States and the African Peace Settlement of 1919', *Journal of African History*, IV, No. 3, (1963), pp. 413-434

Majumdar, Lt.-Col. Birenda, 'Development of the transport system in the Indian Army from 1760 to 1914', *Army Quarterly*, LXXVII, (1959), pp. 250-260

Meneses, Filipe Ribeiro de, 'Too Serious a Matter to be Left to the Generals? Parliament and the Army in Wartime Portugal 1914-18', *Journal of Contemporary History*, XXXIII, No. 1, (1998), pp. 85-96

Monson, Jamie, 'Relocating Maji Maji: The Politics of Alliance and Authority in the Southern Highlands of Tanzania, 1870-1918', *Journal of African History*, XXXIX, (1998), pp. 95-120

Osuntokun, Akinjide, 'Disaffection and Revolts in Nigeria during the First World War, 1914-1918', *Canadian Journal of African Studies*, V, (1974), pp.

Page, Melvin E. 'The War of *THANGATA*: Nyasaland and the East African Campaign, 1914-1918', *Journal of African History*, XIX, No. 1, (1978), pp. 87-100

Rathbone, Richard, 'World War I and Africa: Introduction', *Journal of African History*, XIX, No. 1, (1978), pp. 1-9

Savage, Donald C. and Forbes Munro, J., 'Carrier Corps Recruitment in the British East Africa Protectorate, 1914-1918', *Journal of African History*, VII, No. 2, (1966), pp. 313-342

Smith, Alan K., 'The Idea of Mozambique and its Enemies, *c.* 1890-1930', *Journal of Southern African Studies*, XVII, No. 3, Sept 1991, pp. 496-524

Solf, Wilhelm, 'Schnee und von Lettow-Vorbeck', *Die Deutsche Nation*, (1920), pp. 87-95

Spies, S.B., 'The Outbreak of the First World War and the Botha Government', *South African Historical Journal*, 1969, pp. 47-57

Stronge, Capt. H.C.T., 'Bush Warfare Against Trained Troops', *Journal of the Royal United Services Institution*, LXXII, (1927), pp. 603-613

Stone, Glyn A., 'The Official British Attitude to the Anglo-Portuguese Alliance, 1910-1945', *The Journal of Contemporary History*, X, No. 4, October 1975, pp. 729-748

Vincent-Smith, J.D., 'The Anglo-German Negotiations over the Portuguese Colonies in Africa, 1911-14', *The Historical Journal*, XVII, No. 3, 1974, pp. 620-629

– , 'Britain, Portugal and the First World War, 1914-1918', *European Studies Review*, IV, No. 3, (1974), pp. 207-238

– , 'The Portuguese Republic and Britain, 1910-1914', *Journal of Contemporary History*, X, No. 4, (1975), pp. 707-727

Warhurst, P.R., 'Smuts and Africa: a Study in Sub-Imperialism', *South African Historical Journal*, XVI, (1984), pp. 82-100

Woodhouse, Maj. H.L., 'Railway Organisation for the Indian Army', *Journal of the Royal United Services Institute*, Volume LVI, pp. 95-102

Woodward, D.R., 'Britain in a Continental War: The Civil Military Debate over the Strategical Direction of the War of 1914-1918', *Albion*, XII, (1980), pp. 37-65

Yearwood, Peter J., 'Great Britain and the Repartition of Africa 1914-19', *Journal of Imperial and Commonwealth History*, XVIII, No. 3, (October 1990), pp. 316-341

Notes

FOREWORD

1 Lettow-Vorbeck, *My Reminiscences of East Africa.*
2 Meinertzhagen, *Army Diary.*
3 Hordern, *History of the Great War: Military Operations East Africa August 1914- September 1916.*
4 Boell, *Die Operationen in Ostafrika.*
5 Miller, *Battle for the Bundu*; Mosley, *Duel for Kilimanjaro*; Gardner, *German East Africa: the Story of the First World War in East Africa*; Sibley, *Tanganyikan Guerrilla*; Hoyt, *Guerrilla: Colonel von Lettow-Vorbeck and Germany's East African Empire.*
6 Strachan, Hew, *The First World War: To Arms,* I.

CHAPTER ONE

1 Hordern, *Military Operations*,7. The correct name for the German colony was Deutsch-Ostafrika, but it will be referred to as German East Africa throughout. The northern British colony was formally known as the East Africa Protectorate, but usually called British East Africa.
2 Kaponen, *Development for Exploitation, German Colonial Policies in Mainland Tanzania 1884-1914*, pp.306 and 310-311.
3 CAB 8/5, No. 404M, *Colonial Defence – Employment of Armed Native Levies in the East and West African Protectorates,* May 1909; No. 411M, *Zanzibar – Defence of Town and Island,* December 1909 and No. 424M, August 1910; No. 417M, *General Principles Affecting the Oversea Dominions and Colonies,* July 1910; No. 431M, *East and West African Protectorates – Position in the Event of War with a European Power,* January 1911; CAB 8/6, No. 460M, *Oversea Defence – Position of Regular Officers Serving with the King's African Rifles and West African Frontier Force in the Event of a European War in which Great Britain is Involved,* April 1913.
4 CAB 8/5, No. 451M, *Rhodesia Report by the Inspector-General of the Overseas Forces on the Defence of Southern and Northern Rhodesia,* August 1912; CAB 11/117, *Defence Plan for the Uganda Railway and East African Protectorates,* February 1912.

5 CAB 8/5, No. 417M, 1-3.
6 CAB 11/117, *Defence Plan*, 1-16.
7 Wack, *The Story of the Congo Free State*, pp.530-544.
8 BA/MA, N14/14, Boell Papers, *Denkschrift über Mobilmachungsvorarbeiten für den Fall eines Krieges mit Grossmacht für Deutsch-Ostafrika*, 27 Apr 12.
9 BA, R1001/6879, 15 Aug 14, Chancellor's Decree.
10 Fischer, *Germany's War Aim Aims in the First World War*, pp.38-39; French, *British Strategy*, pp.9-10 and 14; Pélissier, *Naissance de Mozambique*, Volume II, 650-651 and 656; Teixeira, *L'Entreé du Portugal dans la Grande Guerre*, pp.114-119; Vincent-Smith, 'The Portuguese Republic and Britain, 1910-1914', *Journal of Contemporary History*, X, No. 4, (1975), 714-717; Langhorne, 'The Anglo-German Negotiations Concerning the Future of the Portuguese Colonies in Africa', *Historical Journal*, XVI, No. 2, (1973), 378-379; Newitt, *Portugal in Africa*, pp.33-35; Willequet, Jacques, 'Anglo-German Rivalry in Belgian and Portuguese Africa?', Giffard and Louis, *Britain and Germany*, p.265.
11 Hatton, 'Harcourt and Solf', *European Studies Review*, I, No. 2 (1971), pp. 123-140; Berghahn, 'Germany and the Approach of War in 1914', pp. 113, 132-133; Ritter, *The Sword and the Sceptre The Problem of Militarism in Germany*, III, *The Tragedy of Statesmanship - Bethmann Hollweg as War Chancellor (1914-1917)*, pp. 27-28.
12 Hankey, *The Supreme Command*, I, p.168; French, *British Strategy*, pp.27-28; Oxford and Asquith, *Memories and Reflections 1852-1927*, II, p.25.
13 Halpern, *Naval History*, pp.6-9 and 66-70.
14 Halpern, *Naval History*, p.69.
15 CAB 8/5, No. 411M, *Zanzibar – Defence of Town and Island*; Kennedy, 'Imperial Cable Communications and Strategy, 1870-1914', in Kennedy (ed.), *The War Plans of the Great Powers, 1880-1914*, pp.75-98.
16 Kennedy, 'Imperial Cable Communications', pp.91-92; Arendt, *Kamina ruft Nauen*, pp.132, 136 and 167-174; Boell, *Die Operationen*, p.18.
17 Chatterton, *Königsberg Adventure*, p.12.
18 Corbett, *Naval Operations*, I, pp.151-153.
19 Hordern, *Military Operations*, pp.559 –561.
20 Moyse-Bartlett, *The King's African Rifles*, p.701.
21 Hordern, *Military Operations*, p.15; Moyse-Bartlett, *The King's African Rifles*, pp.260-264.
22 Boell, *Die Operationen*, p.30.
23 Meinertzhagen, *Army Diary*, pp.86 and 103.
24 *Campagnes coloniales belges*, I, pp.24-27; Wéber, 'L'efforts belges', I, BBSM, (1927) No. 5 , pp.411-412. Jadot, 'Une batterie de montagne des troupes coloniales belges dans l'Est Afrique allemand', I, *BBSM*, 1924, No. 2, pp.171-172; Bayot, 'Les Operations Militaires, II(1)', BBSM, (1934) No. 1, pp.32-33.
25 MNE, UN, 3° Piso, Armário 7, Maçao 13, Capilha 1, Letter, Minister of Colonies to Ministry of Foreign Affairs, 27 Aug 14; Telegram, Governor of Moçambique to Minister of Colonies, 30 Aug 14.
26 Fischer, *Germany's War Aims*, pp.102-103; Mombauer, *Helmuth von Moltke and the Origins of the First World War*, pp.235-237; Craig, *The Politics of the Prussian Army*, pp.294-295.
27 Iliffe, *Africans: The History of a Continent*, p.208; Monsun, 'Relocating Maji-Maji', *Journal of African History*, 39, 1998, pp.115-120; Pakenham, *The Scramble for Africa*, p.622; Zirkel, Kirsten, 'Military Power in German Colonial Policy', in Killingray and Omissi, *Guardians of Empire*, pp.98-104.

28 Zirkel, Kirsten, 'Military Power', pp.97-98 and 101-104; Schnee, *Deutsch-Ostafrika im Weltkrieg*, pp.18-23 and 34-36; Lettow, *Reminiscences*, pp.20-22.
29 Petter, Wolfgang, 'Das Offizierkorps der Deutschen Kolonialtruppen 1889-1918', *Das Deutsche Offizerkorps 1860-1960*, ed. Hofmann, pp.164-165.
30 GstA, VI, HA, Schee 20a, 183.
31 Lettow, *Mein Leben*, pp.9-15, 30-36, 46-115.
32 Boell, *Die Operationen*, p.29.
33 BA R1001/829, 20 Sep 13, Letter K Nr. 1715, Solf to Schnee.
34 Lettow, *Mein Leben*, pp.120-121.
35 CAB 11/117, *Defence Plan*, p.6-7.

CHAPTER TWO

1 Methner, Unter drei Gouverneuren, 342-343; Marinearchiv, Der Kreuzerkrieg in den ausländischen Gewässern, I, 11-14; Marinarchiv, Kreuzerkrieg, II, 122 – 126 and 132-136; Schnee, Deutsch-Ostafrika im Weltkrieg, 25-27; King-Hall, Naval Traditions, 243-245.
2 Corbett, Naval Operations, I, 152-153.
3 BA, R1001/875, Bericht über den Krieg in Deutsch-Ostafrika, Schnee to Reichskolonialamt, 7 May 1919, 1-3. Henceforth, Bericht - Schnee.
4 Fischer, Germany's War Aims, 93-94.
5 CAB 21/3, Joint Naval and Military Committee for the Consideration of Combined Operations in Foreign Territory, 5 Aug 14.
6 CAB 5/3, 'Proceedings of a Sub-Committee of the Committee of Imperial Defence, August 5, 1914', 1.
7 Churchill, *The World Crisis*, I, p.283.
8 CAB 21/3, 'Proceedings of a Sub-Committee of the Committee of Imperial Defence Assembled on the 14th August, 1914', 14 Aug 14; French, *British Strategy*, p.15.
9 Churchill, *The World Crisis*, I, p.283.
10 French, *British Strategy*, pp.27-28.
11 Callwell, *Experiences of a Dug-Out*, 175-177; CAB 5/3, 13 Sep 14, 111-C, *Committee of Imperial Defence Expedition Against German East Africa*, 1.
12 CAB 21/3, 'Joint Naval and Military Committee', Part 7 – East Africa, 7 and 17 Aug 1914.
13 Hordern, *Military Operations*, pp.30-31.
14 CAB 21/3, 'Joint Naval and Military Committee', Part 7 – East Africa, 9 and 10 Aug 1914.
15 Wynn, *Ambush*, pp.21, 24-25 and 46-47; Johnson Papers, 77/109/1, 'Notes on the Account of the Action at Tanga by Major General Sir E.C.W. Mackenzie', pp.2-3; Meinterzhagen, *Army Diary*, pp.109, 123 and 158-159; *India Army List*, April 1906, April 1913 and October 1914.
16 CAB 21/3, 'Joint Naval and Military Committee', Part 7 – East Africa, 17 Aug 1914.
17 IWM, PP/MCR/150, King Papers, Diary 25, 26, 30 Aug and 1 Sep 1914; Hordern, *Military Operations*, pp.60-62; IWM, 80/13/1, Aitken Papers, 'Account of the Indian Expeditionary Force to German East Africa', 1-2, Henceforth, *Aitken Account*; CAB 21/3, 'Joint Naval and Military Committee', Part 7 – East Africa, 28 Aug 1914.
18 Hordern, *Military Operations*, pp.62-63.
19 CAB 5/3, 'Expedition Against German East Africa', 3 Sep 1914; Harcourt Papers, 10 Sep 1914, Telegram Harcourt to Belfield.
20 Hordern, *Military Operations*, pp.66-67; CAB 5/3, CID Paper 112-C, 'Expedition Against German East Africa – Draft of Instructions Proposed for Issue to the GOC Expedition "B"', 28 Sep 14; CAB 21/3, *Proceedings*, 29 Sep 14.
21 Hordern, *Military Operations*, pp.51-52 and 530.
22 CAB 8/5 Appendix II to CID No.431 M, 24 Jan 11, 'East and West African

Protectorates Position in the Event of War with a European Power'; Hordern, *Military Operations*, p.60.

23 FO 371/1882, Folio 37617, 9 Aug 14, Letter Count Lalaing to Grey; Folio 37617, 13 Aug 14, Letter FO to CO.

24 FO 371/1882, Folio 37617, 10 Aug 14, Minute; Folio 38483, 12 Aug 14, Telegram 46, Hardinge to Grey.

25 IWM, 49538, *Schutztruppe Kriegstagebuch*, pp.5, 8 and 23, Aug 14. Henceforth, *Schutztruppe KTB*.

26 Lettow, *Reminiscences*, pp.18-19.

27 BA, R1001/6879, 15 Aug 14, Chancellor's Decree.

28 Petter, 'Deutsche Kolonialtruppen', 168-169; WO 157/1112, Intelligence Summary IEF B, 16 Oct 14.

29 IWM, 49538, *Schutztruppe, KTB*, 10 Aug 14, Telegram, GHQ to Lindi. BA, R1001/865, 20 Dec 14, Letter M245/15, Ambassador Lisbon to FO; GstA, VI, HA, Nl Schnee, No. 16, pp.22, 204-208.

30 BA, R1001/875, *Bericht-Schnee*, p.4; Boell, *Die Operationen*, pp.68-70; IWM 49538, *Schutztruppe, KTB*, 23 and 24 Aug 14.

31 FO 371/1882, Folio, 39213, 13 Aug 14, Telegram 64, Grey to Carnegie; 15 Aug 14, Telegram 47, Carnegie to Grey; FO 371/1883, Folio 38669, n.d. [13 Aug 14], Minute.

32 FO 371/1883, Folio 38309, 13 Aug 14, Letter, CO to FO; Folio 39795, 21 Aug 14, Letter FO to CO; Folio 41798, 21 Aug 14, Telegram 50, Carnegie to Grey.

33 FO 371/1882, Folio 38791, 13 Aug 14, Letter CO to FO.

34 FO 371/1882, Folio 42613, 22 Aug 14, Letter Villiers to Grey; 24 Aug Folio 44712, 2 Sep 14, Letter Grey to Villiers.

35 FO 371/1882, Folio 52758, 24 Sep 14, Letter US Ambassador (Hines) to Grey; Folio 58894, 13 Oct 14, Letter 172, Villiers to Grey; 8 Oct Folio 60662, 17 Oct 14, Telegram Bertie to Grey; Folio 70703, 10 Nov 14, Telegram 192, Villiers to Grey; Folio 707003, 20 Nov 14, Letter Grey to Page.

36 Harcourt Papers, dep 507; Telegram Harcourt to Buxton, 22 Sep 14 and telegram Harcourt to Belfield, 3 Oct 14 for the Belgians; Telegram No. 3, Harcourt to Buxton, 27 Aug 14 and dep 590 FO Print; Telegram 176, Grey to Carnegie, 26 Aug 14 for the Portuguese; CAB 21/3, Telegram Grey to Bertie, 14 Aug 14 and Andrew, Christopher and Kanya-Forster, *France Abroad*, pp.62-63 for the French.

37 Louis, *Ruanda-Urundi*, pp.216-217; *Campagnes Coloniales Belges*, II, p.125.

38 Vincent-Smith, 'Britain, Portugal and the First World War, 1914-16', *European Studies Review*, IV, No. 3, (1974), pp.210-211.

39 Stone, 'The Official British Attitude to the Anglo-Portuguese Alliance, 1910-1945', *The Journal of Contemporary History*, X, No. 4, October 1975, pp.729-730; Vincent-Smith, 'Britain, Portugal and the First World War, 1914-19', *European Studies Review*, IV, No. 3, (1974), pp.210-211; *Teixeira, L'Entrée du Portugal*, pp.188-194.

40 ADM 137/9, 12 Aug 14, Telegram 104, Britannia, Simonstown to Admiralty.

41 Boell, *Die Operationen*, pp.35-37; GStA, VI, HA, Schnee, 22, Nr 16, 201-202.

42 ADM 137/9, 18 Aug 14, Telegram 119, CinC Cape to Admiralty.

43 IWM, 49538, *Schutztruppe, KTB*, 23 Aug 14, Telegram GHQ to Bagamoyo; 8 Sep 14, Telegram, GHQ to *8 FK*.

44 ADM 137/9, 17 Aug 14, Telegram 116, CinC Cape to Admiralty; 17 Aug 14, Telegram 102, Admiralty to CinC. Cape; 26 Aug 14, Telegram 128, Admiralty to CinC Cape.

45 ADM 137/9, 27 Aug 14, Telegram 156, CinC. Cape to Admiralty; 30 Aug 14, Telegram, Admiralty to SNO Zanzibar.

46 ADM 137/10, 27 Aug 14, Telegram 156, CinC Cape to Admiralty; 19 Aug 1914, Letter, CO to Admiralty; ADM 137/10, 26 Aug 14, Letter, Admiralty to CO.

47 BA/MA, N14/14, Boell Papers, *Denkschrift über Mobilmachungsvorarbeiten für den Fall eines Krieges mit Grossmacht für Deutsch-Ostafrika*, 27 Apr 12; Boell Papers, N14/14; WO 157/1112, Intelligence Summary, IEF B, 10 Oct 14.

48 Schnee, *Deutsche-Ostafrika im Weltkrieg*, pp.58-60; IWM, 49538, *Schutztruppe Kriegstagebuch*, 5, 8 and 23 Aug 14. Henceforth, *Schutztruppe KTB*.

49 GStA, VI, HA, Schnee, 24, No. 14, 1917, *Report of Referant Brandes*, 11; Arning, *Vier Jahre Weltkrieg*, pp.50-51; Lettow, *My Reminiscences*, pp.21 and 27-28.

50 Craig, *Politics of the Prussian Army*, pp.281-282 and 294-302; Mombauer, *Moltke*, pp.95-96, 139 and 205.

51 Moyse-Bartlett, *The King's African Rifles*, pp.266-267.

52 BA/MA, N103/36, *Lettow Personlichestagesbuch*, Aug 14. Lettow kept a series of pocket books throughout the war that effectively acted as his personal war diary. They were usually very terse records of operations. Henceforth, Lettow, PTB; *Marinearchiv, Kreuzerkrieg*, II, pp.132-134.

53 Boell, *Die Operationen*, pp.28-29.

54 IWM, 49538, *Schutztruppe, KTB*, 23 Aug 14, Telegram, GHQ to Tanga; Arning, *Vier Jahre Weltkrieg*, pp.52-53.

55 Boell, *Die Operationen*, p.54.

56 Hordern, *Military Operations*, pp.46-47; IWM, 49538, *Schutztruppe, KTB*, 8 Oct 14, Telegram, Baumstark to GHQ; Boell, *Die Operationen*, p.56.

57 Boell, *Die Operationen*, pp.57-58; Hordern, *Military Operations*, pp.39-41; Schnee, *Deutsch-Ostafrika*, pp.101-102.

58 Hordern, *Military Operations*, pp.24-26; Schnee, *Deutsch-Ostafrika*, pp.102-103.

59 Boell, *Die Operationen*, pp.58-59.

60 Campagnes coloniales belges, I, 160; Bayot, 'Les Opérations Militaires', I, *Bulletins belges des sciences militaires*, 1934, I, No. 6, pp.532-533; Boell, *Die Operationen*, pp.58- 60; Schnee, *Deutsch-Ostafrika*, pp.106-107.

61 Campagnes coloniales belges, I, 27; Schnee, *Deutsch-Ostafrika*, pp.115-116.

62 Boell, *Die Operationen*, pp.64-65; Hordern, *Military Operations*, pp.176-178.

63 Schnee, *Deutsch-Ostafrika*, p.117; Boell, *Die Operationen*, pp.66-67; Hordern, *Military Operations*, pp.171-174.

64 Boell, *Die Operationen*, p.70.

65 FO 371/1882, Folio 52448, 22 Sep 14, Telegram Harcourt to Buxton.

66 FO 371/1882, Folio 54712, 2 Oct 14, Telegram 120, Grey to Villiers; Folio 56273, 8 Oct 14, Letter Asquith to Grey.

67 Marinearchiv, *Deutschen Kolonien*, pp.176-178; Hordern, *Military Operations*, p.23.

68 Hordern, *Military Operations*, pp.166-170; Schnee, *Deutsch-Ostafrika*, p.116.

69 FO 371/1883, Folio 42412, n.d. [23 Aug 14], Letter Grey to Officials; Folio 42412, 24 Aug14, Telegram, Harcourt to Governor of Nyasaland; Folio 44271, 28 Aug 14, Note Teixeira-Gomes [Portuguese Minister] to Grey; Folio 42172, 22 Aug 14, Telegram No. 52, Carnegie to Grey; Folio 44048, 26 Aug 14, Telegram, Buxton to Harcourt.

70 Hordern, *Military Operations*, pp.37, 47 and 51-52.

71 FO 371/1882, Folio 56273, 6 Oct 14, Minute.

72 FO 371/1882, Folio 71865, 17 Nov 14, Minute.

73 Cann, John, 'Mozambique, German East Africa and the Great War', *Small Wars and Insurgencies*, XII, No. 1, (2001), p.119.

74 Newitt, *History of Mozambique*, pp.398-

406; Newitt, *Portugal in Africa*, pp.84-85; Vincent-Smith, 'Britain, Portugal and the First World War', pp.210-211.

75 Corbett, *Naval Operations*, I, pp.280-281; Halpern, *Naval History*, pp.124-125; ADM 137/32, 5 Sep 14, Memo Churchill to 1st Sea Lord; 30 Sep 14, Telegram H1219, Viceroy to WO and Admiralty.

76 WO 95/5344, WD 61st Pioneers, 22, 29 Sep and 7, 8 Oct 14; Hordern, *Military Operations*, pp.68-69.

77 *India Army List*, April 1913 and October 1914; IWM, 88/6/1, Wapshare Papers, Diary for 1914 and *The Times*, 24 Dec 32, Obituary for Lieutenant General Sir Richard Wapshare.

78 Singh, Maj. K. Brahma, *History of Jammu and Kashmir Rifles 1820-1956*, pp.108-111.

79 *India Army List*, April 1913 and October 1914; IWM 88/6/1, Wapshare Papers, Eastbourne newspaper cutting 'Major-General M.J. Tighe – Eastbourne Resident to command in East Africa, *c.* 1915.

80 Marinearchiv, *Kreuzerkrieg*, II, pp.85 and 209. SMS *Emden* sank some sixteen merchant ships in September-October 1914, while *Königsberg* sank only one merchant ship, but destroyed one British light cruiser in the same period; ADM 137/14, 4 Nov 14, Note 1st Lord to Chief of Staff; 5 Nov 14, Telegram Admiralty to SNO, Mombasa.

81 Boell, *Die Operationen*, p.77. A common German designation was the *Abteilung* (detachment) that took the senior officer's name. It was usually abbreviated to Abt; Arning, *Vier Jahre Weltkrieg*, pp.102-103.

82 IWM, PP/MCR/150, King Papers, Diary, 26 Oct 14; WO 138/41 Aitken Personal File, 28 Aug 20, Letter Admiralty to War Office, enclosing statement by Rear Admiral Caulfield [sic], 1; WO 157/1112, Intelligence Summary IEF B, 29 Oct 14.

83 WO 95/5289, WD IEF B, 31 Oct 14; CAB 45/6, 'Memorandum of the Operations at Tanga' to cover letter of 31 Jul 14 [sic – note attached to letter of 20 Feb 17]; PP/MCR/150, King Papers, Diary, 9 Nov 14; IWM, P80, Cooke Papers, 'Field Notes on German East Africa, General Staff India, August 1914', 65; IWM, PP/MCR/150, King Papers, Diary, 27, 29 and 31 Oct 14.

84 Hordern, *Military Operations*, pp.97-98; Boell, *Die Operationen*, pp.82-83.

85 ADM 137/32, 30 Oct 14, Zanzibar to Admiralty; 31 Oct 14, *Chatham* to Admiralty; 31 Oct 14, Admiralty to CinC China Station, East Indies Station and Cape Station; 1 Nov 14, Telegram *Goliath* to Admiralty; 4 Nov 14, *Goliath* to Admiralty.

86 Boell, *Die Operationen*, p.77.

87 Anderson, *Battle of Tanga*, pp.66-68.

88 Anderson, *Battle of Tanga*, pp.69-76.

89 Anderson, *Battle of Tanga*, pp.77-118.

90 Anderson, *Battle of Tanga*, pp.118-122.

91 Looff, *Tufani*, pp.26-29 and 36-38; Marinearchiv, *Kreuzerkrieg*, II, pp.141-148.

92 ADM 137/8, 20 Sep 14, Telegram 234, CinC Cape to Admiralty; 15 Oct 14, Telegram 439, CinC Cape to Admiralty.

93 Looff, *Tufani*, pp.48-58; Marinearchiv, *Kreuzerkrieg*, II, pp.150-159; Chatterton, *Königsberg Adventure*, pp.20-21; ADM 137/14, 20 Oct 14, Telegram 20, Intelligence Officer, Colombo to Admiralty; Halpern, *A Naval History*, pp.76-77.

94 ADM 137/3, 23 Sep 14, Telegram, Buxton to Harcourt; 27 Sep 14, Telegram 189, Admiralty to CinC Cape; Chatterton, *Königsberg Adventure*, 35.

95 ADM137/32, 1 Oct 14, Telegram 198, Admiralty to CinC Cape; Telegram 199, Admiralty to CinC East Indies; 13 Oct 14, Telegram 225, Admiralty to CinC East Indies.

96 ADM 13713, 3 Nov 14, Telegram 354, CinC Cape to Admiralty; 8 Oct 14, Telegram 285, CinC Cape to Admiralty; Corbett, *Naval Operations*, I, pp.338-339.
97 ADM 137/14, 3 Nov 14, Telegram *Chatham* to Admiralty; Marinearchiv, *Kreuzerkrieg*, II, pp.159-165; Looff, *Tufani*, pp.68-71.
98 ADM 137/13, 31 Oct 14, Telegram, *Chatham* to Admiralty; 3 Nov 14, Telegram 585, *Chatham* to Admiralty; Telegram Zanzibar to Admiralty; 10 Nov 14, Telegram, Governor Straits Settlements to Admiralty; Corbett, *Naval Operations*, I, pp.374-375.
99 FO 371/1882, Folio 61632, 24 Oct 14, Letter FO to CO.
100 FO 371/1883, Folio 71503, 14 Nov 14, Telegram, Harcourt to Smith; Folio 74961, 19 Nov 14, Telegram Smith to Harcourt.
101 Marinearchiv, *Krieg zur See – Deutschen Kolonien*, p.184; Boell, *Die Operationen*, p.64; Hordern, *Military Operations*, p.179.
102 FO 371/1882, Folio 66873, 3 Nov 14, Letter CO to FO; Folio 71852, 17 Nov 14, Minutes; Folio 78948, 7 Dec 1914, Letter FO to WO.
103 Bayot, 'Operations Militaires', I, 541; Bayot, 'Les Opérations Militaires', II(1), *BBSM*, 1934, II, No. 1, 24-25; *Campagnes coloniales belges*, I, p.169.
104 FO 371/1882, Folio 81461, 9 Dec 14, Letter Callwell to Nicholson.
105 FO 371/1882, Folio 75245, 25 Nov 14, Telegram, Grey to Bertie; Folio 78100, 2 Dec 14, Telegram 524, Bertie to Grey; Folio 78585, Telegram 527, Bertie to Grey; and Folio 78585, 5 Dec 14, Telegram 1130, Grey to Bertie.
106 FO 371/1882, Folio 82994, 18 Dec 14, Telegram 214, Grey to Villiers; Folio 87274, 23 Dec 14, Letter Kidston to Grey.
107 WO 33/714, No. 1490, 2 Dec 14, Telegram S66, Wapshare to Kitchener; No. 1586, 9 Dec 14, Telegram 2393, Kitchener to Wapshare.
108 WO 95/5289, WD IEF B, 14 Dec 14, Telegram S87, Wapshare to Kitchener.
109 Arning, *Vier Jahre Weltkrieg*, pp.121-122.
110 Boell, *Die Operationen*, pp.85-88.
111 Hordern, *Military Operation*, pp.120-121; Boell, *Die Operationen*, p.88.
112 WO 33/714, No. 1680, 17 December 1914, No. 95, Wapshare to Kitchener; No. 1723, 23 December 1914, Telegram 2251, Kitchener to Wapshare; WO 95/5289, WD IEF B, 2 Jan 15, Telegram 2615, Troopers to Wapshare.
113 WO 33/714, No. 1718, 23 Dec 14, Telegram S 109, Wapshare to Kitchener; No. 1723, 23 Dec 14, Telegram 2551, Kitchener to Wapshare.
114 WO 95/5289, WD IEF B, 6 Jan 15, Telegram S139, Wapshare to Kitchener; 6 Jan 15, *Appreciation of the Situation – Tanga.*
115 Boell, *Die Operationen*, p.85.
116 IWM, 49538, *Schutztruppe, KTB*, mid-Nov 14, *Report about the Field Commissariat, for the Period 5th September to middle of November 1914.*
117 Schnee, *Deutsch-Ostafrika*, pp.118-121; IWM, 49538, KTB, Extracts from *General von Lettow's Private Diary*, p.17; Deppe, *Mit Lettow-Vorbeck*, pp.136-137.
118 BA/MA, Boell Papers, N14/17, *Die Organisation des Nachschubwesens*, pp.19-20 and 30-31; Hodges, Carrier Corps, 143.
119 Schnee, *Deutsch-Ostafrika*, p.107; Marinearchiv, *Deutschen Kolonien*, pp.176-180.

CHAPTER THREE

1 Hankey, *The Supreme Command*, I, p.249.
2 ADM 137/178, 12 Feb 15, Telegram 63 Admiralty to CinC Cape; 12 Feb 15, Telegram 7 *Weymouth* to Admiralty; WO 33/858, No. 35, 12 Feb 15,

Telegram 3050, Kitchener to Wapshare; No. 51, 15 Feb 15, Telegram 229, Wapshare to Kitchener.

3 Corbett, *Naval Operations*, II, pp.236-239.

4 Harcourt Papers, dep 583, 4 Jan 15, Telegram 2, Kidston to Grey; dep 507, 14 Apr 15, Telegram 4, Buxton to Harcourt; FO 371/2229, Folio 1456, 4 Jan 15, Letter CO to WO; Folio 1456, 5 Jan 15, Minute; Folio 1456, 7 Jan 15, Minute.

5 WO 33/858, No. 1878, 10 Jan 15, Telegram 2698, Kitchener to Wapshare.

6 Campagnes coloniales belges, I, 170-173; Bayot, 'Les Opérations Militaires', II, pp.389-393.

7 MNE, UN, 3°Piso, Armário 7, Maço 13, Capilha 11, 12 Feb 15, Letter, J Rodrigues Mon[?] to Carnegie; Newitt, *A History of Mozambique*, pp.367-368.

8 Halpern, *Naval History*, pp.306-308 and 328-329.

9 Looff, *Tufani*, p.80.

10 Lettow, *Reminiscences*, pp.18-22; Deppe, *Mit Lettow-Vorbeck*, pp.25-28.

11 Lettow, *Reminiscences*, pp.64-66; Deppe, *Mit Lettow-Vorbeck*, pp.80-81.

12 Boell, *Die Operationen*, pp.104-105.

13 BA/MA, N103, Lettow, *PTB*, 12-14 Jan 15; Arning, *Vier Jahre Weltkrieg*, pp.124-125.

14 Hordern, *Military Operations*, pp.123-125; Boell, *Die Operationen*, p.89; Lettow, *My Reminiscences*, pp.60-61; Arning, *Vier Jahre Weltkrieg*, pp.127-130.

15 Hordern, *Military Operations*, p.128; Boell, *Die Operationen*, pp.90-91; Lettow, *My Reminiscences*, pp.60- 63; BA/MA, N103, Lettow, KTB, 23 and 24 Jan 15; Boell, 90; WO 33/714, No. 2001, Telegram S185, Wapshare to Kitchener.

16 WO 33/714, No. 2001, 23 Jan 15, Telegram S185, Wapshare to WO.

17 WO 33/714, No. 1976, 21 Jan 15, Telegram 2810, Kitchener to Wapshare.

18 WO 33/858, No. 23, 6 Feb 15, Telegram S215, Wapshare to WO; Hordern, *Military Operations*, p.130; WO 95/5290, WD GHQ, 21 Feb 15.

19 WO 95/5290, WD GHQ, 6 Mar, 15 Apr and 27 May 15.

20 WO 33/858, No. 308, 2 Aug 15, Telegram 322, Tighe to Kitchener; WO 95/5289, WD GHQ, 27 and 30 Mar 15. The Rampur Infantry were considered to be unwilling to the fight the Germans while 2 soldiers deserted from the 17th Cavalry.

21 Boell, *Die Operationen*, p.94; Arning, *Vier Jahre Weltkrieg*, pp.132-133.

22 Keen 'The Campaign in East Africa', JUSI Vol XLVI, 1917, 78; Deppe, *Mit Lettow-Vorbeck*, pp.82-84; WO 95/5290, WD GHQ, 1 Apr 15.

23 WO 95/5290, WD GHQ, 5 Jul 15.

24 Boell, *Die Operationen*, pp.108-109: Lettow, *Reminiscences*, p.66; Deppe, *Mit Lettow-Vorbeck*, pp.86-88.

25 Boell, *Die Operationen*, pp.104-107; Arning, *Vier Jahre Weltkrieg*, pp.56-57.

26 Marinearchiv, *Krieg zur See – Kreuzerkrieg*, II, pp.186-187; Christiansen, Carl, *'Durch' Mit Kriegsmaterial zu Lettow-Vorbeck*, pp.1-4 and 25-28; ADM 137/3853, *German Narrative of Events Leading up to the Loss of the 'KONIGSBERG' by Fregatten-Kapitän Looff*, 17 Oct 15, 1; Halpern, *Naval History*, pp.36-37; King-Hall, *Naval Traditions*, pp.265-266; Corbett, *Naval Operations*, III, pp.6-8.

27 WO 95/ 5290, WD GHQ, 23 and 25 Jun 15; Marinearchiv, *Deutsche Kolonien*, pp.149-150.

28 WO 33/858, No. 15, 17 Feb 15, Telegram 229, Wapshare to Kitchener.

29 WO 33/858, No. 147, 3 Apr 15, Telegram 3854, Kitchener to Wapshare; No. 168, 12 Apr 15, Telegram 3992, Kitchener to Wapshare.

30 WO 33/858, No. 215, 14 May 15, Telegram 4663, Kitchener to Tighe; Hordern, *Military Operations*, p.155.
31 BA/MA, Boell Papers, N14/17, *Die Organisation des Nachschubwesens*, p.45; Boell, *Die Operationen*, p.112.
32 WO 95/5290, WD GHQ, 16 Jun 15, 'Intelligence Notes on Bukoba and Neighbourhood'.
33 WO 95/5290, WD GHQ, 26 and 30 Jun 15; Hordern, *Military Operations*, pp.150-153; Boell, *Die Operationen*, p.112.
34 Boell, *Die Operationen*, pp.110-111; Regimental Headquarters, Queen's Lancashire Regiment (RHQ QLR), WD 2 LNL, Entry 29 Jul 15.
35 Boell, *Die Operationen*, pp.112-113; Hordern, *Military Operations*, pp.155-158.
36 Boell, *Die Operationen*, p.108; WO 95/5290, WD GHQ, 1 and 30 Jun 15; Hordern, *Military Operations*, p.155.
37 Boell, *Die Operationen*, pp.128-129.
38 Ibid., pp.154-155.
39 Hordern, *Military Operations*, pp.162-163.
40 WO 95/5290, WD GHQ, 24 Jun 15.
41 WO 95/5290, WD GHQ, 30 Jun, 16 and 21 Jul 15.
42 WO 33/858, No. 315, 14 Aug 15, Telegram 325, Tighe to Kitchener; WO 33/858, No. 320, 16 Aug 15, Telegram 328, Tighe to Kitchener.
43 WO 33/858, No. 418, 2 Oct 15, Telegram 343, Tighe to WO; No. 518, 5 Nov 15, Telegram 360, Tighe to WO.
44 IWM, 49538, *KTB*, II, Annex 13, 1 Sep 15, pp.11-18.
45 Boell, *Die Operationen*, pp.114- 115.
46 IWM, 49538, *KTB*, II, Annex 25, 6 Jun 15, pp.12-13.
47 IWM, 49538, *KTB*, II, Annex 7, 1 Aug 15, *Detachment Muansa*, pp.1-7; Boell, *Die Operationen*, p.110.
48 NAM 6506-16-1, *Priestland Papers*, 'Patrol to Blow up the Uganda Railway', Jul 15.
49 NAM 6506-16-1, *Priestland Papers*, 6 Aug 15, *Kommando der Schutztruppe an das Batallion Tanga*.
50 NAM 6506-16-1, *Priestland Papers*, 'Patrol to Blow up the Uganda Railway 27 Aug 15'.
51 Hordern, *Military Operations*, pp.109-112, 118, and 136-158.
52 RHQ QLR, WD 2 LNL, 31 Jul 15.
53 RHQ QLR, WD 2 LNL, 31 Aug 15.
54 RHQ QLR, WD 2 LNL, 2 Oct 15.
55 RHQ QLR, WD 2 LNL, 8 Dec 15.
56 RHQ QLR, WD 2 LNL, 27 Dec 15.
57 NAM 6112-611, *Davidson Papers*, 27 Mar 15, Letter Maj Davidson to Kitty [Davidson].
58 WO 33/858, No. 243, 4 Jun 15, Telegram8/4/1, Tighe to Kitchener.
59 WO 95/5290, WD GHQ, 1 Jun 15.
60 Deppe, *Mit Lettow-Vorbeck*, pp.82-93.
61 MNE, UN, 3°Piso, Armário 7, Maço 13, Capilha 9, 30 Apr 15, Note Theophilo José da Trindade to Minister of Colonies.
62 *Campagnes coloniales belges*, I, pp.170-171; Wéber, 'L'Effort Belge', I, pp.409-412 and 418.
63 Bayot, 'Opérations Militaires', II(1), pp.36-46.
64 WO 95/5289, WD GHQ, 25 Feb 15, Telegram 239S, Wapshare to Malleson; WO 95/5289, WD GHQ, 10 Mar 15, Telegram 168, Malleson to Wapshare, 5 Mar; 14 Mar 15, Telegram 3537, WO to Wapshare.
65 Bayot, 'Les Opérations Militaires, II', 396-403.
66 *Campagnes coloniales belges*, I, pp.191-192; Bayot, Les opérations militaires', II', pp.480-494; Wéber, 'L'effort belge', III, *BBSM*, 1928, I, No. 1, pp.17-18.
67 ADM 123/142, 3 Jun 15, Letter, Admiralty to Spicer-Simson; Shankland, *The Phantom Flotilla*, London: Collins, 1968, pp.22-26.
68 Newbolt, *Naval Operations*, IV, pp.80-81; Marinearchiv, *Deutsche Kolonien*, p.178.
69 ADM 123/142, *Report of Proceedings*,

Nos. 2-4, 30 Jul-28 Sep 15; Spicer-Simson, 'The Operations on Lake Tanganyika in 15', *Journal of the Royal United Services Institute*, LXXIX, 1934, pp.755-758.

70 ADM 123/142, 25 Oct 15, Telegram C, Resident Commissioner, Salisbury to High Commissioner.

71 IWM, 49538, *KTB*, II, Annex 25, 6 Jun 15, 5-6; Boell, *Die Operationen*, 29 May 15, Telegram Lettow to Wahle, pp.117 and 130.

72 IWM, 49538, *KTB*, II, Annex 13, 1 Sep 15, 9-10; Boell, *Die Operationen*, pp.117-118.

73 Boell, *Die Operationen*, p.120; Hordern, *Military Operations*, pp.184-185.

74 IWM, 49538, *KTB*, II, Annex 13, 1 Sep 15, 9-10.

75 Vincent-Smith, 'Britain, Portugal and the First World War', pp.226-230.

76 MNE, UN, 3°Piso, Armário 7, Maço 13, Capilha 20, 17 Jul 15, Telegram, Minster of Colonies to Governor General.

77 Pretorius, Major P.J., *Jungle Man The Autobiography of Major P.J. Pretorius*, pp.16-22.

78 Chatterton, *The Königsberg Adventure*. pp.156-157.

79 King-Hall, *Naval Traditions*, pp.268-269.

80 Jones, *The War in the Air*, III, pp.8-10; Corbett, *Naval Operations*, III, pp.64-65.

81 ADM 137/3853, *German Narrative of Events*, 3; Looff, *Tufani*, pp.99-103.

82 ADM 137/3853, *German Narrative of Events*, pp.5-6.

83 Corbett, *Naval Operations*, III, pp.64-67; Jones, *War in the Air*, III, pp.10-14; Chatterton, *Königsberg Adventure*, pp.184-196.

84 WO 33/858, No. 381, 13 Sep 15, Telegram 337, Tighe to War Office.

85 IWM, 49538, KTB, *Lettow's Private Diary*, pp.8-9 and 17-18.

86 IWM, 49538, KTB, *Lettow's Private Diary*, pp.17-18 and 40-41; GstA, VI HA, Schnee Papers 22, Nr 16, *Mein Verhältnis zu Lettow-Vorbeck*, 1920, pp.194-196.

87 IWM, 49538, KTB, II, *Lettow Report*, 1 Nov 15, 3-4 and 14; 1Jan 16, pp.18-21; *Boell, Die Operationen*, pp.121-132.

88 Bayot, 'Les Opérations Militaires', I, pp.150-151.

89 Bayot, 'Les Opérations Militaires, V', *BBSM*, 1936, II, No. 3, pp.257-258.

90 *Campagnes coloniales belges*, I, pp.292-294; Bayot, 'Les Opérations Militaires, V', pp.262-270.

91 Boell, *Die Operationen*, p.127.

92 Boell, *Die Operationen*, pp.131-133.

93 ADM 123/142, 2 Nov 15, Telegram A, Resident Commissioner, Salisbury to High Commissioner; Spicer-Simson, 'Lake Tanganyika', pp.760-761.

94 IWM, 49538, KTB, II, *Wahle Report*, 10 Dec 15, pp.4-9.

95 IWM, 49538, KTB, II, *Lettow Report*, 1 Jan 16, 18; ADM 123/142, 31 Dec 15, Telegram A, Resident Commissioner, Salisbury to High Commissioner.

96 Spicer-Simson, 'Lake Tanganyika', 761-762; Marinearchiv, *Deutschen Kolonien*, pp.192-193; ADM 123/142, 1 Jan 15 [sic], Telegram A, Resident Commissioner to High Commissioner; Shankland, *Phantom Flotilla*, pp.142-144.

97 WO 33/858, No. 570, 24 Nov 15, Telegram 10285, WO to CinC India.

98 WO 33/858, No. 573, 24 Nov 15, Telegram 363, Tighe to WO.

99 WO 33/858, No. 584, 27 Nov 15, Telegram, Tighe to WO; No. 584, 27 Nov 15, Telegram, Tighe to WO; Hordern, *Military Operations*, p.218; Keen, pp.80-81.

100 WO 33/858, No. 572, 24 Nov 15, Telegram 363, Tighe to WO; No. 584, 27 Nov 15, Telegram, Tighe to WO.

101 IWM, 49538, KTB, II, Annex 25, 22 Nov 15; *Lettow Report*, 24 Dec 15, 1-2; WO 33/858, No. 657, 10 Dec 15, Telegram 375, Tighe to WO.

102 WO 33/858, No. 629, 6 Dec 15,

Telegram 371, Tighe to WO; No. 647, 7 Dec 15, Telegram 10837, War Office to Tighe; No. 666, 13 Dec 15, Telegram 397, Tighe to War Office.

103 WO 33/858, No. 657, 10 Dec 15, Telegram 375, Tighe to WO; No. 629, 6 Dec 15, Telegram S371, Tighe to WO; No. 655, 9 Dec 15, Telegram 376, Tighe to WO; No. 695, 17 Dec 15, Telegram 1329/24, Tighe to WO.

104 WO 33/858, No. 711, 22 Dec 15, Telegram 381, Tighe to WO; No. 759, 9 Jan 16, Telegram 387, Tighe to CIGS; Boell, *Die Operationen*, p.115.

105 MNE, UN, 3°Piso, Armário 7, Maço 13, Capilha 14, 28 Oct 15, Letter, Minister of Foreign Affairs to Minister, London; 24 Dec 15, Letter A Soares to Minister of Colonies.

106 Cann, 'Mozambique', pp.122 and 126-127.

CHAPTER FOUR

1 Turner, *British Politics*, pp.62-63; French, *British Strategy*, pp.100-102.

2 Hyam, Ronald, *South African Expansionism*, pp.23-24.

3 Strachan, *The First World War*, pp.554-555.

4 Harcourt Papers, dep 471, 2 Nov 14, Letter Buxton to Harcourt; Buxton Papers, dep 9930, File Sep 14, 24 Sep 14, Letter Buxton to Harcourt.

5 Hancock and van der Poel, *Selections from the Smuts Papers*, III, 30 Aug 15, Letter Smuts to J.X. Merriman, 310.

6 Hyam, *South African Expansionism*, pp.26-28; Harcourt Papers, dep 472, 18 May 15, Letter Buxton to Harcourt; Buxton Papers, dep 9930, File May 1915, 15 May 15, Letter Buxton to Harcourt.

7 Buxton Papers, dep 9930, File May 15, 25 May 15, Telegram D 166 Smuts to Buxton citing 22 May 15, Telegram B45 Botha to Smuts; WO 33/858, No. 163, 10 Apr 15, Telegram 3970, WO to Buxton; Harcourt Papers, dep 583 dep 507, 14 Apr 15, Telegram 4, Governor General of South Africa to Secretary of State for the Colonies.

8 Buxton Papers, dep 9930, File May 15, 27 May 15, Press Cutting *Cape Argus*.

9 Meintjes, *General Louis Botha*, p.273; Buxton Papers, dep 9930, File Aug 15, 11 Aug 15, Letter Buxton to Bonar Law.

10 Buxton Papers, dep 9930, File Aug 15, 19 Aug 15, Letter Buxton to Asquith; 28 Aug 15, Telegram Buxton to Bonar Law.

11 WO 33/858, No. 322, 19 Aug 15, Telegram 7135, WO to Tighe; No. 324, 19 Aug 15, Telegram 7137, WO to Tighe; No. 332, 24 Aug 15, Telegram D 1578, Smuts to WO; No. 380, 13 Sep 15, Telegram 336, Tighe to WO.

12 WO 33/858, No. 404, 21 Sep 15, Telegram 8087, WO to Tighe.

13 Turner, John, *British Politics*, pp.68-69; French, *British Strategy*, p.159; Yorke, *A Crisis of Colonial Control: War and Authority in Northern Rhodesia: 1919-19*, p.132. Cites Bonar Law to Buxton, 3 Sep 15.

14 French, *British Strategy*, pp.72, 81 and 160-161.

15 WO 106/310, 'The Military Situation in East Africa', CIGS 8 Oct 15. In this report, General Sir A.J. Murray cited General Tighe's Telegram 322 of 2 Aug 15, his despatch of 31 Jul 15, and his Telegram 325 of 14 Aug 15; WO 33/858, No. 407, 24 Sep 15, Telegram 8212, WO to Smuts; No. 408, 24 Sep 15, Telegram 8213, WO to Smuts.

16 WO 33/858, No. 517, 5 Nov 15, Telegram 359, Tighe to WO; No. 520, 7 Nov 15, Telegram 9650, WO to Tighe.

17 CAB 24/1, 18 Nov 1915, Paper G38, *Future Operations in East Africa*.

18 IWM, Northey Papers, *Undated Lecture Notes*; Hordern, *Military Operations*, pp.187-190. Cites WO Letter to CO, 22 Nov 15. Repeated in WO 33/858, No. 846, 25 Feb 16, Telegram 13744,

Robertson to Smuts.

19 WO 33/858, No.544, 17 Nov 15, Telegram 10013, Murray to Kitchener; No. 548, 18 Nov 15, Telegram 74, Kitchener to Murray;. No. 555, 22 Nov 15, Telegram 10199, WO to Tighe; No. 531, 12 Nov 15, Telegram Buxton to Bonar Law.

20 Gilbert, *Winston S. Churchill*, Companion III, 1296. Cites 3 November 1916, Letter Curzon to Churchill; Buxton Papers, File Aug 15, 13 Aug 15, Letter Stamfordham to Buxton; File May 15, 9 May 15, Telegram Buxton to Harcourt; 11 May 15, Telegram Harcourt to Buxton; 19 May 16, Letter Bonar Law to Buxton; File Aug 15, 9 Aug 15, Telegram Bonar Law to Buxton.

21 Hordern, *Military Operations*, p.213; CAB 22/3, *An Appreciation by the General Staff on the Situation in East Africa*, 10 Dec 15; Callwell, *Experiences of a Dug-Out*, pp.178-179.

22 CAB 22/3, *Minute by the Secretary of State for War*, 14 Dec 15; CAB 22/3, War Committee Meeting of 15 Dec 15.

23 CAB 22/3, War Committee Meeting of 28 Dec 15. Robertson's agreement was contained in the *CIGS Note* of 23 Dec 1915.

24 WO 106/310, 'Appreciation on the Situation in East Africa', General H.L. Smith-Dorrien, 1 Dec 15, 3-4. Smith-Dorrien put great emphasis on the need for careful and thorough preparation on account of the climate and endemic diseases. He thought that the government believed that GEA could be completely subjugated by April 1916, but warned that no decisive result could occur before July or August 1916.

25 GstA, VI HA, Schnee Papers 22, Nr 14, *Auszüge aus dem Bericht des Referanten Regierungs und Baurat Brandes über die Tätigkeit der Civilverwaltung während des Kriegs in Deutsch Ostafrika*, 1917, p.10; Marinearchiv, *Deutschen Kolonien*, pp.197-198.

26 Marinearchiv, *Deutschen Kolonien*, pp.200-201.

27 Schnee, *Deutsche-Ostafrika*, pp.174-175; Marinearchiv, *Deutschen Kolonien*, pp.200-204.

28 IWM, 49538, *KTB*, II, 6 and 8 Feb.

29 IWM, 49538, *KTB*, II, *Lettow Report*, 1 Jan 16, pp.1-5.

30 IWM, 49538, *KTB*, II, *Lettow Report*, 1 Jan 16, pp.21-28.

31 WO 33/858, No. 759, 9 Jan 16, Telegram 387, Tighe to CIGS; No. 792, 19 Jan 16, Telegram 1023, Smith-Dorrien to WO; No. 800, 22 Jan 16, Telegram 1035, Smith-Dorrien to WO.

32 WO 33/858, No. 803, 25 January 1916, Smith-Dorrien to CIGS; No. 809, 31 Jan 16, Telegram 1082, Smith-Dorrien to WO; Boell, *Die Operationen*, pp.108-109; Woodhouse, 'Railway Demolitions and Repairs', *Royal Engineer Journal*, p.50.

33 *Campagnes coloniales belges*, I, pp.218-219 and pp.236-237.

34 Marinearchiv, *Deutschen Kolonien*, pp.192-196; Spicer-Simson, 'Lake Tanganyika', pp.762-764; Wéber, 'L'effort belge', II, 511-512.

35 Boell, *Die Operationen*, pp.133-134.

36 Marinearchiv, *Deutschen Kolonien*, pp.171-172.

37 WO 33/858, No. 770, 12 Jan 16, GOC Cape Town to WO; Smuts Papers, Box 197, 29 Nov 15, Letter Smuts to A.B. Gillett; Buxton Papers, 1 Feb 16, Telegram, Buxton to Bonar Law; 8 Feb 16, Telegram Buxton to Bonar Law.

38 WO 33/858, No. 810, 31 Jan 16, Smith-Dorrien to WO; Buxton Papers, 1 Feb 16, Telegram, Buxton to Bonar Law.

39 Buxton Papers, 1 Feb 16, Telegram, Private Buxton to Bonar Law.

40 Buxton Papers, 3 Feb 16, Telegram Bonar Law to Buxton; CAB 22/3, War Committee Meeting of 3 Feb 16.

41 Buxton Papers, Semi-Official Letter File, 12 Feb 16, Smith-Dorrien to Buxton.
42 Strachan, *The First World War*, pp.559 and 567-568.
43 Hancock and van den Poel, *Selections from the Smuts Papers*, II, 13 Apr 16, Letter Botha to Smuts, 356; Meinertzhagen, *Army Diary*, p.166.
44 Hordern, *Military Operations*, p.222.
45 Buxton Papers, Telegram Buxton to Bonar Law, 1 Feb 1916; WO 33/858, No. 820, 8 Feb 16, Telegram 13018, CIGS to Smuts.
46 Smuts, *Military Despatches from the Commander-in-Chief, East Africa Forces, Despatch dated 29 April 1916*, p.187. Henceforth Smuts, *Despatch I*; Orr, 'Some Afterthoughts on the War in East Africa', *Journal of the Royal United Services Institute*, LXIX, (1924), p.697.
47 WO 106/310, *Appreciation on Situation in East Africa*, General H.L. Smith-Dorrien, 1 Dec 1915, 4.
48 Lettow, *Reminiscences*, pp.108-109.
49 IWM, 49538, *KTB*, II, 12 and 13 Feb 16; RHQ QLR, WD 2 LNL, 12 Feb 16.
50 Hordern, *Military Operations*, pp.231-234.
51 FO 371/2598, Folio 41935, 3 Mar 16, Letter 17, MacDonell to Grey, 4 Feb covering Letter Chief of Cabinet to Governor General to MacDonell, 18 Jan; Folio 46256, 10 Mar 16, Letter, WO to FO, 9 Mar; AHM, 5a Repartição, 2a divisão, 7a secção, caixa 10, pasta 11, 24 Mar 16, Telegram 375, Governor General to Ministry of Colonies; 30 Mar 16, Telegram 404, Ministry of Colonies to Governor General.
52 Strachan, *The First World War*, I, p.605.
53 Boell, *Die Operationen*, p.142.
54 WO 33/858, No. 867, 6 Mar 16, Telegram GO210, Smuts to CIGS.
55 Göring, *Kriegserlebnisse*, pp.30-37.
56 Lettow, *Reminiscences*, pp.110-111.
57 Hordern, *Military Operations*, pp.244-245.
58 Lettow, *Reminiscences*, pp.114-115; Arning, *Vier Jahre Weltkrieg*, pp.151-152; Hordern, *Military Operations*, p.246; Boell, *Die Operationen*, pp.168-169.
59 WO 33/858, No. 879, 15 Mar 16, Telegram GOF 110, Smuts to CIGS; No. 882, 17 Mar 16, Telegram 14500, CIGS to Smuts.
60 Buxton Papers, 16 Mar 16, Smuts to Buxton.
61 Boell, *Die Operationen*, pp.173-174; WO 33/858, No. 890, 21 Mar 16, Telegram GOF205, Smuts to CIGS.
62 Hordern, *Military Operations*, pp.254-258; Boell, *Die Operationen*, pp.175-177.
63 WO 95/5313, Advanced GHQ (A/GHQ) AQ WD, 26 Mar 16, Telegram Z95, van Deventer to GHQ; Telegram QC254, GHQ to IGC; A/GHQ AQ WD, 1 Apr 16, Memorandum AQMG to GOCs 2nd SA Inf, 3rd SA Inf and 2nd EA Inf.
64 Boell, *Die Operationen*, p.178; WO 33/858, No. 913, 27 Mar 16, Telegram GOF283, Smuts to CIGS.
65 IWM, 49538, KTB, II, 14, 17 and 18 Apr 16.
66 FO 371/2596, Folio 63200, 3 Apr 16, Telegram 14879, CIGS to Smuts, 28 Mar; Telegram GOF308, Smuts to CIGS, 2 Apr; Folio 17150, 15 Apr 16, Telegram 62, Macdonell to Grey, 12 Apr.
67 WO 33/858, No. 893, 22 Mar 16, Telegram NF 56, Northey to CIGS; *Campagnes coloniales belges*, II, pp.54 and 132.
68 IWM, 49538, *KTB*, II, 7 Mar 16, *Wintgens* Report, 1-2.
69 Woodhouse, 'Notes on Railway Work in East Africa, 1914-1918', *Royal Engineers Journal*, pp.38-40.
70 WO 33/858, No. 938, 6 Apr 16, Telegram GOF338, Smuts to CIGS; No. 940, 7 Apr 16, Telegram GOF247, Smuts to CIGS; WO 95/5313, A/GHQ AQ WD, 4 Apr 16, Telegram

PC96, Post Commandant New Moshi to Adminstaff, Old Moshi.

71 WO 33/858, No. 972, 21 Apr 16, Telegram F5003, Smuts to CIGS; No. 975, 23 Apr 16, Telegram F5020, Smuts to CIGS; Boell, *Die Operationen*, p.182.

72 WO 95/5313, A/GHQ AQ WD, 11 Apr 16, Telegram Z168, van Deventer to GHQ; 19 Apr 16, Telegram 101T, IGC to Adminstaff; WO 33/858, No. 992, 1 May 16, Telegram F5057, Smuts to CIGS; Hordern, *Military Operations*, p.276

73 WO 33/858, No. 976, 24 Apr 16, Telegram 15715, Lloyd George to Smuts; No. 989, 30 Apr 16, Telegram F5048, Smuts to CIGS.

74 Boell, *Die Operationen*, pp.184-185; Lettow, *Reminiscences*, pp.133-134.

75 Reid, *Footslogging in East Africa*, pp.43-45; Boell, *Die Operationen*, p.185; Lettow, *Reminiscences*, pp.136-137; Hordern, *Military Operations*, p.280.

76 WO 33/858, No. 1016, 11 May 16, Telegram F5101, Smuts to CIGS; Hordern, *Military Operations*, pp.279-285.

77 WO 95/5313, A/GHQ AQ WD, 20 May 16, Telegram GOC33, van Deventer to Smuts, 19 May.

78 AHM, 5a Repartição, 2a divisão, 7a secção, caixa 10, pasta 1; Ribeiro de Meneses, 'Too Serious a Matter to be Left to the Generals? Parliament and the Army in Wartime Portugal 1914-18', *Journal of Contemporary History*, XXXIII, No. 1, (1998), pp.85-86 and 90.

79 AHM, 5a Repartição, 2a divisão, 7a secção, caixa 43, pasta 1, *Expediçãoa Moçambique em 1916: Relatório das operações efectuadas até 24 de dezembro do mesmo ano par General José Ferreira Gil*, pp.2-4 and 19-25. Henceforth *Relatório – Gil*.

80 Cann, John, 'Mozambique, German East Africa and the Great War', *Small Wars and Insurgencies*, XII, No. 1, (2001), pp.126-127.

81 *Campagnes coloniales belges*, II, pp.158-167.

82 IWM, 49538, KTB, II, 3 May 16, Telegram Wahle to GHQ; Telegram Wintgens to Wahle; *KTB*, II, 4 May 16, Telegram, GHQ to Wahle; 9 May 16, Telegram, Wahle to GHQ.

83 *Campagnes coloniales belges*, II, pp.199-214 and 258.

84 WO 33/858, No. 1027, 19 May 16, Telegram F5153, Smuts to CIGS.

85 Brett Young, *Marching on Tanga*, pp.106-107.

86 WO 95/5313, A/GHQ AQ WD, 4 Jun 16, *Notes of a Conference*.

87 WO 95/5312, A/GHQ WD, 2 Jun 16; Hordern, *Military Operations*, pp.288-294; WO 95/5313, A/GHQ AQ WD, 19 Jun 16, Telegram GOC64, van Deventer to GHQ; 20 Jun 16, Telegram OA283 Genstaff to Adminstaff, 19 Jun; Hordern, *Military Operations*, pp.310-311.

88 WO 95/5313, A/GHQ AQ WD, 1 Jul 16, Telegram GOC77, van Deventer to Smuts, 30 Jun; Hordern, *Military Operations*, pp.311-312 and 324-325.

89 WO 106/308, *Memorandum on the Situation which may arise as the result of Portugal complying with the request made by the British government that German shipping in the Tagus should be commandeered*, [n.d.] [likely early 1916].

90 Teixeira, *L'Entreé du Portugal dans la Grande Guerre*, pp.356-360; Stone, 'The Official British Attitude to the Anglo-Portuguese Alliance', *The Journal of Contemporary History*, X, No. 4, (October 1975), p.732; Smith, 'The Idea of Mozambique and its Enemies, c. 1890-1930', *Journal of Southern African Studies*, XVII, No. 3, Sept 1991, pp.502-504.

91 FO 371/2598, Folio 56114, 24 Mar 16, Letter, WO to FO, 21 Mar; WO 106/308, *Memorandum*.

92 AHM, 5a Repartição, 2a divisão, 7a secção, caixa 10, pasta 11, 20 Mar 16,

Telegram 350, Governor-General to Ministry of Colonies; Vincent-Smith, 'Britain, Portugal and the First World War', 235-236; Arquivo Militar Histórico (AHM), 2a divisão, 7a secção, caixa 10, pasta 11, 30 Mar 16, Telegram 404, Governor of Lourenço Marques to Commander, Porto Amelia; Stone, 'The Official British Attitude to the Anglo-Portuguese Alliance', 732.

93 AHM, 5a Repartição, 2a divisão, 7a secção, caixa 10, pasta 11, 15 Mar 16, Telegram 320, Governor General to Ministry of Colonies; 17 Mar 16, Telegram 331, Governor General to Minisitry of Colonies.

94 FO 371/2599, Folio 66746, 8 Apr 16, FO Minute; Telegram GOF324, Smuts to CIGS, 4 Apr; Folio 69128, 11 Apr 16, Letter Bonar Law to Grey.

95 WO 33/858, No.930, 3 Apr 16, Telegram GOF314, Smuts to CIGS; No. 931, 4 Apr 16, Telegram GOF324, Smuts to CIGS; 950, 11 Apr 16, Telegram GOF366, Smuts to CIGS.

96 WO 33/858, No. 983, 26 Apr 16, Telegram F5028, Smuts to Lloyd George.

97 WO 33/858, No. 1010, 8 May 16, Telegram 16239, CIGS to Smuts.

98 *Campagnes coloniales belges*, II, pp.259-285 and 335-345; Hordern, *Military Operations*, pp.422-424.

CHAPTER FIVE

1 Northey Papers, WD Nyasaland and North-Eastern Rhodesia Frontier Force (henceforth Norforce), 4 Dec 15-16 Feb 16.

2 Northey Papers, WD Norforce, 19 Feb 16-19 Mar 16; 15 Apr 16, NF 122, *Instructions to Commanders, Preliminary and Supplementary to Operation Orders, as to the Forthcoming Advance into German Territory, and Investment and Capture of Enemy's Bomas.*

3 WO 33/858, No. 1002, 4 May 16, Telegram NF 182, Northey to CIGS; Hordern, *Military Operations*, pp.462-463.

4 WO 33/858, No. 1047, 29 May 16, Telegram NF 360, Northey to CIGS; Hordern, *Military Operations*, pp.462-468.

5 Hordern, *Military Operations*, pp.468-469. Cites Smuts of 3 and 9 Jun 16 to Northey.

6 Hordern, *Military Operations*, pp.471-473.

7 WO 95/5329, WD Norforce, 1, 3 and 5-6 Aug 16.

8 WO 95/5329, WD Norforce, 18 and 19 Aug 16.

9 WO 95/5329, WD Norforce, 22-31 Aug 16.

10 FO 371/2596, Folio 100376, 19 May 16, Telegram, Buxton to Bonar Law; 24 May 16, Telegram, Bonar Law to Buxton; ADM 123/142, *Report of Proceedings*, Nos. 5-21, 1 Oct-4 Aug 16; Shankland, *Phantom Flotilla*, pp.204-210.

11 Wéber, 'L'Effort belge', II, 527-528; III, 28-35.

12 ADM 123/142, 19 Aug 16, Telegram, Bonar Law to Buxton; 20 Jul 16, Telegram, Buxton to Bonar Law; Spicer-Simson, 'Lake Tanganyika', 763; Wéber, 'L'effort belge', III, 18-19; Newbolt, *Naval Operations*, IV, pp.83-85; Marinearchiv, *Deutschen Kolonien*, p.196.

13 *Campagnes coloniales belges*, II, 4790493; Hordern, *Military Operations*, pp.445-449.

14 WO 95/5291, WD GHQ, 2 Sep 16, Telegram F5213, Smuts to CIGS.

15 WO 95/5291, WD GHQ, 3 Sep 16, Intelligence Report.

16 GSWA, Box 24, 23 Jul 16, Telegram IG23, Aeroplanes to 2 Div; 24 Jul 16, Telegram K11A, 2 Div to BGGS.

17 GSWA, Box 25, 4 Aug 16, Telegram OA538, Smuts to van Deventer.

18 Collyer, *South Africans*, pp.184-185.

19 AHM, 5a Repartição, 2a divisão, 7a

secção, caixa 43, pasta 1, *Relatório* – Gil, 50-51; AHM, 5a Repartição, 2a divisão, 7a secção, caixa 10, pasta 11, 14 Jul 16, Telegram 758, General, Palma to Ministry of Colonies; 7 Aug 16, Letter 1583, Commander, Palma to Ministry of Colonies.

20 Boell, *Die Operationen*, pp.187-188.

21 WO 33/858, No. 1072, Telegram F5267, Smuts to CIGS.

22 WO 33/858, No. 1083, 20 Jun 16, Telegram F5280, Smuts to CIGS; Boell, *Die Operationen*, 192; Collyer, *South Africans*, pp.147-148.

23 WO 95/5312, WD A/GHQ, 23 Jun 16; WO 33/858, No. 1090, 25 Jun 16, Telegram F5289, Smuts to CIGS; Boell, *Die Operationen*, pp.192-193; Hordern, *Military Operations*, pp.303-306.

24 WO 95/5312, WD A/GHQ, 29 Jun 16; 26-28 Jun 16; Buchanan, *Three Years of War in East Africa*, p.104; Young, *Marching on Tanga*, pp.183-184.

25 WO 95/5313, WD A/GHQ AQ, 2 Jul 16, *Memorandum on the Transport Situation*; Hordern, *Military Operations*, p.307.

26 WO 33/858, No. 1096, 28 Jun 16, Telegram 18912, CIGS to Smuts.

27 WO 33/858, No. 1102, 2 Jul 16, Telegram F5319, Smuts to CIGS.

28 WO 33/858, No. 1105, 5 Jul 16, Telegram F5329, Smuts to CIGS.

29 WO 95/5312, WD A/GHQ, 10 Jul 16; Hordern, *Military Operations*, pp.313-323.

30 WO 95/5312, WD A/GHQ, 12 and 13 Jul 16.

31 WO 33/858, No 1119, 18 Jul 16, Telegram OA584 Smuts to CIGS; WO 95/5312, A/GHQ WD, 23 Jul 16.

32 WO 95/5313, WD A/GHQ AQ, 28 Jul 16, AQMG to BGGS, *Notes on Transport & Supply Situation 28th July 1916*.

33 WO 33/858, No. 1107, 6 Jul 16, Telegram OA440, Smuts to CIGS; FO 371/2599, Folio 239004, 27 Nov 16, Telegram 87, Villiers to Grey.

34 WO 33/858, No. 1107, 6 Jul 16, Telegram OA440, Smuts to CIGS.

35 WO 33/858, No. 1111, Telegram 19426, CIGS to Smuts; No. 1133, 30 Jul 16, Telegram F5427, Smuts to CIGS; No. 1164, 18 Aug 16, Telegram 21748, CIGS to Smuts; CAB 45/44, Colonel Fendall's Diary, 18 Aug 16.

36 WO 33/858, No. 1056, 2 Jun 16, Telegram 17453, CIGS to Smuts; No. 1111, 11 Jul 16, Telegram 19426, CIGS to Smuts; No. 929, 3 Apr 16, Telegram GOF310, Smuts to CIGS; WO 33/858, No. 1119, 18 Jul 16, Telegram OA584, Smuts to CIGS.

37 WO 95/5312, WD A/GHQ, 25 Jul 16; Lettow, *Reminiscences*, pp.143-144; Collyer, *South Africans*, p.174.

38 WO 33/858, No. 1113, 14 Jul 16, Telegram OA547, Smuts to CIGS.

39 WO 95/5312, WD A/GHQ, 5 Aug 16; WO 33/858, No. 1145, 6 Aug 16, Telegram F5475, Smuts to CIGS; Hordern, *Military Operations*, pp.334-335; Collyer, *South Africans*, p.174.

40 Hordern, *Military Operations*, p.349; WO 33/858, No. 1148, 10 Aug 16, Telegram F5496, Smuts to CIGS.

41 WO 95/5312, WD A/GHQ, 10-11 Aug 16.

42 WO 95/5312, WD A/GHQ, 15-19 Aug 16; Hordern, *Military Operations*, pp.340-347; WO 95/5313, WD A/GHQ AQ, 18 Aug 16, Telegram OA899, Genstaff to IGC/Adminstaff.

43 WO 95/5313, WD A/GHQ AQ, 13 Aug 16, Telegram K342, van Deventer to GHQ; GSWA, Box 25, 16 Aug 16, Telegram K354, van Deventer to Smuts.

44 WO 95/5312, WD A/GHQ, 25 and 28 Aug 16; GSWA, Box 25, 20 Aug 16, Telegram X510, Collyer to van Deventer; 22 Aug 16, Telegram V72, 2 Div to BGGS.

45 WO 33/858, No. 1194, 29 Aug 16, Telegram 22178, CIGS to Smuts.

46 WO 33/858, No. 1210, 6 Sep 16,

Telegram F5635, Smuts to CIGS.

47 WO 95/5312, WD A/GHQ, 20-22 Aug 16.

48 Hordern, *Military Operations*, pp.354-355; Collyer, *South Africans*, pp.203-204.

49 WO 95/5312, WD A/GHQ, 25-27 Aug 16; WO 95/5291, WD GHQ, 29 Aug 16, Telegram F5578, Smuts to CIGS.

50 WO 95/5312, WD A/GHQ, 31 Aug and 1-2 Sep 16.

51 Marinearchiv, *Deutschen Kolonien*, pp.203-205; Schnee, *Deutsche-Ostafrika*, p.176.

52 WO 95/5312, WD A/GHQ, 8 and 9 Sep 16.

53 WO 95/5312, WD A/GHQ, 6 Sep 16.

54 Hordern, *Military Operations*, pp.369-371.

55 WO 95/5312, WD A/GHQ, 7 Sep 16.

56 WO 95/5312, WD A/GHQ, 14-15 Sep 16; Hordern, *Military Operations*, pp.370-371.

57 WO 95/5291, WD GHQ, 22 Sep 16, Telegram OA412, Smuts to CIGS; 27 Sep 16, Telegram OA491, Smuts to CIGS.

58 WO 153/111, Map of East Africa; Crowe, *General Smuts' Campaign*, Sketch 4; CAB 45/73, Sketch 74, 'The Strategic Situation, 1 December 1916'.

59 WO 95/5300, WD DMS, 24 Sep 16, Letter, DMS to DA&QMG; WO 95/5313, A/GHQ AQ WD, 23 Sep 16, Telegram QC81, Adminstaff, Morogoro to Adminstaff Dar-es-Salaam; 30 Sep 16, Telegram QC149, AQMG Morogoro to DAQMG Dar-es-Salaam.

60 Moyse-Bartlett, *The King's African Rifles*, pp.332-333 and 701.

61 WO 95/5292, WD GHQ, 15-16 Oct 16; 24 Oct 16, Telegram F5892, Smuts to CIGS; Collyer, *South Africans*, pp.239-240; Macpherson and Mitchell, *Medical Services*, IV, pp.458-459.

62 WO 33/858, No. 1313, 17 Oct 16, Telegram D280/1973, Botha to War Office; CO 551/101, *Court of Enquiry*, 26 Oct 16, Letter Lt.-Col. Kirkpatrick, Commanding 9th Regiment South African Infantry to General Officer Commanding 3rd South African Infantry Brigade, 248-250; Brown, *King and Kaiser*, pp.301-302; WO 33/858, No. 1388, 17 Nov 16, Telegram OA84, Smuts to CIGS.

63 Hancock and van der Poel. *Selections from the Smuts Papers*, II, 16 Aug 16, J.C. Smuts to S.M. Smuts, p.394.

64 Boell, *Die Operationen*, pp.233-234; Lettow, *Reminiscences*, p.158.

65 WO 95/5292, WD GHQ, 8 Oct 16, Telegram OA615, Smuts to CIGS; WD GHQ 10 Oct 16.

66 Orr, 'Smuts v. Lettow: A Critical Phase in East Africa; August to September 1916', *Army Quarterly*, XIII, (1925), p.294.

67 WO 95/5313, WD A/GHQ AQ, 1 Sep 16; Woodhouse, 'Notes on Railway Work in East Africa', pp.43-44.

68 WO 95/5313, WD A/GHQ AQ, 7 Sep 16, *General Supply Situation 7/9/16*; WO 95/5313, WD A/GHQ AQ, 5 Oct 16, Memorandum Hoskins to A/GHQ.

69 Blenkisopp and Rainey, *History of the Great War: Veterinary Services*, pp.416-417; Crowe, *General Smuts' Campaign*, pp.217-218.

70 WO 95/5292, WD GHQ, 30 Nov 16, Telegram OA198, Smuts to CIGS; CAB 44/7, 1-2.

71 WO 33/858, No. 1248, 20 Sep 16, Telegram OA411, Smuts to CIGS.

72 FO 371/2599, Folio 201178, 8 Oct 16, Minute; 9 Oct 16, Letter 161, Villiers to Grey, 7 Oct; Folio 180485, 18 Sep 16, Letter, FO to CO; Folio 189188, 22 Sep 16, Letter, CO to FO; Folio 215965, 24 Oct 16, Letter, WO to CO; Folio 226488, 8 Nov 16, Letter, Villiers to Hardinge; 4 Dec 16, Telegram, Hardinge to Villiers.

73 FO 371/2599, Folio 231045, 17 Nov 16,

Telegram 80, Villiers to Grey; Folio 231635, 17 Nov 16, Telegram 81, Villiers to Grey; Folio 237330, 26 Nov 16, Telegram 57, Grey to Villiers.

74 WO 95/5292, WD GHQ, 30 Nov 16, Telegram OA198, Smuts to CIGS; WD GHQ, 20 Dec 16; FO 371/2856, Folio 7930, 2 Jan 17, 'Belgian feeling over question of Tabora & other points', 'Extract of a letter from Sir F. Villiers to Mr Balfour'; FO 371/2599, Folio 257079, 19 Dec 16, Minute; 19 Dec 16, Letter, WO to FO; Folio 257829, 21 Dec 16, Minute; 21 Dec 16, Telegram 94, Villiers to Grey, 20 Dec; Folio 258817, 21 Dec 16, Letter, CO to FO.

75 WO 95/5292, WD GHQ, 10 Nov 16, Telegram 6150, Bonar Law to Smuts, 9 November.

76 Boell, *Die Operationen*, pp.250-251.

77 WO 95/5329, WD Norforce, 16, 17 and 21 Sep 16; GSWA, Box 26, 11 Sep 16, Telegram K475, 2 Div to Smuts; Boell, *Die Operationen*, p.254.

78 WO 95/5329, WD Norforce, 20 Sep 16; Boell, *Die Operationen*, pp.253-254.

79 Boell, *Die Operationen*, p.255.

80 MSS Afr.s.1715 (300), Williams, Col. H.P., *History of 1 KAR*, p.158; CAB 44/4, 2-3; Meinertzhagen, Army Diary, maps 17-19; CAB 44/4, 1, Sketch 67; Boell, *Die Operationen*, p.287.

81 WO 95/5329, WD Norforce, 16 and 30 Sep and 1 Oct 16; WO 95/5291, WD GHQ, 24 Sep 16, Telegram OA445, Smuts to CIGS.

82 Boell, *Die Operationen*, pp.286-287.

83 WO 95/5292, WD GHQ, 3 Oct 16, Telegram OA569, Smuts to CIGS; 13 Oct 16.

84 WO 95/5329, WD Norforce, 28 Aug and 16 Sep 16; Boell, *Die Operationen*, p.254.

85 MSS Afr.s.1715 (300), *History of 1 KAR*, pp.159-160.

86 WO 95/5292, WD GHQ, 14 Oct 16, Telegram F5839, Smuts to CIGS; WO 95/5329, WD Norforce, 14 Oct and 27-29 Nov 16; CAB 44/4, 8-9, Sketch 67.

87 WO 95/5292, WD GHQ, 26 Oct 16, Telegram F5910, Smuts to CIGS; Boell, *Die Operationen*, p.289; CAB 44/4, 9-12 and 17.

88 WO 95/5292, WD GHQ, 27 Oct 16, Telegram F5917, Smuts to CIGS; Boell, *Die Operationen*, pp.290-291.

89 WO 95/5292, WD GHQ, 1 Nov 16, Telegram F5948, Smuts to CIGS; WO 95/5329, WD Norforce, 2 and 3-4 Nov 16.

90 Boell, *Die Operationen*, pp.256-257; CAB 44/4, 17-20; MSS Afr.s.1715 (300), *History of 1 KAR*, pp.160-161.

91 CAB 44/4, 27; WO 95/5329, WD Norforce, 2, 7 and 8 Nov 16; MSS Afr.s.1715 (300), *History of 1 KAR*, pp.161-162. WO 95/5329, WD Norforce, 30 Oct16; Boell, *Die Operationen*, p.257; WO 95/5329, WD Norforce, 2 Nov 16.

92 WO 95/5292, WD GHQ, 1 Nov 16; 7 Nov 16, Telegram OA969, Genstaff to CIGS; GSWA, Box 27, 12 Oct 16, Telegram K651, 2 Div to BGGS; CAB 44/4, 39-42.

93 WO 95/5329, WD Norforce, 8 and 9 Nov 16; CAB 44/4, 29-30.

94 WO 95/5292, WD GHQ, 17 Nov 16, Telegram NF 1498, Norforce to Genstaff, 16 Nov; WO 95/5329, WD Norforce, 11 and 12 Nov 16; Boell, *Die Operationen*, pp.293-294; CAB 44/4, 28-30;

95 WO 95/5329, WD Norforce, 13, 14 and 18 Nov 16; CAB 44/4, 31-32; MSS Afr.s.1715, *History of 1 KAR*, p.163.

96 WO 95/5329, WD Norforce, 17 Nov 16.

97 WO 95/5329, WD Norforce, 18 Nov 16; Boell, *Die Operationen*, p.294; CAB 44/4, 48.

98 WO 95/5329, WD Norforce, 27-29 Nov 16; MSS Afr.s.1715, *History of 1 KAR*, p.163.

99 WO 95/5292, WD GHQ, 7 Nov 16,

Telegram OA969, Genstaff, Morogoro to CIGS, London; WO 95/5292, WD GHQ, 14 Nov 16, Telegram OA 24, Genstaff, Morogoro to Norforce and Genstaff, Dar-es-Salaam, 13 Nov.

100 WO 95/5292, WD GHQ, 19 Nov 16; WO 95/5329, WD Norforce, 17 Nov 16; Boell, *Die Operationen*, pp.255-256.

101 WO 95/5292, WD GHQ, 29 Nov 16.

102 WO 95/5292, WD GHQ, 25 Nov 16, Telegram X945, Smuts to CIGS.

103 There were two places known as Kilwa; Kilwa Kivinje was near the mouth of the Matandu River and was usually known as Kilwa; Kilwa Kiswani was located on an island to the south of Kilwa Kivinje and had an excellent deep water anchorage. It would be subsequently developed as the port.

104 WO 95/5292, WD GHQ, 1 Nov 16, Telegram F5948, Smuts to CIGS.

105 Moyse-Bartlett, *The King's African Rifles*, p.336.

106 Boell, *Die Operationen*, pp.235-238.

107 Boell, *Die Operationen*, pp.238-240; CAB 44/5, 15.

108 Boell, *Die Operationen*, pp.241-242.

109 WO 95/5292, WD GHQ, 1 Nov 16, Telegram F5948, Smuts to CIGS; 7 Nov 16, Telegram OA969, Genstaff, Morogoro to Genstaff, Dar-es-Salaam; Smuts, *Despatch III*, p.138.

110 WO 95/5292, WD GHQ, 1 Nov 16, Telegram F5948, Smuts to CIGS; CAB 44/5, 4-7.

111 CAB 44/6, 8; WO 95/5329, WD Norforce, 30 Nov 16.

112 WO 33/858, No 1262, 26 Sep 16, Telegram X757, Smuts to CIGS; FO 371/2596, Folio 178923, 9 Sep 16, Telegram Governor Nyasaland to Bonar Law, 5 Sep; 9 Sept 16, Telegram Bonar Law to Governor Nyasaland, 7 Sep; Folio 210722, 21 Oct 16, Telegram 127, MacDonell to Grey, 20 Oct.

113 WO 95/5312, WD A/GHQ, 3 Sep 16; AHM, 5a Repartição, 2a divisão, 7a secção, caixa 43, pasta 1, *Relatório – Gil*, pp.132-133; Pélissier, *Naissance de Mozambique*, II, p.692; Cann, 'Mozambique', p.133.

114 WO 95/5292, WD GHQ, 22 Oct 16.

115 AHM, 5a Repartição, 2a divisão, 7a secção, caixa 10, pasta 13, *Relatório sôbre aas Operacões contra os Portuguese durante os Meses de Setembro a Dezembro de 1916*, p.1-4; Lettow, *Reminiscences*, p.165-166.

116 WO 95/5292, WD GHQ, 7 Nov 16, Telegram OA968, Genstaff to CIGS, London; FO 3712599, Folio 223719, 8 Nov 16, Telegram 424, Carnegie to Grey, 7 Nov; Folio 228448, 14 Nov 16, Letter, WO to FO; Folio 255734, 18 Dec 16, Minute.

117 WO 95/5292, WD GHQ, 5 Dec 16; AHM, 5a Repartição, 2a divisão, 7a secção, caixa 10, pasta 13, 5-9; Pélissier, *Naissance de Mozambique*, II, pp.692-693.

118 AHM, 5a Repartição, 2a divisão, 7a secção, caixa 43, pasta 1, *Relatório – Gil*, pp.155-165; Meneses, 'Too Serious a Matter', p.90.

119 FO 371/2596, Folio 263260, 28 Dec 16, Letter 156, MacDonell to Foreign Secretary, 21 Nov.

120 WO 33/858, No. 1438, 11 Dec 16, Telegram OA267, Smuts to CIGS; FO 371/2596, Folio 252437, 14 Dec 16, Telegram 631, Grey to Carnegie, 15 Dec; WO 95/5292, WD GHQ, 14 Dec 16, Telegram F 6187, Smuts to CIGS; Lettow, *Reminiscences*, p.166.

121 CAB 44/6, 11; MS Boell, N14/30, 26. Kapitel, 1903-1906.

122 Boell, *Die Operationen*, p.242; Lettow, *Reminiscences*, pp.161-163.

123 Boell, *Die Operationen*, p.246; CAB 44/5, 21.

124 WO 95/5292, WD GHQ, 7 Nov 16, Telegram OA969, General Staff Morogoro to General Staff, Dar-es-Salaam; Boell, *Die Operationen*, p.246; Moyse-Bartlett, *The King's African Rifles*, p.338.

125 WO 106/273, *History of 3 KAR*, Plan of Kibata, 58a; WO 95/5330, *History of 1st/2nd KAR*, 5-6. Thatcher, *The Fourth Battalion, Duke of Connaught's Own 10th Baluch Regiment in the Great War*, pp.144-145 CAB 44/5, 22.
126 CAB 44/5, 23-27; Moyse-Bartlett, *The King's African Rifles*, p.339.
127 Lettow, *Reminiscences*, pp.168-169; Boell, *Die Operationen*, p.247; Thatcher, *10th Baluch Regiment*, p.146; CAB 44/5, 25-26; WO 95/5330, *History of 1st/2nd KAR, 6.*
128 Clifford, Sir H.C., *The Gold Coast Regiment in the East Africa Campaign*, pp.51-55.
129 Thatcher, *10th Baluch Regiment*, pp.154-155; CAB 44/5, 33-35; WO 95/5330, *History of 1st/2nd KAR*, 7.
130 WO 95/5292, WD GHQ, 22 Dec 16, Telegram OA355, Smuts to CIGS, 21 Dec. WO 95/5292, WD GHQ, 1 Jan 17, Telegram OA443, Smuts to Adminstaff, 31 Dec; CAB 44/6, 12-13;
131 CAB 44/6, 13-15.
132 WO 95/5329, WD Norforce, 13 Dec 16; WO 95/5292, WD GHQ, 19 Dec 16, Telegram P32, GOC 2 Div to Genstaff, 18 Dec; 20 Dec 16, Telegram OA341, Genstaff to CIGS.
133 GSWA, Box 29, 18 Dec 16, Telegram P32, 2 Div to BGGS.
134 Schnee, *Deutsch-Ostafrika*, 274; CAB 44/7, 30, Sketches 74, 83 and 84.
135 CAB 44/7, 7-9; GSWA, Box 29, 22 Dec 16, Operation Order 24.
136 CAB 44/7, 12-14.
137 GSWA, Box 29, 24 Dec 16, Telegram D1484, Brigzar [1 SA Mounted Brigade] to 2 Div; 28 Dec 16, Telegram D1491, Brigzar to 2 Div; CAB 44/7, 16-18.
138 GSWA, Box 29, 28 Dec 16, Telegram KT422, Col. Taylor to 2 Div; Telegram Col. Kirsten to 2 Div; CAB 44/7, 19.
139 GSWA, Box 29, 27 Dec 16, Letter ADMS to GOC 2 Div; CAB 44/7, 22; WO 95/5202, WD GHQ, 2 Jan 17, Telegram P71, GOC 2 Div to GHQ; WO 95/5292, WD GHQ, 7 Jan 17, Telegram OA567, General Staff to CIGS
140 WO 95/5329, WD Norforce, 1-18 Jan 16; CAB 44/7, 22-23.
141 WO 95/5329, WD Norforce, 19-31 Jan 16.
142 MS Boell, N14/30, 26. Kapitel, 1904; CAB 44/6, 11.
143 Smuts, *Despatch III*, 147; CAB 44/6,22-30.
144 CAB 44/6, 25-27; Downes, *With the Nigerians*, pp.66-67; MS Boell, N14/30, 26. Kapitel, 1918-1919; WO 95/5292, WD GHQ, 4 Jan 17, Telegram OA518, Smuts to CIGS, 3 Jan.
145 MS Boell, N14/30, 26. Kapitel, 1920; CAB 44/6, 36-39.
146 WO 95/5292, WD GHQ, 5 Jan 17, Telegram X1133, Smuts to CIGS 4 Jan; 7 Jan 17, Telegram OA567, Genstaff to CIGS; CAB 44/6, 32-44.
147 MS Boell, N14/30, 26. Kapitel, 1923-1924; WO 95/5292, WD GHQ, 7 Jan 17, Telegram OA567, Genstaff to CIGS.
148 MS Boell, N14/30, 26. Kapitel, 1923-1927; Downes, *With the Nigerians*, pp.68-69.
149 WO 33/858, No. 1313, 17 October 1916, Telegram 280/1973, Botha to War Office, 355; MS Smuts, Box 100, 17 January 1917, Letter Buxton to Mrs Smuts; CAB 44/6, 108-110, covering memorandum 'Supply and Transport Situation', by AQMG 9 Jan 17; GSWA, Box 29, 2 Jan 17, Telegram P71, 2 Div to Genstaff.
150 WO 33/858, No. 1500, 11 January 1917, Telegram X1182, Smuts to Secretary of State for War, 412.
151 CAB 45/19, *Nigeria Regiment Record*, 11; MS Boell, N14/30, 26. Kapitel, 1924-1938; CAB 44/6, 44-50.
152 CAB 44/6, 85-91.
153 MS Boell, N14/30, 26. Kapitel, 1941-1952; WO 95/5292, WD GHQ, 7 Jan 17, Telegram OA567, Smuts to CIGS;

WO 95/5330, *History of 1st/2nd KAR*, pp.8-9.

154 MS Boell, N14/30, 26. Kapitel, 1959-1971; Lettow, *Reminiscences*, pp.174-175.

155 WO 95/5292, WD GHQ, 18 Jan 17, Telegram F6339, Smuts to CIGS; 31 Jan 17, Telegram OA27, Genstaff Dutumi to Genstaff, Dar-es-Salaam; WO 106/273, *History of 3 KAR*, pp.60-61.

156 Hoskins, Lt.-Gen. A.R., *Despatch from the General Officer Commanding-in-Chief East Africa Relating to Operations in East Africa 20th January to 31st May 1917*, dated 30 May 1917, published in the *London Gazette* 'Supplement', No. 30447, 27 December 1917, 156-157. Henceforth, Hoskins, *Despatch*.

157 WO 95/5292, WD GHQ, 25 Jan 17, Repeat of Telegram OA846, CIGS to Hoskins, 22 Jan; WO 33/858, No. 1516, 20 Jan 17, Telegram 28209, CIGS to Hoskins.

158 WO 95/5292, WD GHQ, 14 Feb 17, Telegram OA261, Hoskins to CIGS; Hoskins, *Despatch*, 157; Meinertzhagen, Army Diary, 193.

159 WO 95/5292, WD GHQ, 18 Feb 17, Telegram GO687, First Division to Genstaff; Thatcher, *Tenth Baluch Regiment*, pp.169-170.

160 Riddell, *Lord Riddell's War Diary*, 19 Mar 17, p.166; Long Papers, 947/547, 29 Mar 17, Letter Derby to Long; 947/602, 11 May 17, Letter Buxton to Long; Roskill, *Hankey*, p.388; and Hughes, Matthew, Britain and the Middle East, p.24.

161 WO 33/858, No. 1313, 17 Oct 17, Telegram D 280/1973, General Botha to War Office, 355; Fendall, *The East African Force*, pp.87-88; CAB 44/9, 13. Cites telegram Hoskins to CIGS 4 May 17.

162 WO 33/858, No. 1516, 20 Jan 17, Telegram 28209, CIGS to Hoskins; CO 691/19, Pike, Surg.-Gen. W.W. and Balfour, Col. Andrew, *Report of Medical & Sanitary Matters in German East Africa 1917*, Nairobi: Swift Press, 1918, 6. Henceforth, Pike Report; Long Papers, 947/545, 22 Apr 17, Letter Sir Charles Crewe to Long; WO 95/5329, WD Norforce, 28 Feb 17; Downes, *With the Nigerians*, 267.

163 Louis, *Ruanda Urundi*, pp.208 and 216-217.

CHAPTER SIX

1 Turner, *British Politics*, pp.112-116 and 153; French, *Lloyd George Coalition*, p.17.

2 French, *Lloyd George Coalition*, pp.6–7.

3 RM 3, 21 Apr 17, Letter Solf to Chief of Admiralty Staff, General Staff and Foreign Office; 28 Apr 17, Letter Ludendorff to Solf; RM 3, 28 Nov 16, Letter Solf to Chief of Admiralty Staff.

4 Fischer, *Germany's War Aims*, pp.317-319 and 586-590; Fischer, *Griff nach der Weltmacht*, pp.258-260.

5 Hoskins, *Despatch*, 163; Moyse-Bartlett, *King's African Rifles*, p.701. On 1 July 1916, the regiment was over 8,000 strong; six months later on 1 January 1917, it numbered over 15,000.

6 WO 95/5292, WD GHQ, 24 Feb 17.

7 Hoskins *Despatch*, p.159.

8 Boell Papers, N14/30, 26. Kapitel, 1990.

9 CO 533/216, Folio 7624, 31 Dec 19, Governor to Milner [SSC], Report on Wartime Manpower, Appendix 1, Tables 2 and 3.

10 WO 95/5292, WD GHQ, 6 Feb 17, Telegram OA109, Hoskins to Genstaff covering OA 56 Hoskins to Governor Uganda, 5 Feb; 6 Feb 17, Telegram OA110, Hoskins to Genstaff covering OA 54 Hoskins to Governor Nigeria, 5 Feb; 9 Feb 17, Telegram Governor, Nairobi to Hoskins, 9 February covering Telegram Governor, Nigeria to Hoskins; Killingray, David and Matthews, James, 'Beasts of Burden: British West African Carriers in the

First World War', *Canadian Journal of African Studies*, XIII, No. 1, (1979), pp.8-11.

11 CO 533/216, Folio 7624, 31 Dec 19, Letter Acting Governor to Secretary of State for the Colonies, covering *Report by Lt Col O.F. Watkins CMG, CBE, DSO, Director of Military Labour to the BEA Expeditionary Force: On the period August 4th, 1914 to September 15th*, 1919, pp.451-469. Henceforth, *Watkins Report*; Hodges, *The Carrier Corps*, pp.56-60.

12 CO 533/216, *Watkins Report*, Appendix 1, Table 3; Hodges, *The Carrier Corps*, pp.99-102; Hodges, 'Military Labour in East Africa', in Page, Melvin (eds.), *Africa and the First World War*, p.139.

13 *Campagnes coloniales belges*, III, pp.14-15.

14 WO 95/5292, WD GHQ, 24 February 1917, Telegram Hoskins to Hannyngton.

15 WO 95/5293, WD GHQ, April 1917. The WD enclosed 'Printed Notes from War Diaries, Part CCLXXXV, EAEF Force 'B', General Staff, Army Headquarters, India, April 1917, *Confidential Print of Key Extracts for Army Departments*. Director Supply and Transport, East African Force, 18 to 31 January 1917, Appendix A to DA&QMG, General Headquarters, No. ST 34 dated 18 January 1917, 15-16.

16 Woodhouse, 'Notes on Railway Work in East Africa', *The Royal Engineers Journal*, XXIX, (1923), pp.42-44.

17 WO 95/5292, WD GHQ, 27 Jan 17, Telegram OA947, Hoskins to CIGS.

18 Macpherson and Mitchell, *Medical Services Volume 4*, pp.475-477.

19 WO 95/5292, WD GHQ, 22 Feb 17, Telegram G218, Hoskins to CIGS.

20 WO 95/5292, WD GHQ, 1 Mar 17, Telegram, G337, Hoskins to CIGS.

21 WO 33/858, No. 1696, 21 Mar 17, Telegram 31391, CIGS to Hoskins; WO 95/5292, WD GHQ, 29 Mar 17, Telegram G702, Hoskins to CIGS.

22 WO 158/477, 17 Apr [May] 17, Letter No. 5, Macdonell to Foreign Secretary and Hoskins, covering Despatch dated 16 May 17.

23 FO 371/2857, Folio 55352, 26 Jan 17, Letter 13, Macdonell to Foreign Secretary.

24 Ranger, 'Revolt in Portuguese East Africa: the Makombe Rising of 1917', in *St Antony's Papers*, (ed) K. Kirkwood, Number 15 African Affairs No. 2, 55-59.

25 Ranger, 'Revolt', 72-73. Cites Buxton to Resident Commissioner, 11 Apr 17.

26 WO 95/5293, WD GHQ, 27 Apr 17, Telegram G165, Hoskins to CIGS; CAB 44/9, 39-40.

27 FO 371/2856, Folio 7930, 2 Jan 17, 'Extract of a letter from Sir F. Villiers to Mr Balfour'; Albert 1er, [Belgium], *Les Carnets de Guerre*, ed Thielemans, Entry 1 Nov 16, 290-291 and 14 Feb 17, 289.

28 WO 95/5292, WD GHQ, 1 Mar 17, Telegram G337, Hoskins to CIGS; 28 Feb 17, Telegram NF2410, Norforce to Hoskins, 27 Feb; 7 Mar 17, Telegram 30514, CIGS to Hoskins, 6 Mar.

29 *Campagnes coloniales belges*, III, p.13-14; WO 95/5292, WD GHQ, 10 Mar 17, Telegram 30755, CIGS to Hoskins; 16 Mar 117, Telegram 10077, Huyghé to Hoskins, 16 Mar.

30 WO 95/5293, WD GHQ, 3 Apr 17, Telegram 32025, CIGS to Hoskins, 2 April; 14 Apr 17, Telegram 32670, CIGS to Hoskins, 14 Apr; FO 371/2857, Folio 72473, 8 Apr 17, Telegram 31, Foreign Office to Sir F. Villiers.

31 WO 95/5293, WD GHQ, 21 Apr 17, Telegram P16, Hoskins to CIGS, 19 Apr; *Campagnes coloniales belges*, III, pp.29-35.

32 *Campagnes coloniales belges*, III, pp.34-35.

33 *Campagnes coloniales belges*, III, p.131.

34 *Campagnes coloniales belges*, III,

pp.294-295.

35 WO 95/5293, WD GHQ, 9 Apr 17, Telegram 32324, CIGS to Hoskins, 8 Apr; 27 Apr 17, Telegram G165, Hoskins to CIGS.

36 WO 95/5293, WD GHQ, 19 Apr 17, Telegram 32999, CIGS to Hoskins, 18 Apr.

37 WO 33/953, No. 1787, 28 Apr 17, Telegram G165, Hoskins to CIGS; Boell Papers, N14/30, 26. Kapitel, 2032- 2044.

38 WO 95/5292, WD GHQ, 1 Mar 17, Telegram, G337, Hoskins to CIGS; 7 Mar 17, Telegram 30514, CIGS to Hoskins, 6 Mar.

39 WO 95/5292, WD GHQ, 18 Mar 17, Telegram NF2541, Norforce to Hoskins, 17 Mar; 19 Mar 17, Telegram G601 General Hoskins to Norforce.

40 WO 95/5292, WD GHQ, 2 Jan 17, Telegram P71, GOC Div to BGGS; 13 Jan 17, and 26 Feb 17.

41 WO 95/5292, WD GHQ, 14 Feb 17, Telegram OA261, Hoskins to CIGS; 22 Feb 17, Telegram G218, Hoskins to CIGS; CAB 44/9, 17.

42 Boell, *Die Operationen*, p.253.

43 Lettow, *Reminiscences*, pp.173-176; Göring, *Kriegserlebnisse*, pp.96-98.

44 Boell Papers, N14/30, 26. Kapitel, 1987.

45 Boell Papers, N14/30, 26. Kapitel, 1977-1980.

46 CAB 45/19, *Nigeria Regiment Record*, 3 and 18; WO 106/273, *History of 3 KAR*, 55.

47 Clifford, *The Gold Coast Regiment*, pp.68-69.

48 Macpherson and Mitchell, *Medical Services*, IV, pp.477-479.

49 CAB 45/19, *Nigeria Regiment Record*, p.19.

50 WO 95/ 5293, WD GHQ, 1-30 Apr 17.

51 CAB 45/19, *Nigeria Regiment Record*, pp.20-22.

52 Boell, *Die Operationen*, pp.319-320.

53 WO 33/953, No. 1770, 19 Apr 17, Telegram G21, Hoskins to CIGS; Moyse-Bartlett, *The King's African Rifles*, pp.360-361.

54 Clifford, *Gold Coast Regiment*, pp.82-86; CAB 44/9, pp.18-22.

55 WO 95/5293, WD GHQ, 19 Apr 17, Telegram OA402, 1 Div to Hoskins, 18 Apr; WD GHQ, 19 Apr 17, Telegram OA405, 1 Div to Genstaff.

56 Boell, *Die Operationen*, p.319; Lettow, *Reminiscences*, p.181.

57 CAB 44/9, 70, Sketch 94; Orr, 'From Rumbo to the Rovuma', pp.109-110; Hoskins, *Despatch*, p.167.

58 Boell, *Die Operationen*, p.315.

59 CAB 44/9, 33, Sketch 96.

60 Boell, *Die Operationen*, p.325; MSS Afr.*c.* 1715 (300), *History of 1 KAR*, p165.

61 IWM, 49538, *KTB, IV*, 22 Mar 17; Hoskins, *Despatch*, pp.159-160.

62 IWM, 49538, *KTB, IV*, 13 Apr 17.

63 Boell, *Die Operationen*, p.321.

64 WO 95/5329, WD Norforce, 31 Mar 17; CAB 44/9, 33-34.

65 Hoskins, *Despatch*, p.160.

66 Boell, *Die Operationen*, p.325; WO 95/5320, WD Norforce, 24 Feb, 10 and 11 Mar 17.

67 Boell, *Die Operationen*, p.326; WO 95/5329, WD Norforce, 8 Mar 17; WO 95/5329, WD Norforce, 22-26 Mar 17; Hoskins, Despatch, 168.

68 WO 33/953, No. 1727, 31 Mar 17, Telegram G738, Hoskins to CIGS.

69 WO 95/5329, WD Norforce, 2 May 17; WO 95/5293, WD GHQ, 9 May 17, Telegram P19, Edforce to Genstaff.

70 *Campagnes coloniales belges*, III, pp.132 and 309-310; Boell, *Die Operationen*, p.327.

71 WO 95/5329, WD Norforce, 11 and 27 Apr 17; CAB 44/9, 34-35.

72 WO 95/5329, WD Norforce, 22 Apr 17.

73 CAB 44/9, 35-36; CAB 45/73, Sketch 98 'The Strategic Situation First June 1917'.

74 CAB 44/9, 36-37.

75 WO 95/5329, WD Norforce, 6 May 17.

76 IWM, 49538, *KTB, IV*, 6 May 17; WO 95/5329, WD Norforce, 9 May 17.
77 WO 158/477, 17 Apr [May] 17, Letter No. 5, Macdonell to FO and Hoskins, covering Despatch dated 16 May 17.
78 CAB 44/9, 40-41.
79 WO 95/5329, WD Norforce, 25 and 29 May 17; Ranger, 'Revolt', 62-64; Pélissier, *Naissance de Mozambique*, II, pp.764-765; Newitt, *History of Mozambique*, pp.418-419.
80 WO 95/5329, WD Norforce, 14 and 18 May 17; CAB 44/9, 40.
81 CAB 44/9, 41-42.
82 WO 95/5329, WD Norforce, 1 Jun 17.
83 WO 95/5329, WD Norforce, 29 May 17.
84 WO 95/5293, WD GHQ, 9 Apr 17, Telegram 32324, CIGS to Hoskins.
85 MS Robertson, I/33/48, 2 May 17, Letter Smuts to Robertson; Smuts Papers, Box 100, 13 Apr 17, Letter Smuts to Robertson.
86 CAB 23/2, 23 Apr 17, War Cabinet Meeting 124.
87 MS Robertson, I/33/46/1, 23 Apr 17, Letter Robertson to Smuts; I/33/47/2, 23 Apr 17, Telegram Smuts to Botha; Smuts Papers, Box 100, 9 Apr 17, Letter Robertson to Smuts; CAB 23/2, 1 May 17, War Cabinet Meeting 128.
88 Fendall, *The East African Force*, 101; Boell Papers, N14/32, 28. Kapitel, 2245.

CHAPTER SEVEN

1 Marder, *From Dreadnought to Scapa Flow*, IV, p.102.
2 French, *The Strategy of the Lloyd George Coalition*, pp.74-88 and 94-97.
3 WO 33/953, No. 1868, 29 May 17, Telegram G666, Hoskins to CIGS; WO 33/953, No. 1852, 22 May 17, Telegram 340907, CIGS to van Deventer.
4 *Campagnes coloniales belges*, III, pp.125-127; WO 95/5293, WD GHQ, 27 Apr 17, Telegram G165, Hoskins to CIGS; 10 Jun 17, Telegram G843, van Deventer to CIGS; WO 33/953, No. 1852, 22 May 17, Telegram 340907, CIGS to van Deventer.
5 Beyers and Basson, *Dictionary of South African Biography*, V, pp.809-810; South African National Defence Force, Personnel Archive and Reserves, AG(1) (A)P1/41391/1, *Record of Service of Lieutenant General Sir Jacob Louis van Deventer in the Union Defence Force.*
6 WO 33/953, No. 1901, 11 Jun 17, Telegram G843, van Deventer to CIGS.
7 WO 33/953, No. 1901, 11 Jun 17, Telegram G843, van Deventer to CIGS.
8 CAB 44/9, 67.
9 WO 95/5293, WD GHQ, 26 May 17, Telegram NF2957, Norforce to Hoskins, 25 May.
10 WO 95/5329, WD Norforce, 9 Jun 17.
11 WO 158/477, 19 Mar 17, Telegram 617, Macdonell to Hoskins, 18 Mar 17; 7 Apr 17, Telegram 778, Macdonell to Hoskins, 6 Apr.
12 WO 158/477, 4 Apr 17, Letter, Sheppard to Macdonell.
13 WO 158/477, 20 Mar 17, Letter, Macdonell to Hoskins.
14 FO 371/2857, Folio 105917, 25 May 17, Telegram Macdonell to FO.
15 WO 95/5293, WD GHQ, 10 Jun 17, Telegram G843, van Deventer to CIGS.
16 *Campagnes coloniales belges*, III, pp.126-128 and 329-330; WO 95/5293, WD GHQ, 20 Jun 17, Telegram G976, BGGS to Northey and Tytler.
17 *Campagnes coloniales belges*, III, pp.129-130 and 297-298; WD GHQ, 20 Jun 17, Telegram G976, BGGS to Northey and Tytler.
18 WO 95/5293, WD GHQ, 27 Jun 17, Telegram G91, Genstaff to Hanforce, GOC Lindi, OC Iringa and General Edwards; .28 Jun 17, Telegram G107, van Deventer to CIGS; WO 95/5329, WD Norforce, Jul 17, Attachment by

War Office, MO2(B), 29 Jun 17, 'East Africa – Prospective Advance'.

19 Van Deventer, *Despatch*, I, 172; WO 95/5329, WD Norforce, Entry 8 Jun 17, Telegram G775, van Deventer to Northey, 7 Jun; CAB 44/9, 72.

20 *Campagnes coloniales belges*, III, pp.133-134.

21 *Campagnes coloniales belges*, III, pp.135-136.

22 WO 95/5329, WD Norforce, 24 and 29 Jun 17.

23 WO 95/5293, WD GHQ, 4 Jun 17, Telegram O884, Colonel Grant, Kilwa to BGGS; WD GHQ, 7 Jun 17, Telegram G776, Genstaff to Colonel Grant Kilwa; WO 33/953, No. 1905, 12 Jun 17, Telegram G860, van Deventer to CIGS.

24 WO 33/953, No. 1874, 1 Jun 17, Telegram X18572, van Deventer to CIGS WO 33/953, No. 1901, 11 Jun 17, Telegram G843, van Deventer to CIGS.

25 Cann, 'Mozambique and German East Africa', pp.131-133.

26 Boell Papers, N14/30, 26. Kapitel, 2031-2032 and 2044; On 1 April 1917, they had numbered 6,534 and 2,854 respectively, with effective battle strengths of 4,419 and 1,712. The revised figures are an estimate.

27 CAB 44/10, 9, footnote 1; Boell Papers, N14/32, 28. Kapitel, 2247; Boell, *Die Operationen*, p.333.

28 WO 95/5293, WD GHQ, 10 Jun, Telegram G843, van Deventer to CIGs; CAB 45/73, Sketch 100.

29 CAB 44/10, 8-10.

30 WO 33/953, No. 1907, 12 Jun 17, Telegram G880, van Deventer to CIGS; Boell Papers, N14/30, 26. Kapitel, 2055 and 28. Kapitel, 2247.

31 Boell, *Die Operationen*, pp.333-336; Boell Papers, N14/32, 28. Kapitel, 2250-2251.

32 CAB 45/67, 18 Jun 17, Letter Admiral Charlton to Admiralty.

33 Boell Papers, N14/32, 28. Kapitel, 2252-2255.

34 IWM, 49538, *KTB*, III, 12 Jun 17; Boell Papers, N14/32, 28. Kapitel, 2258-2260 and 2270-2273; WO 95/5330, History of 1st/2nd KAR, 14-15; Boell, *Die Operationen*, pp.337-339.

35 WO 33/953, No. 1952, 1 Jul 17, Telegram G162, van Deventer to CIGS; Boell Papers, N14/32, 28. Kapitel, 2292-2293.

36 WO 95/5293, WD GHQ, 14 Jun 17, Telegram O955, Beves to BGGS, 13 Jun.

37 CAB 44/9, 73-75; Boell Papers, N14/32, 28. Kapitel, 2287-2288.

38 WO 33/953, No. 1969. 7 Jul 17, Telegram G244, van Deventer to CIGS; Orr, 'Rumbo to the Rovuma The Odyssey of 'One' Column in East Africa in 1917', *Army Quarterly*, VII, (1924), pp.110-111.

39 Campagnes coloniales belges, III, 56-57 and 105-107.

40 Ridgway, 'With No. 2 Column', I, *Army Quarterly*, V, (1922), pp. 22-23.

41 WO 106/273, *History of 3 KAR*, 70.

42 WO 33/953, No. 2002, 22 Jul 17, Telegram G447, van Deventer to CIGS; Orr, 'Rumbo to the Rovuma', 114-115.

43 Ridgway, 'With No. 2 Column', I, 26-28.

44 WO 95/5293, WD GHQ, 13 Jul 17, *Note on Situation at Lindi and Note on the relative importance of the Kilwa (A) and Lindi (B) lines of advance by Brigadier-General O'Grady*; CAB 44/10, 7.

45 WO 95/5329, WD Norforce, 3 and 31 Jul 17; CAB 44/9, 48.

46 Boell Papers, N14/32, Boell, 29. Kapitel, 2621-2622; CAB 44/9, 48-49.

47 Boell Papers, N14/32, 29. Kapitel, 2621-2622.

48 WO 95/5329, WD Norforce, 2-3, 6 and 7 Jul 17.

49 WO 95/5329, WD Norforce, 8 Jul 17.

50 WO 95/5329, WD Norforce, 10-12 and 12 Jul 17, Telegram NF4139, Norforce

to BGGS; 13 July, Telegram G300 BGGS to Norforce.
51 WO 95/5329, WD Norforce, 15, 24, 26 Jul and 1 Aug 17.
52 WO 95/5329, WD Norforce, 1, 5 and 8 Aug 17.
53 WO 95/5329, WD Norforce, 9-10, and 14-16 Aug 17. The meeting was partly made possible by Northey's completion of a motor road from Songea to Iringa, nearly 480 km long.
54 WO 95/5329, WD Norforce, 21-22, 28 and 30-31 Aug 17.
55 French, *Lloyd George Coalition*, 77; CAB 23/3, 29 Jun 17, War Cabinet Meeting 172, Appendix I, 'Shipping Allocated to Overseas Expeditions Outside France'. The figures for troop and horse ships are 24 of 70; for hospital ships seven of thirty-two.
56 CAB 23/3, 23 Jul 17, War Cabinet Meeting 193.
57 WO 33/953, No. 2002, 22 Jul 17, Telegram G447, van Deventer to CIGS; CAB 23/3, War Cabinet Meeting 194, 24 Jul 17. Although several artillery batteries were also agreed, only a mounted regiment was sent to East Africa
58 *Campagnes coloniales belges*, III, 141.
59 WO 33/953, No. 2008, 24 Jul 17, Telegram G474, van Deventer to CIGS; *Campagnes coloniales belges*, III, pp.140-141.
60 *Campagnes coloniales belges*, III, pp.142-143.
61 WO 95/5294, WD GHQ, 7 Aug 17, Telegram G650, van Deventer to CIGS; 8 Aug 17, Telegram G675, van Deventer to CIGS.
62 WO 33/953, No. 2050, 6 Aug 17, Telegram G632, van Deventer to CIGS.
63 CAB 44/10, 7 and 19-21; WO 106/273, *History of 3 KAR*, pp.19-20.
64 Lettow, *Reminiscences*, p.204.
65 CAB 44/10, 22-23.
66 Boell, *Die Operationen*, pp.346-348; CAB 44/10, 23-24; Lettow, *Reminiscences*, p.205.
67 Boell, *Die Operationen*, p.348; CAB 44/10, 25-28.
68 *Campagnes coloniales belges*, III, pp.117-118; CAB 44/8, 73-78.
69 WO 95/5294, WD GHQ, 2 Sep 17, Telegram G059, BGGS to Hanforce and Lincol.
70 WO 33/953, No. 2116, 3 Sep 17, Telegram G095, van Deventer to CIGS; CAB 44/8, 120.
71 *Campagnes coloniales belges*, III, pp.364-366, 7 Sep 16, Letter van Deventer to Huyghé.
72 *Campagnes coloniales belges*, III, p.141.
73 Cann, 'Mozambique', pp.136-137.
74 WO 158/478, 29 Aug 17, Letter 11, Macdonell to van Deventer, 14 August;. AHM, 5a Repartição, 2a divisão, 7a secção, caixa 12, *Relatório das operações contra os alemaes no leste Africano de 12 de Setembro do 1917 a 8 da Julho de 1918 par General Thomasz de Sousa Rosa, henceforth Relatório – Rosa*, pp.55-60; WO 95/5924, WD GHQ, 10 Sep 17, BGGS to GSO1, 'Establishing a Belgian Force at Mocimboa da Praia'.
75 WO 158/478, 5 Oct 17, Telegram G450, van Deventer to Macdonell; WO 95/5294, WD GHQ, 30 Sep 17, Telegram 83, Macdonell to van Deventer, 29 Sep.
76 WO 158/469, 24 Sep 17, Telegram G345, Sheppard to Macdonell
77 WO 158/469, 18 Oct 17, Letter No. 19, Macdonell to van Deventer; WO 158/478, 6 Oct 17, Telegram NF4662, Norforce to Genstaff, 5 Oct; 8 Oct 17, Telegram 390S, van Deventer to Genstaff, for onward transmission to the Portuguese, 7 Oct.
78 WO 158/478, 8 Oct 17, Telegram 391S, van Deventer to CIGS, 7 Oct.
79 WO 158/469, Paper 16, Letter No. 20, Macdonell to van Deventer, 18 Oct 17; AHM, 5a Repartição, 2a divisão, 7a secção, caixa 12, *Relatório – Rosa*, pp.66-73.

80 Van Deventer, *Despatch*, I, pp.183-185.
81 WO 158/478, 7 Sep 17, Telegram No. 127/5, Capt Cohen to Force Intelligence, 5 Sep.
82 WO 158/478, 14 Sep 17, Telegram No. 144-1, Cohen to Force Intelligence, 12 Sep.
83 CAB 45/19, *Nigeria Regiment Record*, pp.33-35.
84 WO 33/953, No. 2165, 21 Sep 17, Telegram G320, van Deventer to CIGS; No. 2167, 22 Sep 17, Telegram G322, van Deventer to CIGS; Ridgway, 'With No 2 Column', II, 248-249; IWM, 49538, KTB, III, 23 Sep 17.
85 Orr, 'Rumbo to the Rovuma', 116-117; CAB 45/19, *Nigeria Regiment Record*, 36-39.
86 WO 95/5294, WD GHQ, 26 Sep 17, Telegram G359, van Deventer to CIGS; 29 Sep 17, Telegram G389, van Deventer to CIGS.
87 Lettow, *Reminiscences*, pp.208-210; WO 33/953, No. 2215, 13 Oct 17, Telegram 5WO, van Deventer to CIGS.
88 Ridgway, 'With No 2 Column', II, 250-253; Orr, 'Rumbo to the Rovuma', 120; WO 95/5294, WD GHQ, 11 Oct 17, Telegram 4WO, van Deventer to CIGS; 14 Oct 17, Telegram 7WO, van Deventer to CIGS; 15 Oct 17, Telegram 6WO, van Deventer to CIGS.
89 WO 95/5294, WD GHQ, 13 Oct 17, Telegram 6WO, van Deventer to CIGS.
90 WO 33/953, No. 2171, 23 Sep 17, Telegram G330, van Deventer to CIGS; CAB 44/10, 29-31.
91 CAB 44/10, 32-33; Boell Papers, N14/32, 28. Kapitel, 2582.
92 WO 95/5294, WD GHQ, 28 Sep 17, Telegram G378, van Deventer to CIGS; CAB 44/10, 38.
93 CAB 44/10, 36-37.
94 Orr, 'Von Lettow's Escape into Portuguese East Africa, 1917', *Army Quarterly*, XIII, (1925), pp.50-51.
95 WO 95/5294, WD GHQ, 26 Oct 17, Telegram 17WO, van Deventer to CIGS; 30 Oct 17, Telegram 21WO, van Deventer to CIGS.
96 WO 33/953, No. 2192, 2 Oct 17, Telegram G419, van Deventer to CIGS.
97 CAB 45/72, Map 9508, 'The Strategic Situation 20th December 1917'; WO 95/5294, WD GHQ, 23 Sep 17, 'Instructions to O.C. 25th Cavalry', 16 Sep; Downes, *With the Nigerians*, p.197.
98 CAB 44/10, 39-40.
99 WO 95/5294, WD GHQ, 15 Oct 17, Telegram 6WO, van Deventer to CIGS; CAB 44/10, 41-42. Cites Telegram 552, BGGS to Linforce 15 Oct 17; 'Chief wishes you to push on now as fast as possible towards Massassi. Give enemy no time to make defensive positions and make every endeavour to capture his guns. Enemy is now much shaken, and a determined advance on your line combined with operations outlined in my 549 will probably have decisive effect.'
100 Lettow, *Reminiscences*, 210; WO 33/953, No. 2222, 16 Oct 17, Telegram 8WO, van Deventer to CIGS.
101 CAB 44/10, 42-43; Downes, *With the Nigerians*, p.197.
102 CAB 44/10, 44; Downes, *With the Nigerians*, 198-203; CAB 45/19, *Nigeria Regiment Record*, pp.47-51; Boell, *Die Operationen*, pp.373-374.
103 CAB 44/10, 46-47; Boell Papers, N14/36, 30. Kapitel, 2802; Boell, *Die Operationen*, p.374.
104 WO 33/953, No. 2224, 17 Oct 17, Telegram 10WO, van Deventer to CIGS.
105 CAB 44/10, 49-52; CAB 45/19, *Nigerian Regiment Record*, pp.48-49.
106 Boell, *Die Operationen*, pp.375-376.
107 CAB 44/10, 53-59, footnote 1.
108 WO 95/5294, WD GHQ, 19 Oct 17, Telegram 12WO, van Deventer to

CIGS; Boell, *Die Operationen*, p.375; WO 95/5330, *History of 1st/2nd KAR*, pp.25-28.

109 CAB 44/10, 67-72; Boell, *Die Operationen*, p.377; WO 33/953, No. 2229, 20 Oct 17, Telegram OA559, van Deventer to CIGS. Van Deventer was dissatisfied with Beves' performance and removed him from command, although he did acknowledge that the latter had been suffering from malaria which may have affected his judgement.

110 WO 95/5294, GHQ WD, 9 Oct 17, Telegram 42750, Director of Military Intelligence (DMI) to van Deventer, 8 Oct; 14 Oct 17, Telegram 43200, DMI to van Deventer.

111 Goebbel, *Afrika zu unsern Fußen*, pp.49-50 and 66-67.

112 Goebbel, *Afrika zu unsern Fußen*, pp.95-96; WO 95/5293?, Marinearchiv, *Deutschen Kolonien*, pp. 212-214.

113 WO 158/478, 13 Oct 17, Telegram 92, Colonel Macdonell to Genstaff; WO 33/953, No. 2204, 7 Oct 17, Telegram 391S, van Deventer to CIGS.

114 WO 33/953, No. 2256, 31 Oct 17, Telegram 22WO, van Deventer to CIGS; van Deventer, *Despatch*, I, p.189.

115 FO 371/2857, Folio 198268, Oct 17, Minutes.

116 WO 33/953, No. 2239, 24 Oct 17, Telegram 717, van Deventer to CIGS.

117 *Campagnes coloniales belges*, III, pp.219-221 and 387-388; WO 33/953, No. 249, 28 Oct 17, Telegram 18WO, van Deventer to CIGS.

118 *Campagnes coloniales belges*, III, pp.221-222.

119 WO 95/5294, WD GHQ, 2 Nov 17, Telegram 23WO, van Deventer to CIGS.

120 Lettow, *Reminiscences*, pp.216-218.

121 WO 95/5294, WD GHQ, 9 Nov 17, Telegram 29WO, van Deventer to CIGS; WO 33/953, No. 2268, 6 Nov 17, Telegram 878, van Deventer to CIGS; No. 2270, 7 Nov 17, Telegram 26WO, van Deventer to WO; AHM, 5a Repartição, 2a divisão, 7a secção, caixa 12, *Relatório – Rosa*, 124-125.

122 WO 95/5293, WD GHQ, 6 Nov 17, Telegram 26WO, van Deventer to CIGS; WO 33/953, No. 2271, 7 Nov 17, Telegram X900, van Deventer to CIGS; No. 2272, 8 Nov 17, Telegram 44997, CIGS to van Deventer; No. 2291, 17 Nov 17, Telegram 45875, CIGS to van Deventer.

123 *Campagnes coloniales belges*, III, pp.222-223.

124 WO 33/953, No. 2276, 9 Nov 17, Telegram 28WO, van Deventer to CIGS.

125 Orr, 'Von Lettow's Retreat', 52-53.

126 WO 33/953, No. 2280, 11 Nov 17, Telegram 30WO, van Deventer to CIGS.

127 Orr, 'Von Lettow's Retreat', 53-54; WO 106/273, *History of 3 KAR*, p.84.

128 WO 33/953, No. 2288, 16 Nov 17, Telegram 34WO, van Deventer to CIGS; Lettow, *Reminiscences*, pp.219-222.

129 *Campagnes coloniales belges*, III, pp.223-224 and 389.

130 WO 33/953, No. 2294, 18 Nov 17, Telegram 36WO, van Deventer to CIGS; Lettow, *Reminiscences*, p.220; Orr, 'Von Lettow's Retreat', p.55.

131 *Campagnes coloniales belges*, III, pp.224-227; WO 33/953, No. 2311, 25 Nov 17, Telegram 42WO, van Deventer to CIGS.

132 Ridgway, 'With No 2 Column', II, pp.256-257.

133 WO 95/5294, WD GHQ, 19 Nov 17, Telegram 37WO, van Deventer to CIGS; 21 Nov 17, Telegram 38WO, van Deventer to CIGS; Lettow, *Reminiscences*, pp.223-224; Orr, 'Von Lettow's Retreat', pp.56-57.

134 WO 95/5295, WD GHQ, 25 Nov 17, Telegram 43WO, van Deventer to CIGS; WO 95/5295, WD GHQ, 27

Nov 17, Telegram 44WO, van Deventer to CIGS, 26 Nov.

135 IWM, 49538, KTB, IV, 24 Nov 17; Ridgway, 'With No 2 Column', II, 258; Pretorius, *Jungle Man*, pp.182-185.

136 WO 95/5294, WD GHQ, 30 Nov 17, Telegram 46WO, van Deventer to CIGS, 28 Nov.

137 WO 95/52394, WD GHQ, 3 Dec 17, Telegram 47022, CIGS to van Deventer, 2 Dec.

138 WO 95/5294, WD GHQ, 5 Dec 17, Telegram 402, van Deventer to CIGS, 4 Dec.

139 WO 33/953, No. 2317, 27 Nov 17, Telegram 299, van Deventer to CIGS; No. 2325, 29 Nov 17, Telegram 46804, CIGS to van Deventer; WO 95/5294, WD GHQ, 3 Dec 17, Telegram 47022, CIGS to van Deventer, 2 Dec; *Campagnes coloniales belges*, III, pp.227-228.

CHAPTER EIGHT

1 Boell, *Die Operationen*, p.399; Göring, *Kriegserlebnisse*, p.144.

2 Lettow, *Reminiscences*, pp.236-237.

3 Boell Papers, N14/36, 1. Kapitel, 1.

4 Boell, *Die Operationen*, p.399.

5 Boell Papers, N14/36, 1. Kapitel, 2.

6 Boell Papers, N14/36, 1. Kapitel, 3.

7 Göring, *Kriegserlebnisse*, pp.144-145.

8 Lettow, *Reminiscences*, pp.229-232; Schnee, *Deutsch-Ostafrika*, p.311; Boell Papers, N14/36, Kapitel 1, 3; AHM, 5a Repartição, 2a divisão, 7a secção, caixa 12, *Relatório – Rosa*, pp.143-145; WO 95/5294, WD GHQ, 4 Dec 17, Telegram 50WO, van Deventer to CIGS.

9 Boell Papers, N14/36, 1. Kapitel, 5.

10 Boell, *Die Operationen*, 399-400; Schnee, *Deutsch-Ostafrika*, p.314.

11 Boell Papers, N14/36, 1. Kapitel, 8-9 and 20-21.

12 Schnee, *Deutsch-Ostafrika*, p.320; Boell Papers, N14/36, 1. Kapitel, 14-15 and 30.

13 WO 95/5294, WD GHQ, 2 Dec 17, Letter van Deventer to Schnee; Boell Papers, N14/36, 1. Kapitel, 6 and 11-12.

14 WO 95/5294, WD GHQ, 12 Dec 17, Telegram 52WO, van Deventer to CIGS, 11 Dec; 13 Dec 17, Telegram 53WO, van Deventer to CIGS.

15 WO 95/5294, WD GHQ, 29 Dec 17, Telegram 68WO, van Deventer to CIGS, 28 Dec; 1 Jan 18, Telegram 71WO, van Deventer to CIGS, 31 Dec.

16 French, *Lloyd George Coalition*, pp.169 and 180-181 Hughes, *British Strategy in the Middle East*, p.27; Marder, *From Dreadnought to Scapa Flow*, IV, p.277.

17 Smith, 'The British Government and the Disposition of the German Colonies in Africa, 1914-1918', 283-285 in Louis, 'Great Britain and German Expansion in Africa, 1884-1919'; Giffard and Louis, *Britain and Germany*, pp.40-42 and; French, *Lloyd George Coalition*, pp.63-64; CAB 24/4, 8 December 1917, Paper G182, *German and Turkish Territories Captured in the War*, by Lord Curzon, p.10.

18 Smith, 'Disposition of the German Colonies', pp.288-289.

19 WO 33/953, No. 2203, 6 Oct 17, Telegram 380, van Deventer to CIGS; Louis, 'Great Britain and German Expansion', pp.40 and 45-46; CAB 24/4, 8 Dec 17, Paper G182, *German and Turkish Territories Captured in the War, by Lord Curzon.*

20 WO 33/953, No. 2412, 29 Dec 17, Telegram X9842, GOC to WO, 271-274. Out of a total strength of 52,000 over 11,000 Indian, 10,000 British and 3,700 South African troops remained in theatre.

21 WO 33/953, No. 2334, 2 Dec 17, Telegram 47022, CIGS to van Deventer.

22 Moyse-Bartlett, *The King's African Rifles*, p.390.

23 WO 33/953, No. 2441, 8 Jan 18,

Telegram W965, van Deventer to CIGS.

24 WO 95/5330, WD Norforce, 1 Jan 18.

25 Admiralty (NID), *A Handbook of Portuguese Nyasaland*, London: 1920, 51.

26 WO 95/5295, WD GHQ, 3 Jan 18, Telegram 1B, van Deventer to WO, 1 Jan.

27 WO 158/478, 1 Dec 17, Telegram 46895, CIGS to van Deventer, 30 Nov.

28 FO 371/3128, Folio 655, 2 Jan 18, Telegram 3, FO to Carnegie.

29 FO 371/3128, Folio 655, 31 Dec 17, Telegram A1495, van Deventer to CIGS, 29 Dec.

30 FO 371, 3128, Folio 2132, 3 Jan 18, Letter WO to FO.

31 FO 371/3128, Folio 5578, 10 Jan 18, Telegram 16, Carnegie to FO, 9 Jan.

32 WO 95/5294, WD GHQ, 4 Dec 17, Telegram 49WO, van Deventer to CIGS, 2 Dec.

33 Boell, *Die Operationen*, pp.406-407; WO 95/5294, WD GHQ, 29 Dec 17, Telegram 68WO, van Deventer to CIGS, 28 Dec.

34 WO 95/5295, WD GHQ, 29 Jan 18, 'Minutes of Conference between the Acting Governor General of Mozambique and General van Deventer'.

35 WO 95/5295, WD GHQ, 12 Feb 18, Telegram 36S, van Deventer to CIGS.

36 AHM, 5a Repartição, 2a divisão, 7a secção, caixa 12, *Relatório – Rosa*, pp.182-185; WO 95/5295, WD GHQ, 12 Feb 18, Telegram 36S, van Deventer to CIGS.

37 AHM, 5a Repartição, 2a divisão, 7a secção, caixa 12, *Relatório – Rosa*, II, pp.35 and 64-68.

38 Lettow, *Reminiscences*, p.242.

39 IWM, 49538, KTB, IV, 7 Jan 18, GHQ Order; Boell Papers, N14/36, 2. Kapitel, 72.

40 WO 95/5330, WD Norforce, 4 and 7 Jan 18; IWM, 49538, *KTB*, IV, 10 Jan 18; Boell Papers, N14/36, 2. Kapitel, 49.

41 WO 95/5330, WD Norforce, 14 and 18 Jan 18; Van Deventer Despatch, II, 121.

42 Moyse-Bartlett, *The King's African Rifles*, p.390.

43 Boell Papers, N14/36, 2. Kapitel, pp.32-33 and 49.

44 Boell, *Die Operationen*, p.404.

45 Boell Papers, N14/36, 2. Kapitel, 61-62;

46 WO 95/5330, WD Norforce, 20 Jan 17; Boell Papers, N14/36, 2. Kapitel, 66-67.

47 WO 33/953, No. 2513, 16 Feb 18, Telegram G173, van Deventer to CIGS; Lettow, *Reminiscences*, p.245.

48 WO 95/5330, WD Norforce, 4 Feb 18; IWM, 49538, KTB, IV, 5 Feb 18; Boell Papers, N14/36, 2. Kapitel, 62-64.

49 Van Deventer Despatch, II, 122; Boell, *Die Operationen*, p.404; CO 691/15, WD Norforce, 22 Feb 18.

50 Boell Papers, N14/36, 2. Kapitel, 84.

51 AHM, 5a Repartição, 2a divisão, 7a secção, caixa 12, *Relatório – Rosa*, II, 35; WO 95/5294, WD GHQ, 28 Feb 18.

52 CO 691/15, WD Norforce, 10 Mar 18; Moyse-Bartlett, *The King's African Rifles*, 391; WO 95/5330, *History of 1st/2nd KAR*, p.37.

53 Boell, *Die Operationen*, p.406

54 WO 33/953, No. 2601, 6 Apr 18, Telegram G429, van Deventer to CIGS.

55 Clifford, *The Gold Coast Regiment*, pp.238-239; WO 95/5330, *History of 1st/2nd KAR*, pp.37-38.

56 WO 33/953, No. 2619, 19 Apr 18, Telegram 177WO, van Deventer to CIGS; Boell Papers, N14/36, 2. Kapitel, 113.

57 IWM, 49538, *KTB*, IV, 18 Apr 18; Boell, *Die Operationen*, p.407.

58 Clifford, *The Gold Coast Regiment*, p.256; van Deventer, *Despatch*, II, 125.

59 IWM, 49538, *KTB*, IV, 3 May 18; WO 33/953, No. 2647, 4 May 18, Telegram 191WO, van Deventer to CIGS; WO

95/5330, *History of 1st/2nd KAR*, pp.39-40.
60 *Die Operationen*, p.408; Göring, *Kriegserlebnisse*, p.188; WO 33/953, No. 2650, 6 May 18, Telegram G269, van Deventer to WO; WO 95/5330, WD Norforce, 5 May 18.
61 Clifford, *The Gold Coast Regiment*, p.269; Boell, *Die Operationen*, p.409.
62 WO 95/5330, WD Norforce, 22 May 18; IWM, 49538, *KTB*, IV, 21 May 18; Göring, *Kriegserlebnisse*, pp.186-188; WO 95/5330, *History of 1st/2nd KAR*, pp.41-42.
63 Boell, *Die Operationen*, p.410; Boell Papers, N14/36, 2. Kapitel, 166-167; WO 33/953, No. 2674, 24 May 18, Telegram 210WO, van Deventer to WO.
64 WO 33/953, No. 2679, 27 May 18, Telegram 214WO, van Deventer to CIGS; CO 691/15, WD Norforce, 27 May 18.
65 Boell, *Die Operationen*, 412.
66 WO 95/5295, WD GHQ, 21 Jun 18; WO 33/953, No. 2688, 1 Jun 18, Telegram 218WO, van Deventer to WO.
67 Boell, *Die Operationen*, 412; WO 95/5330, *History of 1st/2nd KAR*, p.43.
68 WO 33/953, No. 2688, 1 Jun 18, Telegram 218WO, van Deventer to CIGS; CO 691/15, WD Norforce, 1 Jun 18.
69 CO 691/15, WD Norforce, 2 Jun 18.
70 Boell, *Die Operationen*, 413.
71 CO 691/15, WD Norforce, 15, 20 and 24 Jun 18.
72 IWM, 49538, *KTB*, IV, 14 and 25 Jun 18.
73 FO 371/3128, Folio 112227, 27 Jun 18, Letter FO to WO.
74 FO 371/3128, Folio 115649, 26 Jun 18, Telegram G962, van Deventer to WO, 25 Jun.
75 FO 371/3128, Folio 115649, 29 Jun 18, Letter WO to FO.
76 AHM, 5a Repartição, 2a divisão, 7a secção, caixa 12, *Relatório – Rosa*, II, 219-220.
77 WO 33/953, No. 2718, 17 Jun 18, Telegram 234WO, van Deventer to WO; No. 2729, 22 Jun 18, Telegram 238WO, van Deventer to WO.
78 Boell Papers, N14/36, 3. Kapitel, 216-218; WO 106/273, *History of 3rd KAR*, 89a.
79 Göring, Kriegserlebnisse, 202-203; Moyse-Bartlett, *The King's African Rifles*, pp.399-400; WO 106/273, *History of 3rd KAR*, pp.90-91.
80 IWM, 49538, *KTB*, IV, 2-3 Jul 18; Boell, *Die Operationen*, 415; WO 106/1460, Schnee Diary, [2-4] Jul 18, pp.146-147.
81 Boell Papers, N14/36, 3. Kapitel, 230; WO 95/5330, WD Norforce, 4 Jul 18.
82 WO 33/953, No. 2755, 6 Jul 18, Telegram G161, van Deventer to CIGS.
83 AHM, 5a Repartição, 2a divisão, 7a secção, caixa 12, *Relatório – Rosa*, III, pp.5-6 and 166.
84 Boell, *Die Operationen*, p.416; CO 691/15, WD Norforce, 13 Jul 18.
85 Boell, *Die Operationen*, p.417; Moyse-Bartlett, *The King's African Rifles*, p.402; WO 106/273, *History of 3rd KAR*, pp.92-93; CO 691/15, WD Norforce, 22 and 23 Jul 18.
86 WO 33/953, No. 2782, 25 Jul 18, Telegram 7WO, van Deventer to CIGS; WO 106/1460, Schnee Diary, 22-23 Jul 18, 152-153.
87 CO 691/15, WD Norforce, 24 Jul 18.
88 Moyse-Bartlett, *The King's African Rifles*, p.402; WO 106/273, *History of 3rd KAR*, pp.93-94.
89 WO 33/953, No. 2787, 31 Jul 18, Telegram No. 11WO, van Deventer to CIGS.
90 WO 106/1460, Schnee Diary, 24-31 Jul 18, 154-155; Lettow, *Reminiscences*, pp.290-291.
91 Boell, *Die Operationen*, pp.417-418.
92 Van Deventer *Despatch*, II, p.131.
93 WO 33/953, No. 2798, 11 Aug 18, Telegram 18WO, van Deventer to

CIGS; Göring, *Kriegserlebnisse*, p.220; WO 106/1460, Schnee Diary, 10 Aug 18, 3.

94 Boell, *Die Operationen*, pp.418-419; Wenig, *Kriegs-Safari*, pp.192-94.

95 Moyse-Bartlett, *King's African Rifles*, p.405.

96 Boell, *Die Operationen*, p.419; WO 106/1460, Schnee Diary, 27 Aug 18, 5; Lettow, *Reminiscences*, pp.294-295.

97 CO 691/15, WD Norforce, 31 Aug and 1 Sep 18; Moyse-Bartlett, *The King's African Rifles*, p.406.

98 IWM, 49538, *KTB*, IV, 30-31 Aug 18.

99 WO 95/5295, WD GHQ, 1 Sep 18; Boell Papers, N14/36, 3. Kapitel, 307.

100 WO 106/1460, Schnee Diary, 1 Sep 18, 17.

101 Moyse-Bartlett, *The King's African Rifles*, pp.407-408; CO 691/15, WD Norforce, 1 Sep 18; WO 106/1460, Schnee Diary, 6 Sep, 21-22.

102 IWM, 49538, KTB, IV, 6 Sep 18; Boell, *Die Operationen*, p.420; WO 106/1460, Schnee Diary, 8 Sep 18, 24-25; Wahle, *Erinnerungen*, p.55.

103 WO 106/1460, Schnee Diary, 17 Sep 18, 25.

104 WO 95/5295, WD GHQ, 19 Sep 18; Moyse-Bartlett, *The King's African Rifles*, p.409.

105 Moyse-Bartlett, *The King's African Rifles*, p.409.

106 CO 691/15, WD Norforce, 25 and 26 Sep 18.

107 Wenig, *Kriegs-Safari*, pp.216-217; Boell Papers, N14/36, 3. Kapitel 321-322; WO 106/1460, Schnee Diary, 19 Sep 18, 31-32.

108 Boell, *Die Operationen*, p.421; WO 106/1460, Schnee Diary, 14 Sep 18, 26-27.

109 WO 106/1460, Schnee Diary, [29] and 30 Sep and 2 Oct 18, 42.

110 WO 33/953, No. 2857, 7 Oct 18, Telegram 53WO, van Deventer to WO; Boell, *Die Operationen*, 421; WO 106/1460, Schnee Diary, 5-8 Oct 18, 44-50.

111 WO 33/953, No. 2858, 9 Oct 18, Telegram 54WO, van Deventer to WO.

112 WO 106/1460, Schnee Diary, 15 Oct 18, 66-67; Wahle, *Erinnerungen*, p.57; Boell, *Die Operationen*, p.422.

113 Boell, *Die Operationen*, p.422.

114 WO 106/1460, Schnee Diary, 1 Nov 18, 81-82.

115 WO 33/953, No. 2883, 31 Oct 18, Telegram 68WO, van Deventer to WO; No. 2884, 31 Oct 18, Telegram 69807, WO to van Deventer; IWM, 49538, *KTB*, IV, 5 Nov 18.

116 Boell, *Die Operationen*, p.424.

117 WO 33/953, No. 2913, 16 Nov 18, Telegram 70934, WO to van Deventer.

118 WO 158/475, 1 Oct 18, Letter van Deventer to Secretary of State for War.

List of Illustrations

List of Plates

List of Maps

Numbers refer to pages

Index

Battles & Campaigns

A series of illustrated battlefield accounts covering the classical period through to the end of the twentieth century, drawing on the latest research and integrating the experience of combat with intelligence, logistics and strategy.

Series Editor

Hew Strachan, Chichele Professor of the History of War at the University of Oxford

Published

Ross Anderson, *The Battle of Tanga 1914*
Ross Anderson, *The Forgotten Front: The East African Campaign 1914-1918*
William Buckingham, *Arnhem 1944*
David M. Glantz, *Before Stalingrad*
Michael K. Jones, *Bosworth 1485*
Martin Kitchen, *The German Offensives of 1918*
M.K. Lawson, *The Battle of Hastings 1066*
Marc Milner, *The Battle of the Atlantic*
A.J. Smithers, *The Tangier Campaign*
Tim Travers, *Gallipoli 1915*

Commissioned

Stephen Conway, *The Battle of Bunker Hill 1775*
Brian Farrell, *The Defence & Fall of Singapore 1941–1942*
Martin Kitchen, *El Alamein 1942–1943*
John Andreas Olsen, *Operation Desert Storm*
Michael Penman, *Bannockburn 1314*
Matthew C. Ward, *Quebec 1759*